Legacies of the First World War
Building for Total War 1914–18

Legacies of the First World War

Building for Total War 1914–18

Edited by Wayne Cocroft and Paul Stamper

Published by Historic England, The Engine House, Fire Fly Avenue, Swindon SN2 2EH
www.HistoricEngland.org.uk

Historic England is a Government service championing England's heritage and giving expert, constructive advice.

© Historic England 2018

Images (except as otherwise shown) © Historic England Archive, © Crown Copyright. Historic England Archive, or Source: Historic England Archive.

First published 2018

ISBN 978 1 84802 288 1

British Library Cataloguing in Publication data
A CIP catalogue record for this book is available from the British Library.

All rights reserved
No part of this publication may be reproduced or transmitted in any form or by any means, electronic or mechanical, including photocopying, recording, or any information storage or retrieval system, without permission in writing from the publisher.

Application for the reproduction of images should be made to Historic England. Every effort has been made to trace the copyright holders and we apologise in advance for any unintentional omissions, which we would be pleased to correct in any subsequent edition of this book.

For more information about images from the Archive, contact Archives Services Team, Historic England, The Engine House, Fire Fly Avenue, Swindon SN2 2EH; telephone (01793) 414600.

Brought to publication by Jess Ward, Publishing, Historic England.
Typeset in Georgia Pro 9.5/11.75pt
Edited by Merle Read
Proof read by Kim Bishop
Indexed by Sue Vaughan
Page layout by Hybert Design Ltd, UK
Printed in the Czech Republic via Akcent Media Limited.

Front cover: Cunard's works, Liverpool. Women workers machining large calibre artillery shells. [BL24001/006]
Frontispiece: Recruiting poster designed by Lieutenant General Sir Robert Baden-Powell, July 1915. An idle young man looks on at a group of servicemen and people engaged in war work. [© The National Army Museum / Mary Evans Picture Library]
Px: Ships of the British Grand Fleet, the main fleet of the Royal Navy, in 1914. [© Robert Hunt Library/Mary Evans Picture Library]
Back cover: War memorial, Bury, Lancashire, relief by Joseph Hermon Cawthra depicting the civilian contribution to the war effort. [DP220274]

Contents

	Notes on contributors	vi
	Acknowledgements	viii
	Preface	ix
1	Introduction *Sir Hew Strachan*	1
2	The army *Peter Kendall*	8
3	The naval war *Serena Cant and Mark Dunkley*	35
4	Defending the coast *Paul Pattison and Roger J C Thomas*	66
5	The aerial war *Jeremy Lake*	93
6	The workshop of the world goes to war *Wayne Cocroft*	119
7	Civic and civilian architecture *Katie Carmichael*	147
8	Feeding the nation *Paul Stamper*	166
9	Back to Blighty: British war hospitals, 1914–18 *Kathryn A Morrison*	180
10	Remembering the dead *Roger Bowdler*	199
11	Epilogue *Wayne Cocroft and Paul Stamper*	213
	Notes	218
	Bibliography	226
	Index	234

Notes on contributors

Martyn Barber is an archaeologist who has worked at Historic England or its predecessors since 1990. He is currently Senior Investigator in the Aerial Investigation & Mapping Team. He has published on a wide range of subjects, from Neolithic flint mining to the First World War aerodrome at Stonehenge, and is the author of *A History of Aerial Photography and Archaeology* (2011).

Roger Bowdler worked for Historic England for almost 30 years, latterly as Director of Listing. He led the organisation's work on the First World War, notably its campaign to raise the profile of war memorials through an ambitious programme which added 2,500 memorials to the National Heritage List. His interest in all forms of remembrance is long-standing, and he served as chairman of the Mausolea & Monuments Trust. He is currently writing a book on tombstones.

Serena Cant is a Marine Information Officer at Historic England and for over 20 years has specialised in documentary research on wreck sites, with a special interest in the First World War and in wrecks in a naval context. She has published widely on England's maritime history, including *England's Shipwreck Heritage: From logboats to U-boats* (2013).

Katie Carmichael is an architectural historian and currently an Investigator in the Historic Places Investigation team at Historic England. She has published on the heritage of the Luton hatting industry and the buildings of Boston, Lincolnshire. She was until recently the conference secretary of the Society of Architectural Historians of Great Britain.

Wayne Cocroft is an archaeologist with Historic England. For over 25 years he has specialised in the investigation of former military sites and has published extensively on the history and archaeology of explosives manufacture and the Cold War. He is currently manager of the Historic Places Investigation team (East) based in Cambridge.

Mark Dunkley, a professional diver, is a marine archaeologist with Historic England, with responsibility for the protection of underwater cultural heritage. He regularly works with marine enforcement agencies to detect and prosecute underwater heritage crime and advises the UK National Commission for UNESCO on marine matters.

Andrew Hann is head of the historians' team at English Heritage. He specialises in research into country houses and historic designed landscapes, and has published widely on the social history of the country house, as well as on consumption and material culture and agrarian change. He has researched the history of Wrest Park in Bedfordshire since 2007, working closely with the volunteer history team based at the site. With them he curated an exhibition on the First World War hospital at Wrest in 2014.

Peter Kendall is an archaeologist who has worked at Historic England or its predecessors for 35 years. As a Principal Inspector of Ancient Monuments in the south-east of England, much of his work has focused on barracks, dockyards, fortifications and military sites in general. He has published research about the Royal Engineers at Chatham including *The Royal Engineers at Chatham 1759–2012* (2012).

Jeremy Lake has published widely on many aspects of heritage and landscape conservation and research, initially with the National Trust, then in private practice and between 1988 and 2016 with Historic England. He played a leading role in the development of approaches to the assessment of 20th-century military heritage and specialises in understanding the landscapes, historic buildings and other heritage assets of rural areas. He now runs his own heritage consultancy.

Dan Miles is an archaeologist, currently the Research Resources Officer in the Capacity Building Team at Historic England. He has a particular interest in conflict archaeology, with much of his research focused on Wiltshire.

Kathryn A Morrison is an architectural historian, currently Head of Historic Places Investigation (North & East) at Historic England, and a former Chairman of the Society of Architectural Historians of Great Britain. Over the last 25 years – working for the Royal Commission on the Historical Monuments of England, English Heritage and Historic England – she has published on a wide range of topics including hospitals, workhouses, retail buildings, factories, motoring heritage and country houses.

Paul Pattison is an archaeologist and historian who has been involved in the investigation and study of historic monuments and landscapes of all types and periods for over 30 years. He is currently a Senior Properties Historian at English Heritage, specialising in research on military sites and their presentation to the visiting public, including authorship of six guide books.

Paul Stamper worked for Historic England for 20 years in various roles associated with the management of England's historic landscape and buildings. Previously he was on the Shropshire staff of the Victoria County History. He has published widely on medieval and later rural history and archaeology, and was a long-time editor of the journal *Landscapes*. He now runs his own heritage consultancy and is a Visiting Fellow at Leicester University.

Sir Hew Strachan was knighted in 2013 for services to the Ministry of Defence. He has been Professor of International Relations at the University of St Andrews since 2015. Previously he was Professor of the History of War at All Souls College, Oxford. In 2016 he was awarded the Pritzker Prize for Lifetime Achievement for Military Writing. His publications include *The Politics of the British Army* (1997), *The First World War: To Arms (2001), The First World War: A New Illustrated History* (2003) and *The Direction of War* (2013).

Roger J C Thomas is an Assistant Listing Adviser with Historic England, currently based in York. Previously he was English Heritage's Military Support Officer. For over 40 years he has specialised in the investigation of former military sites and has published extensively on the history of a wide variety of types of site, with an emphasis on the 19th and 20th centuries.

Acknowledgements

This book embodies the results of research on the impact of the First World War on England carried out by colleagues from English Heritage and Historic England, knowledge often acquired across many decades. It also incorporates summaries of commissioned research undertaken over the centennial commemoration period, including work carried out by Martin Brown on trench systems, Antony Firth on the war at sea, and Jane Phimester on wireless stations. Thank you to our commissioning team who oversaw these projects. Sebastian Fry undertook initial research into the national factory system which was built on by David Kenyon, and Matthew Edgeworth reported on the Grain firing point. We are also grateful for access to the latest research from a project to study the remains of the First World War camps on Cannock Chase by Edward Carpenter, David Knight, Cara Pearce, Rebecca Pullen, Fiona Small, David Went and Helen Winton. Rebecca also produced important new research on the Cliffe explosives works, Medway. The results of this research may be viewed in more detail on the Historic England website. Chapter 5 has greatly benefited from past discussions with Paul Francis, Steven Woolford, formerly Imperial War Museum, Duxford, and Ian Flint and the staff of the Stow Maries Great War Aerodrome Trust.

We also thank our photographers for their superb work that has added so much to the design of this book: Steven Baker, Anna Bridson, Alun Bull, Steve Cole, James Davies, Patricia Payne, Chris Redgrave and Jerry Young. We are also grateful to Damian Grady for aerial photography taken in support of the project.

John Vallender has prepared the illustrations, some based on drafts produced by our former colleagues Trevor Pearson and Philip Sinton.

Nicky Hughes, a volunteer in our Communications Team, has been a stalwart supporter of all our First World War related activities. She ensured a high media presence and researched images, while her incisive questioning has sharpened our presentations. Our former colleague Beth McHattie was also instrumental in raising the profile of the effect of the war on England. Robin Page helpfully alerted us to archaeological work being undertaken in Germany on traces of the First World War.

Among those who read and commented on particular chapters of the book we would like to thank Professor Nick Bosanquet and Dr Merrick Moseley. In addition, Sir Hew Strachan kindly read the whole volume in typescript.

Nigel Wilkins in our Archives offered invaluable assistance in tracking down many of the images used in the book. Paul Liss, of Liss Llewellyn Fine Art, kindly assisted in obtaining a copy of Figure 10.1. Finally, we would like to thank the publications team – John Hudson, Clare Blick and Jess Ward – for bringing this project to fruition.

Preface

Wayne Cocroft and Paul Stamper

A century ago, our forebears in the Office of Works and the Royal Commission on Historical Monuments (England) largely suspended their work for the duration of the First World War; in Essex, where work did continue, some RCHM investigators were detained as potential spies. Royal Commissioner Major Sir Schomberg Kerr McDonnell, GCVO, KCB, FSA, was an early casualty, killed in the trenches in 1915. Many members of staff, including a young archaeologist Mortimer Wheeler, were commissioned into the forces, while others were transferred to the War Office.[1] One particularly notable contribution was that of Frank Baines, of the Office of Works, who rendered great service to the country through the design of munitions factories, associated housing estates and other government construction projects.[2] Before the Royal Commission was suspended in 1916 it was charged by the Home Office with recording the damage to monuments caused by air raids; sadly, most of these records, with the possible exception of photographs of Lincoln's Inn Chapel, appear to be lost.[3] This one example illustrates how the unfolding magnitude of the conflict reached down into all aspects of national life as manpower and resources were redirected to the war effort.

A hundred years later the popular image of the war is dominated by the Western Front and the loss of hundreds of thousands of lives, commemorated on memorials in almost every community in England. This was the first total war between the major industrialised nations, and to supply the troops in the trenches and on other battle fronts, the Royal Navy, merchant marine and a rapidly expanding air force, required the mobilisation of the nation's resources and people on an unprecedented scale. Since the 1960s, and in particular following the publication of Arthur Marwick's groundbreaking book *The Deluge*, which analysed the social effects of the war, the study of the social history of the war and in particular the role of women have been popular topics.[4] The physical effect the war had on England's countryside and built environment has been surprisingly little explored, and relatively few sites and buildings have been protected. Shortly before the outbreak of the Second World War, at the February 1939 meeting of the Ancient Monuments Board, the scheduling of pillboxes of the 'last War' was discussed, but deferred to later generations.[5] It was only in the early 1990s that English Heritage experts began research on the First World War in the context of wider thematic studies of airfields, coastal fortifications, hospitals and munitions factories and the like. This book brings together the work of these authors, often over many years, alongside new research undertaken as part of the centenary programme on wireless stations, trench systems, submarines, and the legacy of the war at sea in the North Sea and Dover Straits.

This book also represents the culmination of a number of projects that Historic England has undertaken as part of the government's centennial programme. These have included new research into poorly understood classes of features and structures constructed for the war effort. With the exception of trench systems, relatively few survive sufficiently intact to merit national protection, although a notable survival is the early wireless station at Stockton-on-Tees.[6] Internationally, the United Kingdom has one of the greatest concentrations of local war memorials, commemorating the men, women and children who lost their lives fighting for their country, or in air raids or devastating explosions in munitions works. Funded by the Department for Digital, Culture, Media and Sport, Historic England has worked with the Imperial War Museum, Civic Voice and War Memorial Trust to improve the understanding, recording and conservation of these memorials and to increase their protection through listing, work greatly assisted by many volunteers. Historic England has also funded the Council for British Archaeology to develop the Home Front Legacy project, which has encouraged people to report and document traces and events of the war in their localities, and to record if they still survive.

While the focus of this book is on England, where relevant sites elsewhere in the British Isles are brought in to the discussion, as indeed is the wider European, and world, context. The book brings together what has been discovered about the legacy of the First World War in England, and begins to set the agenda for future research. It helps to mark the contribution and sacrifice not only of those who served in the armed forces, but also of those who provided support, in myriad ways, on the home front. These reminders the inquisitive can find all around us, as we now see in sharper focus.

1

Introduction

Sir Hew Strachan

On the afternoon of 3 August 1914, bank holiday Monday, the Foreign Secretary, Sir Edward Grey, stood before the House of Commons to give an account of recent events across Europe. That morning he had heard of Germany's ultimatum to Belgium, demanding passage for its army so that it could invade France, and of Belgium's rejection of the German request. The King of the Belgians had appealed to Britain for aid. 'What can diplomatic intervention do now?' Grey asked, before proceeding to give his own answer to that question. Policy had failed and failure to go to war would result in greater failure, with Germany dominating not just Belgium but all the Low Countries, and possibly France. If that were allowed to happen, 'just opposite to us there would be a common interest against the unmeasured aggrandisement of any Power'.[1]

Put more bluntly, Britain could not afford to have an over-mighty and hostile European state facing it across the English Channel, its principal waterway to the wider world. Whether it was the France of Louis XIV or Napoleon, or the Germany of Wilhelm II or Adolf Hitler, it was in Britain's interests to seek to balance such a threat, and – if need be – to form an alliance to fight it. In 1914 the growth and interdependence, both political and economic, of the British Empire did not create an alternative locus for British interests. Rather it confirmed their connections: geographically and geopolitically Britain was both of Europe and of the world (Fig 1.1). In addressing one, it was not rejecting the other.[2]

These links found their most obvious manifestations in the City of London and the Royal Navy. The City's shipping, banking and insurance markets underpinned a system of global trade, financed by the gold standard (which in this case meant the convertibility of the pound

Fig 1.1
Whitehall, London. The War Office, photographed in 1911, was designed by William Young and completed in 1907, and was the administrative centre of the British military effort. To accommodate its increased staff the War Office took over many other buildings in London, as well as erecting temporary accommodation.
[OP03709]

sterling) and carried overwhelmingly in British-owned vessels. Just under a half of the world's merchant tonnage was British, and it operated as cross-traders on international routes as much as it carried goods to and from different points across the Empire. As a result, Grey reminded his parliamentary colleagues on 3 August, war would affect Britain whether it remained neutral or not. He acknowledged that it would 'suffer ... terribly in this war', but 'little more than we shall suffer if we stand aside'. Britain had 'to protect our commerce, to protect our shores, and to protect our interests'. Its principal weapon in the coming conflict, at least as Grey portrayed it on that Monday afternoon, was the fleet (Fig 1.2).

There were many ideas as to how this fleet would be used, but no consensus. Was its purpose to seek a decisive battle with the German navy? Some, captivated by the memory of Trafalgar, harboured such visions. For others, its function – especially if the conflict were to be long – was to wage economic warfare against Germany. A blockade would prevent it from importing commodities vital to its military effort and could starve its population into revolution or surrender. So imprecise was some of this thinking that a few thought that economic war, if it caused crisis on the world's stock exchanges, could precipitate a general collapse and end the war in short order.[3] Nor were battle and blockade necessarily alternatives. The latter could precipitate the former, as the German navy would be forced to fight to reopen its own trading routes. And success in battle could enable Britain to tighten its economic stranglehold on Germany. For others the prime role of the Royal Navy was not offensive but defensive, to keep the sea lanes open and to protect trade. As the war lengthened, Britain's capacity to corral the world's resources for its allies became increasingly important. Those partners, Belgium, France and Russia, and later Italy, had access to the sea, but as continental European powers fighting a Central European alliance waged their war on land more than on the water. Their armies had operational plans ready in order to fight at least their opening campaigns. Britain by and large did not: on 3 August 1914 it still had to choose its strategy.

The main bases of the Royal Navy had been developed along the south coast, from Portsmouth to Plymouth. They reflected the legacy of two centuries shaped by war, or the fear of war, with France. However, in 1904 Britain and France had settled their differences, and in 1912 had signed a naval agreement which made

Fig 1.2
Whitehall, London. The Admiralty, the might of the Royal Navy reflected in stone and brick, was designed by Leeming and Leeming of Halifax, 1894–5. This was at the heart of British naval operations, and wireless aerials strung between the two copper domes allowed the Admiralty to keep in worldwide contact with its vessels. It was also home to the Room 40 codebreakers.
[DP017344]

France principally responsible for security in the Mediterranean, and Britain for the North Sea and Atlantic approaches. After 1905 the Royal Navy reoriented itself to face Germany. The ports of the German navy lay to the east and gave onto the Baltic and the North Sea, not to the south. In 1909 the Channel Fleet was folded into the Home Fleet. The First Sea Lord, Jackie Fisher, concentrated Britain's capital vessels, battleships and battlecruisers, in home waters, even if the battlecruisers, with their lighter armour and greater speed, were better designed for oceanic warfare than combat in the North Sea. Now the more logical bases lay not to the south and west of the North Foreland, but to its east and north. In the decade before the war's outbreak, the Admiralty began to develop Scapa Flow in the Orkneys. This would be the principal anchorage of the Grand Fleet during the war itself, and – moving south down Britain's east coast – Invergordon, Rosyth on the Firth of Forth (the wartime home of the battlecruisers) and Harwich (a harbour for light cruisers) followed suit. The infrastructural ramifications were significant, requiring not just quays and dry docks, but also accommodation and railway links. Because the navy was simultaneously matching and overtaking the German navy's construction targets for new ships, its budget for shore-based installations was limited, and they were far from ready when war broke out.[4]

The war at sea had a further effect on the distribution of employment and investment on mainland Britain. By positioning the Grand Fleet at Scapa Flow and using the 10th Cruiser Squadron to close off the main northern route into the Atlantic, and by simultaneously blocking the English Channel, Britain maximised its geographical position to shut Germany's exits from the North Sea. But the corollary was to convert that sea itself into a no-man's-land, sown with mines and home to submarines. The fishing ports of the east coast, from Aberdeen to Grimsby, were badly affected, and so too was both coastal and international trade on that side of Britain. On the other hand, the harbours on the west coast, Liverpool and Glasgow, and Queenstown (today Cobh) in southern Ireland, flourished, especially as the trade with North America grew. The routes across the Atlantic, which brought (in chronological order) wheat, armaments and – finally – American soldiers, tied up shipping space for less time than did the long hauls to Australia and New Zealand or the Far East.

When Grey addressed the House of Commons on 3 August 1914, he gave only passing attention to the army's role in a future war, merely suggesting that the British Expeditionary Force might be distributed around the Empire to protect its territories from direct attack. This was not what the recently created general staff of the army had in mind. It had been working on plans (and this was where Britain did have a war plan) to deploy the army to north-western Europe. These thoughts had gained particular traction in 1910, with the appointment of Henry Wilson as Director of Military Operations, and after 1911, when the crisis over Morocco created an imminent threat of war.[5]

Richard Burdon Haldane, appointed secretary of war in late 1905, at the same time as Grey became foreign secretary, had set about the formation of the British Expeditionary Force (BEF) to deal with imperial defence, not to support the balance of power in Europe. However, he had not anticipated that it would be divided into penny packets, as Grey seemed to imagine might be the case on 3 August 1914. The army was responsible for the domestic order of the colonies and for the protection of their frontiers, but it aimed to fulfil that duty with forces in place and with locally raised units, pre-eminently the Indian Army. The BEF was designed to reinforce those elements in the event of a challenge from a major power, and especially the invasion of India by Russia. The Anglo-Russian entente of 1907 reduced that threat (if it had ever existed) and freed military planners to focus not on Russia and India, but on Germany and north-west Europe.

If in the event of major war the bulk of the regular army was destined to go overseas, whether to the Empire or to Europe, it would leave the British Isles themselves unprotected. The navy was the first line of home defence, but the advent of the steamship, and the fact that its movements were less fettered by the wind or by tides, fed fears of invasion from the 1840s onwards. Those who called for increased spending on the army used this danger as their principal argument. Aldershot and its surrounding area was chosen as a home in which to train the army, in part because it could be rapidly deployed from this base to different points on the coast to repel foreign forces. From the mid-19th century onwards, fortifications were constructed along the Essex, Kent and Sussex coasts in particular to deter, or if need be to counter, a French landing. After 1904 the Committee of Imperial

Defence conducted enquiries into the danger of a German invasion, but for all the sensationalist fiction to the contrary was dismissive of the dangers. Nonetheless, Haldane's reorganisation of the auxiliary forces of the army, the militia and volunteers rested on the rationale of home defence, not least if the BEF was overseas and the fleet was deployed in remote waters.

Haldane's 'citizen army', the Territorial Force, was formed in 1908, with a target strength of 300,000. Although it never recruited to its full establishment before 1914, it created a military footprint across the country (Fig 1.3). Many of its buildings were the products of an earlier reorganisation in 1881, when Henry Childers completed the reforms to the army commenced by Edward Cardwell in 1867–74. The regular infantry battalions were linked in pairs, the intention being that one should serve at home and the other abroad. They were given regional titles, associating them with particular counties or areas of Britain, where they also recruited. The militia and volunteers formed higher numbered battalions of the same regiments with the same local links, and these connections between the units of the regular army on the one hand and particular communities were perpetuated by the Territorial Force (Fig 1.4). When the army expanded after 1914 it created new 'service' battalions, but ones which revelled in the history and traditions acquired by British regular regiments over two centuries of soldiering: a narrowly professional force became a possession of the people.

Castellated depots appeared in county towns, and many smaller places boasted drill halls and rifle ranges.[6] None of this infrastructure was adequate to house the mass army created in the First World War, but it did enable its enlistment. The existing recruitment offices were not sufficient to match the rush of volunteers, and Territorial drill halls provided alternatives. Although the Territorials were enlisted for home service, they could commit themselves to an 'imperial service obligation'. From 21 August 1914 those units in which 80 per cent had so volunteered could complete to war establishment. By the war's end, 318 Territorial battalions had gone overseas.[7]

Fig 1.3
Cirencester, Gloucestershire. By 1914 the Royal North Gloucester Militia Armoury, Cecily Hill (built 1857), was home to the 4th Battalion of the Gloucester Regiment.
[BB98/13827]

Fig 1.4
Parading at a Northamptonshire drill hall or assembly point, probably in the first weeks of the war. Several things (as well as their respectable dress and well-polished shoes) suggest these are reservists: their age, and that most seem to know how to 'stand easy' with their hands behind their backs and feet properly spaced.
[Courtesy Paul Stamper]

The First World War therefore represented a profound strategic shift for Britain. The profile of the navy in Britain's war effort, although remaining of enormous importance, declined, while that of the army rose. Britain created a mass army, but in the process sent abroad the bulk of the force it had earmarked for home defence should the navy be unequal to the task. The fear of invasion was particularly strong in the early stages of the war. On 1 November 1914 the aura of British maritime supremacy was severely dented at Coronel, off the coast of Chile, when Graf von Spee's East Asiatic Squadron destroyed a British squadron in 30 minutes. The Admiralty's response, to detach three battlecruisers to go to the Pacific and South Atlantic, meant that for alarmists the margin of superiority enjoyed in home waters by the British Grand Fleet over the German High Seas Fleet was too small for error. Once Spee's squadron was dispatched to the deeps on 8 December, the battlecruisers turned for home.

That winter the fear of a German invasion seemed real enough, and it never entirely dissipated thereafter. In November and December, German battlecruisers raided Yarmouth and Scarborough. Tucked up to the north, the Grand Fleet relied heavily on the signals intelligence available to it as a result of the capture of German code books in 1914. They enabled the only clash between the two fleets, at Jutland on 31 May 1916. However, the threat from the German navy did not come only from the sea. It was also airborne. In January 1915 German naval Zeppelins bombed the British coast, and from April they were joined by the army's airships, with raids directed not just at naval installations but also on London itself. The majority of British civilian deaths as a result of enemy action in the First World War were caused by the German navy: over 15,000 died at sea and 1,266 from air and sea bombardment.[8] In June 1917 the German army abandoned its dirigibles in favour of fixed-wing aircraft, and Gotha bombers attacked London for a full year until May 1918, when they were diverted to France to give more direct support to the army's ground operations.[9] Britain was itself a battlefront for much of the war.

That in itself cannot explain the size of the home force maintained by the British army, especially by 1917–18 as the danger of an actual invasion receded. In November 1916, 1.79 million British soldiers were at home, as opposed to just over 2 million deployed overseas in the theatres of war. Over the course of 1917, the commitment to the war rose to a peak of 3.3 million men by December and still stood at 3.22 million in November 1918. The size of the BEF did not, however, rise in step with the demands on the Western Front, especially after the French army passed its peak strength in 1917 and before the Americans arrived in numbers from May 1918. Nor was the home army significantly reduced. Between March and May 1918, as the Germans unleashed the first of their Western Front offensives, the forces at home fell from 1.66 million men to 1.48 million, but they recovered almost immediately thereafter and by September, as the BEF moved over to the offensive and took heavy losses in consequence, stood at 1.63 million.[10]

It would be easy to conclude that some of the soldiers at home were unfit for overseas service by dint of age or wounds, but many of these were incorporated in the Volunteers, who also included those exempted from conscription, normally because they were in reserved occupations. Between 1916 and 1918 the Volunteers' strength, which was additional to the home army totals, ranged between 273,000 and 292,000. Soldiers who were sent to Britain because of wounds and were expected to recover do figure in the home army totals: of the 130,000 service personnel who died in the First World War and are buried in Britain, about 90,000 succumbed in hospital from wounds incurred overseas. However, the home army's overall size makes a further point: the threats at home were not just that of a German invasion. They included, especially after the Easter Rising in Dublin in 1916, the possibility of another Irish nationalist insurrection, and from 1917 the fear of resurgent internationalist socialism.

The popular image of Britain as a nation which went to war united in its enthusiasm for the cause has not stood up to scholarly scrutiny. It makes insufficient allowance for differences in age, class, employment and geography. Many school leavers and undergraduates may have joined up with alacrity, but those who were married needed first to put their affairs in order and to ensure that their families would be cared for if they were killed. Many may have joined up because they needed work. The war's outbreak precipitated short-term unemployment as peacetime industries lost markets and businesses closed, while the conversion to war production had yet to take up the slack. The rush to the colours peaked six weeks after the war's outbreak, in September, not in August, 1914, and personal considerations may have been more influential

Fig 1.5
The war asked much of many families. Here a studio portrait taken in Wellingborough (Northamptonshire), probably of siblings, records their service in the St John's Ambulance Brigade, as a munitioneer and as a soldier in the Royal Fusiliers.
[Courtesy Paul Stamper]

Fig 1.6 (opposite)
St James's Park, Whitehall, London, photographed in 1921. The glittering lake in the park was drained for fear that it might act as a marker for German aerial attacks. Temporary government offices were built on the lake bed, including outposts of the Ministries of Blockade and Shipping, the War Office pensions office, and the Passport Office. To the top of the picture are Horse Guards Parade, the Admiralty and the War Office.
[EPW006161]

in determining individual responses than events at the front (Fig 1.5). By the end of 1915 the flow of recruits had slowed. By now too the sense of inequity created by the losses sustained by those who had joined up voluntarily created a popular consensus in favour of conscription, which was adopted in the summer of 1916.[11]

The winter of 1916–17 was tough for all the belligerents. The harvest had been poor and food was in short supply, although Britain was less affected than Central and Eastern Europe. Hopes for a negotiated peace at the year's end were dashed. While official trades unionism in Britain remained focused on conditions of employment, the unofficial shop stewards prompted fears of socialism. In 1917 war-weariness led Parliament to establish a National War Aims Committee. Inspired in part by the earlier example of the Parliamentary Recruiting Committee, its aim was to reaffirm the purposes for which Britain was fighting, especially after November 1917 when the Bolsheviks in Russia captured the moral high ground by calling for a peace without annexations or indemnities. As German strength waned, fear of Bolshevism stepped into the vacuum.

The British government gave itself a powerful agent for the management of its own population when it passed the Defence of the Realm Act. Designed on the outbreak of the war to catch spies, by its end it had curtailed civil liberties, its regulations leaving lasting legacies from the management of pubs' opening hours to the introduction of daylight saving. The popular-

isation in 1914 of 'business as usual' was not a statement that the values of Liberal Britain were to be the basis for waging the war, but an indication of national resolve to carry on in the knowledge that they would not.

First the Liberal government, and then – from May 1915 – the coalition showed it was ready to place itself between employers and workers in the regulation of trade relations in order to maximise national output for state purposes. From the winter of 1914–15 the government set about the conversion of industry for war production. State-owned factories were sufficient to maintain the output of guns and shells required for a small army before the war, as well as to maintain quality control. But private armaments firms, of which Vickers was the best known, made the bigger items, such as heavy artillery and warships, financing the investment required in plant by overseas sales. During the First World War the state met its own demands through partnerships with private industry, bringing in what Lloyd George called 'men of push and go' from business to organise output, and creating umbrella organisations which encouraged small concerns to convert production from the civilian applications of peacetime to the needs of war. In May 1915 Lloyd George himself became the first minister of munitions. The department's success lay in its capacity to distribute output across the country through a regional network by creating a national framework for existing industries.

Other new ministries followed, mostly after Lloyd George became prime minister in

December 1916 – for trade, the Ministries of Blockade and Shipping; labour, the Ministries of Labour and of National Service; and the press, the Ministry of Information (Fig 1.6). Britain mobilised for war through governmental intervention while retaining the rhetoric of partnership and consent, and came out of it convinced that it had won it for democracy and liberal values. In reality the state never fully retreated from the position the First World War had encouraged it to assume, even if the overt justification was removed in 1919. In many respects, therefore, the experience of 'total war' in 1914–18 foreshadowed that of 1939–45. In both wars Britain's geography made it the offshore base for Europe, providing the link with the wider world without which its values would not have prevailed.

2

The army

Peter Kendall

Introduction

Probably the single greatest achievement by the British state during the war was the creation of a very large army, which increased from an entire strength of 733,514 in 1914 to 3,563,466 British soldiers by November 1918, and a total of over 5.3 million when colonial, Indian Army, and native troops and labourers are included.[1] During the war in total 5 million men volunteered for or were conscripted into the British army, representing 22 per cent of the male population. The army did not just grow in size. In response to new weapons and tactics it became a much more complex and diverse force. Large parts of the infrastructure for waging war, including training schools, were overseas, but nevertheless no part of England was untouched by the war effort, with many buildings and large areas of land devoted to army use.[2] By November 1918, 1,383,311 British and 220,073 colonial soldiers were based in Great Britain, at places used for training and rehabilitation, for home front defence, for the supply of the forces abroad and for military research. Many physical remains survive as evidence of this monumental national undertaking.

The fighting branches of the army

Britain in effect fielded four separate armies, each of which was constituted in a different way. The Regulars of the pre-war army formed the expeditionary force which sailed for the continent at the outbreak of war and served with distinction, but was soon spent. Army reservists and the Territorials (volunteer part-time soldiers) were embodied next. The early fighting revealed the need for a large army, and Lord Kitchener as secretary of state for war called for New Armies made up of wartime volunteers. Initial enthusiasm to serve was huge: in September 1914 alone, 462,901 men volunteered. Pals battalions saw volunteers from the same professions, sports clubs, towns and cities first train and then fight together.

Over 1915 the rate of volunteering declined and this resulted in a fourth type of soldier, the conscript. Britain had never had a mass conscription army and it took time for the inevitability of one to be accepted. In October 1915 the Derby Scheme allowed men to voluntarily attest for service but only to be called to serve as required. This did not address the need for men, and a first Military Service Act in January 1916 made all single men aged 18 to 41 liable for compulsory military service, with married men too from May 1916. Between 1916 and 1918 about 2.5 million men were conscripted.

Quartering the New Armies

Significant reforms to address problems exposed by the army's performance in the Boer War (1899–1902) had included investment in new barracks.[3] These could not house the mass volunteer army of late 1914 as accommodation was available for only *c* 179,000 soldiers.[4] Forces at home were divided into the commands shown in Table 2.1. Aldershot, Hampshire, was the main centre of the army, with additional Great Camps at Shorncliffe, Kent; Colchester, Essex; and the Curragh, Ireland. The Cardwell reforms of 1872 had resulted in localisation depots[5] in the most populous towns for county-associated regiments. In 1914 these depots and Territorial drill halls[6] built from the mid-19th century provided infrastructure for recruitment and training but not sufficient quarters. From 1897 land at Salisbury Plain, Wiltshire, was acquired for new manoeuvring grounds and artillery ranges, with new barracks built there at Tidworth and Bulford. Larkhill was initially a summer camp.[7]

Table 2.1 Increase in available troop accommodation by Home Command

Command	In Aug 1914	By Aug 1915	By Aug 1918
Aldershot	30,990	118,198	135,321
Eastern	39,010	168,291	288,527
London District	8,274	15,459	19,751
Northern	11,544	63,842	248,804
Southern	36,104	223,403	315,346
Western	9,436	55,049	133,388
Irish	35,086	133,938	109,612
Scottish	8,434	68,297	62,887
Total	**178,878**	**846,477**	**1,313,636**

Source: TNA, WO 107/264, and War Office, *Statistics of the Military Effort of the British Empire during the Great War, 1914–1920.* London: HMSO, 1922.

Winter of 1914–15 saw a quartering crisis when tented camps became untenable and with the situation made worse by the arrival of large numbers of colonial troops. The solution was to construct new training centres as vast hutted camps. These took time to build, so as a stopgap troops were billeted on houseowners and in hired buildings. Perhaps the strangest example of the latter were the elaborate plasterboard pavilions and dance halls at Bristol's White City, erected for an international exhibition.[8]

Many of the first new camps were built near Aldershot, around Salisbury Plain in Southern Command (Fig 2.1), and near the Channel ports in Eastern Command. Northern Command increased more slowly, with Catterick, North Yorkshire,[9] selected as a new garrison centre and other large camps at nearby Ripon. Further large northern camps were established at Rugeley and Brocton on Cannock Chase, Staffordshire, and at Clipstone, Nottinghamshire (Fig 2.2). As Britain's colonial allies also mobilised for war, many of their troops came to England before deployment abroad. Australia and New Zealand had camps mainly on Salisbury Plain, while the Canadians were chiefly based around Shorncliffe. In 1917 the United States of America sent over 1 million men to France via England, most through Liverpool (with a major rest camp at Knotty Ash) and then on to south-coast camps close to Southampton, Hampshire.

Fig 2.1 Rollestone Camp, Salisbury Plain, Wiltshire, under construction in 1915. From 1916 it was occupied by Australian training battalions. [Courtesy P Kendall]

*Fig 2.2
Clipstone Camp, Nottinghamshire. Informal gardens were a common feature of many camps and archaeological traces may be found.
[Courtesy P Kendall]*

Many new camps were the size of small towns. Their locations were carefully chosen to be close to open ground suitable for training and to rail transport, often by newly constructed spur lines. Some sites, known to the War Office from pre-war training, were volunteered by their owners for wartime use, but others had to be compulsorily purchased using the Defence of the Realm Act (1914). The fundamental component of each camp was the single hut. British experience of barrack huts stretched back to the Crimean War, and in 1914, in just a few days, Major B H O Armstrong Royal Engineers (RE) produced drawings for 17 different hut types that in combination created an entire camp. The commonest type was a sleeping hut to hold 25 men. Most early examples were built entirely of timber, but later construction based on a light steel frame and concrete block walls became the norm, as timber became scarcer and concrete huts proved more hygienic and less vulnerable to fire. Some of the first training camps were later converted to command depots to rehabilitate recovered soldiers prior to their resuming active service, while huts were also used to create additional accommodation at military hospitals. Huts were built in their tens of thousands but today very few examples survive, at least at their original sites. A group of concrete huts at Ripon is a rare exception.

Army camps in North Yorkshire

Catterick camp in North Yorkshire was created in early 1915 as a wholly new camp to contain 40,000 troops. It remains a major garrison of the British army, and hence very few of its 2,000 wartime concrete huts now remain. Nearby, at Ripon, there is a more coherent survival of just a small part of that site, represented by a group of concrete huts which have survived as they were converted to new uses after 1918. North and South camps were created here in 1915 to hold 30,000 men, and these dwarfed the existing town and its 7,000 residents (Fig 2.3). Picked out in red is the only surviving part, showing just how little of the two great camps now remains. This is the only location identified to date where a large group of army huts has survived, enabling an idea of the overall appearance of an army camp of this period to be gained. The new uses have, however, eroded the simple military character of the huts (Figs 2.4 and 2.5).

Fig 2.3 (right)
Ripon, North Yorkshire. Plan of North and South camps built by 1915. Their area exceeded that of the historic city. The partly surviving sub-camp is marked in red.

Fig 2.4 (below)
Ripon, North Yorkshire. A surviving concrete hut converted into a house.
[DP174562]

Fig 2.5 (bottom)
Ripon, North Yorkshire. Aerial photograph showing the extent of the surviving sub-camp.
[NMR 28751/008]

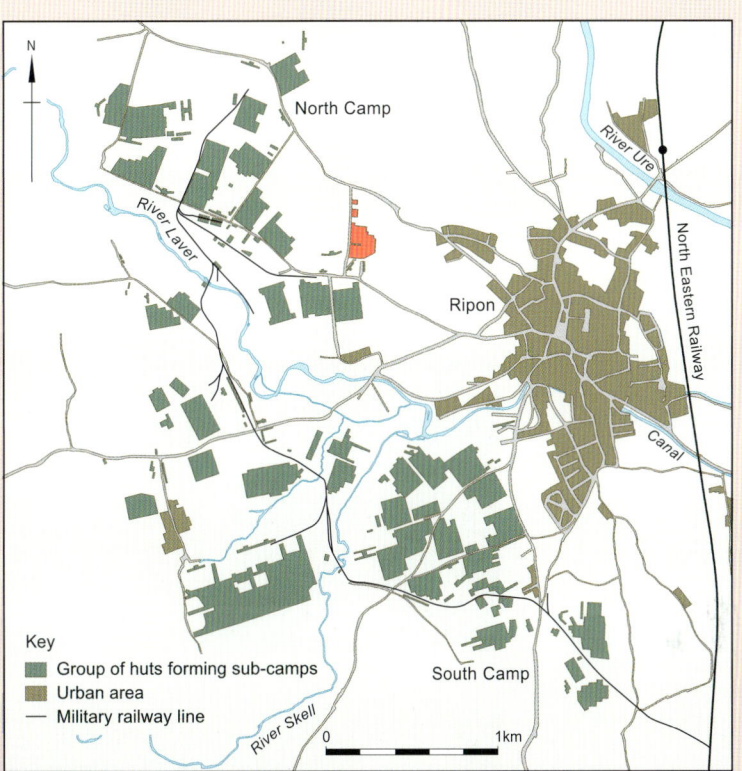

Elsewhere very few timber examples now survive as first built. Some have been restored:[10] the Great War Hut at Cannock Chase is a typical sleeping hut, presented for its 1915 appearance (Figs 2.6 and 2.7). At the end of the war most camps were broken up and the huts auctioned by the Disposals Board for removal by new owners. Around the country a few huts survive as relocated, and scattered, examples, some still in use, albeit much repaired and altered. As the army camps were broken up, anything that could be sold was salvaged. Despite this the camps have often left archaeological remains. Buried structures are frequently visible through aerial prospection (Fig 2.8),[11] and a few sites have been excavated to reveal the remains of buildings (Fig 2.9).[12] Excavation can also produce distinctive artefacts which can help to identify sites, their occupants and uses. Typical items include uniform buttons and unit badges, government-issue crockery, male toiletry items and containers for the food purchased to relieve

*Fig 2.6 (right)
Cannock Chase, Staffordshire. The exterior of the Great War Hut, reconstructed using elements from several original examples.
[DP160764]*

*Fig 2.7 (far right)
The interior of the reconstructed Great War Hut, displayed to represent typical soldiers' living quarters.
[DP160767]*

*Fig 2.8
Seaford, North Camp, Sussex, 1951. Traces of the rectilinear pattern of the First World War camp may be seen running diagonally across the photograph. The circular feature is an old quarry.
[RAF/58/613/RS/4237]*

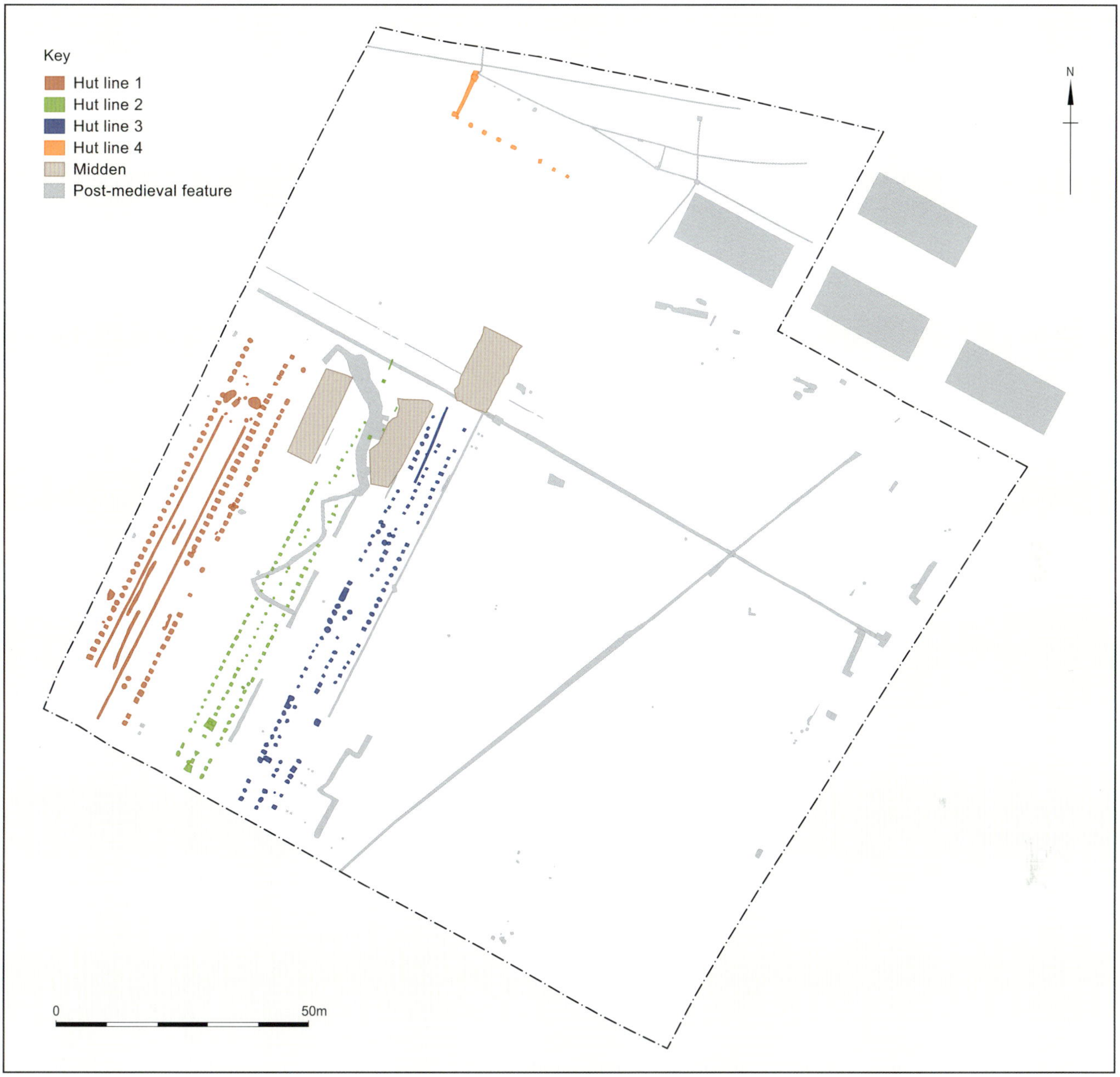

the monotony of the military diet. Some such items may have come from the structures that also grew up at major camps to provide services to the troops. There were shops, banks and cinemas and, for social and spiritual needs, YMCA huts and church institutes. Some army camps grew at least some of the food they needed, and soldiers also created small private ornamental and vegetable gardens. On Salisbury Plain some units chose to permanently record their presence by chalk-cut figures of their regimental emblems, including some by the Australians and New Zealanders (Fig 2.10).

Fig 2.9 (above)
St Martins Plain, Shorncliffe, Kent. Archaeological excavation plan showing rows of posts which supported the huts' floors. [Courtesy Pre-Construct Archaeology]

Fig 2.10 (left)
Fovant, Wiltshire. Chalk-cut regimental badges, above which is the Iron Age hill fort Chiselbury Camp. [NMR 29526/025]

Prisoner-of-war and civil internment camps

One unforeseen consequence of the progress of the war was the need to confine large numbers of prisoners of war (POWs) and enemy aliens.

Military prisoners

In autumn 1914, as the Western Front stagnated into fixed front lines, the number of German POWs captured during military operations and held in Britain was relatively small; by the beginning of 1915 it stood at 6,900, including sailors. From 1916 this figure grew rapidly to 49,815 by November 1917, and a year later had virtually doubled to 91,428. This number, however, represented a small proportion of the up to 328,900 Germans captured by the British, most of whom were held behind the lines in France.[13] Under the recently ratified 1906 Geneva and 1907 Hague Conventions, captured servicemen were entitled to board, lodging and clothing comparable to that of the detaining power's army, and treatment commensurate with their rank.[14] The pressure on the government to find suitable housing for these prisoners, alongside accommodation for vastly expanded British armed forces, was evident in the great variety of places used to hold prisoners. Initially, some were held in tented camps, such as that at Frith Hill, Frimley, Surrey, which appeared little different to a regular army camp except for its barbed wire fences and guard posts (Fig 2.11).

One of the earliest military POW camps was set up in an unoccupied artillery barracks at Dorchester.[15] Photographs, probably taken in 1917, show a well-ordered hutted camp, with a theatre, hospital and chapel.[16] Elsewhere military prisoners were held in vacant factory premises, such as an unfinished mill at Leigh, Lancashire, while others were interned in chartered ships moored off Portsmouth, Hampshire, and Southend, Essex.[17] Officers were housed separately in three camps, such as the one at Donington Hall, Leicestershire.[18] Here rooms in the hall were used as a mess and for reading; officers slept in wooden huts in the grounds, while enlisted men acting as batmen were accommodated in separate huts.[19]

According to the Hague Convention, enlisted men and non-commissioned officers might be expected to undertake work for which they would be paid, although it could not be directly related to military activities. Due to objections by the trades unions, POWs rarely worked in Britain until 1917, but after this date they were employed in agriculture, quarrying, forestry, land reclamation and even airfield construction, as at Yatesbury, Wiltshire (see Chapter 5). Prisoners might be marched to and from work each day or they might be accommodated in small sub-camps. One such has been investigated at Felday, Surrey, where among the discoveries was a deposit of calcium carbonate, probably a waste product from the guards' acetylene searchlights.[20] At Madeley, Staffordshire, a previously undocumented agricultural camp was revealed by an earthwork survey.[21]

Civilian internees

In 1914 there were many thousands of civilians from Germany and the other enemy nations working in England, and the 1911 census identified around 53,000 Germans living in England and Wales.[22] Through provisions in the Aliens Restriction Act (1914) and Defence of the Realm Act the government moved quickly to restrict their movement and liberty. Women, children and elderly men might be repatriated, while

Fig 2.11
A tented camp for German prisoners, probably Frith Hill, Frimley, Surrey. Note the stone-lined gardens decorated with conifer branches.
[Courtesy W D Cocroft]

from October 1914 men of military-service age were interned. Close to London, the exhibition centres at Earls Court, Olympia and Alexandra Palace were taken over to house internees, while elsewhere places as diverse as a wagon works in Lancaster and Newbury race course were pressed into service.[23]

The National Sailors' and Firemen's Union looked to protect the interests of its German members by proposing Alton Abbey, Hampshire, and the Priory, Hyde Vale, Greenwich, as places of internment.[24] They followed this by purchasing Eastcote House, Pattishall, Northamptonshire. Here accommodation was at first in a farmhouse and tents before these were replaced by 24 huts, each 200ft x 30ft x 12ft 6in (61 x 9 x 3.8m).[25] Amenities in the camp included a kitchen, a bakery, a wash house, reading and writing rooms, a swimming pool, vegetable plots and fittingly a model harbour with boats.[26] At Libury Hall, Ware, Hertfordshire, the charitable German Farm Colony, established to assist destitute Germans in England, was paid by the Home Office to house detainees.[27] At Lofthouse, West Yorkshire, a former amusement park, more affluent detainees were permitted to pay for better accommodation within the camp. Photographs show refreshments being taken in a conservatory, while outside were small chalets, typical of allotment-style huts seen on the fringes of many German cities. The largest civil internment camp was at Knockaloe, Isle of Man, which by 1918 housed 24,500 internees.

Some long-term residents Anglicised their names; Edward Kraftmeier, the London agent of the Anglo-German Chilworth Gunpowder Company, changed his name to Edward Kay.[28] In Derby this course of action was prevented by a by-law passed in October 1914 which forbade alien enemies from changing their name on pain of a £100 fine.[29] Anti-German sentiment ran high, and various companies with German-sounding names, such as the Kleine Patent Fire-Resisting Flooring Syndicate, took out adverts to clarify that they were British companies, employing only British labour, under British management and using British materials.[30] In October 1914 the 'King of Prussia Inn' in Halifax was renamed the 'King of Belgium',[31] and similarly the 'King of Prussia' pub in Heanor, Derbyshire, was renamed the 'Market Hotel' in November for 'patriotic reasons'.[32] London had a large German population and riots soon broke out – the worst being in Deptford in October 1914 – with further rioting following the sinking of SS *Lusitania* in May 1915 damaging a number of shops.

Despite the anti-German sentiment, POWs and civilian internees detained in England were generally correctly treated; where privations of poor accommodation and inadequate food did occur it was often due to wartime shortages rather than orchestrated mistreatment. The death rate among prisoners held by the British was about 3 per cent; this was in stark contrast to the experience in Central and Eastern Europe, where losses among some nationalities were 10 times as great.[33]

Traces

A *List of Places of Internment* compiled at the end of the war by the Prisoners of War Information Bureau recorded about 560 places in England where mainly German POWs were held.[34] However, the precise location of many of these places of internment is today unknown, as the published *List* typically provides only a generalised location, and often does not indicate whether the POWs were held in a camp or adapted buildings, such as workhouses or factories. Sometimes the places where prisoners were held still survive, or at least evidence of them does. At Brocton, Cannock Chase, Staffordshire, earthwork traces of the huts can be seen along with pebbles that marked the edges of garden beds.[35] Without supporting documentation there is little to distinguish them from the remains of contemporary army camps. Buried deposits within the camps offer the possibility of learning more about what life was like as a prisoner, including the types of goods they received in Red Cross parcels to remind them of home.

Training soldiers

The first months of fighting on the Western Front forced a realisation that the training of the New Armies had to respond to the reality of trench warfare, as opposed to a war of movement. Training civilians to be infantry soldiers required building up their physical fitness and instruction in the use of rifle, bayonet and trench tactics. Accordingly land was taken up within marching distance of each camp, at which to practice the construction and occupation of trenches and for rifle ranges.

Practice trenches

In 1914 digging trenches was a far from novel tactic, but the combination of static warfare and modern weapons forced the adoption by both sides of trench systems of an unprecedented scale and complexity, the physical remains of which endure as places of pilgrimage. Examples of trench systems were also built in the United Kingdom, some as anti-invasion defences, others as training grounds. Less frequently trenches were built for research and development purposes or as exhibits for the public to visit.

The British army referred to trenches as *fieldworks* or *entrenchments*. An Army Council instruction about infantry training dated 11 March 1915 describes the type of exercise by then made necessary:

> entrenching means not merely digging trenches, but siting them and improving them by traverses, revetments and drainage, the construction of support and communication trenches, supporting points and the rapid erection of wire entanglements. All these details should be taught not just theoretically but practically and continuously, under conditions as nearly as possible akin to those now obtaining in the field. Constant practice is essential, especially in carrying out by night all such work as is referred to above.[36]

The training described above saw the construction of fieldworks, now known as *practice trenches,* used not only to teach recruits how to construct them but also the routines necessary to occupy them for both defensive and attacking purposes. Practice trenches had to accurately replicate the conditions at the front. Some systems combined British and German trench designs, as at Bovington, Dorset, but most consisted solely of British trench systems, often as a single line but sometimes with a second, opposing line, facing. Parallel lines of trenches created defence in depth, with a front line backed up by support or reserve trenches incorporating latrines and first aid posts. Front-line trenches often have a distinctive 'crenelated' appearance to create *traverses* or *fire bays* which prevented blast or bullets from passing down a trench. Communication trenches which permitted movement between the lines of trenches frequently have a zigzag course, again for protection (Fig 2.12). As the war progressed and tactics developed, trench systems became ever more elaborate and incorporated machine-gun and mortar posts, bomb throwing pits and locations for gas warfare. Command posts often took the form of buried dugouts that provided some protection from artillery.

Information, such as war diaries or photographs, sometimes makes it possible to tie archaeological remains to training by a specific unit, and, if so, this adds to the significance of the evidence. At Redmires, near Sheffield, South Yorkshire, an extensive area of trenches is associated with the 12th (Sheffield City) (Service Battalion) of the York and Lancaster Regiment (popularly known as the Sheffield Pals), initially formed in September 1914. British Pathé newsreels include many examples of soldiers digging or occupying practice trenches, but the precise location of these can now be difficult to determine.[37]

Surveys increasingly reveal just how abundant and extensive practice trench remains are. Some survive as visible earthworks, and far more as soil or crop marks (Fig 2.13). Relatively few have seen archaeological investigation, although work has taken place at two of the main centres

Fig 2.12
Beacon Hill, Salisbury Plain, Wiltshire. Training trenches: to the right (immediately left of the track) was the front line, with zigzag communications trenches running to the rear. Also to the rear are shell holes (perhaps hand-dug), which added to the realism of the training landscape.
[NMR 24863/047]

The army

Fig 2.13 (left) Rothbury, Northumberland. Training trenches, first dug in 1915. Front, support and zigzag communication trenches can be seen. [NMR 20683/055]

Fig 2.14 (below) Larkhill, Wiltshire. Training trenches excavated in 2016; the infilled trenches and square-island traverses show clearly against the local chalk bedrock. [© WYG and Wessex Archaeology]

for training of the British army, Salisbury Plain and Cannock Chase.

Salisbury Plain

Land on Salisbury Plain was purchased in the late 19th century for army manoeuvres, and from this grew the extensive training estate still in use to this day. Many units of the New Armies were based here in hutted camps and were soon joined by troops of the colonial allies, most notably the Australians and New Zealanders. Evidence for the training of troops is widespread, notably practice trenches mapped from the air. Recent excavation has added significant new information. At Larkhill new housing for service families prompted the investigation of part of an extensive trench system, thought to have been used by Australian infantry in their preparation for the Somme offensive in 1916 (Figs 2.14 and 2.15). The trenches show an overall correlation to the fieldwork designs of contemporary military manuals, but excavation has confirmed their complexity and also produced small-scale evidence, such as graffiti on the chalk, which allows a more personal connection to the individuals who trained here. North of Larkhill, at Bustard Trenches, the evidence includes practice mines (tunnelling under the trenches), among them a mine crater with the saps (small trenches) used to secure it as a defensive position. Here too there is graffiti by individual soldiers, but this time as arborglyphs, carvings into the tree trunks of a nearby copse.

17

Legacies of the First World War

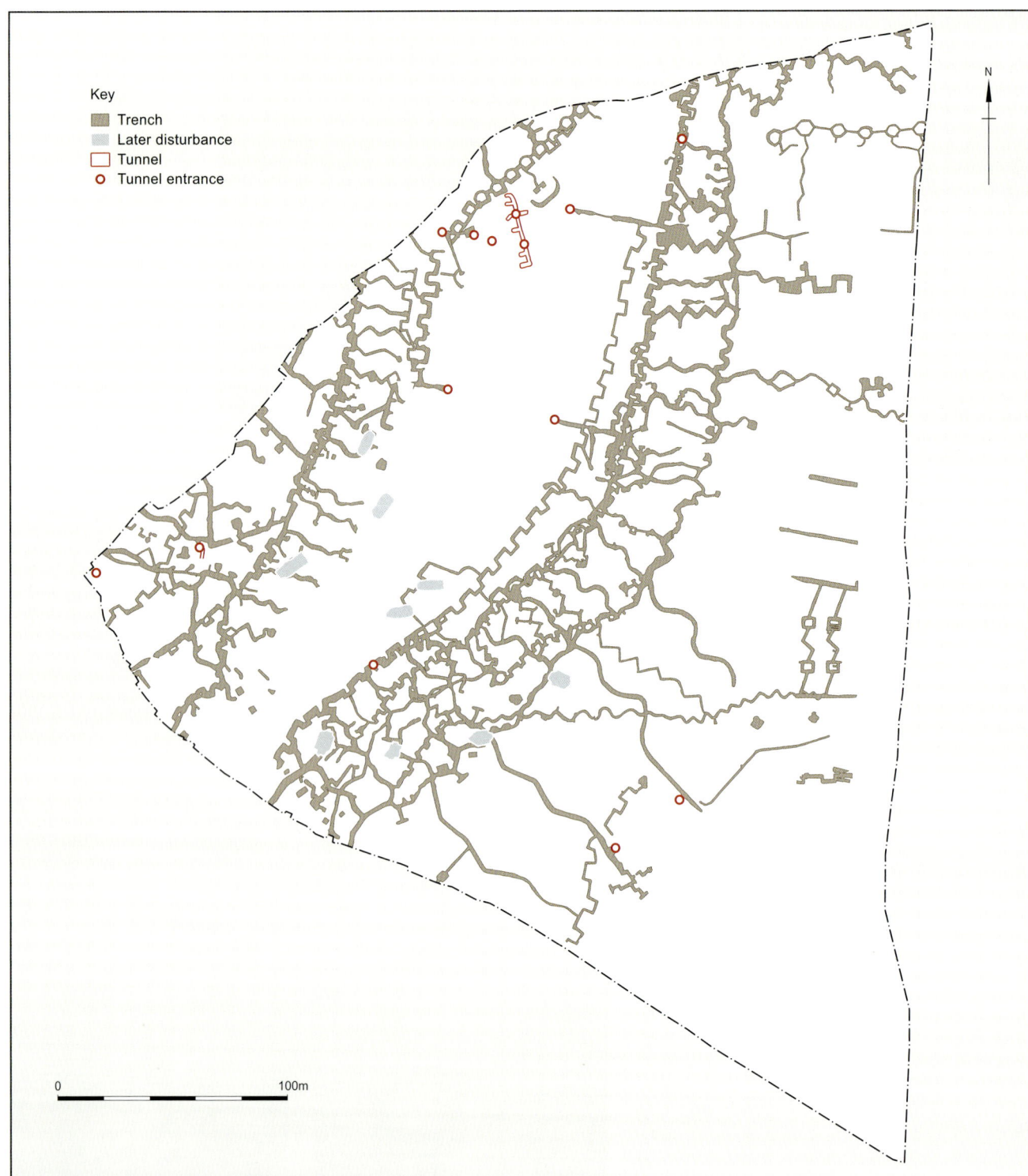

Fig 2.15
Larkhill, Wiltshire. Training trenches excavated in 2016, showing the extensive landscape of trenches and tunnels used in 1916 by Australian troops preparing for the Somme offensive.
[Courtesy WYG]

Cannock Chase

Cannock Chase held 40,000 men in two hutted camps, at Brocton and Rugeley (Fig 2.16). Today this land is an Area of Outstanding Natural Beauty, managed for its landscape significance. While forestry and bracken make the earthwork remains of an extensive First World War military training landscape difficult to detect and understand on the ground, lidar is enabling the mapping of the remains of the camps and their associated training grounds, practice trench systems and rifle ranges (Fig 2.17). Unique to this place is a detailed terrain model made out of concrete, pieces of brick and pebbles. It depicts the town of Messines, in West Flanders, Belgium, and its defences on the eve of its assault by the New Zealand Rifle Brigade in June 1917. Its purpose appears to have been to show how success was achieved to later recruits, but it might also have been intended as a permanent memorial. After the war it could be visited by paying members of the public, but it eventually became buried and lost to view until, in 2013, the model was carefully uncovered and recorded by detailed photography before reburial for its protection (Fig 2.18).[38] Cannock Chase also has quarter-scale representations of a typical set of British trenches, at Rugeley camp,

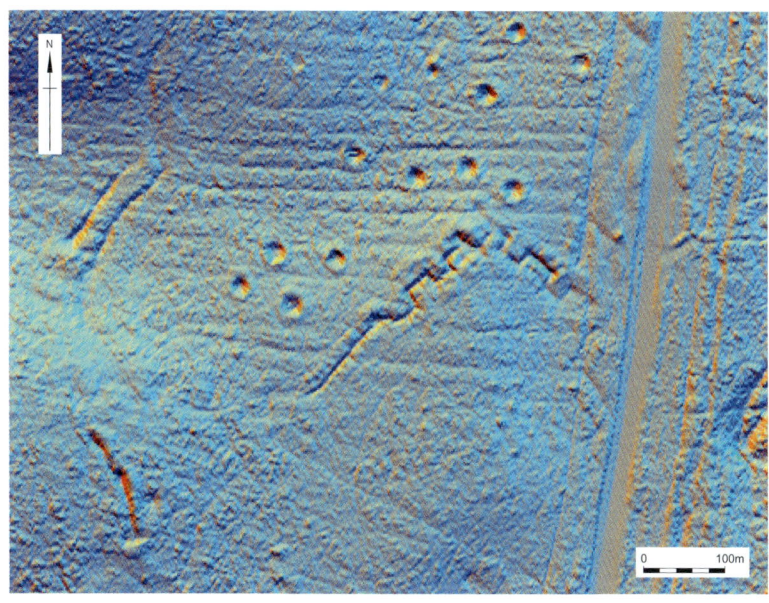

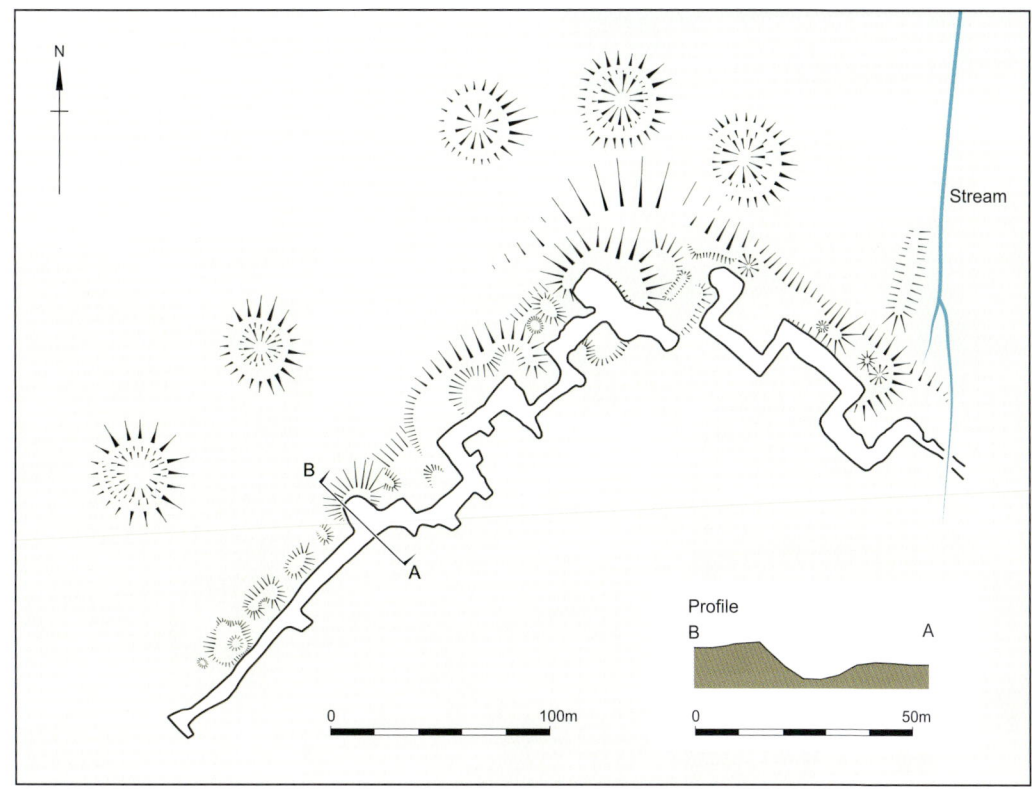

Fig 2.16 (top)
Brocton Camp, Cannock Chase, Staffordshire. In the middle ground, men are digging training trenches.
[Courtesy P Kendall]

Fig 2.17 a & b (above and left)
Sherbrook, Cannock Chase, Staffordshire. Lidar and analytical earthwork survey of a small-scale practice trench.
[Chase Through Time 2016 lidar. Source: Staffordshire CC/Fugro Geospatial BV 2016]

19

too small for actual use. These appear to be another instructional aid.

The public soon became familiar with the trench warfare of the Western Front, and some wanted to experience what it was like. In London, Trafalgar Square was transformed into a French scene, complete with windmill, to help sell war bonds (Fig 2.19), and the *Daily Mail* Active Service Exhibition (1916) included recreations of trenches and dugouts. At Lytham St Annes, Lancashire, practice trenches dug by recruits in 1915 were taken over by soldiers convalescing at a nearby military hospital and presented to tourists for fundraising. Heaton Park in Manchester also had money-raising trenches. There were publicly visible trenches in Kensington Gardens, London, but these were created for a specific purpose as the experimental ground for the British Army School of Camouflage, the replica trenches being used to perfect techniques for concealment and deception.

Fig 2.18
Cannock Chase, Staffordshire. Detail of the Messines model. To the left German prisoners of war in their distinctive 'pork pie' hats are seen working on the construction of the model. Trench lines were accurately modelled, with roads picked out in pebbles. [Royal New Zealand Returned and Services' Association Collection. Alexander Turnbull Library, Wellington, New Zealand Ref: ½-013854-G]

Fig 2.19
Trafalgar Square, London. The Western Front recreated for fundraising purposes, with captured German guns and a trench running across the middle of the picture. Also shown are a windmill, a fake tree used as an observation post and ruined buildings. [Courtesy P Kendall]

Rifle ranges

In 1914 the British army still called using a rifle *musketry*, and its then professional soldiers were expected to be able to fire up to 15 aimed rounds a minute. Bayonet fighting was also taught. While the rows of straw-filled dummies hung on frames for bayonet drill have left no archaeological trace, remains of target practice are more recognisable. Troops were first taught to drill with a rifle. The first shots they fired may have been with small bore weapons on miniature ranges housed in local drill halls or in otherwise standard army huts, using as targets battlefield scenes made by the Hill-Siffken company. No wartime miniature ranges may now survive, but evidence of many full-size rifle ranges exists. Starting in 1914 Colonel J H Cowan (RE) selected sites for over 200 additional ranges on which to train recruits. From firing trenches or butts, soldiers aimed at targets that were raised on wooden frames by range staff operating in a shelter trench. Behind the targets a large earth mound stopped the bullets.[39] The backstop earthwork is frequently the best indicator of a site, but all elements of a range can be present. Cannock Chase provides good examples (Fig 2.20). Not all ranges were earthworks, but surviving brick or concrete examples are rarer. At Burton-on-Trent a brick target wall built *c* 1914 on a monumental scale still bears the scars of the bullets fired at it (Fig 2.21).

Bombing practice

Fighting in the early months of the war saw the improvising of explosive devices to be thrown or catapulted into enemy trenches. This dangerous experimentation in the field was replaced by the introduction in 1915 of the Mills bomb as the standard British hand grenade. The use of these was known as *bombing* and this was an essential part of trench tactics. Over 100 million Mills bombs were supplied during the war, and while all men learnt their use, selected men became specialists at schools of bombing, including Herne Bay, Kent, and Aldershot and Lyndhurst in Hampshire. The site of the Eastern Command School at Godstone, Surrey, has both archaeological remains of a practice trench system and presumably vast numbers of buried grenade fragments. At Chiseldon, Wiltshire, rectangular earthworks mark the sites of bombing training, and elsewhere at Larkhill and Colchester grenade fragments in former trench systems attest to bombing training.[40]

Fig 2.20 (left)
Cannock Chase, Staffordshire. The butt of a rifle range which had 90 separate targets for firing at distances of up to 600yds (550m).
[© Christopher Welch]

Fig 2.21 (below)
Burton-on-Trent, Staffordshire. A 60m wide rifle-range target wall completed c 1914.
[DP197433]

Artillery

Artillery dominated the Western Front battlefields. Shells, not bullets, were responsible for at least 60 per cent of casualties. Guns, their projectiles and the application of science to gunnery were all transformed between 1914 and 1918. In 1914 the Royal Artillery numbered 92,920 men in three branches. The Royal Horse Artillery had light field guns and the Royal Field Artillery (RFA) heavier field guns and howitzers. Both relied on horses for mobility, while the Royal Garrison Artillery (RGA) was responsible for coastal guns and a siege train, made up of the largest guns capable of bombarding fortresses. At the start of the war, field guns were located with the infantry, to fire at visible targets. The majority of available projectiles were air-burst shrapnel shells: these were effective against troops in the open but far less so against a dug-in enemy. Here high explosive (HE) shells were needed to damage trenches, cut barbed wire and, by the splinters of their cases, kill or maim men and animals. HE shells were usually deployed as 'indirect fire' where the target was invisible from the gun battery, whose fire was directed by spotters on the ground or in the air *(see below)*. Mass bombardments were required to soften up enemy-held ground as a preliminary to a frontal infantry assault ('going over the top') and later to provide a creeping barrage to cover attacking troops, but in the opening years of the war HE shell production and quality control was inadequate. In early battles this greatly restricted the effectiveness of the artillery, which sometimes faced severe limitations on the number of shells it could fire.

These problems came to the fore in March 1915 during the Battle of Neuve Chapelle, a British offensive on a relatively narrow front supported by a concentrated bombardment from over 500 guns. This helped the infantry to break the German front line, but then a lack of ammunition and poor infantry–artillery cooperation saw the attack stall. This battle was momentous in many ways. It demonstrated to the British that infantry assaults when accompanied by artillery barrages could break the stalemate of trench warfare, thereby setting a pattern for the offensive operations which followed. Formulae were developed to calculate how many guns were needed for every yard of enemy trench to be attacked.

Another British failure, at the Battle of Aubers Ridge (9 May 1915), helped precipitate the 'Shell Crisis' of May 1915, where press coverage of the problems the artillery faced contributed to bringing down the government, which was replaced by a coalition. In this David Lloyd George headed a new Ministry of Munitions, under which many more guns became available and shell production was transformed. Vast quantities of shells were henceforward delivered by an efficient transport system to stockpiles behind the front. The preliminary bombardment for the First Battle of the Somme (July 1916) saw 1,400 guns fire 1,500,000 shells over eight days, but the performance of the then available fuses meant that HE shells might only explode after entering the ground, making them poor at cutting barbed wire. The introduction of the first British instantaneous percussion fuse no. 106 in late 1916 ensured that a shell was burst by its first contact, including with barbed wire, and overall artillery performance was much improved as a result. By 1918 the Royal Artillery had grown to 548,780 men, and in November 1918 there were 7,578 guns and 15,790,023 rounds available in France.

The adoption of indirect fire as the main use of artillery drove a revolution in gunnery. It required the application of scientific calculations for predicting the arc of shells fired, to allow for meteorological factors and even the progressive wear on gun barrels. Guns firing from cover behind the lines relied on forward artillery observers and secure communications to adjust the fall of shells. Aerial photo reconnaissance and spotting from aircraft and balloons enabled target identification so that reliable map coordinates could be used to direct accurate fire. Sound ranging and muzzle-flash spotting techniques allowed enemy guns to be targeted. The most dangerous use of these new artillery techniques was for the *creeping barrage*. This demanded much of the artillery, as it required a wall of shellfire to move progressively forward towards the enemy with the infantry advancing close behind. Any errors were fatal. This new use of artillery first required experimentation and then practice. Some of this took place at artillery schools in rear areas at the Front, but ranges in England were also used.

The Royal Military Academy at Woolwich, London, and pre-war centres at Shoeburyness, Essex, for the RFA and Lydd, Kent, for the RGA continued to train artillery officers, but such was the demand that 25 other hostilities-only schools were needed. In the late 19th century the ranges at Shoeburyness were a centre

The army

Fig 2.22 (left) Lydd, Kent. A Royal Artillery training camp photographed in 1920. [EPW000066]

Fig 2.23 (below) 'Somewhere in France.' Dragging a large artillery piece to a new advanced position, with caterpillar tracks spreading the weight of the gun. [Courtesy P Kendall]

for artillery experimentation and this continued during the war, including the test firing of shells to establish why such a high proportion were duds. The first Anti-Aircraft School was at Shoeburyness, and the training of war dogs took place there to normalise them to the sound of gunfire. Lydd retained a role for the largest guns but also had a role for the Royal Flying Corps and for the use of balloons (Fig 2.22). The major focus for artillery training was, however, moved to Larkhill on Salisbury Plain – the landscape of which resembled that of northern France – and where the ranges of the Royal School of Artillery remain today.

Before 1914 Larkhill was a summertime training camp, and as part of the drive to house the New Armies, 30 hutted camps (each holding 1,000 men) were constructed. Many troops trained here, including those responsible for the practice trenches investigated in 2016 (*see* pp 16–19). In February 1915 an artillery instruction school was set up at Larkhill manned by staff from Shoeburyness. The Larkhill ranges were primarily to train as many troops as possible to fire guns, but they were also used to experiment with many aspects of gunnery, including wire cutting, sound ranging, smoke screens and the blast patterns of different shells.

By 1917 the standard of training for the artillery was high, but its mobility in the field remained a weakness, even as motorised transport replaced the use of horses (Fig 2.23)

The Royal Engineers

The artillery and the engineers had a shared history. Known as the Sappers, no other branch of the army had such a diverse range of wartime support duties as did the Royal Engineers. They provided vital support for the gunners, building battery positions and the road and rail lines down which the massive shell supply was maintained, but were also trained to fight and to perform a multitude of duties, some of which were new to warfare. In 1914 the Royal Engineers were unprepared for the demands made upon them, both abroad and at home. The strength of the Corps rose from 25,090 in 1914 to 314,318 in 1918.[41]

The historic home of the Royal Engineers was at Chatham, Kent, but despite great expansion there, chiefly using huts, additional training centres were needed by 1915, set up at Newark, Nottinghamshire, and at Deganwy, Wales, alongside other more specialist schools and experimental establishments. At home the Royal Engineers were responsible for the design, supervision and sometimes construction of most of the infrastructure required by the army (and initially by the air force). They designed and oversaw the creation of the huge new army camps and hospitals, and also horse-lines, ordnance depots and prisoner-of-war camps. They remained responsible for coastal fortifications as well as new anti-invasion defences, executed mainly as fieldworks (see pp 82–92). Such constructions increasingly relied on prefabricated elements that could be combined to produce the required kind of facility. The 1914 design of hut encampments is an early example of this, but the corrugated steel sheet half-cylindrical hut developed in 1916 by Captain Peter Nissen (RE) is better known (see p 198). Manufactured in their tens of thousands, these huts were mainly sent to the front. The type was again used during the 1939–45 conflict and all the known surviving examples in England are of that date.

Bridging was a long-standing responsibility of the Royal Engineers. In Kent, pontoon bridges over the Thames at Gravesend and to the Isle of Sheppey were part of anti-invasion planning. On the Western Front the need was for a different portable bridge type capable of rapid deployment, and which after 1916 had to be capable of supporting tanks. The solution was the Inglis bridge, based on steel tubes in a pyramidal shape, first designed by Charles Edward Inglis (RE) in 1914. Only a few examples of this bridge type now exist in England (Fig 2.24).

As the technical troops for the army, the Royal Engineers carried out many roles that after the war were spun off as new units. The Royal Corps of Signals was not founded until 1920, and throughout the war it was the Royal Engineers Signal Service who provided telephone, telegraphic and wireless communication, with training centred on Aldershot and a Signals Experimental Establishment at Woolwich Common. Huge quantities of cable and phone sets were sent abroad, although by the end of the war wireless transmission was more common. Communication was essential to air raid precautions. The Royal Engineers built anti-aircraft gun batteries and operated searchlights to direct their fire. An electric light school at Gosport, Hampshire, trained Royal Engineer units which by 1918 manned 629 searchlights at home.

Secure transportation behind the lines of the Western Front was essential, and the engineers were responsible for the construction and operation of railways, roads and inland waterways. Longmoor, Hampshire, was founded before the war as an instructional railway, and during the conflict over 67,000 men trained there on both broad and narrow gauge track. Some of these men operated the over 80 miles (130km) of military railways in England that connected the new army camps to the mainline rail network. Other important military lines served establishments around Salisbury Plain, including at Porton Down and Larkhill. Often these military railways can still be traced on the ground. That at Cannock Chase became known as the Tackeroo Express, and it today survives as track bed, cuttings and embankments.

The siege conditions at the Western Front saw the reintroduction of historic techniques of mining to tunnel under the enemy lines and to disrupt these with massive explosive charges. Underground warfare became more common

Fig 2.24
Sandtoft, north Lincolnshire. A prefabricated Inglis bridge reused on a Second World War airfield.
[DP197246]

Fig 2.25
Darland Banks, Chatham, Kent. A 1946 photograph of a Royal Engineers' training ground showing practice trenches and mine craters.
[RAF/CPE/UK/1923/RS/4145]

as the war progressed, and ultimately 25 tunnelling companies of the Royal Engineers were formed.[42] These carried out mining operations, as well as being responsible for constructing the subterranean structures known as *dugouts* (deep shelters in which troops could survive enemy bombardment) and *subways* (tunnels to move troops to the forward trenches). Evidence for this critical work survives at Chatham with a 3,000-man capacity dugout built beneath the Great Lines. Mining was also taught nearby at Darland Banks in the fieldworks practice ground, where aerial photographs show the remains of trench systems and craters. The greatest achievement by the RE tunnellers was the 19 deep mines detonated on 7 June 1917 beneath Messines Ridge, Belgium. In preparation, so that calculations of the necessary amount of explosives could be checked, a mine of 5,000 lb of explosive was test fired at Darland under a purpose-built replica of German trenches (Fig 2.25).

Trench warfare required new weapons and tactics, many of which in the early part of the war were improvised by the Royal Engineers Experimental Section. These included hand and rifle grenades, smoke bombs, trench mortars, bulletproof shields and steel helmets. In June 1915 the Ministry of Munitions formed a Trench Warfare Department to test and evaluate weaponry and tactics. This had its main experimental ground at Wembley and also a trench warfare school at Clapham Common (both in London). Testing at Wembley included flamethrowers, some of which were developed by Captain William H Livens (RE). His most significant invention, in July 1916, was a form of mortar, the Livens projector. Used en masse to fire gas-filled bombs, these became essential to an entirely new form of warfare (Fig 2.26).

Fig 2.26
A Livens gas shell projector.
[© IWM Q 014945]

Gas warfare

In April 1915 it was the Germans who carried out the first gas attack of the war on the Western Front, using chlorine at Ypres, but both sides were by then considering its use. First use helped legitimise this deadly new weapon and the British had to both respond in kind and work out a means of defence. Much of the early laboratory work which followed was carried out at London's Imperial College, but field trials were needed. Experiments began with the release of hydrogen sulphide on Cannock Chase.[43] However, the Trench Warfare Department realised it needed a more suitable, permanent, establishment to develop both chemical weapons and defensive measures. Early in 1916 its Scientific Advisory Committee recommended the acquisition of an estate on the chalk downland at Porton Down, Wiltshire, which included a Victorian house and its outbuildings. These were soon joined by two huts, which by the end of the war had grown to an establishment of about 70 buildings including accommodation huts, a canteen, a concert hall, laboratories, a light railway and a farm for raising animals used in experiments.

Trials included the release of gas from cylinders and later the firing of gas-filled artillery shells. To aid these experiments a pair of concentric circular trenches 200 and 400 yards (183 and 366m) in diameter were constructed (Fig 2.27). This allowed gas to be released from within the inner trench and monitored in the outer one regardless of wind direction. Occasionally research staff were present in shell shelters or replica trench systems, gauging first-hand the effects of a gas attack. Earthwork traces of these features remain. Other research included testing captured enemy guns and chemicals to study their effectiveness, while periodically scientists had to respond to the introduction of a new gas by the Germans both to assess its effectiveness – and whether the Allies should adopt its use – and to develop countermeasures. Chlorine was replaced by phosgene in late 1915, and in July 1917 the first German use of mustard gas revealed its deadly effect as a persistent blistering agent.

Porton Down also developed anti-gas defensive measures, including respirators and chemical-soaked curtains used to seal dugout entrances. Instruction with these took place in camps across England, with troops being trained in anti-gas measures and to fight wearing respirators. Archive plans of camps often mark the gas huts in which men were exposed to gas, with and without gas masks. None are known to survive. Some practice trenches were also used for

Fig 2.27
Porton Down, Wiltshire. Air view of two circles of the gas testing trenches.
[NMR 18650/03]

this purpose, and at Seaford, East Sussex, the gas chamber was painted by the Canadian war artist Fred Varley.[44]

At Porton Down itself permanent brick-built facilities were under construction by the time of the armistice, presumably in recognition of the likelihood that chemical warfare was here to stay. The headquarters building of 1918, designed by B F G Wakefield and constructed by the Royal Engineers, was built in a colonial style on an H plan with a central clock tower.[45]

The research and testing facilities at Porton Down have had a continuous history since the First World War, and today house the Defence Science and Technology Laboratories.

The Machine Gun Corps

A far deadlier killer of men than gas was the machine gun, at its most lethal when firing from purpose-built positions to create mathematically precise fields of interlocking fire. In common with most European armies, in 1914 each British battalion had just two heavy Maxim machine guns. Vickers had improved its design in 1912, producing a gun that weighed less and had a higher rate of fire, but this was not yet available in large numbers. It was then rushed into mass production. Even so it remained a relatively heavy, water-cooled, weapon which required a team of six to eight men to operate, and it was too awkward to carry forward in an attack. In summer 1915 the Lewis gun started to reach the battlefield: a lighter, air-cooled weapon with a higher rate of fire capable of use by one man. Its introduction enabled the heavier Vickers guns to be withdrawn from the infantry and to be grouped into machine gun companies. These were formed into a new Machine Gun Corps (MGC) on 22 October 1915.

The new Corps required a training centre in England. This was at Belton Park, Grantham, Lincolnshire (there were also centres at Harrowby Camp and Harlaxton Manor), where in 1914 the Earl of Brownlow had agreed to the establishment of a major camp holding 45,000 men in timber huts. The MGC grew to 124,402 men by October 1918, and overall some 160,500 served in it during the war. Machine guns could be used for indirect fire – firing at an angle into the air – to lay down covering barrages, but were most frequently used in the front line for direct covering fire or to break up enemy attacks. Gun crews, often set forward of the front line, became prime targets for enemy fire, and the Corps suffered 62,049 casualties (12,498 fatal), earning itself the 'Suicide Squad' nickname. At Belton Park air photography and geophysical survey have confirmed a close correlation between the buried remains of the hutted camp and archive plans. Limited archaeological excavation confirmed the broad layout of the camp, although structural remains proved elusive despite a rich assemblage of military artefacts.[46] Nearby in Peascliffe Plantation, in what is now the East Midlands Golf Course, remains of a large stop butt from a machine gun range suitable for 18 gun crews have been identified.

The Corps was disbanded in 1922 when the use of machine guns was reintegrated into infantry training. Today the men of the Suicide Squad are remembered by a stone tablet at Belton House and by a modern sculpture in Wyndham Park, Grantham. The national MGC memorial is at Hyde Park Corner, London, and when unveiled in 1925 it caused controversy about the potential glorification of war, through its use of a statue of David and a biblical quote referring to the slaughter by him of 'tens of thousands' *(see* Fig 10.14).

The Tank Corps

For a short period the name of the MGC was used to help disguise an entirely new weapon of war, and the Machine Gun Heavy Section went on to emerge as the Tank Corps. The tank was designed to break the stalemate of the Western Front by crossing trenches and barbed wire, and to support infantry with machine gun and light artillery fire. Development was by the William Foster agricultural tractor firm at Lincoln, and early field trials took place at Hatfield House, Hertfordshire, in February 1916. The name *tank* was adopted as a security measure.

The first tank crews were formed at Bisley, Surrey, but used a practice ground with replica British and German trenches at Thetford, Norfolk,[47] known as the Elveden Explosives Area, now covered by coniferous plantations. In August 1916 the first tanks for active service were shipped to France from Avonmouth, Bristol, with 32 going into action on 15 September 1916 at Flers-Courcelette during the Somme offensive. Though they were used in too low numbers for their impact to be truly decisive, this first action nevertheless demonstrated the potential of the tank as a weapon. On 2 October

1916 the Commander-in-Chief of the British Expeditionary Force, Douglas Haig, requested 1,000 tanks and the men to use them. General Headquarters quickly recommended the formation of a Tank Corps, but this was not officially created until 28 July 1917. Mass production of tanks was ordered under the supervision of the Ministry of Munitions, through the Mechanical Warfare Supply Department. In November 1917 over 400 tanks achieved an unprecedented breakthrough of German lines as part of the Battle of Cambrai, and by the armistice Britain had built 2,600 tanks. Bovington Camp, near Wool, Dorset, became home to the Tank Corps, and a practice ground larger than that at Elveden was created in 1917.[48] Bovington remains the Armour Centre for the British army, and decades of intensive training has destroyed all but a small part of a once extensive First World War training landscape. Air photos correlate with archive maps showing extensive replica German and British trenches.[49] A separate Experimental Depot for the development of new tanks was at Dollis Hill, London.

Tanks were first officially seen by the public in Britain in newsreels of the 1917 fighting. They caused a sensation which was capitalised upon with six examples, known as Tank Banks, travelling the country on fundraising tours. After 1918 redundant tanks were presented to towns as trophies, and installed in parks and town squares. Many were scrapped in the interwar years and almost all the others became victims of Second World War salvage drives. Only one remains on external public display today, at Ashford, Kent (Fig 2.28).

The support branches of the army

Behind every fighting man there was a chain of support services and depot infrastructure linking every theatre of the war to bases in the United Kingdom. These branches of the army seldom engaged in combat, but this did not prevent them from becoming casualties, especially when delivering support in forward areas. Older men from a civilian business background became administrative officers, making an essential contribution in organising supply chains and other logistic tasks. The unending demand for fighting men saw support roles increasingly filled by those who were too old or unfit for front-line duty, including rehabilitated wounded soldiers. Women were employed in ever-larger numbers as civilian workers and later as the first female soldiers in the British army. The contribution made by these men and women should be remembered alongside the endeavours of the fighting men.

The army was organised from the War Office in Whitehall, London, as headquarters for the Secretary of State for War and the Army Council. Only completed in 1907, this building proved too small for the huge increase in its wartime responsibilities (see Fig 1.1). Its staff grew from 2,000 in peacetime to over 22,000 by 1918, many of them women. Three new ministries would be spun off from it: the Ministry of Munitions of War (1915), the Ministry of Pensions (1916) and the Air Ministry (1918), with the Ministry of National Service taking over responsibility for recruitment from 1917. To create capacity for its expansion, wooden huts known as *Zeppelin Terrace* were erected on the roof, and the nearby National Liberal Club was requisitioned as an annexe. Even so, space remained inadequate, and elements of the War Office occupied parts of wartime emergency buildings built on the Victoria Embankment, and in St James Park by draining the lake (*see* Fig 1.6). The Army Council included the Master General of the Ordnance in command of the Army Ordnance Corps and the Quartermaster General in charge of the Army Service Corps. In 1918 both corps received the prefix 'Royal', by order of the King, in recognition of their wartime contributions. Together they equipped and fed the army and took charge of transportation.

Fig 2.28
Ashford, Kent. Mark 4 tank (listed Grade II), a 'female' version of the tank, armed with six Vickers machine guns.
[DP182278]

The Army Ordnance Corps

At the start of the war the Army Ordnance Corps (AOC) was responsible for the storage and issue of all war materiel with the exception of food, forage and medical stores. It grew from 2,500 personnel in 1914 to over 40,000 by 1918, with an additional 33,000 civilian employees at home (of whom 50 per cent were women). Pre-war planning had not anticipated the scale of the actual fighting and it took time to respond to the needs of the combat forces. Table 2.2 illustrates the huge quantities of materiel that all-out war required.

Table 2.2 Dead weight shipped to France (only), August 1914 to November 1918 (tons)

Food	3,240,948
Forage – oats and hay	5,438,602
Petrol	758,614
Coal	3,922,391
Ammunition	5,253,338
Ordnance stores and clothing	1,761,777
Engineering stores (eg sandbags, picks, shovels or barbed wire)	1,369,894
Railway material	988,354
Timber	842,759
Road stone	761,540
Mechanical transport	158,482
Tanks	68,167
Royal Air Force stores	123,570
Expeditionary Force canteen stores	269,517
Miscellaneous	539,398
Total	**25,497,351**

Source: Forbes, A 1931, *A History of the Army Ordnance Services: The Great War*, 2 edn. London: Medici Society.

Pre-war the AOC's most important facilities consisted of depots at Woolwich; the Royal Army Clothing Depot, Pimlico, London, for uniforms; and the central stores depot on the Grand Union Canal at Weedon Bec, Northamptonshire. This peacetime infrastructure could not cope with the demands soon placed on it.

In June 1915 a 600-acre (240ha) site with good rail connections opened at Didcot, Oxfordshire, with 1,500,000 sq ft (140,000 sq m) of covered storage and 30 miles (48km) of railway sidings. Oxford dons and staff from Eton College volunteered to work there. Little here has survived comprehensive redevelopment. At Bramley, Hampshire, another major ordnance depot was needed by 1917. Constructed either side of the Great Western railway, this became the Royal Army Ordnance Corps School of Ammunition in 1922. Little of its earliest phase now remains. Other large depots were built at Altrincham, Greater Manchester, and Credenhill, Herefordshire. Across the country many other smaller stores were acquired, and often the Army Ordnance Department managed stores adjacent to munitions works where they held supplies accepted for government service.

The AOC also clothed the army: the statistics shown in Table 2.3 give some idea of the scale of this operation.

Table 2.3 Items supplied between 4 August 1914 and 31 March 1919

Boots	46,973,000
Jackets	31,764,000
Trousers	28,297,000
Caps	23,549,000
Greatcoats	8,733,000

Source: War Office 1922, *Statistics of the Military Effort of the British Empire during the Great War, 1914–1920*. London: HMSO.

Please note these figures include uniforms supplied to Allied forces.

The pre-war Royal Army Clothing Depot (demolished) was at the present Dolphin Square, Pimlico, and it struggled to fit out the New Armies (Fig 2.29). Additional depots were soon required at the Olympia and White City exhibition sites in London and in the traditional clothing production areas such as Manchester and West Yorkshire. Dewsbury, West Yorkshire,

*Fig 2.29
Pimlico, London.
Employees model some of the specialist uniforms manufactured by the Royal Army Clothing Depot.
[© IWM Q 030788]*

became a central depot for the reprocessing of old uniforms, including battlefield salvage. By June 1918 the combined clothing depots covered 2,000,000 sq ft (186,000 sq m). At the end of the war uniforms were swapped for the 1,413,760 suits provided to demobilised men and issued by the AOC, chiefly through a depot at Battersea, London.

The Army Service Corps

The Army Service Corps (ASC) was headed by the Quartermaster General, with General Sir John Cowans serving in this role for the entire war. With his staff, he was responsible for the mobilisation of the expeditionary force, for quartering the New Armies and for feeding the massively expanded army at home and abroad. In 1914 the ASC numbered 6,431 men and by 1918 had grown to 325,170. In 1914 it was feeding 186,400 men and 28,742 animals, figures that by 1918 had grown to 3,000,000 and 500,000 respectively. Home production of food and supplies was essential and the army had its own farms, totalling 6,500 acres (2,630ha) by 1918. British production could not meet demand and so the world was scoured for supplies, most for delivery to the United Kingdom, from where after inspection and packing they were re-exported.

The 1869 Foreign Cattle Market (demolished) at Deptford, built on the site of the former naval dockyard, became the Reserve Supply Depot and the chief depot for the army worldwide. This grew to be able to hold a 30-day reserve of supplies. New cranes and wharves permitted transport by ship, but it was on an internal system of light railways and by a new connection to the main rail network that most supplies were moved. The ASC was responsible more generally for transport, and while in 1914 it was still very reliant of horse-drawn wagons, the use of motorised vehicles grew substantially throughout the war. Both the Horse and Mechanised Transport sections of the Corps had significant training facilities in south-east London close to Deptford. At Blackheath, the Rangers House was used to train men to work with horses. At Marvels Lane, Grove Park, the Greenwich Union workhouse of 1902 was requisitioned as a centre for the training of motorised transport soldiers, including mechanics (Fig 2.30). In 1914 the army had just 246 mechanically propelled vehicles, but by the end of the war it had over 28,000 of many kinds, including ambulances, lorries, buses and Holt caterpillar tractors (used to pull heavy artillery). Late in the war, surplus vehicles awaiting repair or disposal were parked on Kempton Park racecourse, Surrey, but when racing resumed the vehicles were moved to a new depot near Slough, Berkshire, from where many

Fig 2.30
Grove Park, Lewisham, London. The Army Service Corps barracks in a former workhouse accommodated servicemen being trained as train drivers and mechanics.
[Courtesy P Kendall]

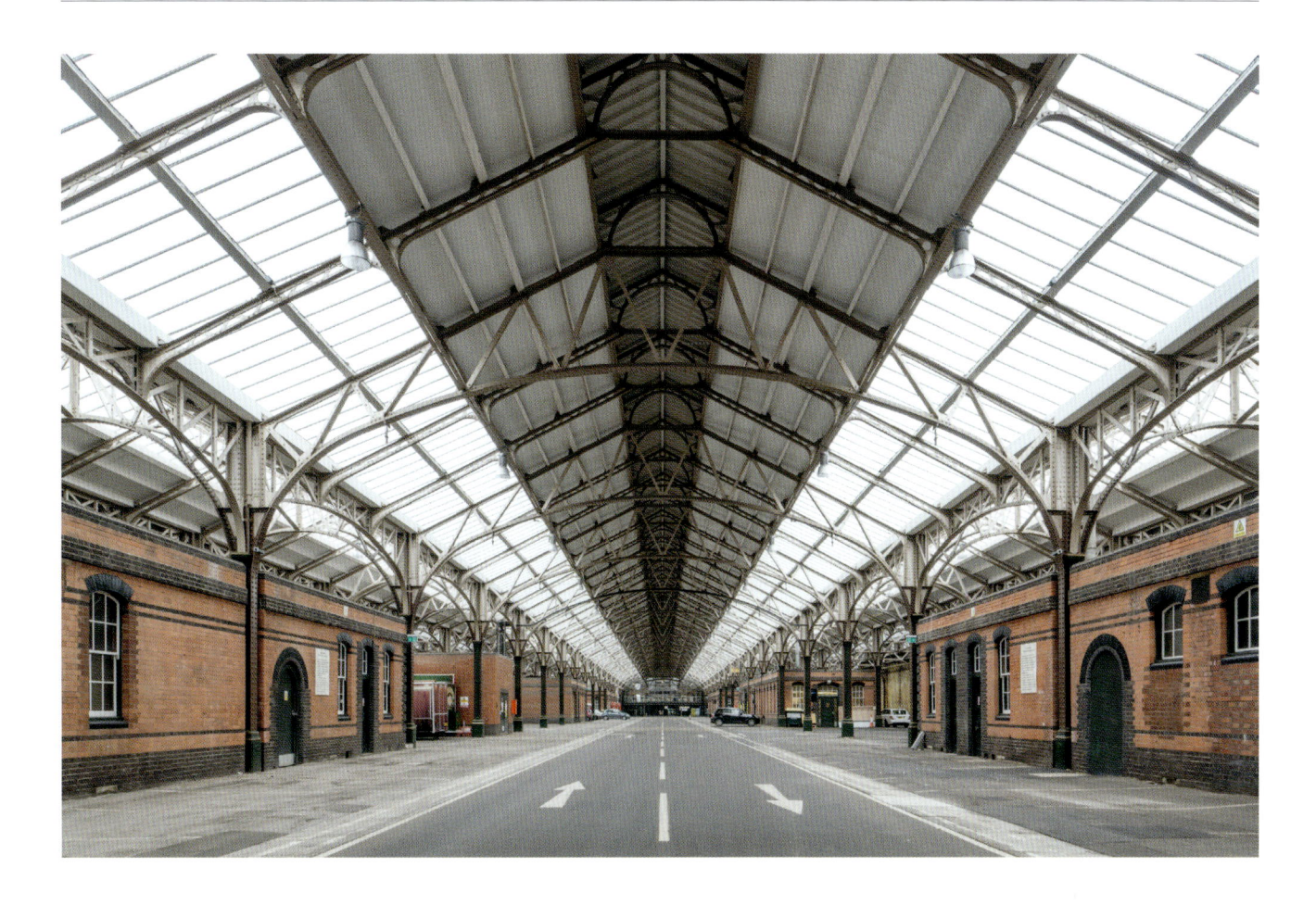

were sold, giving a post-war boost to the British road haulage industry (see Fig 11.3).

In August 1914 it was the ASC which transported the British Expeditionary Force to the continent, and how it was done set the pattern for subsequent movements. That year troops left from Southampton, vehicles and fuel from Avonmouth, and supplies through Newhaven, East Sussex. The last was requisitioned as a controlled secure area, and over the course of the war over 866,000 rail trucks delivered loads to 165 different ships, which made a total of 8,778 voyages to take 6 million tonnes of supplies (including munitions) across the Channel.[50] Avonmouth remained the primary port of embarkation for motor transport and for the import of vehicles from America. The number of troops requiring movement was huge. Many transit ports were needed, particularly as this was the first war in which troops serving abroad were allowed home leave. At Folkestone, Kent, at least 10 million people movements passed through the town, with rest camps set up as barbed wire compounds around some of its fashionable large houses. The steep road to the harbour is now called the Road of Remembrance, and the order to marching troops to 'step short' as they approached it provided the name of a project to remember the wartime role of the town.[51] Along the coast, Dover was an active naval base and thus was used less for troop movements. All ports could be used to repatriate the wounded using empty freighters or hospital ships. At Dover the new Marine Station, incomplete at the start of the war, was hastily finished in early 1915 so that six ambulance trains could simultaneously load the wounded from two ships (Fig 2.31). Here, over the course of the war, 1,260,506 wounded arrived on 4,076 ships before transfer to 7,781 ambulance trains.[52]

Table 2.2 (see p 29) lists the various materials taken across the Channel. The rivers and canals of France provided a ready means of distributing supplies, and in December 1914 an Inland Water Transport Section of the Royal Engineers was formed. Dover proved an inconvenient first base port for them, and from 1916 a new military port was established at Richborough, near Sandwich, Kent.

Fig 2.31
Dover, Kent. Marine Station (listed Grade II), completed in 1914 for the South Eastern & Chatham Railway. Between 1915 and 1919, over a million wounded and sick service personnel who had been returned to England on hospital ships were transferred here onto ambulance trains. Many prisoners of war from both sides were also repatriated through this station.
[DP189076]

Richborough military port

Unlike the railways, which were immediately brought under state control on the outbreak of war, it was not until 1917 that the country's more significant canals came under national supervision via the Canal Control Committee. Its roles included encouraging more goods to be moved on the canals and the regulation of labour. The importance of canals and barges for the carriage of war goods was also recognised by the establishment of the Royal Engineers' Inland Waterways Transport Department. One of its most important tasks was to receive goods by rail for transfer to barges which were towed across the Channel to enter the French canal system.

Barge traffic initially passed via Dover, but in 1916, to alleviate pressure on its docks, work began on a new port at Richborough. Here supplies arrived by rail into one of five marshalling yards capable of holding 3,285 wagons. A new wharf with electric transporter cranes then transhipped goods from the wagons to barges (most of them built in shipyards at the site) which were then towed by tugs to French inland ports.

A logical development saw the introduction of the train-ferry, where up to 54 railway wagons were shunted on to purpose-built steamships and off again in France, saving the time taken to tranship goods to barges. Very heavy items, including tanks, locomotives and siege artillery, were moved in this way. One of the ships could also carry motorised transport, thus introducing the 'roll-on/roll-off' principle used today to move freight by lorry. The new service required construction not only of the ferries but also of new berths with a gantry mounted and counter-balance link span that could cope with the rise and fall of tides, while still maintaining access to the ship. The service became operational just in time to deliver supplies critical to resisting the German spring offensive of 1918. After the war the link span was removed for civilian use at Harwich, Essex, where it remains (Fig 2.32). Prudently, in case the northern French ports were captured, a second train-ferry service was run from Southampton.

By 1918 Richborough had grown into a vast establishment covering over 800 hectares with just under 21,000 employees, including serving and discharged soldiers and 700 women engaged in salvage work (Figs 2.33, 2.34 and 2.35). The port included slipways, foundries, power stations, machine shops, railway repair shops and compressor houses, as well as facilities for building and repairing barges. Blocks for concrete huts were cast on site using the patented 'Winget' machinery, with the same production plant also making the concrete parts of prefabricated Moir pillboxes for use at the front. In 1920 the port was sold into private ownership and in

Fig 2.32 (below) Harwich, Essex. The Grade II listed ro-ro rail bridge moved from Richborough. [DP165499]

Fig 2.33 (opposite, top left) Richborough, Kent. Part of the military port from the north in 1920, showing barges, transit sheds and an accommodation camp near Stonar North Lake. After the war the port received salvage from the Western Front. [EPW000660]

Fig 2.34 (opposite, bottom left) Richborough. The Gantries by John Lavery (1918). [© IWM ART 001387]

Fig 2.35 (opposite, right) Richborough. Plan of the 800 hectare military port, 1918. [Redrawn from TNA, MUN 4/6825]

the late 20th century the site was comprehensively redeveloped. The New Wharf constructed in 1916 and the Stonar Cut to alter the course of the River Stour both survive, but otherwise only a few concrete huts remain alongside a ruinous set of guardroom detention cells and the sewage farm for the site.

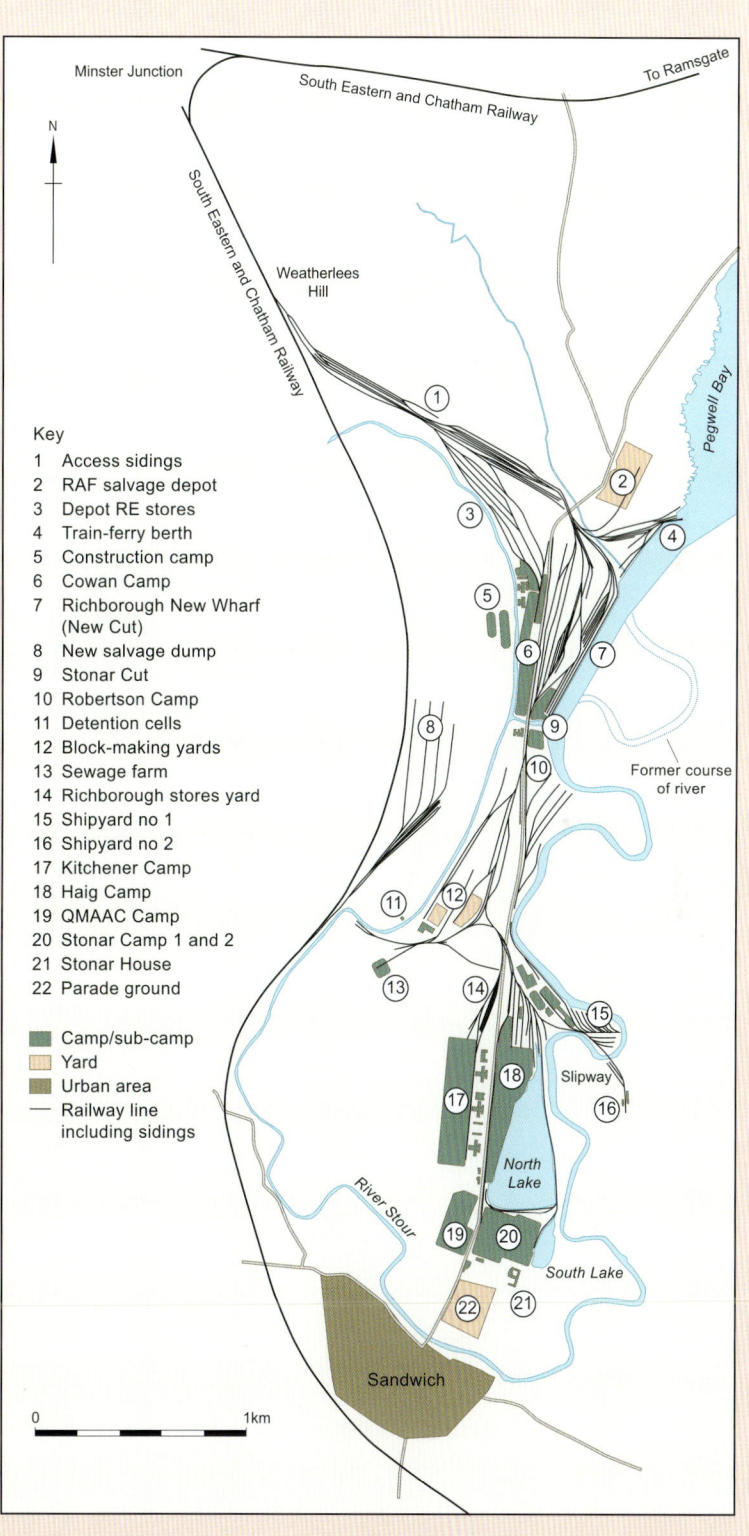

Key
1. Access sidings
2. RAF salvage depot
3. Depot RE stores
4. Train-ferry berth
5. Construction camp
6. Cowan Camp
7. Richborough New Wharf (New Cut)
8. New salvage dump
9. Stonar Cut
10. Robertson Camp
11. Detention cells
12. Block-making yards
13. Sewage farm
14. Richborough stores yard
15. Shipyard no 1
16. Shipyard no 2
17. Kitchener Camp
18. Haig Camp
19. QMAAC Camp
20. Stonar Camp 1 and 2
21. Stonar House
22. Parade ground

- Camp/sub-camp
- Yard
- Urban area
- Railway line including sidings

*Fig 2.36
Shorncliffe, Kent. Headstones marking the graves of members of the Chinese Labour Corps. [Courtesy P Kendall]*

The Women's Army Auxiliary Corps

Richborough is also representative of the major contribution made by women to victory. Materiel salvaged in France was processed there at a depot staffed by 700 female civilian workers. More widely, women often took on work that before 1914 was only done by men. As the war progressed, the ranks of the support arms of the military were combed for men who could be sent on active service, leaving only the aged or unfit. Women made up the numbers and kept the support apparatus of the war functional. Many were civilians, but the logical extension was to recruit women as soldiers. Military female nurses were part of the pre-war army, but after 1914 voluntary organisations enabled women to provide other essential services, and this encouraged the Adjutant General in late 1916 to consider how their recruitment might release men. The Women's Army Auxiliary Corps was formed in March 1917 as a uniformed part of the British army, and overseas service was authorised. Its name was changed to the Queen Mary's Army Auxiliary Corps in April 1918 as royal recognition of its important contribution. The Corps was eventually 39,742 strong, with more than 75 per cent serving at home.

Labour and the Labour Corps

Despite increased mechanisation during the war, most work involving hard labour, such as trench digging, road building or loading of stores, relied on manpower. The ASC and some infantry battalions had labour companies, but these were often in short supply. In January 1917 the Labour Corps was formed and it grew to 389,900 men by the end of the war, representing 10 per cent of the army. Its ranks were men graded unfit for front-line service, including wounded men returning after treatment. A Non-Combatant Corps was formed after the passing of the Military Service Act in 1916 to allow conscientious objectors to serve in labouring roles. Even so, the demand for labour was such that over 300,000 native labourers were hired from across the British Empire (chiefly India, Egypt and South Africa) and from China. These men were never officially part of the British army and served mainly abroad. At Orfordness airfield, Suffolk, the Chinese Labour Corps toiled to improve the sea defences; the resulting banks became known as the 'Chinese Walls'.[53] A small group of gravestones in the Shorncliffe military cemetery at Folkestone is rare evidence of the Chinese labourers, who died far from home (Fig 2.36).

Conclusions

As the guns fell silent in November 1918, soldiers' thoughts turned to home and the resumption of civilian life. Volunteers and conscripts were soldiers only for the period of hostilities, but not all of the men could be released straight away, until peace was certain. Conflict continued on the North-West Frontier, British forces fought against the Bolsheviks in Russia, and the Rhineland was also to be occupied. A well-planned process of demobilisation was initiated, with the numbers being released from the services swollen by repatriated POWs. The same ports that had sent troops and war supplies abroad now welcomed returning personnel. Some horses and war surplus and battlefield salvage which could not be disposed of abroad were also brought back. Soldiers were sent to the largest hutted camps, which acted as Dispersal Centres. At Bulford Camp, in 1919, after riots by New Zealand troops disaffected at the lack of troop ships to take them home, the men were kept busy by carving the enormous chalk figure of a kiwi bird that remains to this day.

3

The naval war

Serena Cant and Mark Dunkley

Introduction

The outbreak of war on 4 August 1914 was initially expected to lead to a shattering Trafalgar-like battle between the British and German fleets with the Royal Navy emerging triumphant.[1] The first naval battle of the war at Heligoland Bight in August 1914, though decisive, was no Trafalgar, and resulted in the Kaiser ordering his fleet to remain in port. As it turned out, naval strategy was instead characterised by the tenacious long-term efforts of the Allied Powers, with their larger fleets and surrounding position, to blockade the Central Powers, depriving them of raw materials and foodstuffs. The Central Powers had to make every effort to break that blockade, alongside establishing their own blockade of Great Britain and France through the use of submarines and raiders.

A key component of the British strategy was to deploy heavy defences and naval patrols to deny the German High Seas Fleet passage to the Atlantic through the English Channel or north around Scotland. The perfect base to maintain guard over that passage was Scapa Flow in Orkney, and the Admiralty began to create a substantial naval base there in 1912.

Britain's declaration of the North Sea as a 'military area' on 3 November 1914, denying German access to imports, further heightened the tension. Despite complaints about breaches of international law, most neutral merchant ships agreed to put into British ports for inspection and were subsequently escorted – minus any cargo bound for Germany – through the British-laid minefields to their final destinations.

The Allied blockade took years to become fully effective, hindered by issues of intelligence-gathering and respecting the rights of neutrals: for example, Austria's Adriatic ports had been subject to a French blockade since the first month of the war.[2] By the end of the war very few supplies were reaching Germany or its allies. The German war economy was badly affected, and many German civilians, as well as those in occupied Belgium, suffered from scurvy, tuberculosis and dysentery as a result of malnutrition. Official statistics attributed nearly 763,000 wartime deaths in Germany to starvation caused by the Allied blockade alone.[3]

Despite the success of the blockade, the Imperial German Navy (Kaiserliche Marine) was far from being confined to port. German warships attacked Great Yarmouth in November 1914, and bombarded Scarborough, Whitby and Hartlepool in December 1914 without retaliation from the Royal Navy (Fig 3.1). Further surface attacks followed on the Kent coast at Margate in February 1915 and Ramsgate in May 1915, while a U-boat attacked Whitehaven,

Fig 3.1
Whitby Abbey, North Yorkshire. Office of Works photographs of war damage to historic fabric. (left) West wall of the abbey prior to the German bombardment of 1914; (right) collapse of window tracery, stair and arcade immediately after the bombardment.
[AL0976/014/01; AL0976/016/01]

Fig 3.2
Admiral of the Fleet John Rushworth Jellicoe, 1st Earl Jellicoe, GCB, OM, GCVO, SGM, DL, 1859–1935. This bust forms part of the Grade I-listed terrace walls surrounding Trafalgar Square, London.
[DP182964]

Fig 3.3
Wills cigarette card issued in February 1917 for the series 'Britain's Part in the War'. The reverse proudly proclaims that 'Britain rules the sea. The sons of her sea-girt isle are sailors all, and her Navy is all powerful…still the seas are free, for night and day her Navy waits and watches.'
[Courtesy Mark Dunkley]

Cumbria, in August 1915. Major engagements with the British Home Fleet included Dogger Bank (January 1915 and February 1916), Jutland (May/June 1916) and the Second Battle of Heligoland Bight (November 1917).

In February 1915 Germany declared the waters around the British Isles to be a war zone, with merchant ships – Allied and neutral alike – to be subject to attack. By September 1915 U-boats had sunk 480 merchant vessels in British waters, including the Cunard liner *Lusitania*, torpedoed off the Irish coast in May 1915 with the loss of 1,201 men, women and children. The international outcry, particularly in the United States, caused the withdrawal of unrestricted submarine warfare, which was, however, resumed on 1 February 1917. Allied shipping losses continued to go up, particularly from late 1916, and the situation worsened after the second declaration of unrestricted submarine warfare. By April 1917 the Allies were losing an average of 167 merchant ships for every U-boat sunk.[4]

Against this background, the war at sea had, for mariners in home waters, become focused on the principal theatres of the North Sea, the English Channel and the Atlantic Ocean. This chapter addresses the five branches of naval activity: the Royal Navy surface fleet, the Royal Naval Reserve, the mercantile marine, the Royal Naval and German submarine services, and the Royal Naval Air Service.

Naval organisation

The possibility of a German invasion of Britain of the kind outlined in Erskine Childers's 1903 novel *Riddle of the Sands* led to the creation of four patrol flotillas along the eastern coast of Britain (the Forth, Tyne, Humber and Dover Patrols). These were augmented by the Northern Patrol covering some 600 miles (965km) of ocean between northern Scotland and the coasts of Greenland and Iceland. Torpedo-boats and submarines would defend individual ports and harbours against attack and were based at the Nore (Thames), Portsmouth, Plymouth, Pembroke and Queenstown (now Cobh, Eire). Further coverage was provided by the Channel Fleet and two patrol flotillas of destroyers and submarines at Harwich.[5]

Instead of dispersing following summer manoeuvres, in July 1914 the Grand Fleet of around 40 warships under the command of Admiral Sir John Jellicoe (Fig 3.2) began to move from Portland to its war station at Scapa Flow, Orkney Islands. Units of the Grand Fleet were also stationed at Loch Ewe on the west coast of Scotland and in Lough Swilly on the northern Irish coast as a precaution against U-boat attack.[6] Subunits within each fleet grouped similar vessels together, eg destroyers or submarines, and were called 'squadrons' or 'flotillas', with the number of warships varying according to requirements (Fig 3.3).

Changes in fuel would have some impact on naval tactics during the war, with the oil-fired *Queen Elizabeth* undergoing sea trials in 1914–15, although most ships continued to be coal-fired. However, oil gave a longer cruising range with the potential for refuelling at sea from 'oilers' (strictly, refuelling vessels, although 'oiler' and 'tanker' were used interchangeably). In addition, greater flexibility in controlling steam pressure allowed for rapid increases of speed, which was particularly useful in anti-submarine operations. Such technologies gave rise to the generation of new infrastructure in and around naval dockyards. At Gosport, Hampshire, for example, a naval oil fuel depot was constructed with 35 planned storage tanks, pipelines and pump houses (Fig 3.4).

The naval war

Fig 3.4
Forton oil fuel depot, Gosport, Hampshire. The move from coal to oil as the main fuel for naval vessels prompted the construction of similar depots of oil storage tanks at many ports. This depot was begun in 1907 and was largely complete by 1919.
[RAF/CPE/UK/2463/V/5177]

The Royal Navy (surface fleet)

The pre-war naval arms race led to both Britain and Germany building warships of previously unknown size and power, followed by the other powers: the United States, France, Italy and Japan. Britain's naval dockyards and commercial shipbuilding industry out-produced those of Germany, with big-gun capital ships, cruisers, smaller warships, support vessels, depot ships and lesser craft numbering more than any other power, and the Royal Navy was also able to draw reserve strength from the world's largest merchant navy and fishing fleet (Fig 3.5).

For the British, the arms race culminated in the *Dreadnought*, launched in February 1906, which was the first large warship to be turbine-driven. Very heavily armed and powered, she rendered all earlier battleships obsolete and gave her name to the new generation of battleship. The battlecruiser was also introduced, less heavily armoured than the battleship for speed

37

Legacies of the First World War

Fig 3.5
Chart of warships and other Admiralty vessels lost during the First World War in UK territorial waters adjacent to England, indicating the volume of naval shipping around the country.

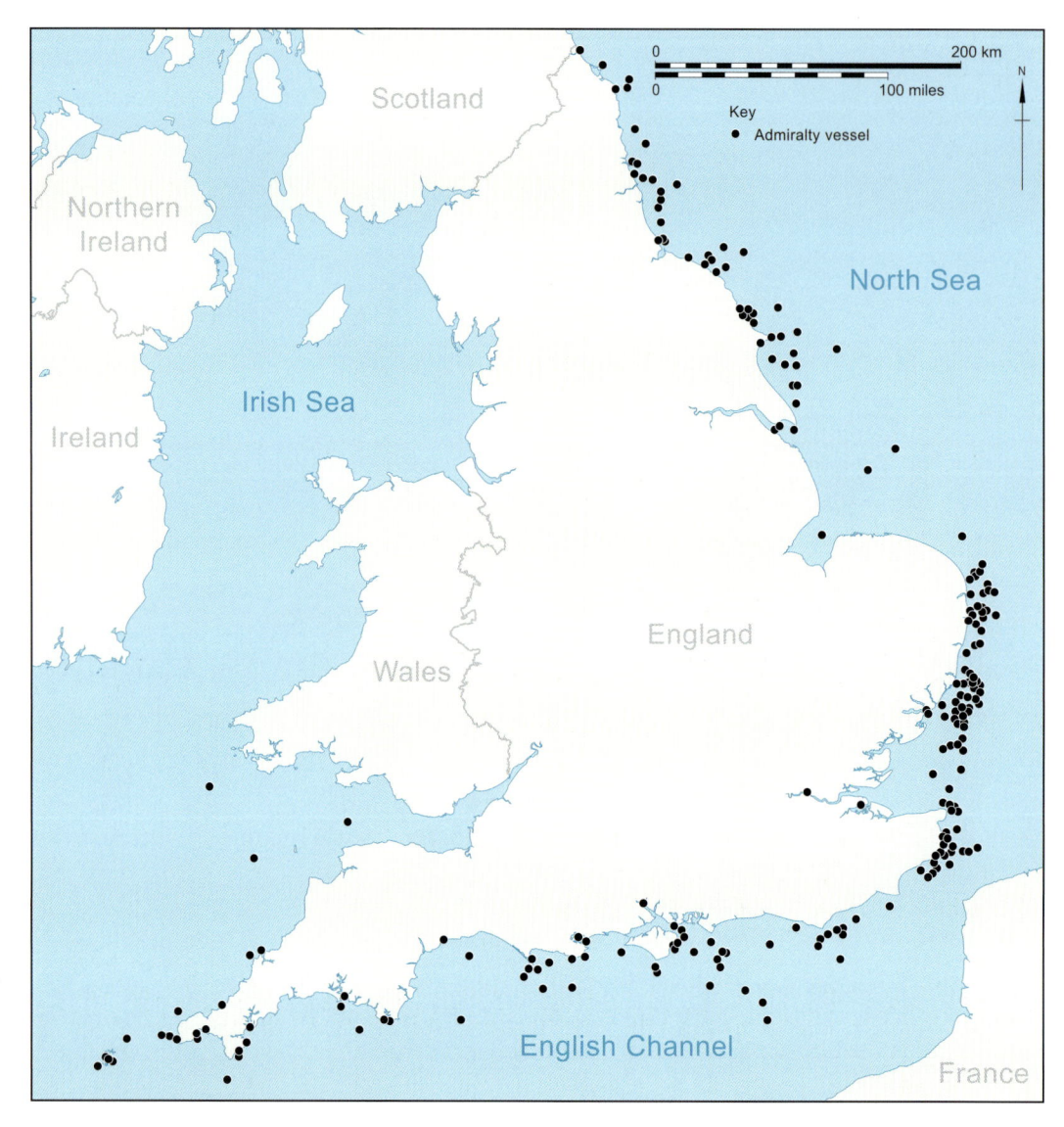

Fig 3.6 (below)
Acoustic multibeam echo-sounder image of HMS Hood, *sunk as a blockship across the southern entrance to Portland Harbour in 1914. The ship can be seen lying upside down with a propeller shaft clearly visible, as well as collapsed parts of the hull. [Courtesy Nautical Archaeology Society]*

and manoeuvrability (which would prove costly at Jutland in 1916). All the major commercial yards, as well as the Portsmouth and Devonport naval dockyards, were involved in building these new types, while the development of Rosyth in Scotland as a base for repair and construction coincided with this period.[7] Innovation continued, and in 1912 HMS *Bristol* became the first warship to run on superheated steam from her 12 boilers, enabling even greater speeds as well as fuel economies.

Although there was some general progress in marine engineering during the First World War, the Admiralty pursued a policy of caution and concentrated on simplifying machinery layout. As the war progressed, the main challenge was to keep ships at sea or in a state of constant readiness. Maintenance had to be reduced to a minimum, and rapid repair through the use of small-scale welding was introduced from 1917 as an alternative to the standard practice of riveting hull plates together.

Naval technology during the war was dominated by the battleship. Battleships were built along the dreadnought model, with several large turrets of equally sized big guns. The size of pre-dreadnought battleships can be seen in the remains of HMS *Hood* (launched July 1891), which was scuttled in late 1914 to act as a blockship across the southern entrance to Portland Harbour, Dorset (Fig 3.6). The museum ship USS *Texas*, launched in 1912, is the only dreadnought still afloat and is a registered US National Historic Landmark moored near Houston, Texas, although the remains of First World War dreadnoughts survive in wreck contexts from the First World War and later.

Besides the transition to oil fuel, general modifications made to warships during the war included taller fore-funnels to keep bridge-work clear of smoke and gases, the addition of balloons (for spotting), and aircraft and anti-aircraft guns. Depth charges and anti-submarine howitzers (such as that from the former armoured cruiser HMS *Leviathan,* Museum of Naval Firepower, Gosport) were also later additions. Other naval weaponry can be found in coastal museums, such as a 4in gun at Bamburgh Castle, Northumberland (Fig 3.7).

Generally, throughout the war British ships had larger guns and were equipped and manned for quicker fire than their German counterparts. By contrast, the German ships had better optical equipment and range-finding. To frustrate their range-finding capabilities, various means of obscuring ship features to confuse the silhouette were employed, such as a painted false bow wave (1915) and 'dazzle' camouflage painting from 1917 onwards.[8] Nicknamed 'Cubist ships', their broken lines and colourful patterns were designed to break up their outlines and disguise the direction of travel. HMS *M33*, a veteran of the Gallipoli campaign of 1915, is displayed in Portsmouth Historic Dockyard, repainted in her wartime dazzle scheme (Fig 3.8).

The Battle of Jutland of 31 May to 1 June 1916 highlighted the differences between British and German ships, the latter being much better compartmentalised and able to deal with damage. The battle's progress and outcomes also hung on differences between British and German explosives, propellants and handling procedures, which had disastrous consequences for a number of British battlecruisers.

Surviving vessels and wreck sites

An understanding of the lines, layout and structure of a First World War warship can be seen both in the few surviving vessels and in wrecks. HMS *Caroline*, the last remaining light cruiser, saw action at the Battle of Jutland before being paid off in 1922, and later became a headquarters ship in Belfast Harbour, where she remains in the care of the National Museum of the Royal

Fig 3.7 (left)
A Mark 5 4in naval gun originally fitted to the cruiser HMS Arethusa *in August 1914, now on display in Bamburgh Castle's Armstrong and Aviation Museum, Northumberland.*
[Courtesy Mark Dunkley]

Fig 3.8
HMS M33*, Portsmouth Historic Dockyard. Designed for coastal bombardment, the M33 was launched in May 1915 and saw action during the long Gallipoli campaign. The ship now forms part of the National Historic Fleet.*
[Courtesy Mark Dunkley]

Fig 3.9
HMS Caroline, *Belfast. The last surviving warship from the Battle of Jutland, the* Caroline *now forms part of the National Historic Fleet and is open to the public after a £12m Heritage Lottery Fund award.*
[The National Museum of the Royal Navy]

Navy (Fig 3.9). A veteran of the battle, HMS *Falmouth* sank in Bridlington Bay following two separate torpedo attacks by U-boats on 20 August 1916, two months after the battle. A recent seabed survey has been combined with imagery from a surviving builder's model to identify features from the wreck in 3D (Fig 3.10).

However, not all wreck sites from the First World War survive as coherently as the *Falmouth*. HMS *Warspite*, a fast battleship in the Fifth Battle Squadron and another Jutland veteran, for example, fought during both world wars before running aground in 1947 at Prussia Cove, Cornwall, where she was dismantled over the next five years (Fig 3.11). Fragments of two boilers and hull plating from the wreck remain *in situ*, while the remains of further boilers lie a short distance away.

Increasingly, the remains of wreck sites from the First World War are being investigated as part of a battlefield-wide approach: this is revealing new meanings which are missed when studying wrecks in isolation. Such 'group value' – understanding individual wreck sites within a seascape context – is playing a growing role in understanding the significance of these modern, but hugely important, heritage assets. Survey, identification and investigation of British and German warships sunk during the Battle of Jutland, for example, is enabling interrogation of official accounts, as well as revealing the extent of unauthorised salvage of metals from the wrecks.[9]

Domestically, defended navigable 'War Channels' between the Firth of Forth and the Thames Estuary that were regularly swept clear of German mines were maintained throughout the First World War and were reinstated during the Second World War.[10] These channels are associated with the wrecks of merchant vessels, fishing vessels and minor warships as well

Fig 3.10
HMS Falmouth, *sunk August 1916. The results of a seabed survey, carried out in partnership with the Maritime and Coastguard Agency, have been combined with a digital 3D image of the original builder's model of the ship held by the Imperial War Museum.*
[https://sketchfab.com/models/53f716eb430245c7afde22ad9e0466a9]

Fig 3.11
HMS Warspite, *aground in Prussia Cove, Cornwall, 1947. Launched in 1913, the ship saw action in both world wars before being decommissioned in 1945. She ran aground under tow, and was dismantled over the next five years.*
[EAW005979]

as the German submarines *UB-41* and *UB-75*. Since the channels were buoyed, it is possible that the remains of the buoys, mooring chains and sinkers that marked out the channels exist underwater.

Onshore, the battle to maintain the safe passage of shipping along the War Channels was fought through the naval bases, which sent out minesweepers, auxiliary patrols and coastal forces, and the Port War Signal Stations, through which shipping communicated as it entered and left port.[11]

had often been built in Britain for their original British owners before being sold into German service before the war. They thus form a small but interesting group of archaeological remains attacked by their former owners while once more under the British flag.

There was no direct commerce with Germany, so German-flagged civilian vessels, as opposed to submarines, have left little archaeological trace in English waters by comparison with the high-profile losses of German ships such as the *Preussen*, wrecked off Kent in 1910.

The Royal Naval Reserve and the merchant navy

Just as Jutland would be no set-piece Trafalgar, from the outbreak of war it was clear that this would be a war at sea unlike any other for the merchant navy. It was one of continuous attrition: not only did the front line come perilously close to the English coast, but the mercantile marine went into daily battle on that front line in civilian or naval reserve roles (Fig 3.12).

Historically, as in the Napoleonic Wars a century earlier, the chief danger for mercantile vessels had been the capture of ships with their cargoes carried away by enemy nations. The internment of German vessels in British ports on the outbreak of war, and their conversion to British vessels, was conventional enough, as illustrated by the *Franz Fischer*, sunk as a British collier on 1 February 1916. These vessels

Fig 3.12
Tower Hill Memorial, Trinity Square Gardens, London, commemorates the missing of the merchant navy and fishing fleet. Designed by Edwin Lutyens, it was unveiled in 1928.
[DP182970]

41

The tale of a shipping office

The confident Grade II-listed Edwardian façade of 14–16 Cockspur Street (Fig 3.13), just off Trafalgar Square, tells a story of the First World War hidden in plain sight.[12] Its exterior decorative scheme, comprising panels sporting figures riding sea creatures, a projecting bow window appropriately bearing the jutting prow of a ship, flanked by figures bearing ship models, and the whole topped with a mask of Neptune, bespeaks its original purpose as the London office of a shipping company.

It was commissioned as its London office in 1908 by the German shipping line Hamburg-Amerika Linie, with part sublet from the outset to the British company Allan Line. It qualified as 'enemy premises' under the Trading with the Enemy Act of 1914, and was put up for sale by auction in July 1917 under the Act as amended in 1916. The auction catalogue reveals its occupation by the Ministry of Munitions 'for the purposes of the present war'.[13]

It was purchased by the British P&O line, which was thereby able to move into a purpose-built shipping office with exterior ornamentation appropriate to its line of business. P&O replaced the original caryatids over the doorcase with two of Britannia and Asia enclosing a grille in which the P&O monogram takes the place of the former HA monogram. The latter was expunged even at fourth-floor level, where it was barely visible from the street, a story in stone of the fortunes of war (Fig 3.14).

Fig 3.13 (below)
Nos 14–16 Cockspur Street, London. Front elevation of the newly opened Hamburg-Amerika Linie House, 1908, now the Brazilian Embassy. Commissioned as part of a set celebrating its completion, the same photographs were used to advertise its sale as enemy property in 1917. It is substantially unaltered apart from changes made by the purchaser in 1917, P&O.
[BL20274/001]

Fig 3.14 (above)
Nos 14–16 Cockspur Street, London. Detail of front elevation, showing the maritime-themed decorative scheme and cartouche with PO monogram superimposed on the original letter A, still visible behind after a century. All five cartouches on the façade, spelling out HAPAG (Hamburg-Amerika Paketfahrt Aktiengesellschaft), were similarly treated.
[DP183754]

If conversion of enemy vessels to British use looked back to the past, conversion of domestic vessels to new purposes and new routes by the Allies demonstrated a new and sometimes desperate approach to naval warfare. The commissioning of the Royal Naval Reserve Trawling Section in 1910, which recognised the potential use of fishing vessels as minesweepers in the event of war, anticipated some of these changes.[14] Small and sturdily built with a shallow draught, trawlers ran less risk of contact with mines lurking invisibly below the surface, while their trawl gear could be easily converted to run sweep cables instead of nets.

The Royal Naval Reserve's trawler crews were mobilised immediately on the outbreak of war to counter the equally immediate threat from minefields. On 27 August HMT trawlers *Thomas W Irvin* and *Crathie* were the first to sink while clearing one of the war's earliest German minefields, laid at the latitude of Tynemouth to catch unwary shipping. On the same day this field also sank a British civilian fishing vessel, the *Barley Rig*; the Icelandic trawler *Skúli Fógeti*; the Danish schooner *Gaea*, outward-bound with coal from Sunderland; and the Norwegian steamer *Gottfried*, inward-bound to Blyth in ballast to pick up coal.

That day prefigured the course of the war in the North Sea and Dover approaches in both the principal victims – fishing vessels (civilian and naval auxiliaries), domestic vessels, Scandinavian shipping and colliers – and location of loss.[15] It was inevitable, given the nature of the task, that the major cause of minesweeper-trawler losses would be the very mines they were working to clear, while collisions occasioned by pair working could not always be avoided.[16]

These losses were not confined to the North Sea coasts, as the case of HMT *Arfon* demonstrates. Built in 1908 for the Peter Steam Trawling Company of Milford Haven, she was a typical example of a trawler, modified with minesweeping apparatus and a 6-pounder gun.[17] She saw the best part of three years' service before striking a mine on 30 April 1917 off St Alban's Head, Dorset, laid by the German submarine *UC-61*. Her remains were finally discovered in 2014, having for many years been believed to lie in another location off the Dorset coast. Her story is characteristic of First World War wreck sites, with many ships of the same type, carrying the same cargoes on the same routes, lost to the same war causes, often lying close to one another.[18] This has resulted in historic confusion and multiple attributions of identity and location, with many sites still unresolved. Virtually untouched for over a century, the *Arfon* represents a time capsule with her wartime fixtures remaining *in situ*. She is in all respects a representative example of the fishing vessels which saw service in a wartime role and in 2016 was designated as such under the Protection of Wrecks Act 1973 (Fig 3.15).

The requisitioning of civilian vessels in support of broader military aims (as distinct from being directly taken into military service) has a long history up to the recent past, with the passenger liner *Queen Elizabeth 2* requisitioned for service during the Falklands War (1982). In the First World War passenger vessels, whether ocean liners or railway company ferries, were converted into troop transports and hospital ships.

Seagoing experience could be put to good use in a wartime context, highlighting the roles women could play on the de facto front line of the sea. An extreme example, perhaps, was a Mrs Mary Roberts, whose experience as a stewardess aboard the *Titanic* fitted her to become a nurse aboard the hospital ship *Rohilla*, only to be shipwrecked again. Fortunately, *Rohilla* was bound for France, rather than returning laden with the sick and wounded, which undoubtedly minimised the loss of life. Seabed remains bear eloquent testimony to the hospital ships which were tragically lost, including HMHS *Anglia*, sunk 1915 (Fig 3.16). Four hospital ships were lost in English waters in 1918, as unrestricted submarine warfare intensified, including HMHS *Rewa*, torpedoed in the Bristol Channel on 4 January 1918, with others lost overseas.

Fig 3.15
Diver examining the wreckage of HMT Arfon *astern, with her propeller visible resting on the seabed.*
[Courtesy Swanage Boat Charters]

Legacies of the First World War

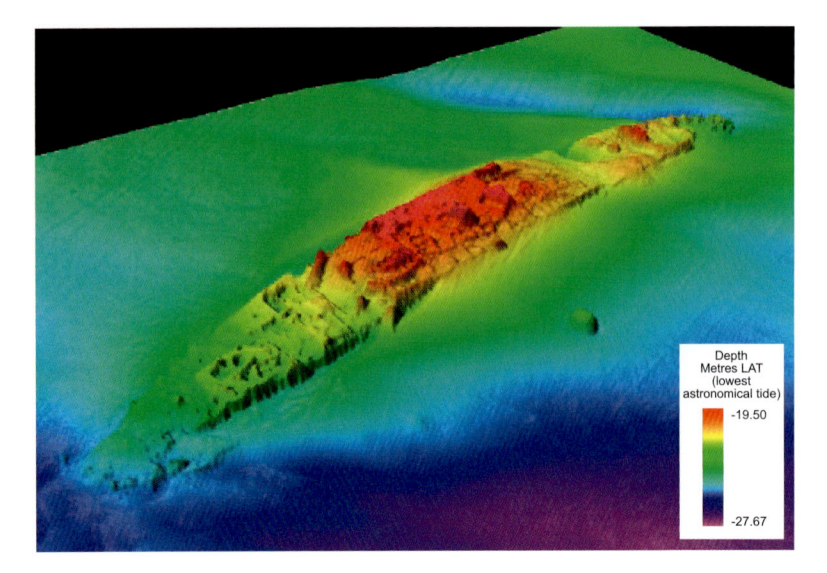

Fig 3.16
Multibeam bathymetry image of HMHS Anglia *as she now lies, with a clear break in her structure towards the top right of the image. Sediment has built up around the wreck. The distinctive cylindrical feature lying off the wreck may be a detached section of funnel casing, but has also been interpreted as a mine.*
[Wessex Archaeology for Historic England]

Despite the continuous criss-crossing of the Channel with troops, troopship losses were infrequent. The two most significant troopship wrecks were both carrying Empire troops but had contrasting outcomes. The SS *Mendi* sank following a collision with the *Darro* on 21 February 1917 with the loss of 646 lives, predominantly members of the South African Native Labour Corps.[19] The *Ballarat* was torpedoed off the Isle of Wight with ANZAC soldiers on 25 April 1917. They were indirectly saved by the Gallipoli tragedy of 1915, since they were mustered on deck ready for a commemorative ANZAC day service and were easily able to evacuate the ship (Fig 3.17).

Fig 3.17
Australian troops mustered and ready to evacuate the Ballarat. *The First World War saw a change in the reportage of shipwrecks, with photography possible from new angles: on board the sinking ship, from boats as they got away, from accompanying ships or as witnessed from the air.*
[© IWM Q 022837]

Civilian vessels also undertook military roles, notably the controversial 'Q-Ships' from 1915. Outwardly retaining the appearance of tramp steamers and other lesser merchantmen, they had in fact been converted to decoy vessels with hidden guns, packed with timber ballast to keep them afloat if torpedoed. They were intended to present tempting targets to submarines as ill-defended lone merchantmen. Once disabled, but not sinking, it was hoped to attract the attacking submarine to the surface to investigate, and sink her by gunfire. As a strategy it soon lost the element of surprise and escalated the tit-for-tat element of reprisals on both sides.[20] A number of Q-Ships survive on the seabed, including *Stock Force* off the south Devon coast, whose exploits would be reprised in a documentary film in 1928 (*see* p 64).

Civilian vessels were also modified to carry armament for self-defence, with an estimated 766 Defensively Armed Merchant Ships in existence by December 1915[21] usually carrying a stern-mounted 1.4in QF gun for self-defence, a typical feature on seabed remains. More than a hundred such defensively armed vessels have been identified within English territorial waters. It was estimated in 1917 that armament boosted the chances of escape by 50 per cent.[22]

Despite high-profile losses of ocean liners such as the *Lusitania*, it is the coal trade which best illustrates the changes forced on British shipping. As a result of the war zone cutting off access to the coalfields of eastern France, British exports of coal to France rose dramatically, including servicing the demands of the British war effort overseas. An increased output from the Welsh ports, already specialists in cross-Channel coal exports, saw an eightfold increase in losses compared with the pre-war period. There is therefore a commensurate rise in the numbers of wreck sites of colliers bound for French ports datable to the First World War era.[23]

The numbers of ships and crew lost to the U-boat blockade continued to rise month after month, with food supplies regarded as a critical issue by April 1917, despite the huge volume of shipping, estimated at 3,000 ships in the 'danger zone' at any one time.[24] Centralised fleet management through the Shipping Controller from 1916 was part of the answer, supplemented in 1917 by a convoy system with escorts, dazzle camouflage of merchant as well as naval vessels, and synchronised zigzagging manoeuvres in convoys to disguise their true direction of travel.

Wartime measures brought their own problems. For example, the cargo steamer *Basil*, requisitioned as a government transport, was running unescorted and without lights with munitions for France, when she was struck by the French steamer *Margaux* on 11 November 1917. The site preserves extensive evidence of the archetypical ammunition of the period otherwise found in 'Flanders fields'. Similarly, on 3 April 1918 the French steamer *France-Aimée* was involved in a collision with a patrol vessel, which happened to have reinforced bows for ramming.

Worst of all, on 24 March 1918, the British oiler *War Knight* would meet her end in a collision in convoy off the Isle of Wight owing to an ill-synchronised zigzag manoeuvre as she and the other lead oiler, *O. B. Jennings*, turned into one another and burst into flames.[25] Dazzle camouflage among the convoy exacerbated the difficulties of a foggy night, and communication by loudhailer rather than wireless, for fear of the enemy, added to the confusion. The remains of *War Knight* (Fig 3.18) and her sister ships, all with the *War* prefix, reflect one of the other measures adopted to counteract the continuing sinkings, facilitated by centralisation: the building of mercantile vessels to a standard pattern, enabling shipbuilding output to rise.

The Shipping Controller also assigned ships to new roles and new routes. In a remarkable agreement with Britain, Scandinavian vessels flew the British flag while retaining their original crews, working coal to British ports and beyond. This solved the problem of vessels from neutral Denmark and Norway being attacked and sunk by Germany, enabled both countries to obtain vital supplies from Britain and went some way to

Fig 3.18
The distinctive spirals of the steam turbine engine of the War Knight *remaining visible among an otherwise very well-broken wreck.*
[© Michael Pitts]

Former Empire Memorial Sailors' Hostel, Tower Hamlets, Greater London

In the years immediately following the First World War there was an appeal to build a hostel lodging for merchant sailors who were between ships and had nowhere to stay. Financed through public subscription, the Empire Memorial Sailors' Hostel was built in 1923 in Tower Hamlets to commemorate the merchant seamen 'of all races across the British Empire' who died in the First World War. It was designed by Thomas Brammall Daniel and Horace Parnacott (Fig 3.19).

Thus it was not only British seamen who stayed there. Britain's declaration of war on Germany and its allies also committed British colonies and Dominions. Over 2.5 million men served in Dominion armies and navies, as well as many thousands of volunteers from the Crown Colonies.[26] Each community therefore has a narrative to contribute.

Among the 25,000 and more merchant sailors who lost their lives on the British side during the war, some 6,600 were Asian and African seafarers known as 'lascars' (from the Urdu and Persian *laskari*, meaning soldier). The word is often thought to refer specifically to sailors from the Indian subcontinent, but originally covered a multi-ethnic community of seamen from East Africa and South-East and East Asia, as well as the subcontinent.

When opened in 1924 the Empire Memorial Sailors' Hostel had 205 single cabins, and over the next five years provided beds for over a million sailors. Demand for rooms fell from the 1960s with the decline of London's Docklands, and the building became a hostel for the homeless, which in turn closed in 1985. In 1994 the building was converted into 50 flats and was renamed The Mission.

Fig 3.19
The former Empire Memorial Sailors' Hostel, built by public subscription in 1923 for sailors who were between ships and had nowhere to stay.
[Courtesy Emma Ridgway]

Fig 3.20
Wills cigarette card, issued in 1917, paying tribute to the Royal Navy submarines, a shift from pre-war attitudes. The reverse of the card reads that the submarines are 'manned by picked crews, and go forth on lonely and desperate errands, performing deeds of thrilling heroism'.
[Courtesy Mark Dunkley]

make up the shortfall in British merchant fleets. Whether sunk before or after the agreement, the remains of some 175 Danish and Norwegian vessels are known to lie in English waters.[27]

Displacement of ships to new routes was also the result of more localised initiatives. For example, very small steamers more suited to their original Mediterranean routes were diverted to fulfil French demand for British coal, such as the 400-ton steamer *Ville d'Oran*, which foundered in the North Sea in September 1916.[28] In a similar vein a short-lived experiment took place in 1917 from the Merseyside ports: small sailing vessels, which would otherwise have worked as barges, ran coal from Ellesmere Port and Runcorn until so many had been picked off by U-boats that the experiment ceased in November that year.[29]

After April 1917 sinkings by war causes began to decrease on the whole, as the new measures at sea bedded in, but would not cease entirely, with spikes in certain months – the seas around Britain remained a front line for all forms of shipping, vulnerable to the depredations of submarines as both minelayers and torpedo attack vessels.

Submarines and U-boats: undersea service on both sides

The Royal Navy initially held an unfavourable view of submarines, with the First Lord of the Admiralty, George Goschen, commenting in 1900 that 'the submarine boat ... would seem to be ... essentially a weapon for maritime powers on the defensive.' This attitude changed after submarines had entered service with foreign navies, and the new First Lord in 1901, Viscount Selborne, announced the purchase of five [submarine] boats 'to assist the Admiralty in assessing their true value'.[30] The submarine service became an independent command in 1912 with its main shore establishment in the obsolete Fort Blockhouse, later HMS *Dolphin*, Gosport, at the entrance to Portsmouth Harbour. Immediately prior to the war the fort had been adapted to accommodate submarine crews while on shore. This work continued during the war, with further additions to existing buildings and new construction work. Anti-submarine experimental and wireless stations were also established here, and in 1917 St Nicholas's chapel on the North Bastion was dedicated to lost submariners (Fig 3.20).[31] For operations in the North Sea a further base was established at Blyth, Northumberland.

Research and experimentation by the Royal Navy progressed slowly through three classes (*A* to *C*) of small boats optimised for coastal patrol and harbour protection. Several of these early submarines lie wrecked off England. The *A1*, sunk in the Solent, 1911, and *A3*, sunk off Portland, 1912, are designated historic wrecks under the Protection of Wrecks Act 1973 (both were sunk with no loss of life). The *A7* is a designated Military Maritime Grave under the Protection of Military Remains Act 1986 on account of its accidental loss in January 1914 with its entire crew. The *B2* lies in the Strait of Dover following collision with the SS *Amerika* in 1912, while the *C29* was mined in the Humber Estuary in August 1915 with the loss of all hands.

The 10 *D*-class boats (Fig 3.21), launched from 1908, were the Royal Navy's first submarines designed for patrolling significantly beyond coastal waters, which was of great importance in the defence of Britain's Empire and its trade. These submarines were the first to carry a wireless transmitter as well as a receiver, and were also fitted with diesel, rather than petrol, engines. These were considerably more economical in fuel consumption (meaning a greater range was given for a fixed quantity of fuel) and, more importantly, the diesel reduced to a minimum the possibility of the buildup of a flammable fuel/air vapour in a submarine.

The *D5* comprises the remains of the only *D*-class submarine lost in English waters (Fig 3.22). A 2015 survey revealed the absence of significant features such as the conning tower, derrick and radio masts on the pressure hull, while the extent of its current burial prohibits a full assessment of its condition.[32] Located some 19km east of Great Yarmouth, the *D5* sank on 3 November 1914 with the loss of 20 lives, out of a complement of 25, after striking a mine while pursuing German ships which had attacked Great Yarmouth to cover a minelaying operation offshore.

Steady improvements in design saw the British *E*-class submarines launched in three groups between 1912 and 1916, and these made up the backbone of the navy's fleet during the First World War. At the outbreak of war in 1914, Britain had 74 submarines, initially divided in to three groups to fulfil specific roles: overseas patrols, surface patrol flotillas working from the

*Fig 3.21
Bow of a British D-class submarine. Note the forward hydroplanes and bow cap with vertically arranged dual torpedo tubes able to fire Mark III 18-inch torpedoes.
[Courtesy wrecksite.eu]*

principal ports and harbour defence flotillas. As the war progressed, emphasis was placed almost entirely on the first role.

The gasoline-powered *U-15*, a type U-13 U-boat or German submarine, was the first submarine casualty of the war: it was rammed and sunk by the British light cruiser HMS *Birmingham* on 9 August 1914 in the North Sea with the loss of all hands. Her engines had apparently failed, as she was lying stopped on the surface in heavy fog when *Birmingham* spotted her and could clearly hear hammering from inside the boat (presumably from attempted repairs). The cruiser fired on her but missed, and as *U-15* began to dive, *Birmingham* rammed her, cutting her in two. A further 200 U-boats were rammed, mined, torpedoed or sunk by gunfire during the war.[33]

Recent research commissioned by Historic England recorded 44 U-boats (a fifth of all wartime U-boat losses) that were lost in England's inshore region, that is, areas of the ocean generally within 12 nautical miles of the coast (Fig 3.23).[34] At the time of writing, only two are protected as Military Maritime Graves – *UB-65* and *UB-81*, with access restricted by the Ministry of Defence. Perhaps unsurprisingly, British submarine losses largely lie further afield, having been lost in operations overseas.

Despite the German naval codes having been broken and signals assessed in Room 40, Old Building of the Admiralty, Whitehall, the centre of British Naval Intelligence during the First World War, shipping losses steadily increased during the war largely because of the U-boat, both torpedo attack and minelaying classes.

*Fig 3.22
The bow cap and vertically arranged dual torpedo tubes of the British D5 submarine, pictured in 2014. It is likely that the bow cap was damaged when D5 struck a German mine in November 1914.
[Courtesy Sylvia Pryer, Dive125.co.uk]*

Legacies of the First World War

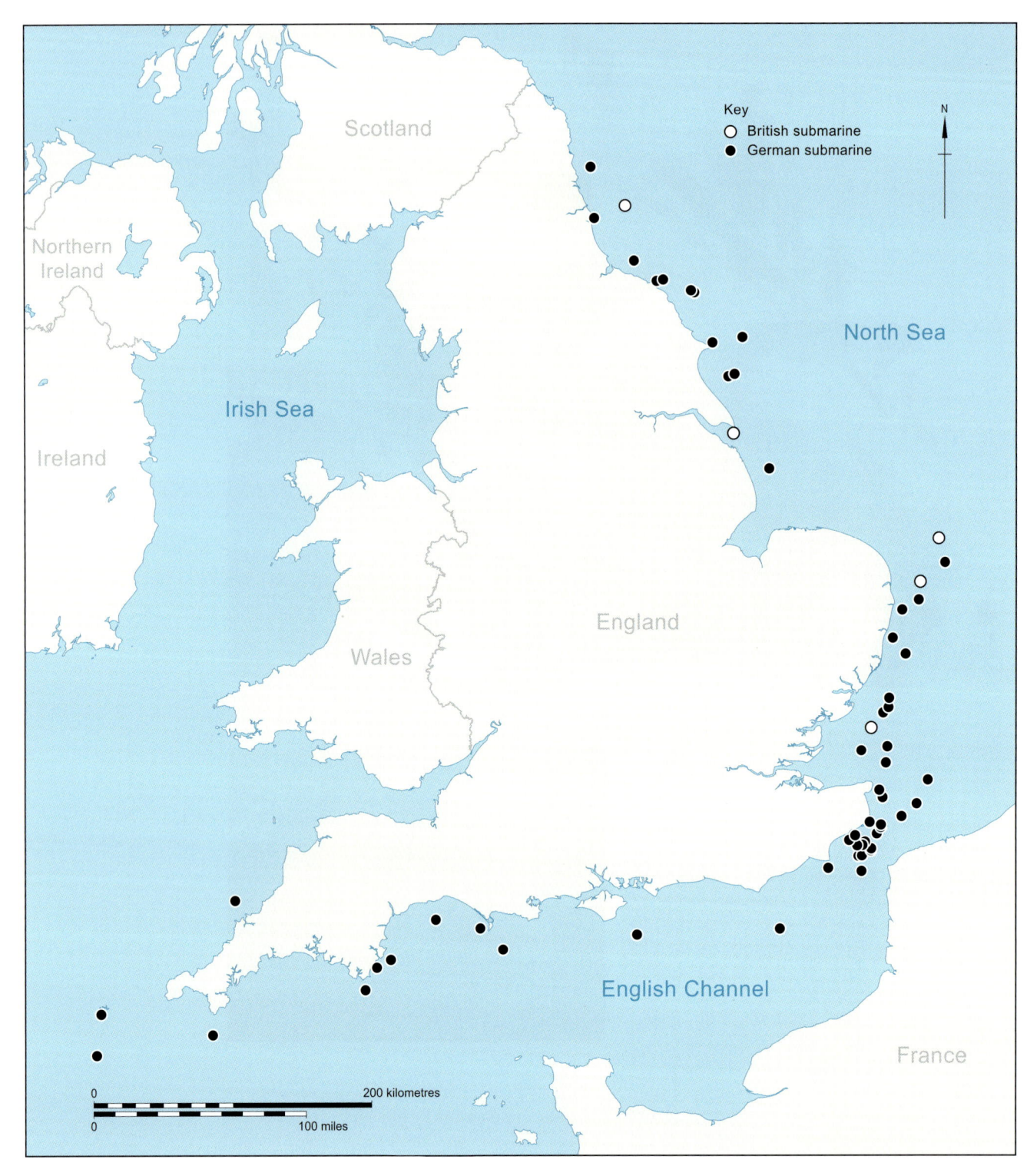

Fig 3.23
Chart showing the location of British submarines and German U-boats sunk during the First World War within territorial waters around the English coast.

Intelligence, in the form of charts, code books, call signs, and technical and personnel data, was gathered from sunken and wrecked U-boats by members of the Admiralty's Salvage Section. Formed at the end of 1915 to meet the increased needs of marine salvage during the war, divers from the unit began work on U-boat investigation in April 1916 with the complete recovery of *UC-5* from the outer Thames Estuary. By March 1918 the Director of Naval Intelligence proposed the development of a special section of divers dedicated to salvage U-boats and to be trained by intelligence officers. This secretive and dangerous work involved squeezing into sunken U-boat hatchways, often manoeuvring past the bodies of deceased submariners, and sometimes using explosives to blast their way in. These specialist divers have since become known as the 'Tin Openers', and their work frequently characterises the remains of U-boats in British waters.

The effectiveness of the German U-boat campaign, particularly following declarations of unrestricted submarine warfare in February 1915 and February 1917, was increased by ineffective Allied countermeasures. A desperate and novel approach to anti-submarine warfare was taken with the training of sea lions to detect and then circle enemy U-boats, uttering loud cries until friendly forces arrived to dispatch the unwary foe. Unsurprisingly, these hopes proved forlorn.[35]

Depth charges, or 'dropping mines' as they were originally called, were introduced throughout the Royal Navy from January 1916 as an offensive countermeasure against U-boats, along with defensive countermeasures. In an attempt to confine the U-boats to the North Sea, barrages (comprising a combination of mines and anti-submarine nets supported by mobile forces, anti-submarine patrols and air forces) were developed. Requiring a huge expenditure of effort and materials, the Northern Barrage stretched between Orkney in Scotland and Bergen in Norway, with the Dover Barrage concentrated between Folkestone, Kent, and Cap Gris-Nez in northern France (Fig 3.24). One element of the Dover Barrage was intended to comprise a series of armed towers linked together with steel nets in order to close the Channel to enemy vessels. By the end of the war, only one had been completed, at immense cost. In 1920 this tower was towed to its new station over the Nab rocks, east of the Isle of Wight, where it remains today, marking the entrance to the main channel into the Solent (*see* Fig 4.16).

Fig 3.24
Chart from December 1917 showing the dispositions of mines and nets of the Dover Barrage, stretching between Folkestone (Kent) and Cap Gris-Nez in northern France.
[By kind permission of naval-history.net]

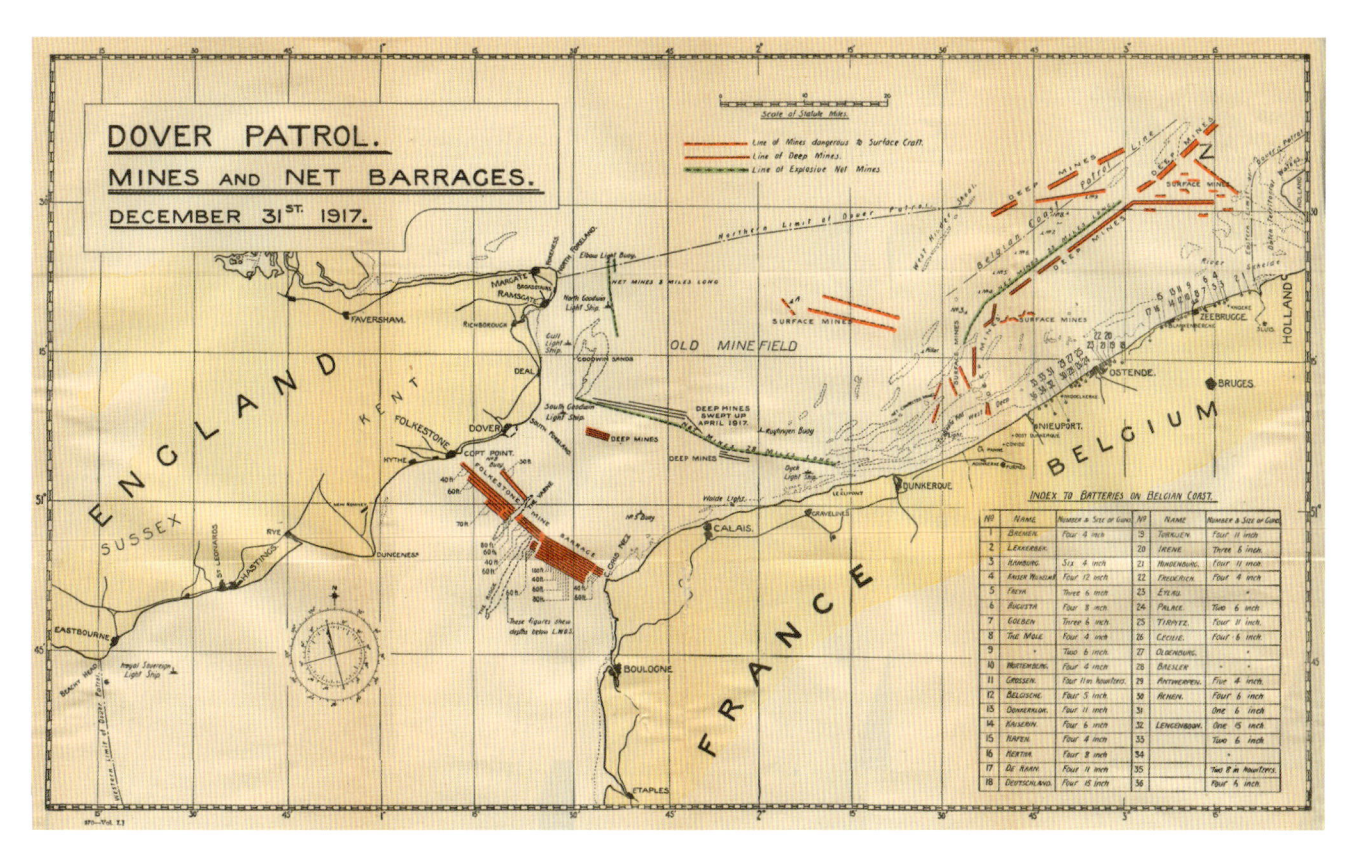

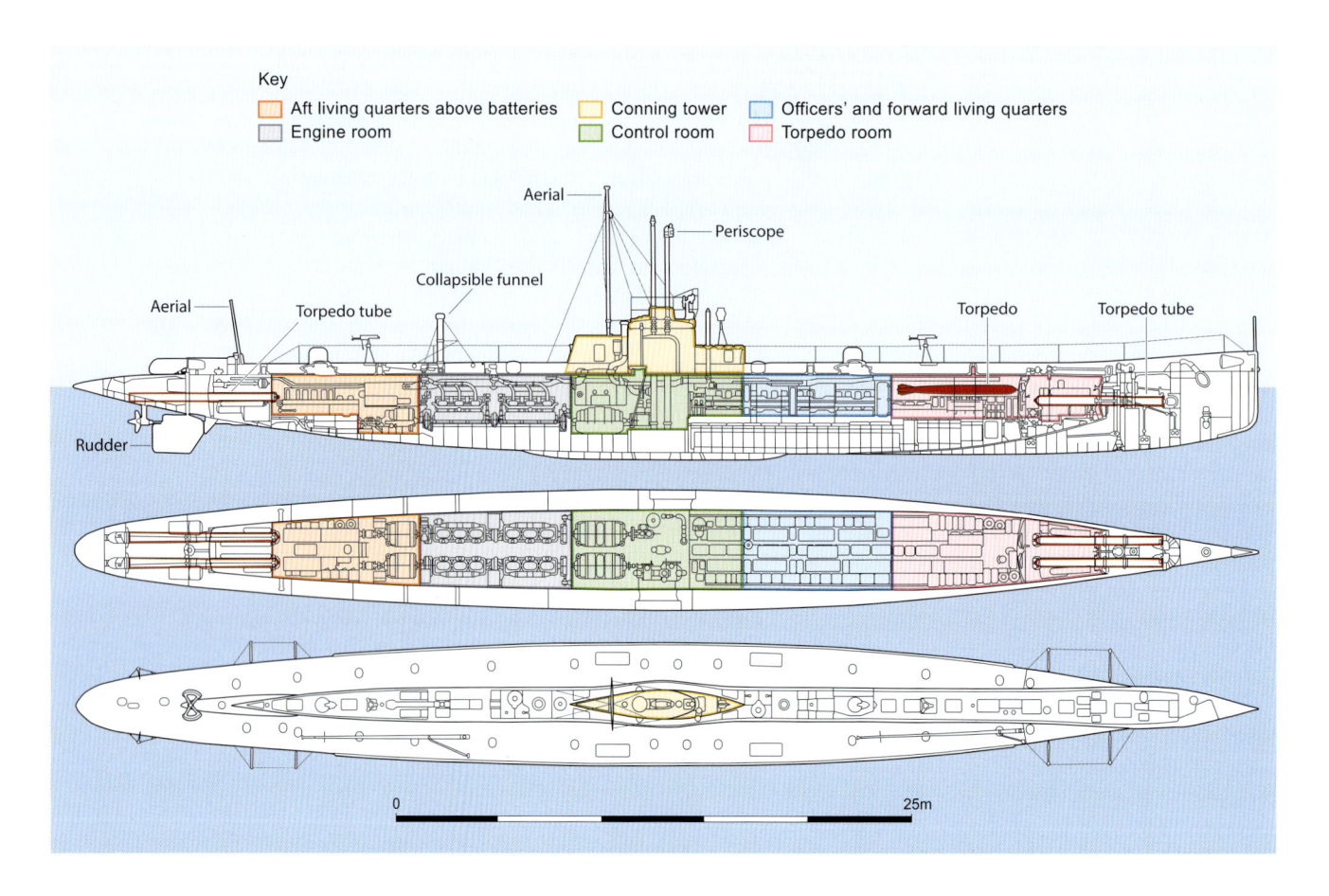

Key
- Aft living quarters above batteries
- Engine room
- Conning tower
- Control room
- Officers' and forward living quarters
- Torpedo room

Fig 3.25
Technical drawing of U-8 based upon sheer drawings for U-boats U-5 to U-8. These submarines were the first German U-boat force to be superior to all foreign competition.
[Redrawn from Rössler, E 2001 The U-boat: the evolution and technical history of German submarines. London: Cassell]

The capture and sinking of the German submarine *U-8* off Folkestone on 4 March 1915 illustrates one of the Dover Barrage's early successes. Launched in 1911 as one of four type *U-5* boats ordered from the Germania shipyard, Kiel (Fig 3.25), *U-8* was passing westwards through the Dover Strait to attack shipping in the Western Approaches, when she ran into the barrage nets. Her attempts to escape attracted the attention of the drifter *Robur*, which called up reinforcements. The destroyer HMS *Ghurka* lowered an explosive sweep and fired a charge when it snagged on an obstruction believed to be the submarine. The commander of the severely damaged U-boat, Kapitänleutnant Alfred Stoß, ordered her to surface, where she was abandoned and later sank, though not before HMS *Ghurka* and HMS *Maori* had opened fire, hitting the area around the conning tower (Fig 3.26).

Innovative acoustic survey commissioned by Historic England in August 2015 collected oceanographic data which confirmed that *U-8* is lying on an even keel, after being on the seabed for over 100 years, with the height of the conning tower extending some 6m above the seabed.[36] Her three periscopes and radio masts remain *in situ*. A buildup of sediment on the western side of the wreck was identified, with possible hull elements having collapsed from their original position onto the seabed (Figs 3.27 and 3.28). The *U-8* was designated a Protected Wreck Site in July 2016 on account of its historical and archaeological importance.

The *U-8* lies within a wider military landscape, as the English Channel was both a transit area and a battlefield for U-boats until August 1918, when the Dover Barrage effectively closed the Dover Strait. German surface raiders attacked the barrage on at least two occasions in actions that have become known as the battles of Dover Strait (26–27 October 1916 and 20–21 April 1917).

Despite the various anti-submarine measures, shipping losses continued to rise steadily during the war. The Allies were losing an average of 65 merchant ships for every U-boat sunk, a figure which, as noted, rose to 167 ships in April 1917.[37] Driven by these U-boat successes, the Royal Navy introduced a convoy system in May/June 1917 whereby groups of merchantmen crossing the Atlantic Ocean sailed under naval protection. The escort ships not only

The naval war

*Fig 3.26
Contemporary postcard showing the sinking of the U-8 by British destroyers off Folkestone, Kent, on 4 March 1915.
[Courtesy Mark Dunkley]*

*Fig 3.27 (far left)
Digital acoustic multibeam echo-sounder image of the U-8, seen lying in good condition on an even keel on the seabed off Folkestone, Kent.
[Wessex Archaeology for Historic England]*

*Fig 3.28 (left)
Digital acoustic side scan sonar image of the U-8 showing that periscopes and radio masts remain in place.
[Data licensed under the Open Government Licence V3.0, from Maritime Coastguard Agency. Prepared by Wessex Archaeology for Historic England]*

guarded against surface gunfire attacks, but also dropped depth charges in areas where U-boats were known to operate.

The convoy system resulted in a rapid decrease in German attacks on Allied shipping during the last 17 months of the war. From April 1918 the construction of merchant ships exceeded losses for the first time since the German declaration of unrestricted submarine warfare in the previous year. Winston Churchill, who served as First Lord of the Admiralty between 1911 and 1915, wrote in 1923 that 'By the middle of 1918 the submarine campaign had been definitely defeated', whereas Rear Admiral Sir William S Jameson claimed that the U-boats had 'been foiled rather than defeated'.[38] During the war, 4,696 British-registered vessels, totalling 9,412,275 tons (9,563,313 tonnes) of shipping, were sunk, of which at least 6,840,744 tons (6,950,517 tonnes) were attributable to submarine torpedo attack, and 40,860 seamen, fishermen and passengers lost their lives.[39]

Meanwhile, raids on Zeebrugge and Ostend in May 1917 and the Battle of Passchendaele (Third Battle of Ypres), July to November 1917, were part of an Allied strategy in West Flanders with the aim of securing the Dutch frontier and capturing the German naval headquarters in Bruges and the U-boat bunkers and floating docks at Ostend and Zeebrugge en route. This land campaign, in support of an ultimately naval objective, resulted in huge casualties on both sides, but illustrates how seriously the U-boat threat was taken. Events culminated in April

Wireless stations and intelligence-gathering

Figs 3.29 Stockton-on-Tees, County Durham. Wireless station's operations room. The window in the gable helped ventilate the battery room. [DP174576]

Fig 3.30 Stockton-on-Tees, County Durham. Wireless station's power house. [DP174579]

Fig 3.31 (below) Stockton-on-Tees, County Durham. Wireless station site plan. [After Ordnance Survey 1916]

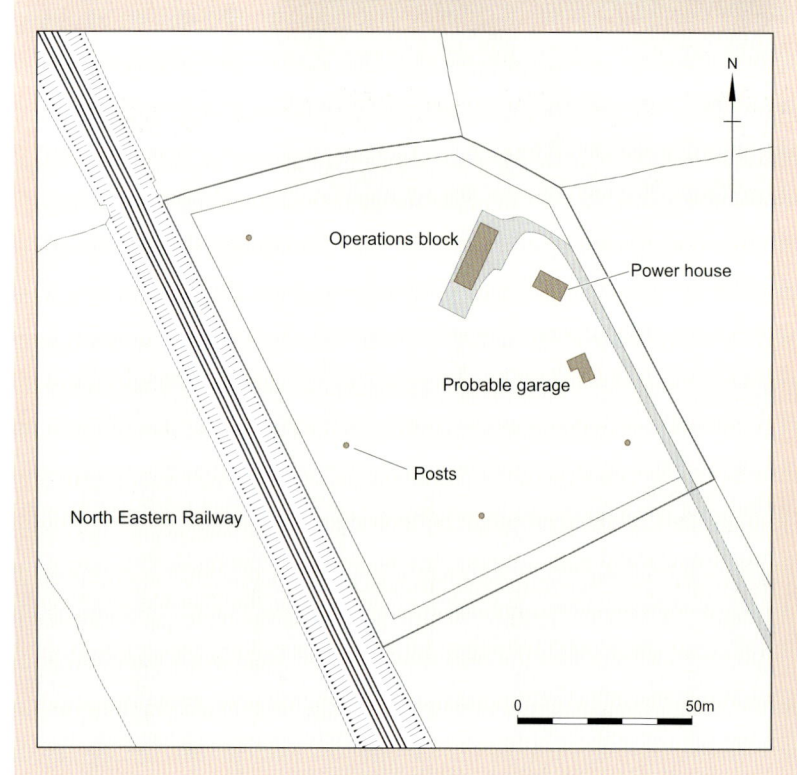

Prior to the First World War, British intelligence-gathering and code-breaking activities were organised on an ad hoc basis for individual military campaigns, notably to support the power politics of the Great Game – the maintenance of Britain's hegemony in India and the surrounding region. Intelligence sources included informants, intercepted letters and, as the 19th century progressed, electrically transmitted telegrams.[40]

At the start of the 20th century most international communications relied on the established technology of submarine copper telegraph cables that spanned the globe carrying critical commercial and diplomatic messages. Germany's cable network was comparatively small, and in one of the first acts of war Britain severed most of its cables, forcing Germany to rely on cables operated by neutral countries, some of which passed through Britain. Messages were also transmitted from the powerful Telefunken wireless station at Nauen, north-west of Berlin. As will be explained, both changes facilitated the interception of German diplomatic communications.[41]

At this time wireless communication was still in its infancy and largely restricted to the maritime sphere with the tapped dots and dashes of Morse code. As the war progressed, the increasing use of wireless technology on land, at sea and in the air presented new opportunities to eavesdrop on an adversary's military and diplomatic communications: a precursor of modern cyberwarfare.

Interception

From at least the late 19th century the Royal Navy had regularly collated information on foreign navies' flag and light signals, and from as early as 1904 had started to collect foreign wireless messages intercepted by British naval vessels.[42] Britain, however, lacked the personnel and infrastructure to collect and systematically exploit this new source of intelligence. Shortly before the war's outbreak the Admiralty completed a dedicated shore-based wireless intercept station at Stockton-on-Tees, County Durham, whose main role was to monitor Royal Navy wireless transmissions to ensure signallers were following regulation procedures (Figs 3.29, 3.30 and 3.31). Its relatively elevated position on the east coast also ideally placed it to intercept signals from the German coast and vessels in the North Sea. Remarkably, at Stockton the operations and generator buildings survive in domestic use, and it provides one of the best examples of an early wireless station. Both structures are brick built, with cement-rendered upper sections beneath tile roofs. The main block is 17.5m by 6.7m and housed the operations room and office, a bunk room and kitchen. A distinctive feature of this building was a separate upper battery room, with a short lifting beam above a lunette window in a gable wall for handling the batteries. They were probably placed here to dissipate any fume leaks.[43]

Shortly after the declaration of war, two amateur radio operators, Colonel Richard Hippisley Royal Engineers (retired), and Russell Clarke, a barrister, reported to the Admiralty that they were able to pick up Morse code messages from the German naval wireless stations at Norddeich in Schleswig-Holstein and Neumünster on the German coast. Hippisley was well respected and in 1913 had been a member of the War Office Committee on Wireless Telegraphy, and after the declaration of war had been commissioned a Commander in Naval Intelligence.[44] To exploit this source, in September 1914 he and Clarke were given permission to work from a hut adjacent to the General Post Office's radio telegraph station at Hunstanton, Norfolk (Figs 3.32 and 3.33).[45] By the end of the war there were up to six direction-finding stations in the Hunstanton area; at least two wartime timber huts believed to be from wireless stations survive incorporated into a house.[46] From these modest beginnings the Admiralty worked with the Marconi Wireless Telegraph Company at its works at Hall Street and at Broomfield, both in Chelmsford, Essex, and at Leafield, Oxfordshire, to refine interception techniques.

Room 40

In late 1914, to remedy the lack of a centralised body to gather, decipher, translate, analyse and disseminate intelligence gathered by the coastal stations and naval vessels, Rear Admiral Henry Oliver established a new section in the Old Admiralty Building, Whitehall, which became simply known as Room 40 (see Fig 1.2).[47] Initially the new department was headed by Sir Alfred Ewing, Director of Naval Education; by 1918 it remained a relatively small operation, employing 74 men and 33 women. British naval communications were sent and received from a telegraph room in the basement of the Admiralty with its aerials strung between the building's imposing cupolas, augmented by landlines to the principal wireless stations. The greatest prize from this work was the interception in January 1917 of a telegram from the German Foreign Minister, Arthur Zimmerman, to the Mexican government in which he offered United States territory in Texas, Arizona and New Mexico in return for Mexico's support of the Central Powers. When revealed, this proposition was instrumental in bringing the United States into the war on the Allied side.[48]

Fig 3.32
Hunstanton, Norfolk. Telegraphic equipment was housed in the coastguard tower completed in 1909.
[DP182221]

Fig 3.33
Hunstanton, Norfolk. The lighthouse and coastguard station, and remaining wartime hut, photographed in June 1920.
[EPW001849]

Wireless stations

By 1918 there were around 90 wireless stations in England, mainly around the coast and concerned with maritime and diplomatic traffic, but there were also many important inland sites (Fig 3.34). These were accommodated in a variety of structures. Some occupied pre-war commercial stations which were taken over or extended by the government, for example at Cullercoats, Tyne and Wear, where a pre-war building and a later addition survive.[49] Elsewhere, they were placed within existing defences, as at Fort Blockhouse, Gosport, and Dover Castle, Kent. Temporary wartime stations were typically placed in wooden huts clad in corrugated iron, timber weather boarding or asbestos sheeting. The minimum requirements for a station were usually a building to house the receiving and transmitting sets, a generator building, aerial masts and, in more remote locations, staff accommodation. Many stations were also provided with a guard hut, a perimeter fence and barbed wire obstacles. Contemporary sources also indicate the official classification of stations into 'Y' stations charged with interception duties and 'B' responsible for direction finding. Further subdivisions of provisioning are also hinted at, including standardised hut types.[50]

By the end of the war the combination of wireless sets with other new technologies, such as aircraft and tanks, foretold the future direction of warfare. On the battlefield, voice transmission by wireless telephony transformed communications between spotter aircraft and artillery units. Pioneering experiments began in summer 1915 at Brooklands, Surrey, into voice communications between aircraft and the ground. These trials continued throughout 1916, and by early 1917 a number of home defence squadrons were equipped with wireless sets capable of communicating with the ground and between machines in the air. Messages warning of intruders were relayed from six ground stations in the London area.[51] By the end of the war about 50 Royal Flying Corps airfields were equipped with wireless sets, as well as a number of Royal Naval Air Service stations and some Trinity House lightships.[52]

Direction finding

In addition to intercepting wireless signals it was found that transmissions could also be used to triangulate the position of hostile stations, ships, submarines, airships and aircraft.[53] Research into this technique had started before the war, notably by two Marconi engineers, Henry J Round and C S Franklin at Devizes, Wiltshire.[54] Round was commissioned into the army and continued his work in France, and later supervised the installation of a line of direction-finding stations between Shetland and Kent. By the end of the war there were 19 such stations. Information about German naval vessels was sent from these to Room 40 in the Admiralty (see p 53), while the positions of German airships and aircraft were reported to Room 417 at the War Office, where they were plotted on map tables and their courses disseminated to the relevant air defence units.[55]

Legacies

At the end of hostilities, temporary wartime facilities were commonly sold and given new uses, leaving few traces of their former purpose. At Devizes the plan of the station may be traced as concrete floor slabs and earthworks. A hut was moved into the local village and converted into a workshop.[56] Here and elsewhere there is the potential for rubbish pits that may yield discarded equipment, especially broken glass and earthenware components that had no scrap value. In surrounding fields concrete blocks for mast bases and tethering guys may remain.

Although many detailed records are lost, it is known that wireless and direction-finding stations contributed to many military tactical successes, including the interception of hostile ships, submarines, airships and aircraft.[57] Their most significant contribution to the naval war came in late May 1916, when they alerted the Admiralty to the imminent sailing of the German High Seas Fleet. Speaking after the war, the First Sea Lord Sir H B Jackson, an early wireless enthusiast, commented that it was the interception of increased German naval wireless traffic from Wilhelmshaven, and later the recognition that a transmitting vessel had moved position, which alerted the Royal Navy to the impending departure of the German fleet. This in turn prompted Jackson to order the British Grand Fleet to sea, which culminated in the Battle of Jutland.[58]

The naval war

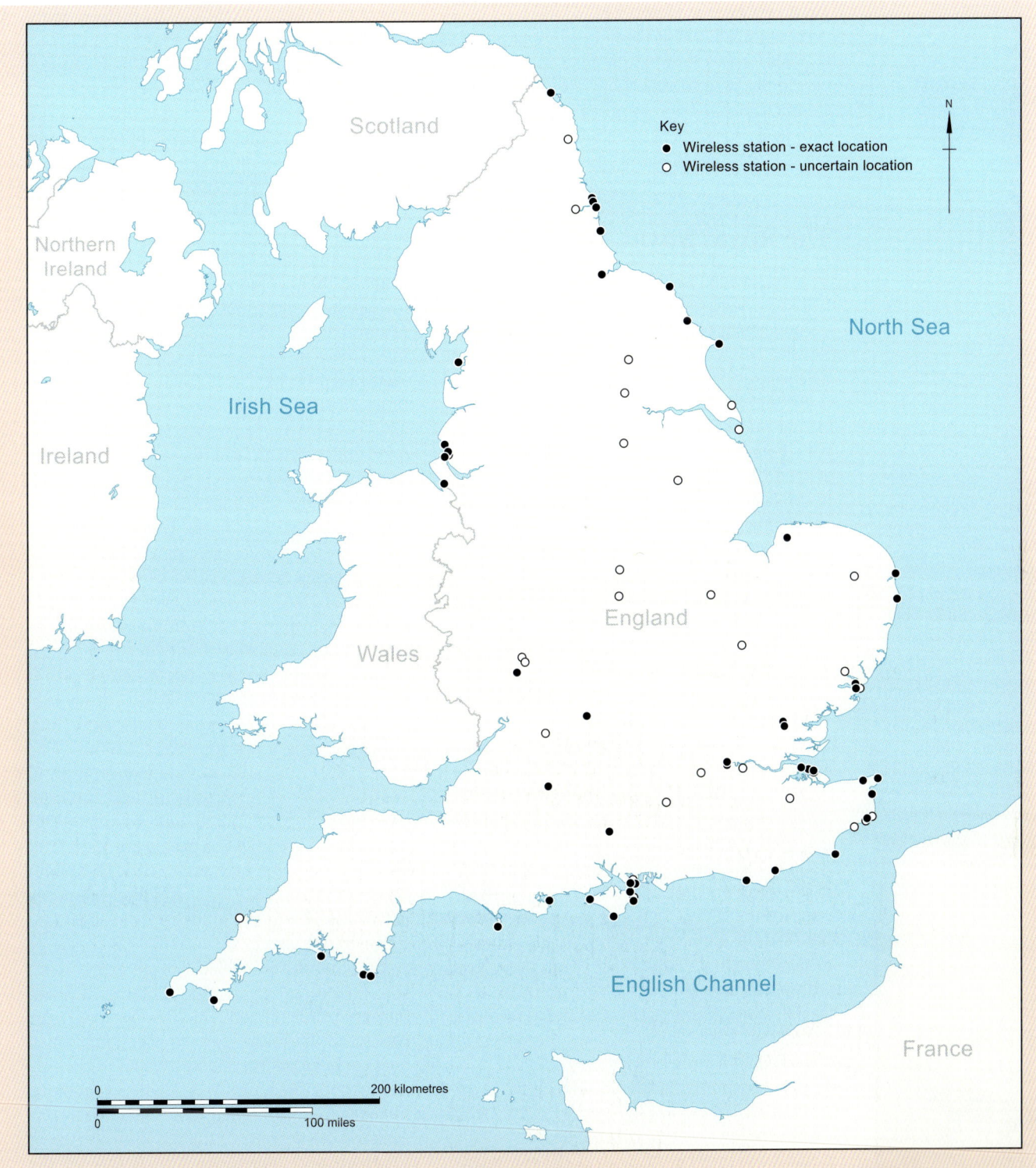

Fig 3.34
Map showing the locations of the principal wireless stations in England at the end of the First World War.

1918 in a raid on Zeebrugge, which was, however, ultimately unsuccessful in blockading the U-boats. In fact that month showed an upward blip in the general month-by-month decline in shipping losses since April 1917, owing to the cumulative effect of all the preventive measures put in place since then.[59]

The Royal Naval Air Service

In a war which saw the first use of powered flight, the defensive barrier of the English Channel and North Sea could no longer be held by the Royal Navy alone. A new means of organised defence was urgently needed.

Prior to the war the Royal Navy took a leading role in the development of aircraft technology, with both flying boats (aircraft with fuselages shaped like boat hulls for take-off and landing on water) and seaplanes (aircraft with floats or landing gear that permitted use on water, in existence before the war). Naval manoeuvres in 1913 using the converted cruiser HMS *Hermes* as a seaplane carrier foreshadowed the formation of the Royal Naval Air Service (RNAS) as distinct from the Royal Flying Corps (RFC) on 1 July 1914, under the direction of the Admiralty's Air Department.[60] A 1913 airship base at Kingsnorth, Kent, became an RNAS station, while a seaplane base on the Isle of Grain was constructed.

By the outbreak of war, the RNAS had 93 aircraft, 6 airships, 2 balloons and 727 personnel, used mainly in patrol and reconnaissance roles rather than in direct combat (Fig 3.35). With these modest resources, the Admiralty required the RNAS to mount a complete coastal patrol from Kinnaird's Head, about 45 miles (72km) north of Glasgow, to Dungeness, Kent, with orders to report any ships, submarines or aircraft spotted. In practice the limited resources at first restricted the patrol area to between the Thames and Humber estuaries.[61]

Experimentation with the launching of aircraft from ships began before 1914. HMS *Campania*, a converted ocean liner, was used as a seaplane carrier from mid-1915, and following modifications in April 1917 which included extending the length of her launch deck, she was able to launch heavier reconnaissance seaplanes. On their return, these had to alight on the sea and were then craned aboard. In rough weather the aircraft sometimes had to be written off.[62] It was not until 1918 that HMS *Argus*, the world's first flat-top vessel capable of carrying military aircraft, was launched.

In June 1917 five Royal Navy light cruisers were modified to include a flying-off platform for Sopwith Pup aircraft, in what was a 'use and ditch' solution as there was no landing-on facility. However, two months later a Sopwith Pup landed on the flight deck of the battlecruiser HMS *Furious*, which marked a turning point in aircraft carrier design.

The intensification of U-boat activity in the English Channel at the beginning of 1915 saw the hastily designed SS (submarine scout) class of semi-rigid airship at RNAS Kingsnorth put into service in less than three weeks (Fig 3.36). Suspended by wire stays below the hydrogen-filled gasbag, the gondola control car of the airship was a BE2c aircraft, without its wings and rudder, which held two crewmen: a wireless operator observer in front, with the pilot seated behind. The airships were to prove a formidable deterrent to the U-boat while performing reconnaissance, mine-hunting and convoy escort duties.

By mid-1917 the inclusion of the American Curtiss *H12* flying boat with an endurance of eight hours, coupled with airships flying from coastal stations, enabled the RNAS to play a significant part in the U-boat war. From July to September 1917 flying boats sank four U-boats, while a seaplane sank another. The RNAS was now able to mount patrols from the Cherbourg peninsula to Cornwall and from Peterhead in Scotland to Rotterdam. Patrols also covered the Irish Sea from a northern limit bounded by a line between the Isle of Mull to north-west Ireland, with airships extending the patrol area to the south between Brest and south-west Ireland.[63]

Eastchurch, on the Isle of Sheppey, Kent, was established as the Naval Wing HQ with the aerodrome named HMS *Pembroke II* (after the naval barracks next to Chatham naval dockyard). In addition to its key role in training naval pilots, the base's War Flight – reinforced by the RFC's No 4 Squadron – became responsible for the defence of the naval dockyards at Chatham and Sheerness. The RNAS, in the forefront of the development of military aviation as a strategic force, conducted trials here of the Handley Page O/100 bomber, which in September 1917 was used on anti-submarine patrols off the River Tees. The bomber was then the largest aircraft that had been built in the UK and one of the largest in the world.

Fig 3.35
Wills cigarette card issued in February 1917, paying tribute to the Royal Naval Air Service, the 'eyes of the battleships' according to the reverse of the card. 'Nothing is hidden from them – the submarine below, the airship above, the bases of the enemy, his great armament factories and the homes of his mammoth airships.'
[Courtesy Mark Dunkley]

Fig 3.36
RNAS Pulham, Rushall, Norfolk. The R33 airship at its mooring in 1921.
[EPW006322]

Fig 3.37 (below)
The Sopwith Baby, a small, fast and agile seaplane used by the RNAS from 1915 as a scout, bomber and anti-Zeppelin fighter (note the upward-firing rockets). This composite example, on display at the Fleet Air Arm Museum, Yeovilton, was built from the original components of two aircraft.
[Courtesy Mark Dunkley]

Eastchurch, together with Larkhill, is one of the two sites in Britain where aircraft sheds built in association with the pre-war pioneers of powered flight have survived. They are among the most historically significant structures associated with the pioneering phase of powered flight to have survived anywhere in Europe or America. Four hangars survive at Eastchurch and are listed Grade II, alongside several other wartime structures and an altered mess building of 1912. Flying at Eastchurch – now the site of an open prison – began in July 1909, when Charles S Rolls (who, together with Henry Royce had co-founded the Rolls-Royce car manufacturing firm) used Standford Hill on Sheppey for tests of his glider, designed and built by the pioneer Short brothers at their nearby Leysdown works.

Convoy channels were protected by aircraft like the Felixstowe F2A Flying Boat, which operated out of Felixstowe and Yarmouth. The F2As frequently engaged German seaplanes in an attempt to control airspace in the southern North Sea. The Felixstowe hull had superior water-contacting attributes and became a key base technology in most seaplane designs thereafter. No aircraft or airships of the RNAS survive, though replicas exist and some composite aircraft can be seen in the Fleet Air Arm Museum in Somerset (Fig 3.37). Of the aircraft themselves, no RNAS airframes are known to survive archaeologically as they were light, relatively flimsy and, with airframes of wood and 'doped' (varnished) fabric, particularly susceptible to fire.[64] A number of offshore RNAS crashes were recorded, such as the loss of a seaplane off Lyme Bay in November 1916 (Fig 3.38).[65]

Fig 3.38
The remains of an SS (submarine scout or sea scout) class airship from RNAS Mullion, Cornwall, being recovered by a trawler.
[The National Museum of the Royal Navy]

RNAS infrastructure survives at Tresco, Isles of Scilly, and Howden, East Yorkshire. From February 1917 aircraft (comprising the Short Type 184 and Felixstowe F5 flying boat) from RNAS Tresco patrolled the Western Approaches providing convoy escort. At RNAS Tresco visible remains include the ramp from the yard onto the beach, bomb store and accommodation block footings.[66] The site is now occupied by the appropriately named Flying Boat Club of the Tresco Estate. At Howden a survey undertaken in 2011 by the Airfield Research Group revealed the floor of an airship shed and other foundations.[67]

Elsewhere, archaeological remains are even less obvious and poorly understood. The concrete perimeter road at the former airship station at Capel-le-Ferne in Kent survives within a modern park for leisure homes (Fig 3.39), while at Polegate (Fig 3.40) an airship station in East Sussex now lost under the post-war housing development between Wannock and Lower Willingdon, Broad Road and Coppice Avenue follows the line of the former station service

Fig 3.39
The perimeter service road of the former airship station at RNAS Capel, Kent. SS class non-rigid airships on anti-submarine patrols flew from this station, the station opened in May 1915, in the Dover Strait area. The site now forms part of a caravan park.
[Courtesy Mark Dunkley]

road. An airship mooring ring (comprising an iron ring set into a sunken concrete cube) can be found *in situ* in a front garden of a property in Wannock Avenue (Fig 3.41). Similarly at RNAS Mullion, a former airship station in Helston, Cornwall, the line of service roads can still be discerned in the Bonython Estate, while the YMCA canteen from the base was relocated after the war to become the village hall at Cury, 4 miles (6km) south of Helston, where it is still in use.

Larger former RNAS structures also occasionally survive, including the main flying-boat hangar at the former RNAS seaplane station at Calshot, Hampshire, which was listed Grade II* in 1988 (Fig 3.42). Similarly, the Network Rail Depot in Wimbledon includes a surprising survival of a rare former seaplane shed. Originally constructed *c* 1918 at Newhaven Seaplane Station in East Sussex, the shed was sold *c* 1921 at an RAF disposals committee auction, dismantled and acquired by the London and South Western Railway, coinciding with the expansion and electrification of its suburban lines in the 1920s. The seaplane shed, including its annexe, was re-erected at Wimbledon Depot in the early 1920s for use as a civil engineering and signal telegraph stores building (Fig 3.43). One of the most complete groups of RNAS hangars survives at former HMS *Daedalus*, Hampshire, with the adjacent slipway for launching seaplanes.

Following the United States' entry into the war in April 1917, American naval aviation

Fig 3.40 (above)
RNAS Polegate, East Sussex. Looking south-east this shows the parade ground, accommodation and service huts. Most buildings were removed when the station closed in 1919. A survey carried out in 1980 found five concrete blocks with rings, used as airship tethers, west of the site at the foot of the Sussex Downs. [The National Museum of the Royal Navy]

Fig 3.41
RNAS Polegate, Wannock Avenue, East Sussex. Airship mooring ring (diameter 0.2m) at former RNAS Polegate, 1915–19. Polegate accommodated four SS class non-rigid airships. [Courtesy Mark Dunkley]

activities were initially focused in France. However, greater numbers of pilots, observers, mechanics and other personnel would be trained in Britain to serve at RNAS and RAF stations to carry out extensive missions, ranging from patrols, to convoy duties, to hunting German airships (Zeppelins). In 1918 the US Navy took control of Killingholme Station, Lincolnshire, and transformed it into the single largest American patrol base in Europe.[68]

It is clear that the surviving remains of former RNAS airfields, seaplane stations, airship stations and balloon stations have not been comprehensively studied, and much has been lost, although other coastal defence structures survive. Further investigation is therefore needed to identify, map and record the largely imperceptible remains to ensure that they are adequately signposted within historic environment records, so as to assist with their future preservation.

Fig 3.42
Former RNAS seaplane station at Calshot, Hampshire. When built in 1918 the main hangar was the largest in Britain for use by fixed-wing aircraft during the First World War, covering an area of 5,704 square metres.
[Courtesy Mark Dunkley]

Fig 3.43
The former seaplane shed originally from Newhaven Seaplane Station, East Sussex, now in use at the Network Rail Depot at Wimbledon, London.
[DP182972]

Sound mirrors

To counteract the threat from the air and to complement the activities of the RNAS, a new form of coastal infrastructure was required to anticipate enemy aerial activity.

The first line of defence was the interception of wireless transmissions from Zeppelins, which had greater range and endurance than contemporary German aircraft, with the Observer Corps providing valuable intelligence when an intruder was actually sighted at the coast. The time lag between these two reports made it difficult to position defensive aircraft. Acoustic sound mirrors offered to fill this gap by providing advance notice of approaching Zeppelins.[69]

Sound, or acoustic, mirrors were one of the first early-warning detection systems and worked by using a curved convex surface to focus sound waves from an airship's engine onto a focal point, where it was detected by a listener or, later, by microphones, so that the airship or aircraft could be heard before it was visible.

Operators using a stethoscope would be stationed near the sound mirror, and would need specialist training in identifying different sounds. Distinguishing the complexity of sound was so difficult that the operators could only listen for around 40 minutes at a time, but at their most sophisticated, the devices could identify the sounds of surface vessels or aircraft up to 25 miles (c 40km) away.

The early story of sound mirrors is not wholly clear, but it is thought that the first experiments were conducted in 1915, with the first mirrors or 'dishes' appearing to have been cut directly into chalk in the Dover area. These early beginnings were soon to give way to larger and more complicated concrete structures intended to form a coastal chain from Southampton to Northumberland.

There were three main types of acoustic structures: 'track plotting mirrors', also known as 'Coast Watchers', were upright concave bowls 3 to 4m in diameter; 'sentry walls' were curved structures up to 61m in length, with microphones in a trench dug in front; and 'discs' were horizontal concave bowls designed for use in pairs to measure speed as aircraft passed overhead.

Surviving examples exist at Selsey, West Sussex; Fan Bay, Kent; Kilnsea, East Riding of Yorkshire; Boulby and Bridge Farm, Redcar and Cleveland; and Fulwell, Sunderland (Fig 3.44).

Fig 3.44
A general view from the south of the 1917 sound mirror below Fan Bay Battery, Kent.
[DP189093]

Fig 3.45
Seaplane Lighter H21. Designed by Thornycroft and built by the Royal Engineers in 1918 at Richborough, Kent. H21 had a long post-war career as a lighter on the Thames, and was acquired by the Fleet Air Arm Museum in 1996.
[Courtesy George Hogg]

At sea the RNAS made use of vessels like Seaplane Lighter *H21* (built 1918) to support seaborne aircraft operations. *H21* now forms part of the National Historic Fleet (administered by National Historic Ships UK) and is stored at the Fleet Air Arm Museum (Fig 3.45). These lighters were towed behind warships at speeds of up to 30 knots and were used to operate both flying boats (particularly the Curtiss *H12*) and fighter aircraft (the Sopwith Camel). At sea the lighters had the capability of being flooded to embark and disembark the flying boats and then pumped out using on-board compressed air bottles to restore their buoyancy. They carried sufficient compressed air to perform two complete operations. For fighter aircraft the lighters were modified by fitting an elevated inclined wooden deck for take-off. There was no way of landing, so the aircraft either had to land ashore or ditch alongside the ship.

By 1918 the RNAS had grown to 67,000 officers and men, 2,929 aircraft, 103 airships and 126 coastal stations. It provided the air arm of the Royal Navy until 1 April 1918, when it was merged with the army's RFC to form a new service, the Royal Air Force.

Traces of the Kaiser's navy

The post-war fate of the German navy also continued to exercise minds well beyond the cessation of hostilities. Following the armistice the U-boat fleet made its way to Harwich, while the German High Seas Fleet of surface warships entered Rosyth. Thence they proceeded to Scapa Flow, Orkney, for internment pending the outcome of the eventual Treaty of Versailles (finally signed on 28 June 1919).

Delays in signing the treaty, and fears that the ships might be seized against the will of the German government, led the local commander Rear Admiral Ludwig von Reuter to order his crews to scuttle the vessels on 21 June 1919. While the majority of the scuttled vessels were later raised and salvaged, the wrecks of three battleships (SMS *König*, *Kronprinz Wilhelm* and *Markgraf*) and four cruisers (SMS *Brummer*, *Dresden*, *Karlsruhe* and *Köln*) remain on the seabed today as Scheduled Monuments (Fig 3.46).

SMS *Baden* was among those refloated, only to be sunk shortly afterwards. It was common for the Royal Navy to expend obsolete vessels as gunnery targets: *Baden* thus met her end in mid Channel on 16 August 1921. In a similar vein

Fig 3.46
Scapa Flow, Orkney Isles, Scotland, 21 June 1919. German crews scuttle and then abandon their ships.
[Courtesy W Cocroft]

the German torpedo-boat destroyers V-*44* and V-*82* were used for gunnery trials, subsequently beached at Portsmouth and sold for scrap. Their remains have recently been located and identified in Portsmouth Harbour.[70]

The torpedo-boat destroyers T-*189* and S-*24* broke tow en route to be scrapped in December 1920, going ashore off south Devon. Such a fate was also characteristic of U-boats bound for scrapping: stripped of navigational equipment, they were very vulnerable to the elements, which would often accomplish the task intended for the shipbreakers. At least six such recorded sites survive today, including a significant group which were deliberately beached off Pendennis Head in Cornwall following experimentation with the captured German submarine salvage vessel SS *Cyclop* (Fig 3.47).

In an echo of the fate of V-*44* and V-*82*, a U-boat whose identity has not been confirmed was abandoned in Humble Bee Creek, Medway, Kent, after being stripped of all its recyclable components, including light bulbs, which were put to industrial use in local factories (Fig 3.48).[71]

Fig 3.47 (above)
The German submarine salvage vessel Cyclop. *Herself a war prize, she was part of the trials which involved beaching several U-boats off Pendennis, Falmouth, in 1921. After failing to get them off the rocks, she was considered unfit for use by the Royal Navy and was sold for breaking. Parts of the submarines remain in situ. Photographed by the officer in charge of operations, Jack Casement.*
[JXC01/02/006; reproduced by kind permission of Patrick and Anne Casement]

Fig 3.48
Aerial photograph of the hulk of a U-boat in Humble Bee Creek, Medway, Kent, where she has lain since the 1920s. Believed to be the UB-122, her identity remains unconfirmed.
[NMR 27106/027]

Post-war losses

A continuing front line and its aftermath: destruction and disposal

With so many minefields sown around the coastline, clearance operations continued until well after the armistice. Not all mines could be accounted for immediately, since many had broken loose and drifted outside their original fields.

Lloyd's *War Losses for the First World War* includes a section devoted entirely to vessels lost to mines following the cessation of hostilities up to 1925.[72] A number were lost around the English coastline, from three particular groups, as follows: minesweepers continuing sweeping activity, British and foreign merchantmen, and fishing vessels, with 1919 being a peak year for losses in English waters.

The last known mine victims were perhaps the most tragic. Having successfully served as a minesweeper for the duration of the entire war, the trawler *Strathord* sank after reverting to her peacetime fishing role. She netted a stray mine in her trawl and blew up on 23 February 1920 with the loss of all hands, including her skipper, who had also resumed his civilian occupation after war service. His brother, in a nearby trawler, witnessed the explosion and brought the news back to Scarborough.[73] A few weeks later the trawler *Taranaki*, which had been involved in sinking *U-40* in 1915, was lost in a similar position to the same cause. In the light of these casualties the Admiralty recommended the adoption of a mine deflector to prevent stray mines entering trawl nets.[74]

By the time the 'docudrama' film *Q-Ships* was made in 1928, based on the adventures of *Stock Force* as documented by her commanding officer, there were no longer any German U-boats available to play their part in the film. Instead an obsolete British submarine, HMSM *H52*, standing in for a U-boat, and a sailing vessel, the *Amy*, representing the victims of the U-boats, were expended off the Eddystone. They could be considered the very last victims of the First World War in English waters (Fig 3.49).

Conclusions

The war at sea was quite unlike the war on land. There were no set-piece battles and no glorious victories, and the Battle of Jutland was the only full-scale direct action to occur between opposing navies: even this was indecisive. In reality, though, the battle was a strategic British victory; British naval superiority was maintained and the trade blockade continued.

The German naval command attempted to retaliate against the British blockade through the resumption of unrestricted submarine warfare in February 1917, rather than undertake another attempt to engage the Grand Fleet head-on. The observation traditionally attributed to a contemporary American correspondent that 'The prisoner has assaulted his jailer, but he is still in jail' sums up the position of the German High Seas Fleet at this time.

The blockade of supplies to Germany (and its allies) continued to weaken the country and directly contributed to the end of the war. Conversely, the U-boat campaign might have tipped the balance, had the convoy system and other countermeasures, together with collective

Fig 3.49
Still from the film Q-Ships *(1928), depicting the sailing vessel* Amy *apparently being blown up by torpedo from a watching U-boat. In reality scuttling charges were placed on board by the Royal Navy, while an obsolete British submarine stood in for the U-boat.*

action on the part of shipping companies, not eventually succeeded in defeating the German submarines. British control of the North Sea meant no less than the difference between independence and invasion.[75]

Though the war saw diversification of shipping in various guises – redirection of ships and routes, and a diversity of measures adopted to counter a continuously evolving threat – the war also had the result of rendering sailing ships largely obsolete as a component of the world's merchant navies. For the first time since the introduction of steamships, the war saw steamship sinkings outstrip those of sailing vessels. Large sailing vessels were already seen as uneconomic by the early 20th century and beginning to be confined to very long-distance routes in which they still held the advantage against steamships, where they could go for long distances without the need to bunker coal. This trend was only accelerated by the war.

The war at sea is reflected offshore in an immense number of wreck sites, moorings and structures that can now be understood and appreciated as a battlefield landscape, and onshore through buildings, infrastructure and systems that were developed to build, man, arm and maintain the prosecution of the naval and mercantile war. It is easy to overlook the loss of life and the archaeological legacy of the actions and daily struggles of mariners and airmen against both the enemy and the elements that occurred, in some cases, only a matter of metres from the shoreline.

4

Defending the coast

Paul Pattison and Roger J C Thomas

Coast defences prior to the First World War

It has been claimed that British coastal defences were, in general, in a high state of readiness in 1914.[1] True, many ports had well-developed defences, but significant deficiencies existed along the east coast, from Harwich to Orkney, where work had only just begun to address the threat from Germany that had crystallised in the early years of the 20th century. Significantly, there were few or no defences between ports.

Since the 1890s much attention had been paid to port defences. Britain had a worldwide trading network upon which its prosperity and economic security depended, notably for the import of food and goods and the export of products from its massive industrial base (see Chapter 8). Several ports also housed the military and naval facilities that made control of the commercial sea lanes possible. The protection of ports had been debated by the Joint Naval and Military Committee on Defence, from 1891, and the Defence Committee, from 1895. Additional influence came with the establishment of the Committee of Imperial Defence in 1904. These bodies prepared memoranda and undertook reviews and reports on defence matters in response to a constantly evolving situation. The Committee of Imperial Defence had standing and ad hoc sub-committees that included, from 1909, the Home Ports Defence Committee, which advised the Cabinet in the years leading up to 1914.[2] It enabled the government to build on advice from earlier reports in the light of new threats.[3]

In the late 19th century the Royal Navy was the dominant armed service in Britain. In 1889, following the Naval Defence Act, it began a new wave of shipbuilding. From 1905 another wave, the Dreadnought programme, was undertaken to ensure Britain remained the pre-eminent world naval power. In that year the old notion that the Royal Navy formed the first line of defence for the nation (the 'Blue Water' doctrine) was formalised in General J F Owen's report on the armament of home ports, which recorded that 'the Admiralty must be the sole authority for advising as to what class of hostile ships may reasonably be expected to attempt to enter certain waters'.[4] The report categorised port defences into three grades, A to C (A being most important), according to the nature and scale of the perceived threat of naval attack, with coast guns and searchlights allocated for their defence proportionately. Thus, each defended port had its armament of fixed coast artillery modified, and standardised at certain calibres (see pp 74–5), with a nationwide net reduction in guns from about 279 to 244.[5]

Despite some reductions in the heaviest guns, port defences were generally strong and formed a second line in case the enemy eluded the Royal Navy. The emerging response to the threat in the North Sea from German naval forces operating out of Wilhelmshaven, Cuxhaven, Kiel and Danzig included the establishment of new naval bases in Scotland at Rosyth on the Forth (1909), Cromarty (1907) and Scapa Flow (1909), though none of them were fully fortified when war began. In 1909 the standard of primary armament for defended ports was confirmed as that determined by the 1905 Owen Committee, though a few additions were proposed in some locations that were considered to be under-gunned, including at Sheerness on the River Medway.[6] The construction of new fixed defences was also proposed at other east coast ports, consistent with their reclassification as war anchorages and smaller naval bases, including Harwich, which became a war anchorage in 1909–10,[7] the Humber from 1913 and the Tyne from 1916, though in the last of these, new defences were not completed by 1918. Extensive defences were also built in the new Scottish naval bases once war began.

Defending the coast

Fig 4.1
The defended ports of the UK and the Channel Islands at the outbreak of war in 1914.

The defended ports and the fortress system

In 1914, coast defences were concentrated in and on the approaches to 33 defended ports (Fig 4.1).[8] Some of these were the naval dockyards; others were naval anchorages or important commercial ports. Each had coast artillery and electric lights in fixed positions, mainly for defence seawards, operated by Territorial artillery and engineers, with garrison infantry and mobile artillery for perimeter defence. In the event of war the garrisons would be increased in accordance with individual defence plans that had been developed from 1905.

When war was declared, each port became a fortress, to which was mobilised a larger garrison headed by a fortress commander. Every garrison made a defensive perimeter, within which martial law operated and where restrictions were imposed on movement and social hours. Each garrison was arranged according to the port's Defence Plan, a printed volume of secret information, distributed only to senior commanders.[9] The plan contained full details of the port and its defence; expected forms of attack and methods of meeting them; troop deployments and duties in peace and war; weapons allocated to fixed defences and other units; the extent of the perimeter, and key places to be defended by whom and how; reinforcements; availability of naval forces and the nature of cooperation; and local civilian assets such as hospitals, railway stations, coastguard stations, harbour facilities and telephone exchanges.

Strength lay in the artillery and engineers of the fixed defences, who were, for the most part, well-trained Territorials who had practised on

Fig 4.2
The land defences of the defended port of Harwich, as recorded in February 1916.
[The National Archives, ref WO78/4423]

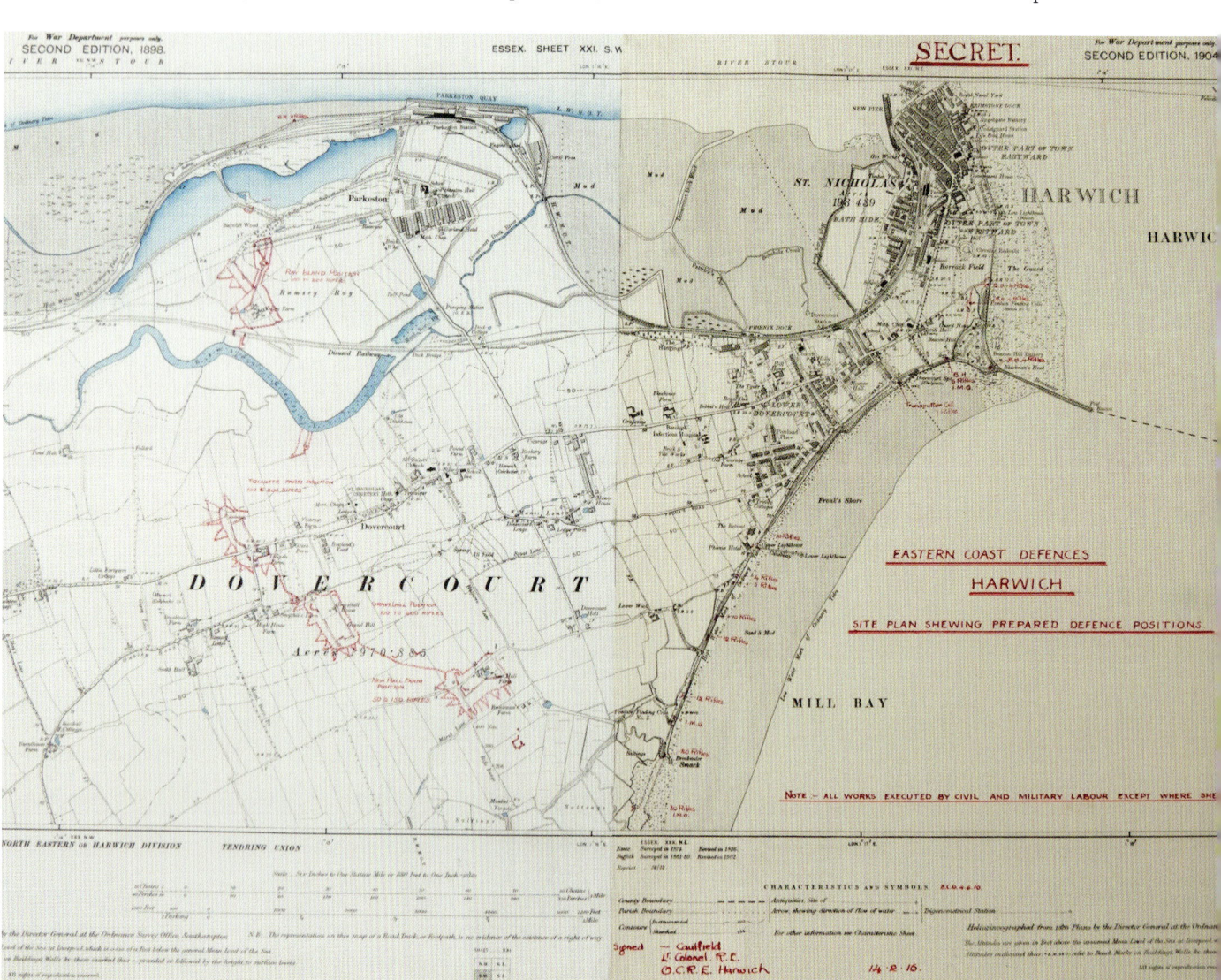

their guns and equipment for several years, had attended yearly camps for intensive instruction and were familiar with technical manuals laid down for the operation of their guns, range and position-finding equipment and defence electric lights.[10]

Pre-planned perimeter defences were probably implemented at all the defended ports, to varying degrees of complexity. Good documentary evidence illustrating the complexity and organisation of defended ports survives for Harwich (Fig 4.2), Portland, Falmouth and Dover.

In addition to perimeter defences and fieldworks, hutted camps for accommodating the soldiers manning the defences were erected in the fortress areas. These varied considerably in size, housing anything from a company (c 160 men) to a battalion (c 800 men). These were often occupied by units in training, or units who had completed their training and were awaiting dispatch to the continent.

The successful defence of the defended ports was dependent upon well-prepared schemes for the coordination of all the armed services, including coastal patrols, coast artillery and searchlights, land defences, and sea obstructions and minefields. Coast artillery was crucial and came under a Commander Royal Artillery, who provided technical advice to the fortress commander. The Royal Navy had its own command structure but worked closely with the fortress commanders, taking responsibility for identifying all warships and submarines approaching a port, the laying of obstructions, boom defence and minefields. The Royal Artillery's roles included both seaward and landward artillery defence with fixed and mobile guns, and the tactical control of the Defence Electric Lights (DELs or searchlights), operated by the Royal Engineers, who were also responsible for the maintenance of the gun batteries, communications and DELs. Infantry units were responsible for the local defence of the gun batteries, DELs, other important installations, manning various entrenchments and guarding possible landing-beaches.[11]

The fortress commander supervised the fire commanders, each of whom was responsible for a fire command comprising a group of coast defence batteries. Each gun battery had a battery commander who controlled up to six guns, all of one type. For night fighting, a DEL could be fitted with a dispersed beam to illuminate an area of water that an attacking ship had to pass through, or used as a fighting light with an intense narrow beam that could be moved to illuminate and track a moving target. Although all DELs were worked and maintained by the Royal Engineers, fixed lights were directed by the fire commander, and fighting lights were allocated to particular batteries and therefore directed by individual battery commanders.[12]

A defended port: Dover

Dover was graded 'B' in the Owen Committee report of 1905,[13] but in 1914 was an obvious target for attack because of Admiralty Harbour, completed in 1909 as a war anchorage for the Royal Navy. It was also a potential bridgehead port for an invading force. From 1914 it became the base of the Dover Patrol, a large, mixed force of ships of all sorts, seaplanes and submarines that conducted defensive operations in the Dover Strait to ensure safe communications to France and Flanders, and offensive operations against German-held positions there. Dover was also the principal port for reception of the wounded from the Western Front, eventually handling the safe transport of 1.2 million casualties during the war.[14]

The harbour and its approaches were defended by 16 coast defence guns in fixed emplacements: five 9.2in guns, six 6in guns and five 12-pounder guns that enabled both counter-bombardment at long ranges and close defence, augmented by 10 machine guns, and 14 searchlights for night fighting. Parts of Citadel Battery and Langdon Battery (both 9.2in) survive (Fig 4.3), as do part of the accommodation

Fig 4.3
Citadel Battery, Dover, Kent. A 9.2in counter-bombardment battery. Looking north-east across gun emplacement no 3, showing the ring of steel holdfast bolts for the gun mounting, and remains of the steel loading gantry.
[© Paul Pattison]

Legacies of the First World War

Fig 4.4
Fort Burgoyne, Dover, Kent. A concrete gun platform for a 6-pounder AA gun, of the early response to aerial attack on the port in 1915–16. An old cannon barrel was used as a pivot for the gun mounting, and part of the perimeter hand rail survives.
[© Paul Pattison]

and magazines of the 6in and 12-pounder batteries on the walls of Admiralty Harbour. The threat from the air was also addressed, initially using converted 6-pounder guns but by 1916 with purpose-made 3in 20cwt weapons. Two emplacements for the 6-pounders survive at Fort Burgoyne, complete with old muzzle-loading barrels for use as gun pivots (Fig 4.4).

Entry to Admiralty Harbour was tightly controlled through cooperation between the navy, army and civilian authorities. The main control building, the Fire Command Post and Port War Signal Station, survives on the edge of the White Cliffs in Dover Castle, with a commanding view over the harbour and approaches (Fig 4.5). It is a composite building begun in 1905, with a single-storey Fire Command Post to coordinate the coast defence guns and searchlights. It was extended in 1915 and given a concrete overhead cover against air attack. In 1914 the Royal Navy built its Port War Signal Station against and over the top of the original Fire Command Post.[15]

Fig 4.5
Dover Castle, Dover, Kent. The Fire Command Post and Port War Signal Station. The former lies under the later (Second World War) concrete cover building; the latter is the brick block at left.
[DP094933]

70

To protect Dover against a landwards attack, a garrison of some 10,020 men was envisaged.[16] In common with most defended ports, this number included draft-training battalions and recruits undergoing basic training. Dover Castle was the garrison headquarters, with troops based there, on the adjacent Western Heights and in additional hutted camps built anew within the defended area. The garrison defended a perimeter encompassing the high ground of the North Downs outside the town, plans for which were contained in the Defence Plan, with the nature of each position and the number of troops allocated.

The perimeter defences were field fortifications constructed immediately following the declaration of war, mainly by civilians, and finished in six weeks.[17] They were recorded on maps of March 1915, the details of which correlate with those of the Defence Plan,[18] and formed an arc, 1–1.5 miles from the town centre, beginning and ending on the White Cliffs to each side of Admiralty Harbour (Figs 4.6 and 4.7). A series of mutually supporting positions occupied the ridges and crests of the downs, commanding the valley of the River Dour and its re-entrants that spread, finger-like, onto the chalk massif, and the main roads from Deal, Canterbury and Folkestone. They also protected the approaches to the 9.2in gun batteries at Langdon Battery and Citadel Battery, as well as other vulnerable points, including coastguard stations.

The maps of 1915 show closed earthwork redoubts supported by fire trenches and open fire trench groups. They incorporated barbed wire entanglements and, at some, communication trenches to outlying fire trenches. Separate entrenched positions were established for field guns. An abatis (felled trees with their bushy tops facing outwards) was used in the redoubts and in other tactical locations, while existing buildings were made defensible, and many hedges and areas of woodland were cleared to provide unimpeded lines of fire and to deny cover. All redoubts were linked by telephone cables, and a series of outposts formed a picket screen a further 0.5–2 miles beyond the main line.

As built, the trenches had head cover against shrapnel. However, the Western Front showed this type of trench could be a deathtrap, when incoming high-explosive shells collapsed the overhead cover onto the occupants. Consequently, the original trenches were replaced in 1916 with open trenches, with shelter in deep dugouts.[19] Simultaneously, the perimeter might have been modified but there is, as yet, no documentary or field evidence. Nor is there any definitive evidence that pillboxes were included in any revisions, the only candidates being two circular pillboxes on the ramparts at Fort Burgoyne.

After the war the perimeter defences were infilled, and much has since been levelled by agriculture or destroyed by urban expansion. However, there are verbal reports of possible earthwork traces of a redoubt on Whinless Down, on the north-west side of the town but these have not been surveyed or investigated.

Coast artillery: range-finding

By 1914 coast artillery had been transformed from an art into a science. Hitting fast-moving and distant targets required the Royal Garrison Artillery (Territorial Force) to be among the most highly trained soldiers in the British army. The main problems were range-finding and judging the course and speed of a target to predict its future position. Other relevant factors were the time in flight of the shell, air pressure, temperature, wind direction and speed, curvature of the earth, the size of the charge, variations in the muzzle velocity, the ballistic coefficient, and the droop and wear of the gun barrel. Three types of rangefinder were in general use: the depression position finder (DPF), the depression rangefinder (DRF), and the Barr and Stroud optical rangefinder, the last available in several horizontal base lengths from 4ft 6in to 30ft (1.37 to 9.14m): a longer base length gave greater accuracy and range. When the DPF was used with heavy and medium guns, it was calibrated for the state of the tide, and once the cross hairs in the rangefinder's telescope was laid on the bow of a ship, the range and bearing were transmitted to the guns automatically on dials and there was no need for layers on the sights; this was known as 'Case III'. If the DRF was used, it too had to be calibrated for the tide and only the range could be obtained, and it was necessary for the gun sights to be manned for laying bearings; this was known as 'Case II'. When a target was at short range, or was within the range of the quick-firing guns, the auto-sight telescopes on the gun were laid on the bow of an attacking ship and tracked, which automatically laid the gun for elevation and range to the target; this was known as 'Case I'.[20]

The 'Fortress System', used for extreme long-range targets, involved several dispersed

Fig 4.6
Dover, Kent. Plan of the landward defences of the fortress, with units allocated to defend them, from the Dover Defence Scheme, August 1912. [After The National Archives, WO33/602]

observation posts, which reported bearings of a given target. The information was cross-plotted on a central plotting table and tracked, allowing the range, speed and course to be determined.

Another method of horizontal range-finding involved a Barr and Stroud optical rangefinder: a pair of swivelling object lenses at either end of an optical tube produced two overlapping images of a target in a binocular viewfinder at the centre, and by converging the angle of the lenses to merge the two images into one, the range and bearing could be read. Of course, these systems relied on the ability of the observer: if he was unable to see the target clearly, it could not be effectively engaged.

Key
- ■ Redoubts
- ● Closed fire trench group
- — Fire trench
- ⌐ Defended building
- ⌐ Defended building held at night
- ↔ Entrenched gun positions
- ○ Vulnerable point to be guarded

No. 1 Sub-section
1. Outpost line - 1 Company
2. Swingate Down - 1 Company
3. Upper Road North - 1 Company
4. Upper Road South - 1 Company
5. Cornhill - 1 Company
6. Prison - Local reserve, 3 Companies
7. Dover Castle

No. 2 Sub-section
8. Outpost line - 1 Company
9. Frith Farm - 1 Company
10. Duke of York's School - 2 Companies
11. Long Hill - 1 Company
12. Fort Burgoyne - Local reserve, 3 Companies

Detached Post
13. Outpost line - 1 Company
14. Archer's Court - 2 Companies
15. Old Park Plantation - 1 Company
16. Old Park - 2 Companies + Local reserve, 2 Companies move here from Castle if required

No. 3 Sub-section
17. Outpost line - 1 Company
18. Gorse Hill - 2 Companies
19. Buckland - 1 Company moves here from Gorse Hill if required
20. Coombe Farm - ½ Company moves here from Whinless Down if required
21. Whinless Down - 2 Companies
22. Elms Vale Farm - ½ Company moves here from Whinless Down if required
23. Workhouse

No. 4 Sub-section
24. Outpost line - 1 Company
25. Lydden Spout Coastguard Station - ½ Company
26. Mount Horeham - 2 Companies
27. Little Farthingloe Farm - ½ Company
28. Botany Bay - 1 Company
29. Round Down - ½ Company
30. Citadel Barracks - Local reserve, 3 companies
31. Grand Shaft Barracks - Local reserve, 3 companies move to Workhouse if required

Defending the coast

Fig 4.7
Dover, Kent. Plan showing the landward defences, as constructed, March 1915. [The National Archives, ref WO78/424]

Coast artillery: development before and during the war

When war was declared in August 1914, the recent modernisation of coast artillery defences placed Britain in a reasonable state of readiness. Several new gun batteries were under construction on the Humber and Thames, while from 1903 to 1906 many had been completed within or adjacent to existing later 19th-century fortifications, for example, the Heugh Battery, Hartlepool, Durham; Tynemouth Castle, Northumberland; Paull Point Battery (Paull Fort), Hull, Yorkshire East Riding; Landguard Fort, Felixstowe, Suffolk; Newhaven Fort and Fort Gilkicker, Hampshire; and Pendennis Castle, Falmouth, Cornwall; others, like Frenchman's Point Battery, South Shields, Durham (Fig 4.8), and Upton Battery, Osmington Mills, Dorset, had been built from scratch.[21] Although these batteries were generally well planned, deficiencies in local defence schemes were identified once they were fully manned and in war service. Shortcomings included the need for additional

Coast artillery: guns and their emplacements

The reorganisation of Britain's coast artillery during the first decade of the twentieth century focused on a standardisation of ordnance and equipment, which would enable the coast gunners to deal with four anticipated forms of attack:

1. bombardment at long range by battleships, battlecruisers or heavy cruisers
2. bombardment at medium range by light cruisers
3. attempted forcing of naval obstructions, that is, minefields and boom defences, or blocking of the entrance to a port or harbour
4. attack by torpedo-boats at night.

By 1914 a further possible form of attack was added: a land raid. Four types of guns were chosen to answer these threats:[22]

1. Ordnance BL 9.2in Mk X
   - Carriage: garrison, Barbette Mk V, permitting 15° elevation
   - Effective maximum range: 17,400yds (15,910m)
   - Highest rate of fire: by day 2.4 rounds per minute, by night 1.7
   - Gun detachment: 15
2. Ordnance BL 6in Mk VII
   - Carriage: garrison, central pivot (CP) Mk II, permitting 16° elevation
   - Effective maximum range: 12,600yds (11,521m)
   - Highest rate of fire: by day 7 rounds per minute, by night 6
   - Gun detachment: 13
3. Ordnance QF 4.7in Mk III
   - Carriage: garrison, CP Mk III, permitting 20° elevation
   - Effective maximum range: 11,800yds (10,790m)
   - Highest rate of fire: by day 10 rounds per minute, by night 8
   - Gun detachment: 12
4. Ordnance QF 12-pounder, 12cwt
   - Carriage: garrison, QF 12-pounder Mk II, permitting 20° elevation
   - Effective maximum range: 8,000yds (7,315m)
   - Highest rate of fire: by day 20 rounds per minute, by night 15
   - Gun detachment: 7

In addition to these four, several other guns were used during the First World War for coast defence, including 12in Mk VIII; 9.2in Mk III rail guns; 7.5in naval howitzers; 6in QF; 4in QF Mk II and V; various types of field gun; and the Maxim .303in machine gun.[23]

The War Department attempted to design a standard concrete gun emplacement for each type of gun. However, owing to the number of guns in use, local geology, topography and site constraints, there was some variety from one site to another. The 6in gun emplacement was the most common; it was smaller than the 9.2in emplacement and was usually built in pairs or threes, with each gun mounted on a ring of threaded steel holdfast bolts. These bolts were cast into a central drum of concrete within a circular pit, with a semicircular concrete shell-deflecting apron to the front and a semicircular raised concrete working platform to the rear. Access to the pit for the gun setters was beneath chequerboard steel sheets at the front and to either side of the working platform. The platform had ready-use ammunition recesses set within it, which faced out onto the gun emplacement floor: those for cartridges had timber frames and doors; those for shells had heavy galvanised steel ones. A cast-iron hatch set within the floor of the working platform gave access to an inclined 'ladder hoist' for the delivery of shells directly from the magazine, and a small recess in the rear wall would have housed a field telephone. A galvanised steel door in the side wall of the emplacement gave access to a vertical 'band hoist' for raising cartridges from the magazine below, and further ammunition recesses were set into the side walls.

Each gun was served by an underground magazine, divided into separate shell and cartridge stores. In the most modern batteries, the magazine entrance was at the base of an external light-well to the rear of the emplacement, which often had an underground war shelter for the gun detachment on the opposite side. Light wells were painted white or lined with white glazed tiles to reflect light into the rooms. A double door normally permitted access into the shell passage, which was lined by shell benches, whereas in adapted fortifications pre-existing magazines had shell and cartridge hoists inserted through the old structure. Unless fused, shells were relatively safe and did not require special precautions. However, the highly inflammable cartridges were stored in zinc cylinders within separate cartridge stores: these could only be entered via a small shifting lobby, where soldiers changed from outdoor uniforms into woollen magazine clothing, to reduce the risk of sparks causing an ignition. The magazines were kept dry by forced ventilation using Howarth vents – narrow, chimney-like ducts to the exterior – and lit by tallow candles or oil magazine lamps secured into glazed light recesses in the walls, covered by brass wire mesh to prevent glass breakage and consequent exposure of naked flames. When a cartridge was required, a cylinder was passed into the shell passage through a side-sliding timber issuing hatch, which was then closed immediately. The lid of the cylinder was removed, and the cylinder placed in the band hoist to be cranked up to the emplacement above.

guns to cover anchorages or channels, the provision of 'war shelters' (or 'laying-down' shelters) to protect duty gun detachments from the elements, the need for perimeter infantry defences, the use of wireless communications and the building of additional accommodation.[24]

The German naval raid on Lowestoft and Great Yarmouth on 3 November 1914 and the bombardment of Scarborough, Whitby and Hartlepool on 16 December 1914 highlighted the vulnerability of the coast to attack and shattered the public confidence in the Royal Navy and the 'Blue Water' doctrine. The threat posed by the German High Seas Fleet was re-emphasised by the Lowestoft raid on 25 April 1916 and the inconclusive Battle of Jutland on 31 May to 1 June 1916, with the result that further coast artillery batteries were built subsequently on the east coast: at Blyth Battery (Fort Coulson), Northumberland, completed in 1916 to defend the Royal Navy's submarine base at Blyth Harbour; Roker Battery, Sunderland, Durham, completed in 1916 for two 4.7in QF guns to protect the River Wear; Fletcher Battery, Isle of Sheppey, Kent, with 9.2in guns, completed in 1917 to provide long-range counter-bombardment fire down the Thames Estuary; Palliser Battery, West Hartlepool, Durham, and Pasley Battery, Coatham, Yorkshire North Riding, commenced in 1918 and both armed with a long-range high-angle 9.2in gun, defending Tees Bay; Haile Sand and Bull Sand sea forts, closing off the mouth of the Humber, Yorkshire East Riding; and the Tyne Turrets (Kitchener and Roberts batteries), Durham and Northumberland, built to provide long-range counter-bombardment defence for Blyth, Newcastle upon Tyne and Sunderland. The construction of some of them was technologically and physically demanding, so that some were not completed until after the armistice.[25] The complexity of these works is exemplified by the Humber defences and the Tyne Turrets.

Fig 4.8
Frenchman's Point Battery, South Shields, Durham. A 9.2in gun battery was completed in 1905, seen here during training. [Courtesy of the late Captain F D Young RGA (FT), via R J C Thomas]

The Humber coast artillery defences

Immediately prior to the First World War, the coast artillery defences of the Humber were minimal, with only the mid-Victorian Paull Point

Legacies of the First World War

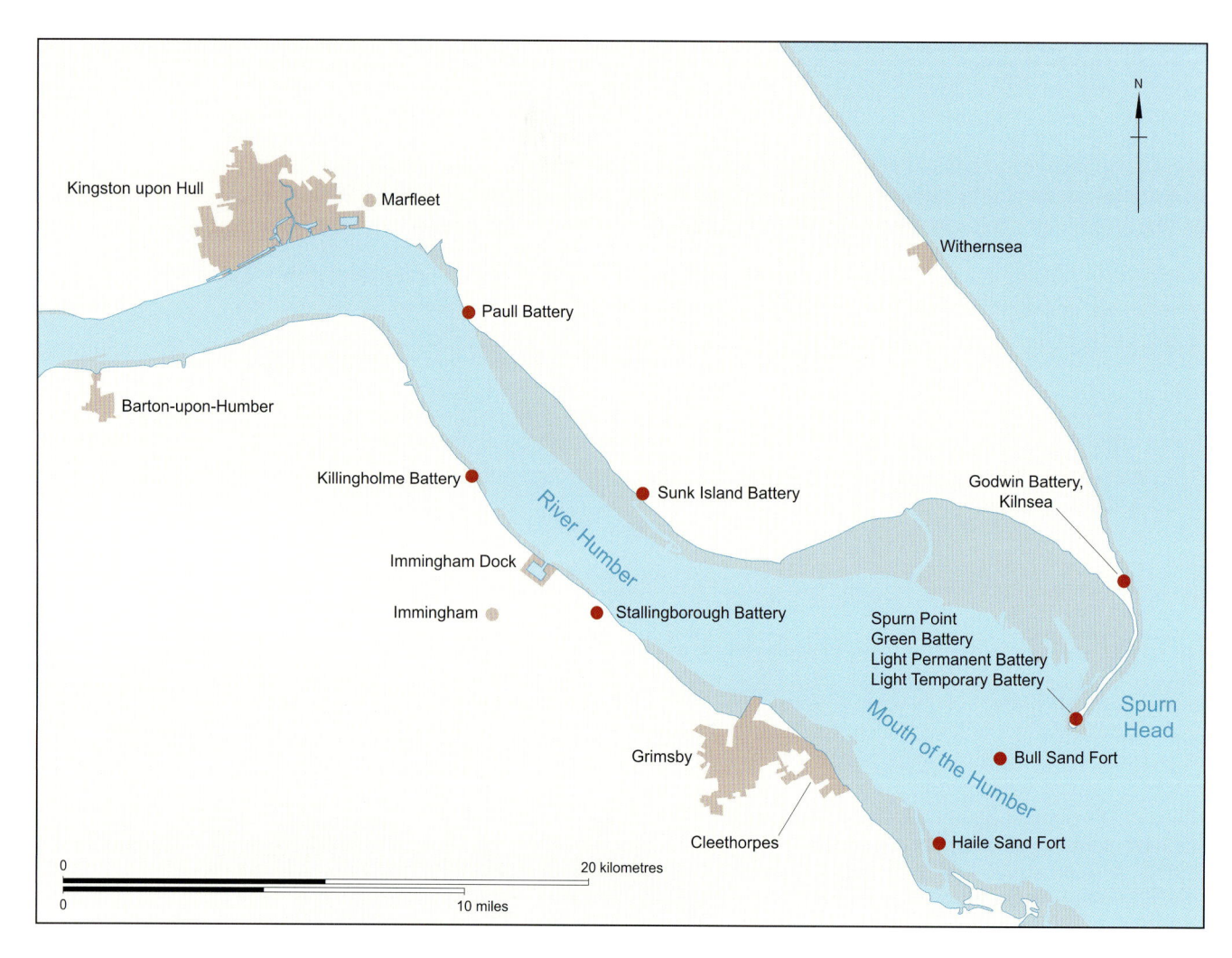

Fig 4.9
Humber defences during the First World War.

Fig 4.10
Godwin Battery, Kilnsea, East Riding of Yorkshire, holdfast drum for the 9.2in gun emplacement, lost to coastal erosion.
[DP169738]

Fig 4.11 (far left)
Bull Sand Fort, Humber Estuary.
[NMR 20620/045]

Fig 4.12 (left)
Haile Sand Fort, Humber Estuary.
[NMR 17085/08]

Battery, rebuilt for 6in and 12-pounder guns in the 1890s. Moreover, this was 19km upstream from the river mouth at Spurn Point (Fig 4.9). In 1905 the Owen Committee concluded that it was sufficient to counter only a class 'C' attack by unarmoured vessels.

The strategic value of the Humber grew in the early 20th century after new docks were built at Marfleet, Yorkshire East Riding, and Immingham, Lincolnshire, and the river had become a naval anchorage, following the construction of an Admiralty fuel oil store at Killingholme, Lincolnshire. Consideration of the defences in 1911 resulted in the rejection of Spurn Point as a site for coast artillery, due to the instability of the sand dunes, and the decision that two batteries, each for two 6in BL guns on concrete gun towers, should be built at Stallingborough, Lincolnshire, and Sunk Island, Yorkshire East Riding, on opposite sides of the Humber. Work on these started in 1913 and was completed in 1915, when Sunk Island was allocated the role of 'Examination Battery', covering all merchant ships entering the examination anchorage for inspection. A concrete Port War Signal Station manned by naval personnel was built adjacent to the battery, responsible for identifying any approaching warships.[26]

Another pair of concrete gun towers, armed with 12-pounder QF anti-torpedo-boat guns, was also built, covering the Admiralty oil jetty at Killingholme. Meanwhile work had started, after all, on new batteries at Spurn Point: Green Battery, armed with two 9.2in BL guns; Light Permanent Battery, armed with two 4in QF guns; and Light Temporary Battery, armed with four 4.7in QF guns. In addition, Godwin Battery, armed with two 9.2in BL guns, was being built a little to the north at Kilnsea, Yorkshire East Riding (Fig 4.10), and a new combined Fire Command Post and Port War Signal Station was under construction to replace the one at Sunk Island. Work had also commenced on two steel 'sea forts' on sand banks in the estuary: Bull Sand Fort, with four 6in BL guns to cover the deep north channel, and Haile Sand Fort, with two 4in QF guns, to protect the shallower south channel from torpedo-boat attack (Figs 4.11 and 4.12). The difficulties of building large structures at sea, on shifting sands and in bad weather, resulted in considerable delay: the smaller Haile Sand Fort was completed by March 1918 but Bull Sand Fort had to wait until December 1919 (Fig 4.13).[27]

Tyne Turrets

Probably the most remarkable coast artillery defences built in Britain during the First World War were those to defend the River Tyne. Its shipbuilding and armaments industries were thought to be vulnerable to long-range naval bombardment and there was a need for long-range guns to counter enemy warships. The need was brought to a head in 1916, when the Admiralty announced to the Army Council that it could no longer undertake the North-East Coast Standing Patrol. In discussion and to some surprise, the Admiralty offered the Army Council two complete 12in BL Mk VIII gun turrets from the pre-dreadnought *Majestic*-class battleship, HMS *Illustrious*, which at the time was moored on the Tyne and was being used as an ammunition store ship.

Fig 4.13
Bull Sand Fort, Humber Estuary. Dignitaries inspect the laying of the heavy reinforcing before the concrete was poured, 8 August 1917.
[IFH 01/015/01]

Two sites were chosen to mount these guns on land: Roberts Battery, north of the Tyne at Hartley, near Seaton Sluice, Northumberland, and Kitchener Battery, south of the river at Lizard Point, Marsden, Durham. Groundworks and construction of the massive concrete gun emplacements began in 1917, much of it by women. Each emplacement had an underground cartridge magazine and shell store, located to either side of a central complex and linked by narrow-gauge tramways. The central complex consisted of a large concrete turret ring, surrounded by electric and hydraulic power plant rooms, and war shelters for the duty detachments. Because the guns had a maximum range of 27,000yds (24.7km), they covered the approaches to Blyth and Sunderland, as well as the Tyne.

A long-base range-finding system was adopted, with a seven-storey directing station built to the rear of 47 Percy Gardens, Tynemouth, Northumberland, which gathered information from transmitting and receiving stations up and down the coast (Fig 4.14). The individual turrets could also be operated in local control from a pair of wireless Battery Observation Posts at Lizard Farm, Marsden, and Fort House, Hartley, each equipped with 30ft (9.14m) Barr and Stroud optical rangefinders (Fig 4.15). Construction continued until September 1921, when both turrets fired 12 proving rounds, only to be placed in a state of 'care and maintenance' in 1922. In April 1926 the War Office scrapped them. The underground structure of Roberts Battery remains buried, but Kitchener Battery was destroyed by quarry operations during the 1960s and 1970s.[28]

The Dover Barrier

Although not strictly coast defence, one other scheme involved the intended use of coast artillery: the Dover Barrier. The Admiralty had considered suggestions for preventing German submarines transiting the English Channel, many of which were impracticable. However, a scheme mooted in 1917 by Admiralty engineer Alexander Gibb was initially rejected but

Defending the coast

accepted upon resubmission in 1918. The work was undertaken in Shoreham Harbour (West Sussex), with concrete boat builders Ver Mehr's chief engineer, Guy Maunsell, involved in the project. The idea was to build several large steel and concrete caisson towers armed with 4in QF guns, erected on buoyant concrete rafts. Each of these had 18 honeycomb chambers, which would be flooded once the tower had been towed into position, sinking it onto the sea bed. The towers would be linked together by a galvanometer system for detecting submarines and by a line of steel anti-submarine nets. By the armistice, only one tower had been completed, at the enormous cost of £1,000,000, though another was nearing completion. In 1920 the completed tower was towed to the Nab Rock (Fig 4.16) off the eastern entrance to the Solent, to replace a lightship, and it continues as a lighthouse today. The second tower was broken up in 1924.[29]

Fig 4.14 (far left)
Percy Gardens, Tynemouth. Directing Station and observation tower for the Tyne Turrets.
[DP169953]

Fig 4.15 (bottom left)
Blyth Battery Observation Post, with a cupola to house a Barr and Stroud rangefinder.
[DP169958]

Fig 4.16 (below)
Nab Tower, about 1920. This 'Mystery Tower' is shown being floated out of Shoreham Harbour. It was intended to be positioned off the coast as a floating defensive emplacement (see p 49).
[OP25301]

79

The Scarborough and Hartlepool raid

In the autumn of 1914 the Imperial German Navy adopted a policy of trying to draw the Royal Navy into battle by using a raiding force to lure the British warships onto the guns of its High Seas Fleet. The first raid on Yarmouth in November 1914 failed to achieve that objective, so Rear Admiral Franz Hipper planned a larger, more daring raid, using several battlecruisers. Unbeknown to the Germans, the British had copies of their code books and, by decoding their wireless transmissions, had discovered that a raid was coming. By 14 December the Admiralty knew that the battlecruisers were about to mount a raid, although they remained unaware that the High Seas Fleet was sailing as well.

Rear Admiral Hipper's raiding force sailed from the Jade River, near Wilhelmshaven (Lower Saxony), on 15 December. It consisted of 4 battlecruisers (*Derflinger*, *Von Der Tann*, *Seydlitz* and *Moltke*), the armoured cruiser *Blücher*, 4 light cruisers (*Strassburg*, *Graudenz*, *Kolberg* and *Strauland*) and 18 destroyers in two flotillas, and was followed out into the North Sea by the High Seas Fleet, under the command of Admiral Friedrich von Ingenohl. Bad weather forced Hipper to send the destroyers and three light cruisers back to port, while the rest continued and later split into two squadrons: *Seydlitz*, *Moltke* and *Blücher* sailed north, parallel to the Yorkshire coast towards Hartlepool; the *Derflinger* and *Von Der Tann* headed towards Scarborough, while *Kolberg* laid a minefield off Flamborough Head. The two battlecruisers commenced firing on Scarborough at 8 am on the 16th and continued for an hour and a half (Fig 4.17), before moving towards Whitby, where the coastguard station was the target, although many shells fell on Whitby Abbey (*see* Fig 3.1) and the town.

Unlike Scarborough and Whitby, Hartlepool was defended by both the Royal Navy and the Army. Unfortunately, only four destroyers were on patrol at the time due to the poor weather. The Hartlepool Fire Command was manned by the 11 officers and 155 men of the Durham Royal Garrison Artillery (TF), commanded by Lieutenant Colonel L Robson RGA (TF). It comprised Heugh Battery, with two 6in guns, and the adjacent Lighthouse Battery, armed with one. The batteries stood on a low headland within 77yds (70m) of each other, separated by a lighthouse, and close to the houses of west Hartlepool. The fire commander received warning of an impending attack at 4.30 am and the guns were supplied with ammunition. The Royal Navy's coastal patrol spotted the German warships at 7.45 am and sent out a warning. HMS *Doon* managed to get one torpedo off, but missed the rapidly approaching warships, before the destroyers, outgunned, were forced to withdraw out of range.

Shortly after gunfire was heard at sea, three warships were spotted by the observation post at South Gare. The naval officer and staff at the Port War Signal Station in the lighthouse at Hartlepool were desperately trying to identify them, when at 8.10 am the ships hoisted German colours and the leading ship opened fire. The first shell from *Seydlitz* exploded between the two batteries, cutting the fire commander's telephone lines, robbing him of effective fire control. The ships came within 5,000yds (4,600m) of the batteries and many of their shells, falling on a flat trajectory, glanced off the ground and ricocheted into the town behind. The gunners of the Heugh Battery engaged the two battlecruisers, while Lighthouse Battery tackled *Blücher*, with hits on *Moltke* and *Blücher*. At 8.25 am the battlecruisers began to fire directly into the town and docks, moving north out of the arc of fire from the Heugh Battery, which turned its fire onto *Blücher* and scored several hits. At about the same time, HMS *Patrol*, a flotilla leader in

Fig 4.17 Scarborough Castle, North Yorkshire. Damage to the barracks building caused by German shelling on 16 December 1914. [FLO1032/02/015]

the harbour, made steam to attack the Germans but was immediately engaged by *Blücher*, hit by two 8in (20cm) salvos and driven aground. HM submarine *C9*, following HMS *Patrol*, drew the enemy's fire but was forced to dive in shallow water and took no further part. The two German battlecruisers then re-engaged the shore batteries as they passed to rejoin *Blücher*, before turning away and disappearing into the mist and smoke drifting over the sea. The Heugh Battery continued to fire until 8.52 am, the last shell at a range of 9,200yds (8,400m). As the fire commander was unable to direct his batteries, most of the engagement was fought at Case II, with high-explosive shells targeting the ships' superstructures. However, when the Heugh Battery turned its fire onto *Blücher*, the guns were laid in the emplacement by the gunners themselves, using only auto-sights, and firing armour-piercing shells at the hulls.

In all, the German warships fired 1,150 shells at Hartlepool, killing 112 people, including two gunners, and wounding more than 200 civilians. The defences replied with 123 shells. The bravery of the gunners in the face of overwhelming enemy shelling was recognised by the award of a Distinguished Service Order to the fire commander, and a Distinguished Conduct Medal and two Military Medals to the three gun captains.[30]

The idea of invasion and raid

Turning to the coastline in general, the notion of a possible invasion or major attack on Britain had been considered before the war and persisted throughout 1914–18, though the size of the force thought likely to undertake it was reassessed on several occasions, prompted by intelligence data on enemy capabilities and on the need to reduce home forces to satisfy the demands of overseas service. However, the means of meeting an invasion remained constant, as expressed by Field Marshal Sir John French in March 1918:

> My system of defence for the United Kingdom is based on the principle of fighting the enemy on the coast and preventing his landing, or should he succeed in doing so, of holding him as near to the coast as possible, and delaying his advance until the various Mobile Formations at my disposal could be brought up as reinforcements.[31]

The size of an enemy invading force was estimated in 1910 by the Committee of Imperial Defence at 70,000 men.[32] That figure was unchanged in January 1913, when the Home Defence Committee commissioned a report on the likelihood of invasion, completed in 1914.[33] It concluded that the enemy was most likely to land at a port to enable resupply, with the aim of striking a decisive blow by taking London.

By July 1915 the fighting troops available to meet such an attack comprised a mobile force in three commands: the Central Force of 145,000 men, covering the area east of Portsmouth to the Wash (until 1916, when it became Eastern Command); Northern Command, with 34,000 men covering the Wash to Berwick-upon-Tweed; Scottish Command, with 22,500 men; and the static garrisons and draft-training battalions of the defended ports.[34]

The general scheme of defence involved coastal patrols by lightly armed units of cyclists and yeomanry, who were charged with watching vulnerable beaches where barbed wire and entrenchments were gradually made, though machine guns and mobile artillery were in short supply. Small troop formations were stationed to defend nodal points further inland, while the main forces with heavier equipment were in barracks in regional towns, ready to deploy at short notice to meet an enemy landing while the forward troops tried to hold it in check.

In July 1915, doubt concerning the ability of the enemy to land 70,000 men at any port resulted in consideration of a smaller force undertaking beach landings.[35] Such attacks would be strategic raids rather than an all-out invasion, with limited but significant objectives such as attacks on wireless stations and armament depots to impede the supply to the main fighting fronts. Landings presented logistical difficulties for defence in some areas, especially on the east coast where there were about 120 miles (200km) of susceptible beaches. However, opinion suggested that 48–72 hours were needed for the enemy to land with heavy equipment and supplies, and though availability of defending troops meant that resistance would be light in some places, this was enough time for the Royal Navy to counter-attack and for larger inland forces to deploy and repel the enemy assault. At the same time it was acknowledged that parts of the home army were too poorly trained and equipped to be totally effective.

In August 1916, as confirmed in January 1917, the War Cabinet increased its estimate of the potential size of a landing force to 160,000 men, for which a force of 500,000 home troops was thought necessary.[36] This remained the estimate in March 1917, but the required defence force was reduced to just over 400,000 men by January 1918,[37] of whom 190,000 were mobile, 161,000 were in coast defence and 128,000 were draft-finding troops at defended ports. By then it was considered that an invasion force of only 30,000 men was the most likely, and accordingly home troops could be further reduced and sent abroad. All beaches within 75 miles (120km) of London were reviewed, and henceforward landings were considered impracticable at most, one exception being a 16km stretch between Aldeburgh and Southwold, Suffolk, which was already strongly defended with barbed wire, machine guns and mobile troops.

Land defence: fieldworks, blockhouses and pillboxes

In addition to those at defended ports, extensive fieldworks were built along exposed stretches of coast, inland and at vulnerable points. These were constructed according to experience gained over the previous 30 years. The British army introduced a bolt-action magazine rifle (the Lee-Metford or Magazine Rifle Mk I) in the late 1880s, and by the time of the Boer War (1899–1902), had adopted the powerful .303 rifle bullet and the 'long' Lee-Enfield Mk I rifle. The accuracy and effectiveness of bolt-action rifle fire was experienced by both sides during that conflict, which resulted in the British adopting new tactics, both in attack and defence: field trenches, barbed wire and infantry blockhouses all became standard defensive measures. Further lessons for the land defence of ports were learnt from the Sino-Japanese War (1904–5), which demonstrated the defensive value of trench systems manned by infantry armed with rifles and machine guns in repulsing multiple large-scale frontal assaults. The engineering principles established in these conflicts were formulated into the manual *Military Engineering: (Part 1) Field Defences*, issued by the War Office in 1908. This was the source for construction in the early part of the First World War, though trench-building methods were modified from experience on the Western Front, and hardened defences made an appearance late in 1916. As we have seen, the potential threat of a major German raid on Britain remained throughout the war, and accordingly the construction of anti-invasion defences continued until 1918.

Redoubts were small strongpoints, each one usually for an infantry section of 10 men, built on high ground or where topography presented a likely line of attack. They were formed as circuits of trenches enclosed by barbed wire perimeters, forming hollow polygonal shapes, possibly with timber or corrugated steel-lined shelters, and with communication trenches crossing the centre from one side to the other. The fire trenches were usually simple, short lengths of crenelated-plan entrenchments, with firing bays separated by projecting traverses to prevent enfilade fire along its length. Initially the trenches were often not fully developed or deepened, but usually had gently sloping sides, a low parapet to the front and a reredos behind, built of spoil from the trench. Over time, many trenches were widened and deepened to reflect the practice in Europe, requiring proper drainage and revetment to prevent flooding or collapse.

Blockhouses were also strongpoints. They varied in size and shape, but were structures with a double timber-framed skin, clad in corrugated steel sheeting, with the intervening space infilled with stone, rubble and sand. The exterior was further encased by sandbag revetments, and a perimeter of barbed wire was set at a distance, both as an obstacle and later to prevent grenade attack.[38]

Field gun positions were often just simple pits dug into the ground, preferably behind walls, on the edge of woods or behind hedges. Where this wasn't possible, a temporary gun emplacement, an epaulement, was built in the form of an irregular earth bank revetted with turf, in front of and to the sides of a gun. It was inadvisable to break the hard ground surface or use dry earth for the banks, as the advantage conferred by the newly introduced smokeless propellants was lost, giving away the gun position as it kicked up dirt and dust on firing.[39]

Pillboxes

Over the course of the war, many blockhouses were replaced by reinforced concrete pillboxes, to a wide variety of designs that tended to be regional or localised. The British army learnt costly lessons during the Battle of the Somme in 1916, when it assaulted well-sited and mutually supporting German concrete infantry posts and machine-gun emplacements. Unfortunately, the British High Command was slow to adopt similar structures as it regarded them as contrary to the aggressive strategy adopted by the army and potentially conducive to soldiers lingering under cover. Nevertheless, their value had not escaped the soldiers and engineers at the front, and improvised concrete defence posts, shelters and observation posts gradually spread on the Western Front and at home. These structures, which in soldiers' slang were termed 'pillboxes' or 'pillar boxes', included observation posts, shelters and infantry posts. 'Pill box' first appeared in print in *The Times* newspaper on 2 August 1917.

Identifying First World War pillboxes can be difficult as many resemble those built during the Second World War: many were reoccupied and integrated into defences during the later conflict. Nevertheless, the appearance and distribution of First World War pillboxes in Britain suggests a degree of centralised design, with circular, oval, square, rectangular, trapezoidal and hexagonal forms being found along the east and south coasts. Commanding Royal Engineers in each district were probably allowed a degree of freedom in the application of the designs, and some may have applied practical modifications from experience gained during service on the Western Front (Figs 4.18 and 4.19).

Among the earliest reinforced concrete infantry structures built in the United Kingdom was a substantial sub-rectangular-plan redoubt, armed with three Vickers machine guns, called Murray's Post, built late in 1915 to defend the landward approaches to Godwin Battery, Kilnsea, north of Spurn Point.[40] Around the same time, a fortified guard room and three blockhouses were built to protect the perimeter of the coast artillery batteries at Spurn Point, and further blockhouses were built at Renney and Hawkins batteries, near Plymouth, Devon. However, it remains uncertain when the first pillboxes were built in England, but some in East Anglia and the South-East may have been built late in 1916. Most were built after mid-1917 and one of the standard designs, with a wide geographical distribution, was a 'lozenge'-plan blockhouse built to a design issued in July 1917, to defend the perimeters of coast artillery batteries. Surviving examples can still to be found as far apart as Fort Bovisand, Plymouth, and Blyth Battery.[41]

Remarkably, subtle variations occurred within the same locations and in the same pillbox design. A round-plan pillbox design found in Norfolk tended to be constructed using interlocking concrete blocks, whereas the same type in Suffolk was usually built *in situ* of poured

Fig 4.18
Pillbox at Barmston Carrs, Barmston, East Riding of Yorkshire.
[DP188423]

Fig 4.19
Pillbox at Folly Hole, Skipsea, East Riding of Yorkshire.
[DP188384]

reinforced concrete. Some of them, particularly along an inland line following the River Ant, have gun embrasures at different heights, the lower ones for a tripod-mounted Vickers machine gun, the higher ones for rifles. The embrasures originally had sliding bulletproof shutters, while a low entrance was closed by double steel doors, but most steel was later removed for scrap. In addition to round forms, hexagonal pillboxes with narrow-splay embrasures were built near Great Yarmouth and along the coast in Suffolk. Others of a similar design were built in Kent, although these usually had wide-splay embrasures, which increased the defenders' fields of fire but increased the likelihood of ricocheting bullets entering the pillbox.

Square and rectangular-plan pillboxes, found in Yorkshire south of Bridlington to the Humber, appear to have been built as an inner lining, intended to be covered and revetted by sandbags or earth, as the 4in (100mm) thick walls were certainly not capable of resisting sustained machine-gun fire, let alone the blast from an artillery shell.

Pillboxes built south of the Humber on the Lincolnshire coast were designed to be shell-proof and are similar in plan to a German pillbox design with three embrasures, built on the Hindenburg Line in 1917. They were constructed of concrete poured *in situ*, reinforced with expanded metal lathing sheets (Expamet), shuttered with timber internally and walled with sandbags externally. Wall thicknesses vary between 3ft 3in and 4ft 5in (1–1.35m), while roofs were very substantial, supported by steel rails, and varied in thickness from 2ft 8in to 4ft 1in (0.86–1.25m). An embrasure with a recess in the wall below was cast into each side wall, designed to receive the front leg of a machine-gun tripod, while a circular roof vent was to draw off fumes generated by sustained gunfire. The lack of an embrasure and additional thickness of the wall on the seaward side were intended to be resistant to artillery fire, while pillbox location below the crest of the adjacent sea bank presented a difficult target.

Several small, eleven-sided concrete guard posts, erected during the First World War around the perimeter of the Royal Navy Armament Depot Chattenden, Medway, have often been described as pillboxes. These tiny structures were sentry or observation posts, the interiors large enough to allow only a single guard to operate a rifle.

Fieldwork systems

Field and documentary studies of fieldwork defence systems in Britain are in their infancy, although some regional work is beginning to reveal their complexity, including some that evolved into well-prepared stop lines. They include the following examples.

East coast defences

Most of East Anglia from the Colne Estuary, Essex, northwards to Hunstanton, Norfolk, has extensive beaches that afforded the opportunity of enemy landings (Fig 4.20). Despite many documentary records of trenches and barbed wire along this coastline, as yet there are no systematic studies of their context. It is likely that they evolved in piecemeal fashion. For instance, trenches were dug on the cliffs north and south of Lowestoft (Suffolk), and a battery of six 4.7in field guns was installed on the southern edge of the town, in response to the German naval bombardment of April 1916. Pillboxes were added later.[42] The Hundred River, Suffolk, would appear to have been a defence line, with pillboxes at Latymer Dam and Rushmere. Also in Suffolk, pillboxes were constructed to strengthen the beaches north of Felixstowe as far

Fig 4.20
Defence lines in East Anglia, as currently known.

Legacies of the First World War

Fig 4.21 (above)
East Lane, Bawdsey, Suffolk. In the foreground is a First World War pillbox and to the rear a Second World War Type 22 pillbox.
[© R J C Thomas]

Fig 4.22 (right)
Circular pillbox at Alderton, Suffolk.
[© P Stamper]

Fig 4.23 (below)
Pillbox at Auburn Farm, Auburn, East Riding of Yorkshire.
[DP188338]

as Bawdsey and Hollesley (Fig 4.21). Pillboxes were also built in the rear of beach defences to guard routes inland, notably at Southwold, Kessingland and Friston.

Further north, at Sheringham, Norfolk, trenches were dug by December 1914, and field guns (60-pounder, 4.4in and 15-pounder) emplaced in batteries or as single guns in several locations between Eccles-on-Sea and Salthouse.[43] These may have formed part of a wider system later augmented by pillboxes. There are several coastal pillboxes between Cley-next-the-Sea and West Runton, with a second group a little further inland between Holt and Aylmerton.[44] That the coastal pillbox line extended further east is confirmed by surviving examples east of West Runton, as far as Sea Palling, as well as a line further inland, with pillboxes along the seaward side of the River Ant linking Stalham, North Walsham and Thorpe Market. A pillbox at Sea Palling bears an inscription scratched into concrete around one of its embrasures, recording construction by the Royal Engineers in July 1918.[45] Further south, Great Yarmouth may have had landwards defences, from which at least two hexagonal pillboxes survive.[46] Together, these may represent the bare bones of an extensive coastal belt of defences, to slow an enemy advance into East Anglia (Fig 4.22).

Complex coast defences have also been revealed during a recent study in East Yorkshire and north Lincolnshire.[47] There, as part of the strengthening of the Humber defences (see pp 75–77), pillboxes were constructed north of the river along the coast from Spurn Head to Bridlington, East Yorkshire, and south of it towards Skegness, Lincolnshire. North of the river, good examples of square pillboxes survive between Fraisthorpe and Skipsea, East Yorkshire, notably around beach exit points at Auburn and Withow Gap (Fig 4.23). Some were constructed on field boundaries with ditches that may have served as communication trenches, while paired pillboxes gave overlapping fire. At Atwick and East Garton, East Yorkshire, semi-sunken rectangular structures surrounded by earth mounds, lacking embrasures and with a single entrance, have been interpreted as command/communications buildings. All appear to have formed part of a 'coastal crust' with at least two lines of mutually supporting defences, interspersed with trenches.

South of the river in north Lincolnshire, the substantial coastal pillboxes of trapezoidal plan

Defending the coast

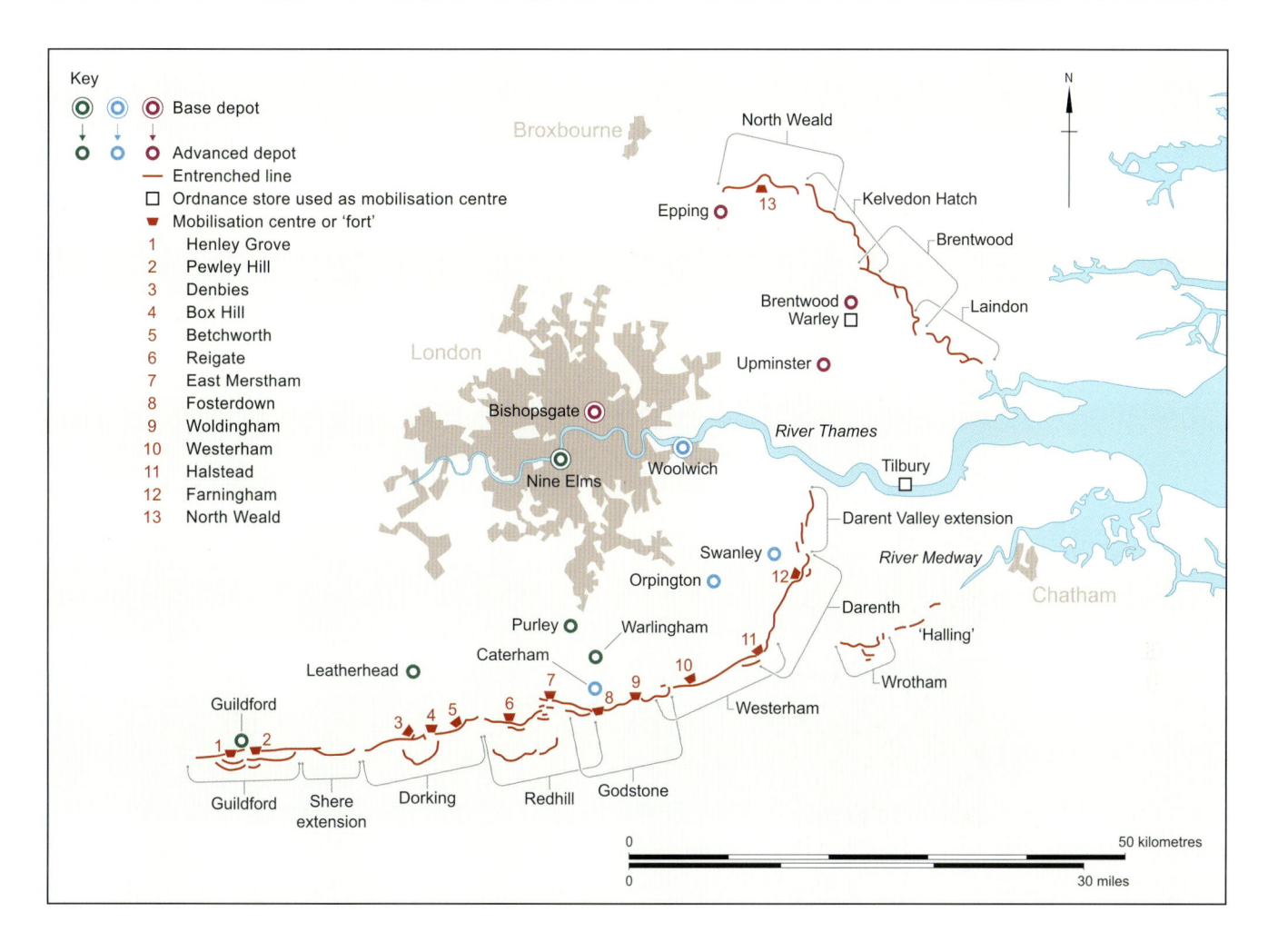

Fig 4.24
The London Defence Line, as drawn in 1902, with First World War modifications.

are represented by four examples surviving in Skidbrooke and North Somercotes.[48] They were built at the back of the beach and spaced at 1,000yd (914m) intervals, with the ground between covered by flanking fire from the Vickers machine guns intersecting at 500 yards (457m), creating a killing zone through which any attacker would have to pass.

The London Defence Line

The London Defence Line was conceived in 1888 and partially constructed from 1892, before abandonment in 1906.[49] It comprised a strong defensive line curving around the south and east approaches to the capital, which was resurrected with some modifications in 1914–15 (Fig 4.24). The modified line followed the North Downs from Buckland Hill near Reigate, Surrey, to Halling, Kent, on the River Medway, where it linked to the Chatham Land Front *(see p 88)*.

The modified line also took the original course down the Darenth valley to Dartford, Kent, resumed on the other side of the River Thames at Vange, Essex, then curved north and west on rising ground to Broxbourne, Hertfordshire, on the River Lea, beyond the original terminus at Epping. The line was articulated around 13 low-profile polygonal mobilisation centres, built of concrete and earth. Some of these formed defensible strongpoints for mobile artillery, although most were stores of ammunition and equipment designed to provide for a defined sector of the line. When the army mobilised, the

Fig 4.25
Reigate Fort, Surrey, a London Mobilisation Centre. The brick entrenching tool store lies at one end of an elongated D-shaped enclosure, with defensive rampart and ditch. The main entrance is on the right.
[DP219129]

87

Legacies of the First World War

Fig 4.26
Troops of the 1st Battalion, County of London Volunteers (United Arts Volunteer Rifles), constructing trenches at Woldingham, Surrey, 1916.
[© IWM Q 023549]

Fig 4.27
A trench of the modified London defences (running left-right below centre), in woodland above Birling, Kent, as revealed by Forest Research lidar.
[Courtesy Kent County Council]

equipment was issued and quickly used to construct field fortifications in the sector, forming a layered defence to a carefully pre-prepared plan, forward of and between each mobilisation centre, on the assumption that they would form a fallback position for field forces that had already deployed to meet an invasion. Many of the centres had been completed by 1906, and there are fine examples surviving at Henley Fort and Reigate Fort, Surrey (Fig 4.25), Fort Farningham, Kent, and North Weald Redoubt, Essex. Some fieldworks between centres were dug from 1915 onwards (Fig 4.26). A single trench of the modified line has been identified from lidar data and subsequently located during fieldwork. It runs for almost 1.5km along the scarp edge of the North Downs above Birling, Kent, overlooking the Medway, and is about 1m wide and 0.5–1m deep, with regular traverses (Fig 4.27).

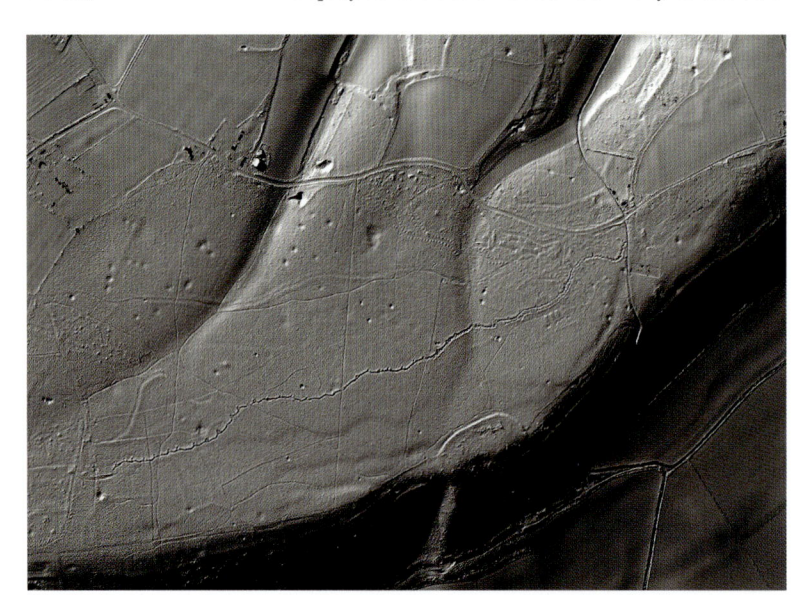

The Chatham Land Front, Kent

Archaeological work[50] has demonstrated the extent and complexity of another fortified line that created a barrier on the approach to London from the south-east coast, linking with the London Defence Line at the River Medway. It began at Detling and ended on the Swale near Kemsley, securing behind it Chatham's naval dockyard and military installations (Fig 4.28). It evolved over the war years to become, in places, a triple line of trenches with barbed wire, earthwork redoubts, pillboxes (the latter

Defending the coast

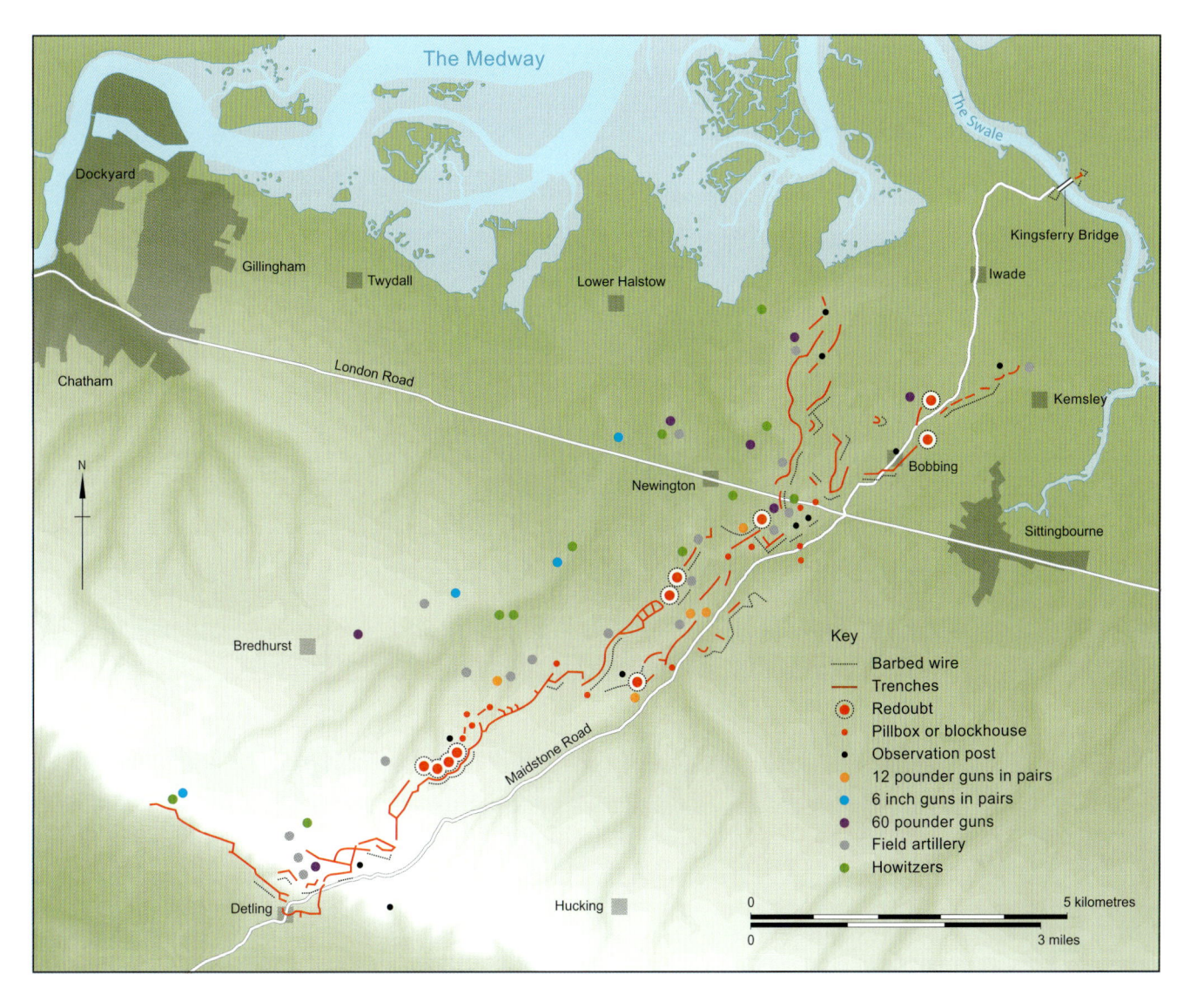

probably from 1917–18) and positions for mobile artillery – though there is no evidence that guns were ever installed.[51] Much of it has been traced from surviving wartime maps and aerial photographs, as well as by fieldwork that has located some physical remains. The principal survivors are pillboxes, three oval (for example, Parsonage Farm, Stockbury) and six square-sided – for example, Wormdale Farm, Newington (Fig 4.29), and Keycol Hill, Bobbing. There are also some earthworks, notably part of a closed redoubt at Cranbrook Woods, Newington, and a section of trench near Detling airfield.

The Sheppey coast defences

The northern edge of the Isle of Sheppey flanks the approach to the River Medway and the Royal Navy dockyards at Sheerness and Chatham, and the mouth of the River Thames. Pre-war, these approaches were heavily defended by a powerful complement of coast artillery at Sheerness and the Isle of Grain. During the war, the defences were augmented with extensive field fortifications which have been the subject of recent detailed study (Fig 4.30).[52] The entire northern coast of Sheppey, comprising 11 miles (17km) of low cliffs and long beaches, was fortified with a continuous line facing seawards, with trenches, barbed wire, earthwork redoubts and pillboxes, additional 9.2in fixed guns at Fletcher Battery (by 1918) and several groups of mobile artillery in field emplacements. Further entrenchments from the main line extended inland, revealing a deeper defensive plan beyond simply defending the beaches. Much of the work seems to be of 1916, with pillboxes added later; some is recorded on detailed contemporary photographs (Figs 4.31, 4.32 and 4.33).[53]

Fig 4.28
The Chatham Land Front showing positions of the main defences.
[Redrawn, after Smith 2016]

Legacies of the First World War

Fig 4.29
The Chatham Land Front. A square-plan pillbox at Wormdale Farm, Newington, Kent. Of its four sides, two have embrasures, a third is blank and the fourth contains a round-headed doorway.
[© Paul Pattison]

Fig 4.30
The Isle of Sheppey, Kent, showing positions of the main defences.
[Redrawn, after Smith 2016]

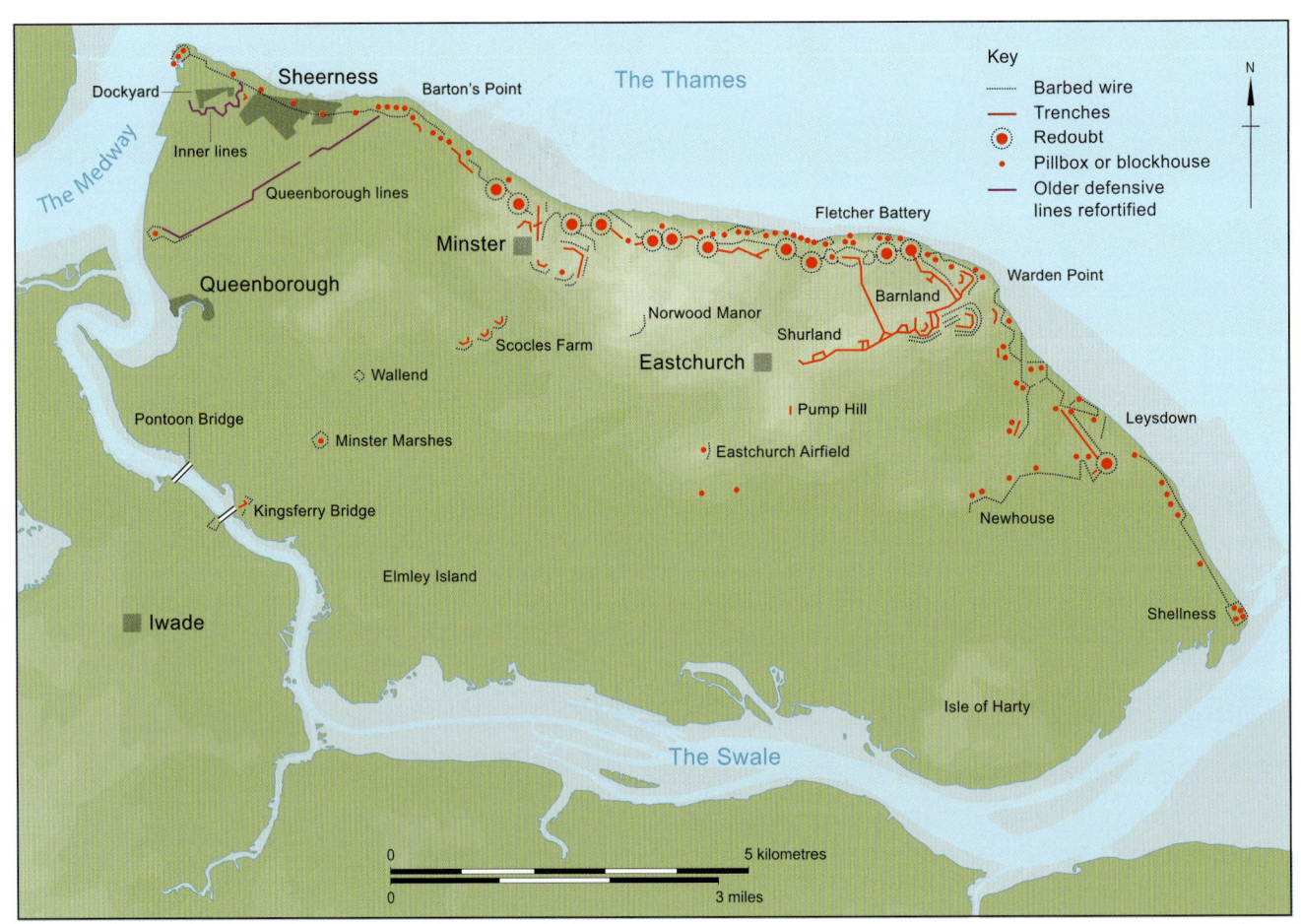

90

Defending the coast

*Fig 4.31 (left)
A trench of the coastal defences near Fletcher Battery, north-east of Eastchurch, Isle of Sheppey, Kent.
[Reproduced by permission of the Royal Engineers Museum, Library & Archive 2/13a/116]*

*Fig 4.32 (bottom left)
A machine-gun pillbox forming part of the beach defences at Ship-on-Shore, Sheerness, Isle of Sheppey, Kent.
[Reproduced by permission of the Royal Engineers Museum, Library & Archive 2/13a/53]*

*Fig 4.33 (below)
Merryman's Hill Redoubt and wire entanglements, Isle of Sheppey, Kent, viewed from the east.
[Reproduced by permission of the Royal Engineers Museum, Library & Archive 2/13a/70]*

*Fig 4.34 (right)
Lodge Hill, Medway. Plan of the earthworks of an infantry redoubt protecting the Ordnance Depot.*

*Fig 4.35 (bottom right)
Lodge Hill, Medway. Plan of the earthworks of an infantry strongpoint protecting the Ordnance Depot.*

Vulnerable points

Field fortifications were also built to protect individual military and civilian installations of strategic importance, including railways, telephone exchanges, oil stores and magazines. The naval magazines at Chattenden and adjacent Ordnance Depot at Lodge Hill, both Medway, were defended by fieldworks built in 1913–14. These comprised four independent redoubts, each for a 13-man section, and two trench groups on high ground around the depot, recorded on a map of progress in September 1913.[54] Two redoubts and a trench group survive as earthworks. One of these is a slightly flattened heptagon in plan, 45–55m across, with a central space of 15m width, surrounded by a low bank, probably originally revetted with an internal firing position, outside which is an encircling ditch (Fig 4.34). A surviving trench group (Fig 4.35), described in 1913 as a 'defensible position with barbed wire and open trench work', has been disturbed by later digging but includes one clearly defined strongpoint, an embanked rectangular space about 22m across with a small bastion-like projection at one corner to enable flanking fire along two sides of the position.

Conclusions

The defence of the coast during the First World War occupied the minds of politicians and military commanders more than is usually acknowledged. The possibility of invasion was considered throughout the war years, though estimates of the size of an attacking force and the troops required to meet it fluctuated considerably. Nevertheless, great effort was put into the protection of the major ports, exposed beaches and other vulnerable points with artillery and infantry defences. Until recently, the recognition and study of these measures had lagged far behind those of the Second World War. At the time of writing, the scale of the First World War defences on the coast, and further inland, is steadily becoming clearer. There is more to discover but it is apparent that defences were extensive and have left a considerable mark in both architecture and landscape along large stretches of the British coastline.

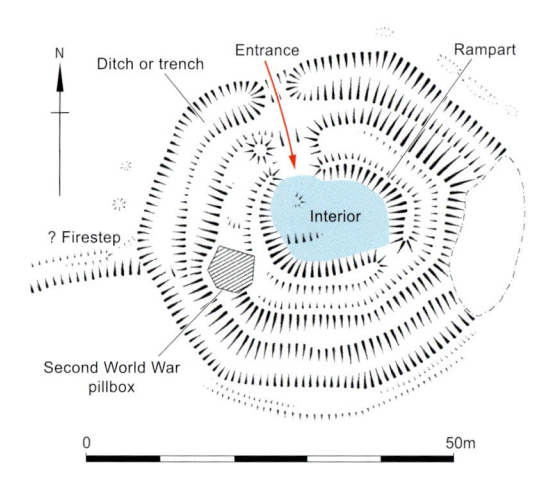

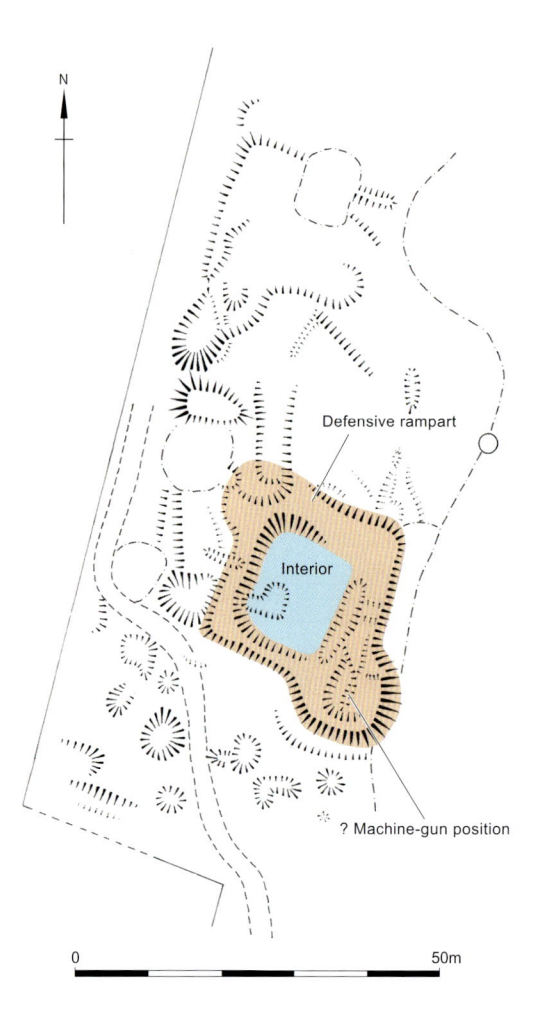

5

The aerial war

Jeremy Lake

To the south-west of Stonehenge lies the site of an airfield that virtually no one knows about. Now only recognisable from crop marks and earthworks (Fig 5.1), it was one of 301 sites that were occupied by the Royal Air Force at the end of the conflict, of which 271 were abandoned and sold by the spring of 1920.[1] As we shall see, around half of the 301 were flying stations, a new type of site that required specialised buildings and areas for a new technology which has had a profound impact on the landscape and culture ever since.

Some sites, such as Bicester and Upper Heyford, Oxfordshire, and Scampton, Lincolnshire, were wholly rebuilt under Lord Trenchard's expansion of the RAF after 1923 and through successive rearmament programmes, developing into sizeable new communities and now often industrial areas. The strategic deployment, form and scale of these sites testifies to the need to support and wage a new form of warfare. New technologies, and ways of organising different ranks, administration and servicing flying

Fig 5.1
Stonehenge, Wiltshire. This aerial photograph, taken in 1943, shows the remains of the airfield at Stonehenge, which is located to the right of the image. Note also the Bronze Age barrows dotted around the site.
[CCC /11796/4519]

machines, are reflected in station buildings and layout. Flying stations had a considerable impact on local communities and their landscapes, bringing new sounds and sights, drawing on local and imported labour – from the Empire to prisoners of war – and also playing a key role in the acceptance of women in uniform in the final year of the conflict.

Foundations

Britain has retained a wholly exceptional range of heritage sites and structures that illustrates the development of military aviation from its earliest years to the end of the First World War. The RAF, formed as the world's first independent air service in April 1918, was by November of that year staffed by 291,170 officers, men and women; it had 22,000 aeroplanes, a massive advance on the total of 95 naval and 63 army aeroplanes in August 1914.[2] With experience of active service beyond Europe in the Middle East and elsewhere, it was poised to gain global influence. These advances were all the more remarkable when it is considered that it was only 10 years since the Wright brothers had demonstrated the application of powered flight to military uses throughout Europe in 1908. Initially, however, despite some enthusiastic protagonists, including Winston Churchill in his role as First Lord of the Admiralty, military flying was dismissed as a 'useless fad' by the Chief of the Imperial General Staff in 1911, while in 1914 General Haig reckoned it less useful than cavalry in a reconnaissance role.[3] Nevertheless, flying machines and their colourful cast of aviators attracted thousands to flying displays, such as at the motor racing circuit at Brooklands in Surrey (where A V Roe had built his own machine and hangar in 1908) and Claude Grahame-White's flying school at Hendon, in the London Borough of Barnet.

Indeed, and although it has been argued that pre-1914 aviation was regarded as an integral part of Britain's small, technological and highly-trained military,[4] the clear impression that is gained is of a slow official recognition of the potential of powered as well as dirigible, or airship, flight. The Royal Engineers' Balloon Section, fresh from its successful deployment in the Boer War (1899–1902), had built Britain's first army aeroplane at Farnborough, Hampshire, which was piloted by the flamboyant American Samuel Cody in October 1908. The first military aviation unit (comprising four Bristol box kites) was created here early in 1911. By April that year, when the headquarters of the newly established Air Battalion – split between airships and aeroplanes, with a balloon store attached to the headquarters building – had been built close to the Balloon Factory at Farnborough, officers in the army and navy were already being trained at their own expense by civilian instructors.[5] While No 1 (Airship) Company remained at Farnborough, making use of the HQ building with its attached balloon store (which still survives),[6] No 2 (Aeroplane) Company moved to Larkhill on the army training grounds at Salisbury Plain. Since April 1909 the War Office had granted permission for the construction of sheds here (Fig 5.2) to civilian aviators and companies, including Sir George White's Bristol and Colonial Aeroplane Company, which in the following year converted the tramworks at Filton, to the north of Bristol, into one of the world's earliest (and still surviving) aircraft factories.[7] Another group of steel-framed hangars dating from early 1912 survives at Eastchurch, where Frank McClean had purchased a new site for the Aero Club and where by the end of 1910 he had made some of its 18 hangars and machines available for the training of naval pilots.[8] The Royal Aero Club's clubhouse at Muswell Manor, also on the Isle of Sheppey and already known as 'the scientific centre of British aviation', hosted the Wright brothers and successfully promoted aviation with the Royal Navy, based at nearby Chatham and Sheerness; the Short Brothers manufactured Wright Flyers at nearby Shellness.[9] In 1911 Eastchurch hosted the Gordon Bennett Air Race, held at Rheims in 1909 and New York in 1910.[10]

Larkhill and Eastchurch thus set the scene for the development of army and naval avia-

Fig 5.2
Larkhill, Wiltshire. Hangars built in June 1910 for the War Office and the British and Colonial Aeroplane Company. A ground-breaking development in the 1910 autumn manoeuvres was the successful transmission of radio messages from an aeroplane to the Bristol hangar. In July 1911 Larkhill served as a control point for the Daily Mail's *'Circuit of Britain' air race. [DP136377]*

*Fig 5.3
Montrose, Angus. This aircraft, built at the Royal Aircraft Factory in June 1912, is shown in front of one of the surviving side-opening hangars at Montrose, shortly before the upper wing collapsed and it crashed, killing the pilot, Lieutenant Desmond Arthur.
[© IWM Q 066015]*

tion on separate paths, which persisted for most of the war, although the Central Flying School at Upavon, Wiltshire, was set up to train officers from both services after the formation of the Royal Flying Corps (RFC) in April 1912. The Naval Wing formally split from the RFC in July and was renamed as the Royal Naval Air Service (RNAS). It had already, in March 1914, assumed responsibility for airships, balloons and a coastal chain of eight Naval Wing bases dating from 1912, concentrated between the Humber and the approaches to London and the Kent dockyards at Chatham and Sheerness.[11] In addition to its key role in training naval pilots, Eastchurch became deeply involved in developing techniques for anti-submarine and shipborne operations, and played a key role for most of the war in the defence of the naval dockyards. In contrast, the largely inland siting of the core RFC bases rendered them far less able than the RNAS to defend coastal harbours and bases, and indeed hostile approaches across territorial waters. Military Wing flyers operating from Larkhill and the RFC's first new squadron station at Netheravon, Wiltshire – under way from late 1913 – focused on the observation of artillery and troop movements on Salisbury Plain. In June 1914, 700 officers and men of the Military Wing – including its new station at Montrose, Angus, in Scotland, where the surviving hangars date from earlier that year (Fig 5.3) – assembled at Netheravon for reconnaissance exercises with the army.[12]

The whole of the Military Wing, joined by new stations at Dover and Gosport, then made its way to St Omer and onwards to active service supporting the Expeditionary Force.

Deployment

These stations formed the nucleus of the wartime flying services. The deployment of sites to deter and fight against attack by sea and air reflects the expanding theatre of war and also key differences between the RFC's focus on reconnaissance support to the army overseas (hence using the term 'scout' rather than 'fighter' for its aircraft) and the RNAS's more expansive and increasingly strategic role in home defence, support of the fleet and offensive operations. The RNAS's aeroplanes and seaplanes played a critical role, alongside patrols by airships and balloons, in denying submarines the chance to operate freely.[13] The RNAS also took the lead in extending air operations to German and occupied sites from as early as December 1914, with raids on German airship sheds and military targets; the first delivery of heavy bombers was made to the Admiralty in 1916 for its bomber wing.[14] Despite the RFC adding to its complement of night landing grounds in answer to the Zeppelin threat from January 1915, the RNAS was better placed to reinforce its existing complement of east coast stations, until the decision was made in February 1916 for the Military Wing to focus on inland defence and the Naval Wing on coastal defence, working in close liaison with kites, balloons and airships.[15]

Inspections had revealed serious shortcomings in this respect, one at RNAS East Fortune (Fig 5.4) in November the previous year noting the lack of properly armed machines for rapid climbing to defend Edinburgh and the Firth of Forth against airships, and sufficient hangarage for only two machines: two other aeroplanes had been dismantled and stored in the officers' house.[16] A barrage system of airfields, landing grounds, searchlights and artillery extending from Edinburgh and the naval dockyard at Rosyth to Dover was put in place from July 1916, replacing the earlier clusters of sites around vulnerable points. A telephone system enabled searchlight crews to communicate with squadron headquarters, thus ensuring that they had enough time to send aircraft from each flight to intercept raiders. This continued as the main line of defence until the end of the war, supplemented by a Home Defence Early Warning System from May 1916, enabling observer posts to communicate the speed and direction of raiders to eight Warning Control Centres. By the spring of 1917 the Admiralty was putting in place a system of seaplane stations to counter the U-boat threat and provide convoy protection to the Western Approaches (Fig 5.5), their ranges of operations overlapping in order to provide sufficient air cover, commanded from the naval dockyard at Devonport; unlike the east coast stations they were unimpeded by the risk of attack and engagement with enemy aircraft, Orkney and Scapa Flow being provided with aerial cover by late 1917.[17]

Fig 5.4 (above)
RNAS East Fortune, Fife. A 1918 painting by John Lavery, showing an airship flying over the airship hangars and a biplane.
[© IWM ART 001276]

Fig 5.5 (right)
Tresco, Isles of Scilly. The seaplane station's surviving slipway. This station played a vital role in extending air cover over the Western Approaches, deterring and attacking U-boats, escorting convoys and on occasion destroying mines which had become dangerously adrift. Tresco was thought vulnerable to enemy raiding parties and several officers brought their dogs with them to bark a warning in the event of a raid.
[NMR 26575/031]

Air attacks on England

Overall, casualties from bombing against defined and chanced-upon targets were relatively small by comparison with the death toll of the Blitz during the Second World War. Five hundred people were killed by bombing from airships up to the last raid on 5 August 1918, while a year of raids from May 1917 by Gotha and Giant bombers killed 836 people and injured over twice as many.[18] Nevertheless, the psychological impact of the raids was profound, and revealed public horror at the prospect of cities incapable of withstanding this type of attack, already conjured in the public imagination by H G Wells's 1912 science fiction novel *The War in the Air* (Fig 5.6).

The first Zeppelin raid – countered by RFC aircraft from Joyce Green, Kent – took place on the night of 19 January 1915, a month after the first bombs had been dropped by a German aircraft close to the Admiralty Pier in Dover.[19] Their immense size and the height at which they flew (higher than most machines could reach at this stage in the war), combined with the stealth of their night-time attacks and seeming impregnability to attack from both ground and air, made them greatly feared. Accordingly, adulation greeted the first pilot – Flight Sub-Lieutenant Reginald Warneford – to destroy one, over Ghent in June 1915, followed by an outpouring of grief in reaction to news of his death only 10 days later.[20] Gotha bombers, operating in daylight from stations around Ghent, made their first appearance on 25 May 1917, turning south from their intended target of London to drop bombs on Folkestone, killing 95 and injuring 195 people.[21] They flew higher, at 21,000ft (6,400m), and faster – some 30mph (48km/h) faster, at around 90mph (145km/h) – than Zeppelins, presenting even greater challenges to interception, with their attacks being concentrated on London, and East Anglian and south-eastern ports and military sites. All this was a cruel irony, in view of the growing success against the Zeppelin menace, in which aircraft played a significant role over the following month.[22] Barrages of shells and the hundreds of fighters scrambled from flight and squadron stations – struggling to climb to a sufficient air height before they could even begin looking for the enemy – seemed powerless in the face of the Gotha campaign, which by 7 July had killed hundreds. On that day members of the Air Board could only join thousands of Londoners in watching the attacks from the balcony of their headquarters in the Hotel Cecil.[23] Concerned at the inadequacy of air raid defences and any official approach to the protection of the civilian population, thousands sheltered in the London underground.[24]

Reaction to the raids paved the way, in the report compiled by General Smuts in the weeks after the first wave of Gotha attacks, for the creation of the world's first independent air force – the RAF – and the doctrine of offensive deterrence which dominated air policy up to and through the Second World War. Another significant consequence of the Smuts report, influencing future control and reporting systems, was the establishment of the London Air Defence Area (LADA) (Fig 5.7). This comprised a unified

Fig 5.6
Cleethorpes, Lincolnshire. Joseph Forrester, a borough councillor and chemist, built this air raid shelter for his family after a series of Zeppelin raids on the town in April 1916.
[DP186208]

Fig 5.7
Clerkenwell, London. A temporary anti-aircraft site opposite the T-junction formed by Margery Street and Amwell Street, on the New River Head site of the Metropolitan Water Board. A 3in 20cwt gun is mounted on a timber platform.
[Courtesy English Heritage Trust]

*Fig 5.8
Lodge Hill, Medway. This artist's reconstruction shows what is now considered to be the earliest surviving anti-aircraft battery in the world. It was relatively close to the coast and was defended from ground attack by a barbed wire fence and fortified blockhouse.
[IC197/002]*

*Fig 5.9
Lodge Hill, Medway. This picture shows an artist's impression of the anti-aircraft battery in action against a Zeppelin.
[IC197/001]*

command structure with intercept squadrons and anti-aircraft guns extending around and east of London, and a control centre outside the Admiralty.²⁵ LADA was supplemented by mobile guns, sound locators and a balloon barrage concentrated around London, the Medway and the Thames – all based on the successful defence of the steelworks at Neuves-Maisons, north-east France. Pre-war telephone exchanges played a key role in sustaining the telephone system which communicated messages from the control centre to gun sites, fighter airfields, the War Office and the House of Commons, while purpose-built airfield huts communicated with pilots in the air.

The most tangible legacies of air attack are the memorials to its victims and the buildings and other structures scarred by bombing. Surviving anti-aircraft emplacements and searchlight positions are concentrated along the east coast and around the approaches to London. Early in 1913 quick-firing guns with a 17,000ft (5,180m) range were fitted to concrete emplacements, designed around a blockhouse and two gun batteries, at Lodge Hill which survives (Figs 5.8 and 5.9) and Beacon Hill, both sites in Medway.²⁶ The sites of anti-aircraft gun emplacements have been recorded by the Great War Archaeology Group at Monkham's Hall near Waltham Abbey in Essex – comprising a platform for stacking shells close to a gun emplacement remodelled before and during the Second World War – and at One Tree Hill in Southwark.²⁷

The aerial war

Fig 5.10
RAF Hendon, Greater London. This 1920 photograph shows part of the London Aerodrome Hotel and the sheds and workshops of Grahame-White's training school and manufacturing business, of the Aircraft Manufacturing Company (Airco) and of the Handley Page Company. Behind are the 1917 hangars of the Aircraft Acceptance Park. Two of these survive, incorporated into the RAF Museum, along with the hotel, main offices, manufacturing shops and viewing platform.
[EPW016610]

Fig 5.11 (below)
Upavon, Wiltshire. Exceptionally, the officers' mess at Upavon was designed by an architect, E W Ellison. Roderick Maclennan, who trained there, reckoned it was 'more like a large hotel than an implement of war'. He described 'Motor parties ... tennis players in white flannels, golfing enthusiasts, male and female, dotted all over the links which stretch away in front of the Mess, and an occasional aeroplane humming and whining overhead' (Maclennan 2009, 39).
[DP004898]

Airfields

Most wartime airfields in England were constructed for training in all aspects of flying, from navigation, bomb dropping, gunnery, and cooperation with naval and army artillery, to the critical business of observation and photography. Training was at first dependent on a small number of air stations and existing civilian schools, the largest of these being at Hendon, which further expanded as a factory and was finally absorbed into an Aircraft Acceptance Park in March 1917 (Fig 5.10).[28] Upavon – with its tempting social opportunities – played a significant role in elementary flying training throughout the war, with pilots transferring here after they had completed preliminary training at a School of Aeronautics (Fig 5.11).[29] All training, in these early days of flying, was hazardous in the extreme, and according to most recent estimates it is reckoned that of the 9,350 Allied pilots who died in the First World War, 1,650 died while under instruction.[30] This was in part down to a nascent technology, but the use of inadequate and outdated aircraft such as the Maurice Farman Shorthorn (christened the 'Rumpty', 'a queer sort of bus like an assembly of birdcages') and the lack of a rigorous system for training instructors as well as novices, in noted contrast to that adopted by pre-war training schools such as Hendon, were also cited as reasons for the appalling casualty rate.[31]

However, following the appointment at the end of 1916 of the veteran pilot Major Robert Smith-Barry as Commanding Officer to No 1 Reserve Squadron at Gosport, there was a marked improvement in both the standard of basic, preliminary and elementary instruction provided by RFC schools (on gunnery, navigation, aero engines, wireless and indeed all aspects of flying) and in-flight training on its airfields. Smith-Barry developed a standardised approach to training, including a flying manual,

99

Air photography

Martyn Barber

Over the course of the war, aerial photography developed from fairly ad hoc beginnings, with its potential barely recognised, to be the key source of intelligence about what was happening the other side of no-man's-land.[32]

The war began more than half a century after the first successful aerial photograph had been taken from a balloon. During the later 19th century more and more such views were taken, but little real progress had been made with putting the detail on those photographs to any kind of practical use. That was despite a long-standing belief that aerial photography, and particularly vertical photographs – those taken with the camera pointing straight down at the ground, producing what was often described as a map-like view – would prove essential to cartography.

The advent and development of powered flight in the decade leading up to 1914 saw growing recognition that the combination of aeroplane and camera could extend the capabilities of airborne observation from a static, distant platform – the observation balloon – to one now capable of capturing a wealth of detail behind the enemy lines. What was more, repeated coverage allowed systematic appraisal of movements and developments over time. The constant analysis of the increasing volume of photographs, and the consequent updating of maps from them, provided the artillery with the clearest possible indication of what and where their targets were, and ensured that the maximum possible information was available when planning attacks or raids, or when trying to predict the intentions of the German army.

During the war considerable advances were made in aerial photography, both in camera technology and in the use of photographs in intelligence. Aerial views allowed maps to be rapidly brought up to date, and when combined with other sources, including information gleaned from prisoners, they gave as full a picture as possible of the enemy's positions and intentions.

One important introduction was automatic cameras. These made it possible to take overlapping photographs which could be joined to create mosaics, covering substantial areas of ground. The overlap also allowed photographs taken in sequence to be viewed in three dimensions through a stereoscope. Experimental flying during 1915 had established both the benefits and the simplicity of stereo cover to the British military, but its full potential was not fully recognised until well after the war had ended.[33]

Similarly, it took a while for the 'intelligence' content of photographs to be fully appreciated – it was one thing to map what was visible on them, but to understand and interpret that detail required a different set of skills altogether. Realisation that there was more to be gained from aerial photographs prompted the appearance of the first printed guides or manuals for interpretation and mapping, as well as the creation of training courses. Much training, covering all aspects of the photographic process, occurred overseas, but this was combined with increasing levels of instruction for pilots, observers and interpreters before they crossed the Channel.

The RFC's School of Photography was established at Farnborough in 1915 and provided training in all aspects of aerial photography. Courses were also taught elsewhere. For example, a surviving syllabus from April 1918 for the No 1 School of Navigation and Bomb Dropping, located immediately adjacent to Stonehenge in Wiltshire, shows that alongside the teaching of navigation, night flying and other essentials, those attending also had lectures on all aspects of aerial photography, including interpretation, the use of the stereoscope and the piecing together of photographic mosaics.

Today, photographs taken over the British Isles soon after the end of the war, especially by the Aerofilms company, provide an essential resource for studying aspects of the home front, capturing as they do aerodromes, camps, training trenches and other establishments while in use. Aerial photographs taken in subsequent decades, including ongoing photography of various forms, from the online vertical coverage provided by the likes of Google Earth to the targeted archaeological reconnaissance flights undertaken by Historic England, also reveal the surviving – and disappearing – traces of activity from the First World War.

the replacement of antiquated machines by the Avro 504, and installation of the 'Gosport Tube' to aid communication between instructors and trainees. Alverbank House, the Victorian villa which became home for Smith-Barry and his wife as well as quarters for flying officers, also served as his office and laboratory.[34]

While elementary flight training continued in tandem with operational duties on some of its bases, including Calshot on the Solent and Eastchurch, the RNAS centralised its officer training for aeroplanes, kite balloons and airships after the purchase in November 1915 of Cranwell in Lincolnshire: dormitory blocks, a drill shed and other structures, built in 1917–18, survive in the East Camp. The need for more pilots led to the formation of the Training Brigade in July 1916, expansion from 37 to 97 reserve (training) squadrons in January 1917 and, from November of that year, the establishment of the Training Depot Station (TDS) programme. By 1918 TDSs provided the penultimate stage in the standard 11-month training programme for pilots, amalgamating two or three training squadrons onto a single site and offering at least 60 hours' flying experience before the final phase of specialised combat training for reconnaissance, fighters, bombers and seaplanes prior to mobilisation (see p 106). With 60 airfields active in this role by November 1918, the TDS programme was the largest airfield construction scheme to date completed in Britain. Standardisation and centralisation emerge as significant themes, accompanied by a host of specialist bases such as Biggin Hill's Wireless Experimentation Establishment, Orfordness's Armament and Experimental Flight (see Fig 5.27),[35] and schools for training fighters and bombing crews, the latter including the No 1 School of Aerial Navigation and Bomb Dropping at Stonehenge (see Fig 5.1).

Centralisation also emerged as a significant theme in the receipt of aircraft from factories and their onward delivery to France and further afield as the theatre of war expanded. The RFC's Aircraft Park was originally based close to the government's Royal Aircraft Factory at Farnborough, which despite some high-profile and unfavourable comparisons to private factories is now widely regarded as a significant innovator and designer of the war's most successful fighter, the SE5. Construction of the R52 wind tunnel building in 1916 (see Fig 6.30) marked a critical period in Farnborough's development, for public censure over the vulnerability of the Royal Aircraft Factory's BE2c fighter had led to the factory's closure as a site for the manufacture of aircraft by the British state. Farnborough, renamed the Royal Aircraft Establishment, was now placed at the heart of cutting-edge developments in aviation technology, a primacy that lasted into the jet age.[36] By the end of the conflict, 29 Aircraft Acceptance Parks, mostly commenced in 1917 and served by their own railway lines, had been established to receive aircraft from local factories, to store and flight-test them and then distribute them to operational squadrons (see Fig 5.18).[37] Triple sheds for the storage of large numbers of aircraft characterised many of these sites (Fig 5.12). The same year saw the establishment of Aircraft Repair Depots for the repair of aircraft and aero engines; they numbered 11 by November 1918.

Building air stations

New types of site were needed to provide shelter for flying machines which faced onto a grass flying field, from which aircraft would take off and land in any direction, or from slipways for seaplanes. By the war aircraft sheds were commonly known as 'hangars' after the French word for an agricultural shed, part of a widely adopted lexicon of French words for aircraft, reflecting France's pre-war leadership in the industry.[38] Military planners also used a variety of designs by private manufacturers with doors in their side or end walls: William Harbrow, for example, used steel frames for the surviving hangars

Fig 5.12
Bracebridge Heath, Lincolnshire. The interior of the triple shed Belfast-truss hangar. It was demolished in 2001.
[BB92/16223]

at Larkhill and Eastchurch, while D Anderson & Co promoted its so-called Belfast trusses as a rapid and cheap means of erecting wide-span agricultural and industrial buildings out of bolted softwood.[39] The size and planning of hangars on military sites tended to mirror developments in the size of aircraft. No single site exemplifies this better than the RNAS seaplane base at Calshot, where the 1913 hangar for small Sopwith Bat Boats was joined by progressively larger hangars, including the immense range of three joined 'F-type' steel hangars built in 1918 for housing Felixstowe F5 flying boats, which considerably increased the range and offensive capacity of anti-Zeppelin and anti-submarine patrols (Figs 5.13 and 5.14).

Fig 5.13
Calshot, Hampshire. This shows the constricted nature of the site as it was in 1917. Two of the surviving buildings can be seen – the 1913 Belfast-truss hangar in the foreground and the Admiralty G-type hangar with its sliding side-opening doors to the rear. Winston Churchill, as First Lord of the Admiralty, an enthusiastic promoter of aviation, made his first seaplane flight here in March 1913, piloted by Tommy Sopwith.
[IWM Q 069384]

Fig 5.14
Calshot, Hampshire 2007. This shows the whole site, including the coastal fort of 1539–40 and the suite of surviving hangars with the massive Sunderland Hangar. This – the largest hangar erected for fixed-wing aircraft until the Second World War – comprises three joined examples of 'F-type' Admiralty hangars. The group exemplifies the development in aero engine and aircraft technology over the First World War better than any other site in Britain.
[NMR 24702/002]

The specifications for hangar and other building types, against which contractors submitted tenders, also reflect a desire – already evident in the approach to planning military barracks since the 1870s[40] – for using standard designs for the organisation of operational units. Captain B H O Armstrong of the War Office's Directorate of Fortifications and Works (DFW) thus designed, in the spring of 1913, a side-opening hangar for a flight of four aircraft (three flights making a squadron of 12 aircraft, on the French model) with two sets of sliding doors and an integral lean-to for hanging flying suits, office space for writing logs and workspace for benches and machine tools. Three of these hangars, all using iron tension bars to provide rigidity to the wide-span timber frame, survive at Montrose, with individual examples at Farnborough and (shortened with one set of doors) at Netheravon. Another set constructed of steel rather than timber, and since re-clad, at the Home Defence Station at Catterick in North Yorkshire (Fig 5.15), exemplifies the degree of variation that was more common before 1917, steel being the standard material specified by the Admiralty's Directorate of Works for its side-opening hangars on seaplane stations.

In March 1916 it was decided to increase the number of aircraft in a squadron from 12 to 18. This led to a complete change in shed design on training stations with the invention of the larger 80ft (24m) span end-opening aeroplane shed. This enabled the construction of sheds in pairs rather than as single units, three pairs making up the standard complement of hangars until November 1918: only the repair section hangar remained as a single-span shed. At first these hangars were built with laminated truss roofs and with doors sliding into timber gantries, as surviving at Montrose and Yatesbury, Wiltshire, but by 1917 the design had changed with the more widespread adoption of Belfast trusses, brick buttresses to the bay divisions and large brick gantries which offered better protection to folded-out doors, as at Old Sarum, Wiltshire (Figs 5.16 and 5.17), Hooton Park, Wirral, and Henlow, Bedfordshire.[41] An increase in the number of aircraft in a TDS unit, from 18 to 24, then prompted another increase in the span to 100ft (30m), with a central brick arcade supporting the arcades in coupled sheds, as at Leuchars, Fife, and North Shotwick, Flintshire. The hangars at Duxford exemplify the decision taken after February 1918 to instal new sliding 'Esavian' doors supplied by the Educational Supply Association of Stevenage, obviating the need for large door gantries. It was not until 1918 that the Air Ministry expressed interest in steel for 100ft-span hangars designed by Dorman Long: only one was built, on the vast Aircraft Repair Depot at Henlow. Home Defence Flight Stations, in contrast to these training and storage sites, required much smaller hangar space for flights of four aircraft for each station: 60ft (18m) span twin sheds which could be extended as required. Two coupled sheds of this type designed in January 1917, replacing earlier wartime hangars, survived until recently at Hainault Farm in Essex (Fig 5.18): concrete block has replaced the original timber-framed and boarded walls

Fig 5.15 Catterick, North Yorkshire. Despite later brick cladding and the demolition of four matching hangars to the north, the four hangars at Catterick make up one of the two most complete groups of the earliest hangar type, designed in 1913 by Captain Armstrong of the Directorate of Fortifications and Works. The other group, of three, is at Montrose, to the north of Dundee. [DP001401]

Legacies of the First World War

Fig 5.16 (right)
The interior of one of the surviving hangars at Old Sarum in 1918, showing the DH4 aircraft used for training in day bombing. Old Sarum's position close to the army training areas on Salisbury Plain ensured its retention after 1919 for the School of Army Co-operation.
[© IWM Q 072548]

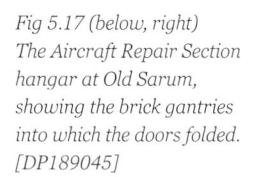

Fig 5.17 (below, right)
The Aircraft Repair Section hangar at Old Sarum, showing the brick gantries into which the doors folded.
[DP189045]

Fig 5.18 (bottom)
Hainault Farm, Essex. The interior of one of the 1917 hangars at Hainault Farm in 1918, showing an Airco DH4 and the fuselage of an Avro 504. Nearly 9,000 of the latter were produced and used for combat. From early 1917 they were also used for training; before that many pilots gained experience on the ground in flightless 'aircraft' known as Penguins.
[© IWM HU 071192]

and its curtained entrance bay. Despite the vulnerability of air stations close to the east coast, and especially in the south-east, to attack, the only documented example of protection being provided for aircraft was in the construction in 1917 of semi-underground sheds at Manston in Kent.[42]

The planners of these sites also had to give thought to the layout and design of military barracks, as well as to the technical buildings. By 1912 it was clear that military aerodromes had different requirements than their civilian counterparts.[43] The most obvious of these was the need to provide facilities close to the flying field for servicing aircraft and housing airmen and support staff, although in the early days officers flying from Larkhill were billeted in the army camp at Bulford and the nearby Bustard Inn. In the summer of 1913 the DFW started work on

104

Fig 5.19
RAF Netheravon, Wiltshire. This shows the airmen's barracks and institute and one of the hangars built in 1918 to admit Handley Page O/400 bombers – the cornerstone of the Inter-Allied bombing force. Netheravon's domestic site has survived in a remarkably complete state. Across Europe only the combined mess and hangar at Schleissheim, north of Munich, established in 1912 as the base of the Royal Bavarian Flying Corps, is comparable.
[NMR 24869/012]

Fig 5.20
Airmen's barracks at Netheravon. Each housed 24 airmen in two 12-man rooms, with the entrance lobby opposite the ablutions area. The softwood frame construction chosen for the buildings, with cover strips placed over the asbestos cement panels, is indicative of the intention of the Directorate of Fortifications and Works to provide a pattern for repetitive reuse.
[DP005148]

the design of the RFC's prototype flying base at Netheravon, under the superintendence of Captain Armstrong and countersigned by Colonel A M Stuart, the DFW's Assistant Director and after 1918 the Air Ministry's Director of Works. It was planned around separate domestic and technical camps, and as so much remains it has claims to be the earliest military airfield, complete with its flying field, to have survived anywhere in the world. The domestic site, with a Sergeants' Mess sited between an Airmen's Institute facing a parade ground flanked by two rows of five barracks blocks and an Officers' Mess facing a grassed square flanked by chalets, has survived in a complete state of preservation (Figs 5.19 and 5.20). The planning of the Officers' Mess and Institute recognised the importance of providing space for reading and more sociable activities such as playing cards and billiards. The workshops, depot offices and sole remaining hangar that have survived on the technical site are associated with a later phase, complete by spring 1914. The temporary officers' and airmen's barracks of 1912 at Upavon were replaced from 1913 in concrete block to plans copied from Netheravon as pupil numbers and the demand for improved accommodation rose.[44]

RAF Duxford

RAF Duxford, near Cambridge, represents the finest and best-preserved example of a fighter base typical of the period up to 1945 in Britain. It has an exceptionally complete group of First World War hangars and technical buildings, as well as a single officers' barrack hut on the 1918 domestic site. It later became one of the core of stations retained for the RAF, first as a Flying Training School and then (from 1 April 1923) as a fighter station. It has technical and domestic buildings typical of both interwar expansion periods of the RAF, and possesses important associations with the Battle of Britain and the American fighter support for the Eighth Air Force.

Tenders for building Duxford and its nearby sister station at Fowlmere as a pair of TDSs (both making one wing) were submitted by P and W Anderson of Glasgow in July 1917. Construction started in October 1917 and continued into 1919 when it was finally curtailed. In March 1918, despite the fact that neither station was complete, they were used to mobilise, or bring together as fighting units prior to active service, DH9 bomber squadrons housed in temporary Bessonneau hangars. These were soon joined by a tented camp for American mechanics working on aero engines, rigging and the assembly of aircraft brought in by rail to Whittlesford. Training, and the use of nearby houses for accommodation, commenced, although it did not formally open as a TDS until September, when 450 personnel from No 35 TDS moved here from Thetford. By 1918 there were also 208 members of the Women's RAF stationed at Duxford, including shorthand typists working in the station headquarters, various technical trades, motorcycle dispatch riders and some domestic workers (Fig 5.21). The on-site WRAF Hostel could accommodate 108; the rest were billeted locally or lived at their local family homes – sometimes as far away as Cambridge and Royston.

Duxford's modular layout, with clear functional zones subdivided and linked by a grid system of roads, reflects the scale and standardised nature of training as it had developed over 1917. The domestic site, subdivided into women's, officers' and airmen's barracks, was built for 850 personnel. They paraded and were assembled here before being marched across the Newmarket to Royston road to the technical site, where they collected their flying kit from the barracks stores before a day of flying instruction and lectures. The layout conformed to the centralised TDS plan, each flying unit having a coupled general service shed with its own flight office and sharing one repair hangar: the Duxford repair hangar was blown up for a scene in *The Battle of Britain* film in 1968, although its

Fig 5.21
Duxford, Cambridgeshire. Probably taken some time in 1918, this shows WRAFs and American airmen fraternising – against the regulations.
[© IWM HU 040579]

associated multifunctional workshop survives. The sheds were built to the 1917 type-design for 100ft-span (30m) hangars for Anderson Belfast-truss roofs, with the annexes to each side wall housing rooms for workshops, stores and changing into flying suits. They all used Esavian folding doors as manufactured by the Educational Supply Association and introduced in February 1918, thus dispensing with the need for the brick gantries which had hitherto been required for housing sliding doors (Fig 5.22). A tower with a hole in its floor attached to one hangar was used to practice dropping bombs.[45] The hangars backed onto an axial route, along the other side of which most of the technical and training buildings were arranged in functional groupings. In November 1918 the motor transport section at the north-east end housed a touring car, 10 light tenders, 10 heavy tenders, 8 motorcycles, 8 sidecars and 5 trailers. Engine-repair and blacksmiths' workshops were placed alongside the repair section, the other buildings being barrack and technical stores, the station headquarters and guardhouse (replaced in the early 1930s), classrooms, and finally (to the south-west) workshops for instruction in gunnery and photography. Slightly detached to the south-west are substantial remains of the shelters and butts for machine-gun training, and to the north-west, the sewage disposal works.[46]

Fig 5.22 Duxford, Cambridgeshire. An aerial view showing the airfield under construction in September 1918, viewed from the west, showing the temporary hangars in the foreground to the right and the domestic site to the left, with the distinctive form of the women's barracks to the rear.
[© IWM Q 114048]

Airfield buildings

The most commonly encountered walling materials on wartime sites are brick laid to a single thickness 4.5in (115mm) wide with roofs of corrugated asbestos, felt or slate. The planning of technical buildings reflected the aircraft technology of the period, from bomb storage, gunnery, synthetic training, motor transport and storage to engine-repair workshops for carpenters, blacksmiths and applying dope for the hardening of fabric (Figs 5.23–5.27). The organising principle of domestic buildings has much in common with post-1850s planning for army barracks, particularly in its careful attention to hierarchies of rank through the provision of separate accommodation for officers and men, although the purpose-built officers' messes and chalets as provided at Farnborough, Upavon (see Fig 5.11) and Netheravon before the war

Fig 5.23
Minchinhampton, Gloucestershire. Australian cadets receive instruction in aerial gunnery, firing into butts of the type which survive at Duxford.
[© IWM Q 111652]

Fig 5.24
Duxford, Cambridgeshire. The interior of the carpenter's shop, photographed in 1918.
[© IWM HU 039317]

Fig 5.25
WRAF's playing tug of war at Duxford in late 1918.
[IWM Q 114860]

Fig 5.26
Stow Maries Airfield, Stow Maries, near Maldon, Essex. Interior view of the headquarters building showing the simple truss construction. Supported on internal piers, it is typical of thousands of military buildings erected during the First World War.
[DP182249]

were rejected in favour of simple hutting, with a servants' room to each hut. A range of facilities were also catered for, from relaxation and socialising (institutes and sometimes cinemas) to shopping, laundry and getting a haircut. Some stations were not considered to require accommodation; Montrose, for example, used nearby Panmure Barracks for the duration of the war. This was especially the case with seaplane stations which commonly accommodated men in coastguard cottages and requisitioned housing.[47] At Fishguard, Pembrokeshire, for example, men were initially (in March 1917) billeted in Goodwick village and housed in railway carriages, while officers lived in the Fishguard Bay Hotel: in the event this arrangement persisted for the duration of the war.[48]

A distinctive new feature was the provision of separate women's accommodation. Women – mainly working on domestic tasks – were a familiar sight on many air stations before the establishment of the Women's Royal Naval Service in 1917 and, at the end of that year, saw official recruitment by the RFC into a wide range of occupations, from cleaners and cooks to drivers, fitters and riggers. The Women's Royal Air Force was formed on 1 April 1918, but numbered no more than 25,000 during the last months of the war. Servicewomen were encouraged to live at home or in lodgings and requisitioned hostels, and cycled or took the bus into work. Arrangements on active stations were makeshift and clearly evidence of a desire to provide separate and distant hutting, often in buildings designed for other purposes and even girded with barbed wire.[49] Women's Hostels, when eventually planned in the summer of 1918, were designed in order to enable WRAFs to gain access from their quarters via short corridors to a centrally placed dining hall, recreation room and other facilities without having to venture outdoors.[50]

Over 170 flying stations, displaying a vast range in their scale and complement, are recorded by station type in the Quarterly Returns of summer 1918.[51] These also record 60 airship stations and 14 balloon stations, store depots and schools which did not require flying fields or slipways for aircraft. Wartime use

Fig 5.27
Orfordness, Suffolk. This airmen's barracks was one of several accommodating some of the 612 personnel stationed at the RFC's Armament and Experimental Flight, which focused on improving gunnery, bomb-sighting and aerial photography. This standard 1918 design could be built from a variety of materials. The example here is made from precast concrete posts and wall slabs manufactured at the National Slab Factory at Yate, near Bristol.
[DP070023]

enhances the historic interest of buildings such as Wantage Hall in Reading – built in 1908 as a quadrangular neo-Tudor hall of residence for what became the University of Reading – which was acquired by the RFC in December 1915 as the No 1 School of Military Aeronautics. Here visitors were famously greeted by the sight of aircraft fuselages hanging from trees and wingless aircraft taxiing around the nearby park.[52] The largest of the specialist schools, developed in the final year of the war, were the RFC's School of Technical Training at Halton Park in Buckinghamshire, with over 11,000 staff and recruits, and the Armament School at Uxbridge, with over 8,000 staff and recruits. The smallest air stations were the landing grounds, chosen and graded for their locations, which were cleared of obstructions and sometimes provided with night-landing flares. Some of these developed into Home Defence Stations, which ranged in size from around 6 acres (2.5ha) for a 1916–18 flight station with 8 aircraft in a twin hangar, 10 officers and 70 men, to more than double that (up to 15 acres [6ha]) for a squadron station of the type developed after 1916 which brought the flights together onto a single site (Fig 5.28).

TDSs were often double the size again. Each comprised three flying units, being built to a standard plan (see pp 107–9) and having three coupled general service hangars and one repair hangar for the provision of serviceable engines and aircraft: aerodromes were built in pairs, the parent having the Wing HQ and repair section. Technical sites were split into four different sections, for aircraft and engine repair, ground instruction, motor vehicles and services. Domestic sites were subdivided into quarters for airmen, officers and women. Aircraft Acceptance Parks and Aircraft Repair Depots were typically more than 35–40 acres (14–16ha) in extent and consistently the largest in size, as were some of their specialist buildings such as Salvage Sheds for aircraft repair and Erecting Sheds for the assembly of aircraft. Examination of the plans, documents and archaeology of these sites often reveals successive and complex phases of rebuilding, calling on the resources of a vast diversity of labour – established construction firms, prisoners of war, labourers, engineers and lumberjacks from across the United States and the British Empire, and immigrant labour from China.[53] No wonder that its administration was so complex, open to abuse and misunderstanding, and subject to post-war scrutiny.[54] The accounts for Duxford, for example, reveal allegations of fraud and pilfering and the difficulty experienced by the Canadian Royal Engineers in understanding the very different British system of contracting.[55] After 1918, sites that continued in use or were selected for the post-1923 expansion of the RAF and for wartime service in 1939–45 further expanded in size – from a 1914–18 average of 167 acres to 400 acres (68–162ha) during the 1930s and 640 acres (259ha) by 1945.[56]

Fig 5.28
A 1918 aerial view of the squadron station at Northolt in west London – developed from February 1914 as a training and Home Defence Station – showing the hangars grouped into flights. Although all were swept away after the war, the routeways along which they and other buildings were arranged strongly influenced the layout when the station was rebuilt in the 1920s and 1930s expansion schemes.
[© IWM Q 111427]

Survival and conservation

As noted above, Britain retains a remarkable range of aerodromes, seaplane stations and other sites which illustrate and provide direct evidence for the development of air warfare from its formative years in observation to the origins of strategic deterrence at the end of the First World War. Internationally, there have been concerted efforts since the 1990s to protect some of the most impressive remains of the birth of aviation, including the flying fields associated with the Wright brothers (managed as landscapes, their hangars having long gone), the remnants of the Pont Long airfield near Pau in France, where in 1909 Wilbur Wright opened a flying school, the base of the Royal Bavarian Flying Corps at Schleissheim near Munich, and the 1880s balloon shed and other structures at Meudon, south-west of Paris.[57] All sites and structures surviving from before August 1914 have particular significance in this global context, including Muswell Manor in Shellbeach, on the Isle of Sheppey (listed at Grade II), where the Wright brothers were famously photographed with the Short brothers in 1909. The Salisbury Plain area, with its surviving pre-war sites at Larkhill, Netheravon and Upavon and its scattered memorials,[58] has particular significance as one of the formative heartlands of military and civil aviation. Together with the training stations at Yatesbury and Old Sarum, the Salisbury Plain group comprises the most coherent grouping of military aviation sites and structures of the 1908–18 period in the world. Netheravon, despite its pre-war date, has the best-preserved suite of barracks buildings of any of the 301 bases in the United Kingdom occupied by the RAF in November 1918, a 1913-pattern hangar built in 1914, some technical workshops and motor transport buildings of the same date and – built at the end of the conflict – a hangar for the Handley Page O/400 bomber. Continuous military use of its grass airfield has also preserved the archaeology of practice trenches for infantry and of earlier land use extending to prehistoric field systems, enclosures and barrows.

Over 130 buildings on 22 sites in England, together with hangars at North Shotwick in Wales and Montrose and Leuchars in Scotland, have now been protected through listing – the vast majority as a result of a thematic survey of military aviation sites and structures conducted in the late 1990s.[59] The criteria for selection focused on the identification of those key sites, in addition to individual buildings or groups which, as a consequence of events on the world stage, military imperatives or varying degrees of public and political support, best reflect the development of military aviation to 1918, and those which are most strongly representative of functionally distinct airfield types, from operational (for seaplanes, bombers and fighters) to the purposes of training and the storage of reserve aircraft. Old Sarum, for example, is the only TDS – indeed the only air station in the whole period up to the end of 1918 – to have retained its full complement of unaltered hangars fronting onto its original grass flying field, and many technical buildings (Fig 5.29). There are only six other surviving groups where a substantially complete set of hangars has survived in a legible state and been designated as listed buildings – Montrose (where three 1916 hangars and three 1913-pattern hangars survive); the 1918 TDS groups at Duxford, Hooton Park and its partner station at North Shotwick;[60] the Eastern

Fig 5.29
Old Sarum, Wiltshire. After Duxford in Cambridgeshire and Leuchars in Scotland, Old Sarum has Britain's most complete surviving group of technical buildings, including a repair hangar (see Fig 5.17), and is strongly representative of a Training Depot Station of the First World War period. Uniquely, it retains its grass flying field with none of the perimeter tracks and other interventions characteristic of the post-1938 period.
[NMR 15362/32]

Command Repair Depot at Henlow;[61] and the seaplane stations at Calshot and Lee-on-Solent, Hampshire.

Calshot and Lee-on-Solent (see Figs 5.13, 5.14 and 5.30) are the best-preserved examples of seaplane stations. Their significance is enhanced by their proximity to the rich military and naval heritage focused around the royal naval dockyard at Portsmouth. The surviving hangar and slipway at Cattewater in Plymouth, close to the 16th-century Mount Batten artillery tower and the naval dockyard guarding the Western Approaches, and slipways at Tresco and Fishguard survive from the seaplane bases sited along Britain's western coastline from early 1917 (see Fig 5.5). The slipway and bases to the hangars remain at Smoogroo, one of the bases around Scapa Flow, which was opened at the outset of the war for fleet aircraft repair and continued to serve as a training airfield and a shore station.[62] Other survivals are buildings at Donibristle in Fife and Catfirth in Shetland.[63] The remains of east coast seaplane stations, which were also engaged in offensive operations across the North Sea, are even more fragmentary. One of these was Killingholme, Lincolnshire, one of the largest naval air bases in Europe, which in November 1918 was staffed by 91 officers and 1,324 enlisted men of the United States Navy's air service. Extending across 135 acres (55ha) of ground along the Humber south of Hull, it comprised a 'city of brick and frame huts' of which the only survival is the pilings for the slipways, which served an immense line of eight hangars fronting a 4ha concrete apron.[64]

Fighter defence was considered more effective than anti-aircraft fire when 'kills' were tallied after the conflict, accounting for 8 Zeppelins and 13 aeroplanes (all after May 1917) in contrast to 2 Zeppelins and 9 aeroplanes felled by guns.[65] Many Home Defence Stations were subject to programmes of rebuilding during the conflict and especially afterwards, making it harder to associate surviving fabric with significant events and personalities than is the case with the Battle of Britain of summer 1940.[66] Thus there is no surviving trace of the airfield at London Colney, where some of the most famous 'aces' of the war – Mick Mannock, Albert Ball and James McCudden – were based for short periods of time.[67] The hangars at Hainault Farm, Essex, were until recently the principal survival from 39 Squadron's bases (the others being at Sutton's Farm, Hornchurch, London Borough of Havering, and North Weald, Essex, which were completely rebuilt for post-war expansion schemes), which guarded the eastern approaches to London: two aircraft from 39 Squadron intercepted and shot down Zeppelins on 24 September 1916, although the hangars were rebuilt later in the war. The remains of the semi-underground hangars at Manston (Kent), from which aircraft sallied forth against Gotha bombers on the way to attack Dover and the Thames Estuary, testify to its perceived vulnerability to attack.[68] Catterick (see Fig 5.15) has retained its original suite of hangars, externally rebuilt around their steel-framed construction (the use of steel, commonly employed by the Admiralty for its seaplane sheds, is unique for an RFC base). 'A Flight' of 76 Squadron, which was responsible for the defence of the Leeds and Sheffield area, was stationed here from late 1916 to November 1918. In the final stages of the war Catterick also became one of over 60 TDSs for the training of pilots in daylight bombing.[69] Reuse as a hospital has also conserved some of the barracks, offices and the lecture hall from the naval airfield at East Fortune near Edinburgh, which also survives as the best-preserved airship base of the period. By the end of 1918 this had become a vast site extending over 1,334 acres (540ha), part of which now hosts Scotland's Museum of Flight.[70]

The most complete surviving Home Defence Station is at Stow Maries in Essex (see p 114), whence after May 1917 aircraft flew on 81 sorties to defend London from Zeppelins, Gotha and later Giant bombers. Stow Maries is remarkable because – despite the loss of its paired hangars – its built fabric airfield and planned layout can be understood and appreciated as a whole. The relationship of coherent surviving groups of buildings to historic station layouts and flying fields has also been fundamental to the selection of sites for designation, with substantially complete groups of hangars and other fabric chosen for designation as conservation areas, notably Duxford near Cambridge (see p 106), Yatesbury (see p 116) and Old Sarum, as well as HMS *Daedalus* at Lee-on-Solent (Fig 5.30). Yatesbury has long been in a deteriorating condition: permission was granted for demolition of one of the three hangars in 2012, but it still retains its flying field and exemplifies the rich potential for using a variety of sources to discover more about these sites. Other surviving hangars, as at Shrewsbury, Shropshire, and Eastleigh, Hampshire, have been re-clad and reused as industrial units, and it was also common for hangars – especially the steel-built ones on seaplane stations – to be

Fig 5.30
Lee-on-Solent, Hampshire. This 1928 view shows the surviving seaplane sheds at the Training Depot Station, developed in 1917 as a satellite to the RNAS base at Calshot. To the rear are the technical and domestic buildings (largely demolished when the base expanded after 1928), while to the right are two of the late Victorian houses requisitioned as an officers' mess and quarters and as the Commanding Officer's House.
[EPW024419]

moved and re-erected on other RAF bases and civilian sites. Roof trusses and, more rarely, substantial sections of buildings were re-erected after the war as covered cattle yards and other farm buildings.

Home Defence Stations are also associated with a much more ephemeral heritage of observation posts, sound locators, and anti-aircraft and searchlight sites, all of which were designed to serve an increasingly centralised control and reporting system *(see p 97)*. The most iconic of these structures are the concrete sound mirrors that probably date from 1917, after an inconclusive initial phase of experimentation in refining the technology for them *(see p 61)*.[71] Many air stations with little or no legible trace of their wartime character are nevertheless valued for their historical associations and as places of commemoration. Leighterton in Gloucestershire is one example of a site whose buildings have been removed and its flying field restored to farmland. Its small cemetery for pilots who perished in training has made it a focus of remembrance for the local community and for relatives and representatives of the Australians and New Zealanders who served there, part of the significant contribution to the air war made by pilots from across the British Empire, who were joined from 1917 by Americans. Similar memorials testifying to the perilous nature of early powered flight are scattered throughout Britain.

The heritage and research potential of historic airfields is now promoted by the Airfields of Great Britain Conservation Trust, which hosts an airfield search facility on its website,[72] and the Airfield Research Group's Airfield Information Exchange, which acts as a forum for exchanging information and research.[73] The RAF Museum at Hendon holds many airfield plans and drawings, while successive gazetteers of sites from 1916 (particularly useful being the RAF's Quarterly Survey) can be consulted at the National Archives and online.[74] They need to be used with some care, as site plans can show the intended rather than the completed layout of buildings and site design: the investigation of sites often raises more questions than answers, sometimes showing where building programmes were curtailed, leaving the footings of buildings or unfinished walling *(see p 114)*. In terms of aerodrome layouts predating the building of permanent structures, investigations may reveal little because of the widespread use of tents and prefabricated buildings. Among the most commonly used of the latter were collapsible Armstrong huts, named after their designer, Captain Armstrong of DFW, and the 9-ton Bessonneau hangars which remained in use from 1917 to 1936 as the RAF's standard portable hangar. Close observation of fabric, and even the unearthing of long-buried artefacts, can either shed further light on how sites developed or raise even more questions for research *(see p 116)*.[75]

Sites with longer operational histories may also have experienced successive phases of rebuilding. One paired hangar has survived at Tadcaster, near York, from the TDS formed in July 1918 from an earlier fighter airfield (for 46 Reserve Squadron, initially for the defence of the Leeds/Sheffield area), and similarly the hangars at Hainault (one from a group of four) and Bekesbourne, Kent, date from a rebuilding later in the war. Individual technical and domestic buildings might be hard to identify with confidence if the site has been substantially redeveloped or planted with woodland. Historic photographs will also reveal temporary hutting and hangars of the type widely used on active service overseas.

Stow Maries

Fig 5.31
Stow Maries, Essex. A rare wartime photograph of the airfield, taken in 1917, showing the lost twin hangars.
[OP25552; Courtesy D Gregory]

Fig 5.32
Stow Maries, Essex. The water tower and, facing the airfield, the pilots' ready room. The original ceilings, doors, dado rails and two fireplaces survive.
[DP182227]

Stow Maries – located close to the Blackwater Estuary in Essex on the eastern approaches to London – is the best-preserved Home Defence Station of the First World War period, despite the loss of its hangars (Fig 5.31); twin sheds of the same type survived until recently at Hainault Farm in the same county. The first aircraft, part of the 37th Squadron of the RFC, which had other flight stations in Essex at Goldhanger and Rochford (now Southend Airport) and its headquarters in Woodham Mortimer Hall, arrived here in October 1916. They first sortied out in May 1917, led by 19-year-old Lieutenant Claude Ridley, a holder of the Military Cross who had evaded capture and returned to Belgium after dropping an agent behind enemy lines in October 1916. Station logbooks record the harrying of enemy bombers, but also pilots' frustration at their inability to shoot down their targets – Ridley recorded near misses by the Gothas' rear guns. By then a Wing Commander, Ridley died of natural causes in 1942 and is buried – with two other comrades who died in flying accidents – in the St Mary and St Margaret churchyard at Stow Maries, a prominent local landmark. One of those airmen is 2nd Lieutenant Gerald Milburn, who crashed through a hedge on the edge of the flying field: the opening is maintained and commemorated as 'Milburn's Gap'.

The site has retained 24 buildings, arranged along a single street with the flying field to the east. The motor transport, workshop and other technical buildings were concentrated to the north and west of the hangars, and the barracks and messes for airmen, senior NCOs, officers and women to the south. The airmen's mess is located close to the pilots' ready room from which they would sortie out to intercept attackers, news of which would be telephoned via the communications room behind the hangars (Fig 5.32). The site had its own reservoir and water tower, and electricity generator hut.

The fuel stores and armoury were provided with lightweight roofs, the wall of the former being strengthened by buttressed brick walls and the latter part-sunken into the ground to help minimise the effects of any explosion.

All these buildings, still under construction in October 1918, represent the result of a gradual replacement in brick of the station's original tents and temporary wooden buildings (Fig 5.33). The officers' barracks were only partly rendered and are clearly unfinished. Despite the presence of a Women's Hostel only three women lived on the site, with 12 more coming on a daily basis to undertake domestic duties. Stow Maries then had a staff of 219, but there were plans for further expansion following its upgrading to Wing Headquarters in June, and the doubling of its original mixed complement of aircraft to eight Sopwith Camels.

In 1919 the site was bought by its former farming tenants, and thereafter it continued in use by the same family until 2009. It was recognized as a rare survival of a First World War airfield in the 1990s. At first it seemed that designation as a conservation area would be the best way of protecting the flying field and its 24 workshop and barracks buildings, but the activities of the Friends of Stow Maries and the Grade II* listing of the site have since opened the door to a new and sustainable future.[76] At its heart lies the purchase of the site by the Stow Maries Aerodrome Trust with the help of grants from Historic England, Natural England and the National Heritage Memorial Fund, and loans from Maldon District Council and Essex County Council (Fig 5.34).

Fig 5.33
Stow Maries, Essex. The blacksmith's shop, a reminder of the traditional approach to fashioning iron for the repair of vehicle and aircraft parts. Inside is a working field forge, transportable for running repairs.
[DP182240]

Fig 5.34
Stow Maries, Essex. The prominent white building is a temporary modern hangar on the site of the wartime one. In the foreground are the motor transport sheds, workshops and attached dope shop, while around the water tower stand the squadron offices, airmen's mess and, facing the flying field, the pilots' ready room. At the far end of the airfield is the gap in the hedge, conserved as a memorial to Lieutenant Milburn, who crashed here.
[NMR 29131/003]

RFC Yatesbury

Dan Miles

There is still much to be learnt about First World War aerodromes, from their establishment and development, including design, layout and individual structures, to the activities that took place there. In recent years archaeological investigations have been undertaken on several aerodromes, including the historic building characterisation survey at Old Sarum (RFC Ford), near Salisbury,[77] and two community projects at Sedgeford, Suffolk, and RFC Yatesbury. The last-named project, undertaken by the Wiltshire Archaeology and Natural History Society Archaeological Field Group, included documentary research alongside a comprehensive programme of field investigations (Fig 5.35) and aerial photographic analysis. The focus of the project was to understand the development of the aerodrome and the training that took place there, and to locate the site of a German prisoner-of-war camp that provided the workforce to build and maintain the aerodrome.

Establishment and development

Yatesbury Aerodrome, 3 miles (5km) west of Avebury, was officially established by the RFC in November 1916 as a TDS to train airmen and ground crew. It specialised in corps reconnaissance. Although plans and some documentary evidence exist for Yatesbury, they provide few details about its establishment and growth.

However, recent analysis of aerial photography has revealed that the aerodrome was developed in phases, initially operating from a temporary canvas aerodrome to the east of where the permanent camp was established some months later. Evidence comes in the form of marks in the grass visible on a photograph taken in November 1918 (Fig 5.36) showing the previous location of Bessonneau hangars (temporary canvas and wood structures) and a tented encampment. A photograph, of April 1917, shows that by then construction was under way on the technical site, including a general service shed, after the official opening date of the aerodrome.

The role of German POWs

Initially it was not known who built the aerodrome. Subsequently research into local newspapers and Red Cross inspection reports showed that 800 German POWs formed the main labour force. However, the exact location of the camp which housed them was not given, and accordingly further research was undertaken to find the camp and get a better understanding of its layout, facilities and what life was like for the POWs. Analysis of aerial photographs revealed evidence of a small military camp just to the east of Camp 1. Its layout, with standard Armstrong-type wooden accommodation huts surrounding centrally laid out communal buildings, is typical of a British army camp of the period. Other features, including a perimeter fence and small sentry boxes, are more characteristic of POW camps. Geophysical survey, test pitting and field walking gathered an extensive collection of finds indicative of an early 20th-century military camp.[78] Of these remains 99 per cent were generic in their nature – hut fixtures and fittings and domestic materials, including white glazed War Office issued crockery – typical of any First World War army site. It was only the other 1 per cent of finds, German uniform buttons (trouser and tunic), belt hooks and a cockade, which provided direct evidence that Germans were detained here.

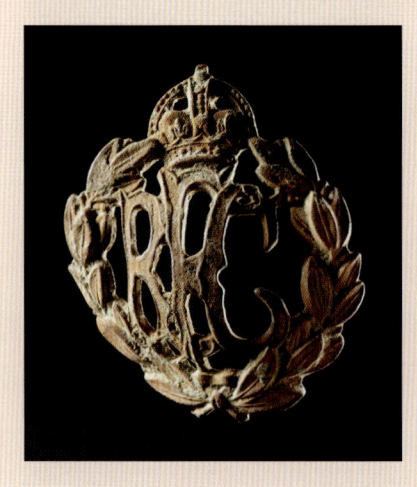

Fig 5.35
Yatesbury, Wiltshire. A Royal Flying Corps cap badge found during archaeological field walking.
[DP195372]

The aerial war

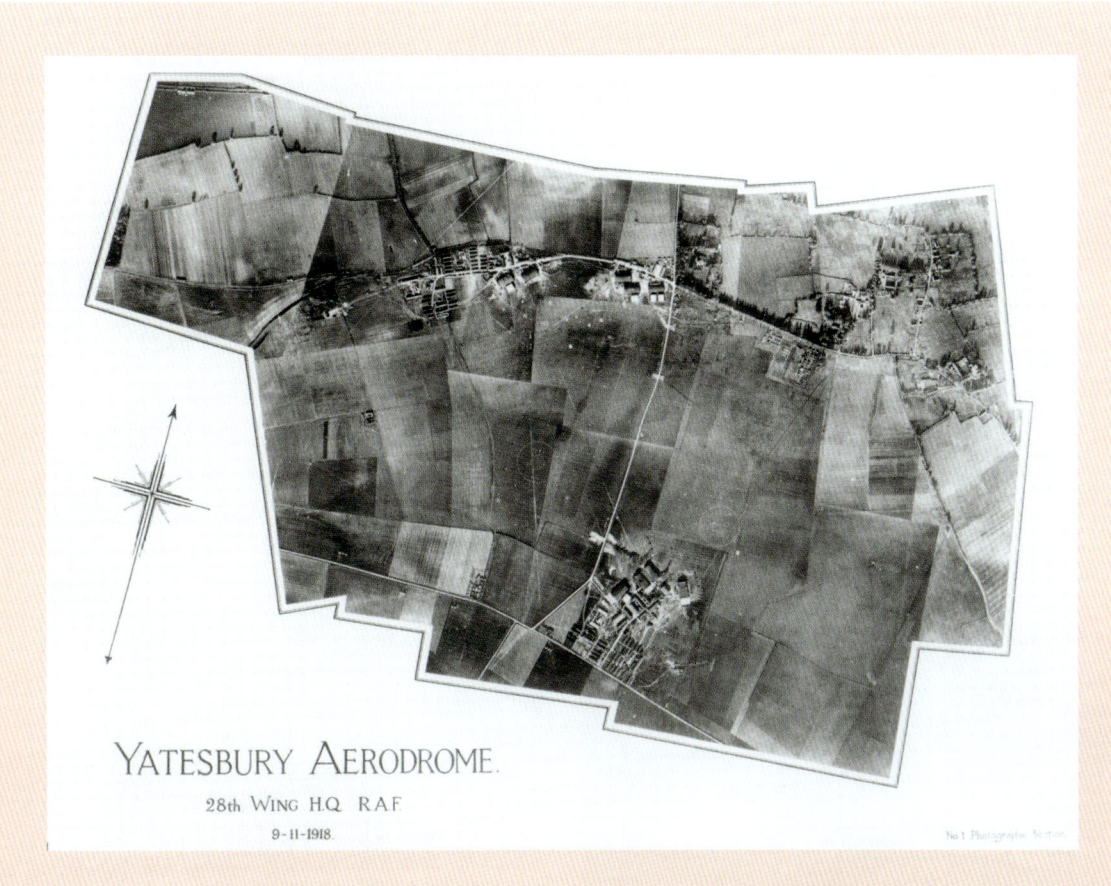

*Fig 5.36
Yatesbury, Wiltshire. Wartime aerial photograph showing the grid laid out on the airfield to assist in the training of observers.
[JXG 14217/01]*

Evidence of training

The project also provided further evidence of the tuition offered at RFC Yatesbury. While documents show that as well as basic training, advanced skills were taught in air corps reconnaissance, they provide few details. Further understanding came from an examination of wartime air photographs of Yatesbury which show a distinct numerical and alphabetical labelled grid system, laid out in white on both landing strips. This miniature grid system represents the coordinate 'squaring' system used on the Western Front, and familiarisation with it made up part of an observer's training in reconnaissance and artillery spotting. Evidence of in-flight training using this system is indicated by the annotations on some aerial photographs taken of Yatesbury and the surrounding countryside. Points of interest – for example crossroads – have been highlighted, and their associated coordinates labelled. The discovery of lead aerial weights, used to weigh down the 160yds (146m) of copper aerial wire that was trailed behind aeroplanes to send wireless signals, indicates there was also training in wireless communication (Fig 5.37). These lost weights support contemporary accounts that describe the difficulty of winding in cables before landing, and how they tended to snag and break off.

*Fig 5.37
Yatesbury, Wiltshire. A lead trailing weight for an aircraft wireless aerial found during archaeological field walking.
[DP195375]*

117

Conclusions

As well as some of the earliest buildings associated with powered flight, Britain has some of the most intact groups of hangars and other buildings dating from the First World War in the world. These form part of a British and international heritage of military aviation that is also found in memorials to pioneer aviators, wartime airmen and the civilian victims of the world's first aerial bombing campaigns. In his report submitted after the first shock wave of Gotha attacks in 1917, General Smuts had made the case for a unified air service and the strategic targeting of sites in Germany. The Air Force Act of November 1917 paved the way for the unification of the RNAS and the RFC as the RAF and for the creation of the Air Ministry in April 1918. What distinguished the RAF from other air forces in the closing stages of the First World War was the development of its independent strategic role: General Smuts, writing in his report following the Gotha raids on 7 July 1917, stated with respect to air power that:

> there is absolutely no limit to the scale of its future independent war use [and] the day may not be far off when aerial operations with their devastation of enemy lands and destruction of industrial and populous centres on a vast scale may become the principal operations of war, to which older forms of military and naval operations may become secondary and subordinate.[79]

The foundations for an independent bomber air force were laid by Sir Hugh Trenchard, appointed as the RAF's first Chief of Air Staff in April 1918 and Commander of the Inter-Allied Air Force from October 1918. In the closing months of the war bases were being developed to launch attacks against Germany by Handley Page O/400 bombers, many of which had been shipped from America for assembly in Britain (Fig 5.38). In Germany, as in Britain, the raids caused unrest and panic, although, as Trenchard himself admitted, 'the damage done both to buildings and personnel is very small compared to any other form of war and the energy expended'.[80] Two bases, at Narborough and Bircham Newton in Norfolk, were built for this purpose in addition to those over the Channel, and a number of hangars for accommodating these bombers were built on TDSs, the most complete of which survive at Netheravon.

Fig 5.38
Netheravon, Wiltshire. This hangar was built in 1918 to house Handley Page O/400 bombers. They were specially designed in order to admit these aircraft, which had 100ft (30m) spans with folding wings.
[DP005154]

6

The workshop of the world goes to war

Wayne Cocroft

War is the harvest of the armament firms

David Lloyd George[1]

Introduction

In the autumn of 1914 the type of open, mobile warfare the British army had prepared for, and envisaged, quickly stagnated into a static confrontation waged from a parallel series of heavily fortified trench lines down what became known as the Western Front. Not only did the army need to learn to fight in these unmatched conditions, but the country's state and private armaments works had to adapt to supply vastly increased numbers of munitions of all types, as well as designing and producing innovative weapons to break the deadlock of the trenches. The chemical industry was called upon to produce explosive substances in unprecedented quantities and to develop new deadly products, such as poison gases. The demands for unparalleled quantities of war materials, and novel goods, drew in many other manufacturers previously unconnected with military supply.

This enormous industrial effort was undertaken by the existing state arsenals and private armaments firms, to which were added adapted factories, backstreet works and from 1915 a network of national factories. Not only were traditional armaments required in vast numbers, but also increasingly technological products that had matured during the preceding decades. The internal combustion engine, airships and aircraft, submarines, torpedoes, machine guns and wireless communications, often now used in combination, changed how war was fought.

The scale of the effort is reflected by the contemporary 12-volume *The official history of the Ministry of Munitions*.[2] A century later, traces of this great enterprise are still to be found. This chapter will explore both how industry responded and the factories and places which were used, modified and created to manufacture the huge quantities of material goods required by Britain's armed forces to wage the Great War.

The state arsenals

In common with the other major belligerent powers, the British state was an important manufacturer of armaments in royal factories and state dockyards. With its origins in the late 17th century the oldest manufactory was the Royal Arsenal at Woolwich. This was effectively a large engineering works, and its principal products included naval gun barrels as well as artillery for the army and its associated carriages. To the east on Plumstead marshes was a filling factory for assembling munitions and proof ranges. A large proportion of the country's requirement for the explosive propellant cordite was produced by the government's Royal Gunpowder Factory at Waltham Abbey, Essex *(see Figs 6.6–6.8)*. Just to its south was the Royal Small Arms Factory, Enfield, Greater London, where, as its name suggests, the main products were rifles, machine guns, swords and bayonets. During the war its most significant product was the Short Magazine Lee-Enfield, the primary weapon of the British infantryman; by the end of the war the factory had produced over 2 million of these weapons.[3] The factory was established in the early 19th century, but was largely rebuilt during the middle of the century to install American-inspired production lines. During the war the workforce rose over fivefold to around 10,000, about 1,500 of whom were women.[4] The factory was bounded to the west by the Lee Navigation, and wartime expansion took place to the east as well as within the established factory boundary. In addition to Enfield, two trade companies – the Birmingham Small Arms Company in Wellhead Lane, Birmingham,

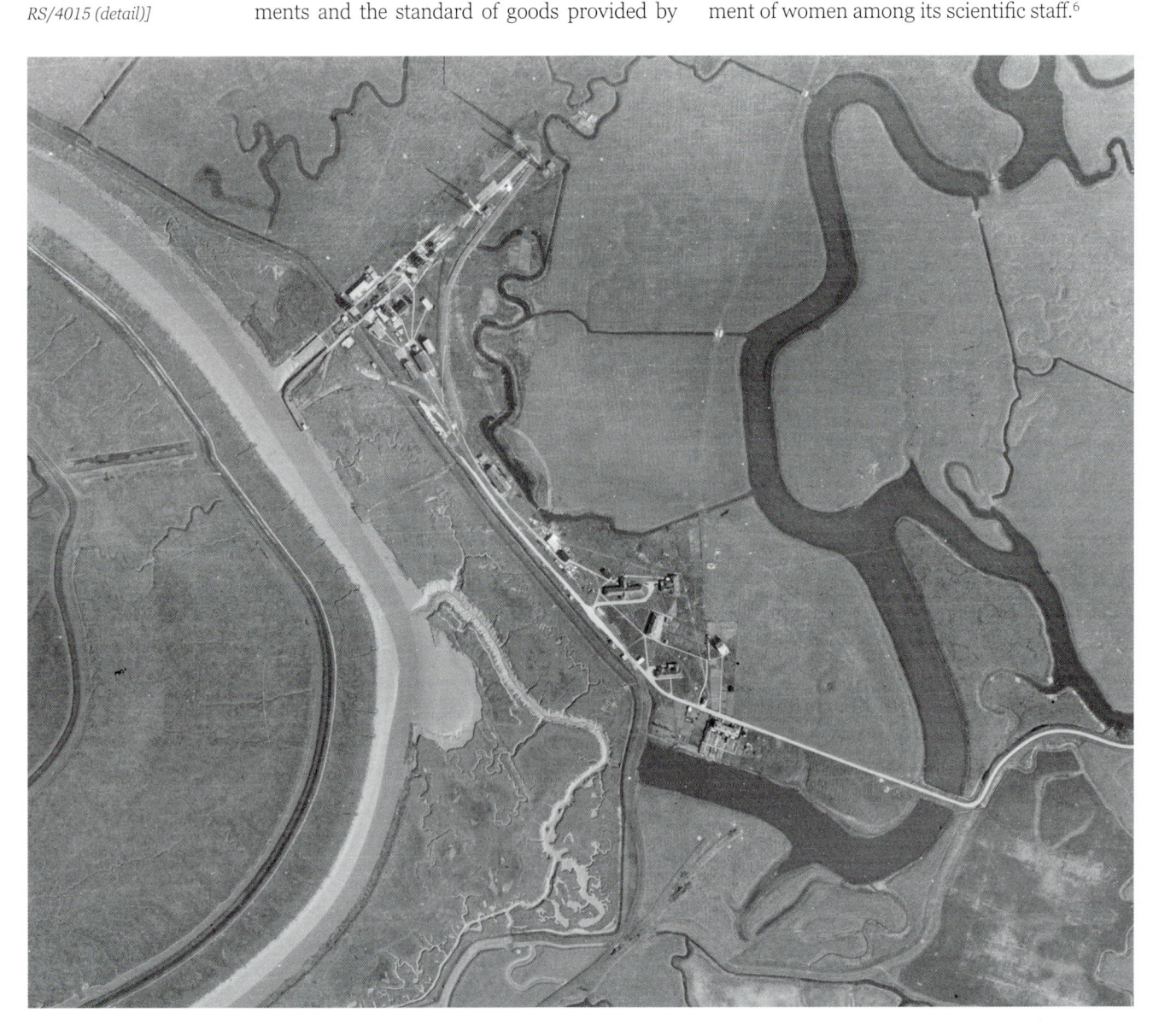

Fig 6.1
Grain Firing Point, Yantlet Creek, Medway. To the top left is the wharf where gun barrels were brought by barge before being transferred onto a rail-mounted transporter. At the opposite end were the masts that supported the wire velocity screens.
[RAF/106G/UK/1444/RS/4015 (detail)]

and the London Small Arms Company, with a factory at Victoria Park – produced the majority of service rifles.

Setting standards

In addition to producing armaments, the state factories acted as quality controllers, repositories of technical knowledge and price regulators. An important task at Woolwich was the production of precisely machined gauges that were used by other factories to ensure the essential interchangeability of components and compatibility of ammunition. From the late 18th century the government had taken an increasingly close and scientific interest in the development of armaments and the standard of goods provided by the state factories and private suppliers. The relatively slow acceptance of scientific and engineering departments in British universities was partly compensated for by expertise within the government establishments and the army's technical officers. As early as the 1860s, under the supervision of the War Office chemist Sir Frederick Abel, one of the first purpose-built chemistry laboratories was constructed at Woolwich.[5] About 1900 a new Research Department was added, which just prior to the outbreak of war employed 11 chemists and 4 physicists. Its work included the development of manufacturing processes for explosives, setting standards for private manufacturers, and the proof and testing of ordnance. Changes during the war included additional buildings and the employment of women among its scientific staff.[6]

Fig 6.2 (left)
Grain Firing Point, Yantlet Creek, Medway. The remains of the gantry path looking towards the former positions of the velocity screens.
[DP187537]

Fig 6.3 (below)
Grain Firing Point, Yantlet Creek, Medway. Electric Power House. This building was built from precast concrete blocks and roofed in red asbestos tiles, a common feature of many wartime buildings. Painted door signs confirm that it housed engine, generating, rectifier and battery rooms.
[DP187526]

Proof ranges, such as those at Purfleet, Essex, ensured the consistency of gunpowder supplied for government service. To test progressively more powerful weapons, in the mid-19th century extensive artillery ranges were established at Shoeburyness, Essex. In 1917, to support the proof and experimental work, a new firing point was built at the eastern end of the Hoo Peninsula at Yantlet Creek, Medway (Fig 6.1).[7] Gun barrels were transported down the Thames from Woolwich by two barges, *Gog* and *Magog*, to a dock where they were moved by travelling crane onto a firing carriage. On the site a wire screen enabled the velocity of a projectile to be measured as it left the barrel. The range was so aligned that guns fired over the Thames onto the Maplin Sands off the Shoeburyness ranges, a distance of up to 26km. Today the remains of the dock, the foundations of the concrete proof stand and a number of concrete block buildings with red asbestos tile roofs survive (Figs 6.2 and 6.3). Increasing government concern about the need for scientific research facilities was also reflected by the establishment of the National Physical Laboratory at Teddington, Middlesex, some of whose early work included research into flight. Further facilities were created to understand the physics of flight at the Royal Aircraft Factory, Farnborough, where a new wind tunnel was constructed in 1916 (*see* Fig 6.31). In addition to the government laboratories, large industrial concerns, such as the Cheshire-based Brunner Mond, supported modest research laboratories.

Explosives manufacture

The foremost needs of the services for explosives were for the propellant cordite, exploder charges for shell fillings and other explosives in lesser quantities. To break the impasse on the Western Front, Field Marshal Sir John French, Commander-in-Chief of the British Expeditionary Force, declared in February 1915 that 'the problem set is a comparatively simple one, munitions, more munitions, always more munitions'.[8] During the opening months of the war the British Expeditionary Force was mainly supplied with shrapnel shells, designed to burst in mid-air and incapacitate the enemy with a lethal shower of lead balls. While these were deadly

Legacies of the First World War

against troops in the open, they were ineffective against field fortifications and trenches. British forces were also equipped with a higher proportion of quick-firing field guns, as opposed to heavy artillery for reducing fortifications.

High explosives

In August 1914 the principal British high-explosive shell filling was picric acid, or Lyddite, which was manufactured from the nitrated coal tar distillate phenol.[9] In contrast, since the beginning of the century the Germans had used TNT. It too was derived from coal tar products, but its main raw ingredient, toluene, required smaller amounts of raw materials. Britain was well placed to secure toluene from coal tar extracted at town gasworks, along with toluene derived from the distillation of benzene from Shell Borneo petroleum. Such was the significance of this latter source that a distillation plant was brought from Rotterdam and re-erected at Portishead, Bristol, and an identical plant was built at Barrow-in-Furness, Cumbria. During the course of the war these two factories produced almost the same amount of toluene as the entire gas industry.[10]

The industrial capacity to produce large amounts of high explosives needed to be built up virtually from scratch. Initially the favoured approach was to adapt existing chemical works, which led to a concentration of production in the north of England at plants previously associated with refining coal tar to produce synthetic textile dyes. Another significant group of factories was located along the River Thames close to London. Prior to the war there was little experience of handling TNT and it was thought to be a fairly safe explosive to manufacture, with fire a greater hazard than detonation. The novelty of the manufacturing process and plant, the inexperience of the workforces and the use of unsuitable premises in urban areas led to two of the worst accidental explosions of the war. In Silvertown, east London, Brunner, Mond and Company converted an idle caustic soda plant to TNT production with disastrous consequences. On Friday, 19 January 1917, the factory was devastated by an explosion that killed 16 employees and 53 people in the densely packed streets surrounding the works; 4 more people died later (Fig 6.4).[11] In Ashton-under-Lyne, Greater Manchester, in a similar urban area of terraced housing, the Hooley Hill Rubber and

Fig 6.4
Silvertown, east London. Part of the Brunner, Mond TNT factory devastated by an explosion on Friday, 19 January 1917.
[SIL01/01/03]

Chemical Company adapted a former cotton mill to TNT production. On 13 June 1917 a fire in the nitrating house resulted in the detonation of 5 tons (5.08 tonnes) of TNT that engulfed two adjacent gasometers. Here 24 employees and 19 local residents died.[12] A year earlier a picric acid factory, at Low Moor, Bradford, West Yorkshire, had exploded with the loss of 34 lives.[13]

While these early adaptations fulfilled the immediate demand for TNT, work soon began on purpose-built factories. The first National Factory was at Oldbury in the West Midlands, where the plant constructed at government expense was managed by Chance and Hunt. Others included a large works at Queensferry, Flintshire, which could produce up to 500 tons (508 tonnes) per week.[14] Brunner, Mond and Company also erected the Gadbrook Works, close to Northwich, Cheshire, for purifying TNT.[15] The company's contribution to the war effort was also critical through research into the production of ammonium nitrate that was mixed with TNT to form a relatively inexpensive shell filling known as amatol. Production was concentrated in its Cheshire heartland, with works at Winnington, Lostock and Sandbach, the Victoria Salt Works, Northwich, and works at Plumley, where footings of the factory remain. An outlying plant was started in September 1917 at Stratton St Margaret, Swindon, Wiltshire (Fig 6.5).[16]

Cordite

Cordite was adopted in the 1890s as the main British military propellant for artillery rounds and rifle cartridges. At this time it comprised a combination of nitroglycerine and nitrocellulose, or guncotton, which was gelatinised in bread-dough-like incorporating machines with the addition of the solvent acetone and mineral jelly in order to reduce gun-barrel erosion. Prior to the war the yearly demand for cordite by Britain's armed forces stood at around 3,600 tons

Fig 6.5
His Majesty's Explosives Factory, Stratton St Margaret, Wiltshire. In the right foreground are the administrative offices and canteen. This factory was designed by the Ministry of Works under the supervision of Frank Baines.
[EPW000941]

Fig 6.6
Royal Gunpowder Factory, Waltham Abbey, Essex. Buildings added to increase wartime cordite production.
[Redrawn from 1917 plan held in Royal Gunpowder Mills Archives]

(3,660 tonnes); the Royal Gunpowder Factory at Waltham Abbey supplied about one-third and seven trade factories the remainder, with the majority going to the Royal Navy.[17]

After the outbreak of war the initial drive to increase cordite production was met by heightened production in existing works, through increasing shifts and the construction of additional process buildings. Elements of the Waltham Abbey factory dated from the 1660s, and over the succeeding centuries it had grown organically, the latest significant changes having taken place about 1900 to accommodate the production of cordite. The resulting layout was inefficient, and with the low-lying Lea valley constrained by the river and canals there was little opportunity for expansion. Nevertheless, along the factory's eastern flank additional cordite

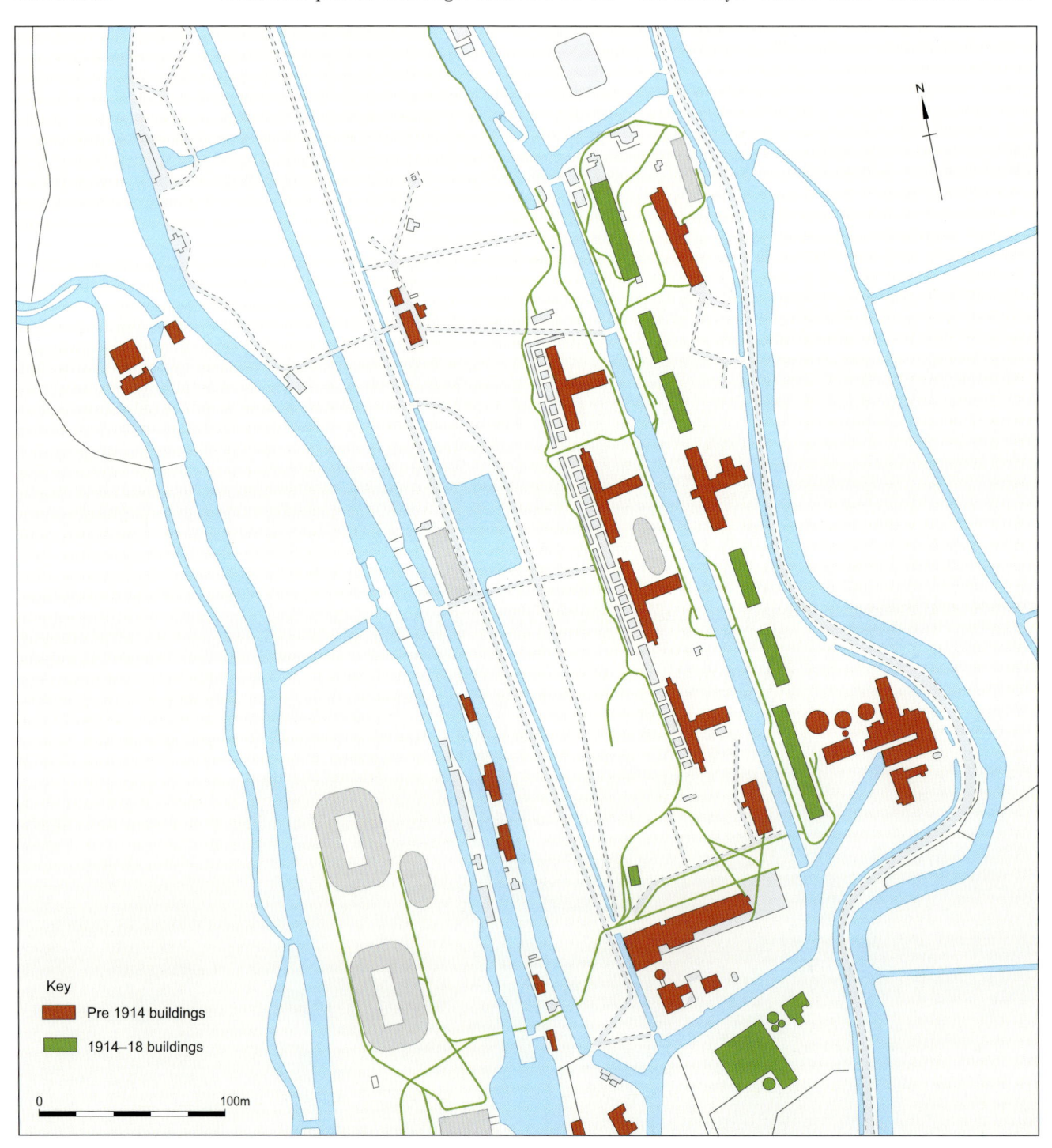

Key
- Pre 1914 buildings
- 1914–18 buildings

incorporating mills and press houses were built with a typical bay form to lessen the effects of any accidental explosions (Figs 6.6 and 6.7).

Acetone was vital in the manufacture of cordite and other important substances such as dope to stiffen the fabric of aircraft fuselages and wings. Prior to the war, America, Canada and Austria were the country's chief suppliers of acetone (along with other chemicals), largely produced by the destructive distillation of wood. In an attempt to conserve supplies, the Research Department at the Royal Arsenal developed a new form of cordite using a less highly nitrated form of cellulose, known as collodion. In place of acetone it was incorporated using diethyl ether-ethanol; the resulting product was known as Cordite RDB. At Waltham Abbey this change in cordite technology was marked by the construction of an ether and mineral jelly store (Fig 6.8).

Curtis's & Harvey explosives factory, Cliffe, Medway

From the late 19th century, in addition to developing the Royal Gunpowder Factory, the government encouraged the private sector to invest in new cordite factories. It did this by alternating contracts between different manufacturers, so that by 1914 there were seven private firms capable of manufacturing cordite.[18] These were some of the largest and most complex explosives factories. They required large areas of flat land, a reliable water supply, good transport links, plant to concentrate sulphuric acid and to manufacture nitric acid, as well as facilities to recover spent acids, and access to a large workforce. Most were self-sufficient and included sections dedicated to the production of guncotton and nitroglycerine.

One of the explosives factories where the government funded expansion was that managed by Curtis's & Harvey on the Thames at Cliffe, Medway. This was an ideal location: it was remote and the flat marshland allowed the works to be efficiently laid out without constraints of topography. Sulphuric acid was readily available from the east London chemical industry, and the river provided a safe means of transport for its products to government establishments or for export.

Cordite production at Cliffe had started here in the first decade of the century, and archaeological evidence suggests that some expansion in capacity may have commenced in 1913. To increase output the works was almost doubled in size in 1916 with the construction of His Majesty's Cordite Factory immediately east of the existing works. This new section included new guncotton and nitroglycerine factories, and was administered by Curtis's & Harvey (Fig 6.9).[19]

Archaeologically, the factory at Cliffe is one of the most complete cordite works, and its remains illustrate the full manufacturing process and supporting infrastructure. On the remaining floor slabs traces of different floor surfaces and machinery bases may be analysed to illustrate the production of acids and guncotton, while earthen mounds mark the position of the nitroglycerine factories. To the east are rows of mounds that surrounded magazines for cordite paste before it was moved to the incorporating house. Here the cordite paste was blended with the solvent acetone to form cordite dough (Fig 6.10). This was then taken to the adjacent press houses, where it was extruded

Fig 6.7 (left, top) Royal Gunpowder Factory, Waltham Abbey, Essex. A wartime cordite press house, typical of most explosives buildings in being compartmentalised to minimise the effects of any accidental explosions. [DP188494]

Fig 6.8 (left, bottom) Royal Gunpowder Factory, Waltham Abbey, Essex. The wartime ether and mineral jelly store. [BB92/26081]

125

Legacies of the First World War

Fig 6.9
Cliffe, Medway. Curtis's & Harvey explosives works. The structures shown on the right (east) were added during the First World War.
[RAF/540/1699/F22/0113]

Fig 6.10
Cliffe, Medway. The cordite production line flowed from right to left. To the right are the bases of the cordite incorporating machines and to their left the cordite press house and left again the acetone recovery stoves. Beyond them was the acetone recovery house and another set of acetone recovery stoves. To the top are bases of the batching houses.
[NMR 26891/007]

under hydraulic pressure into cordlike strands. From here it was taken on the tramway in hand-propelled wagons to the acetone recovery stoves, where the cordite was gently heated to drive off the acetone vapour, which was conveyed to the neighbouring acetone recovery house (Fig 6.11). The eastern acetone recovery stoves are a unique survival and cover 80m by 8m, comprising a central spine wall with 15 small compartments to either side (Fig 6.12). Their walls are constructed from a mixture of brick and reinforced concrete, and some of the concrete is

Fig 6.11
Cliffe, Medway. Remains of the acetone recovery house, with the acetone recovery stoves to the right. To the rear were cordite drying stoves.
[DP141667]

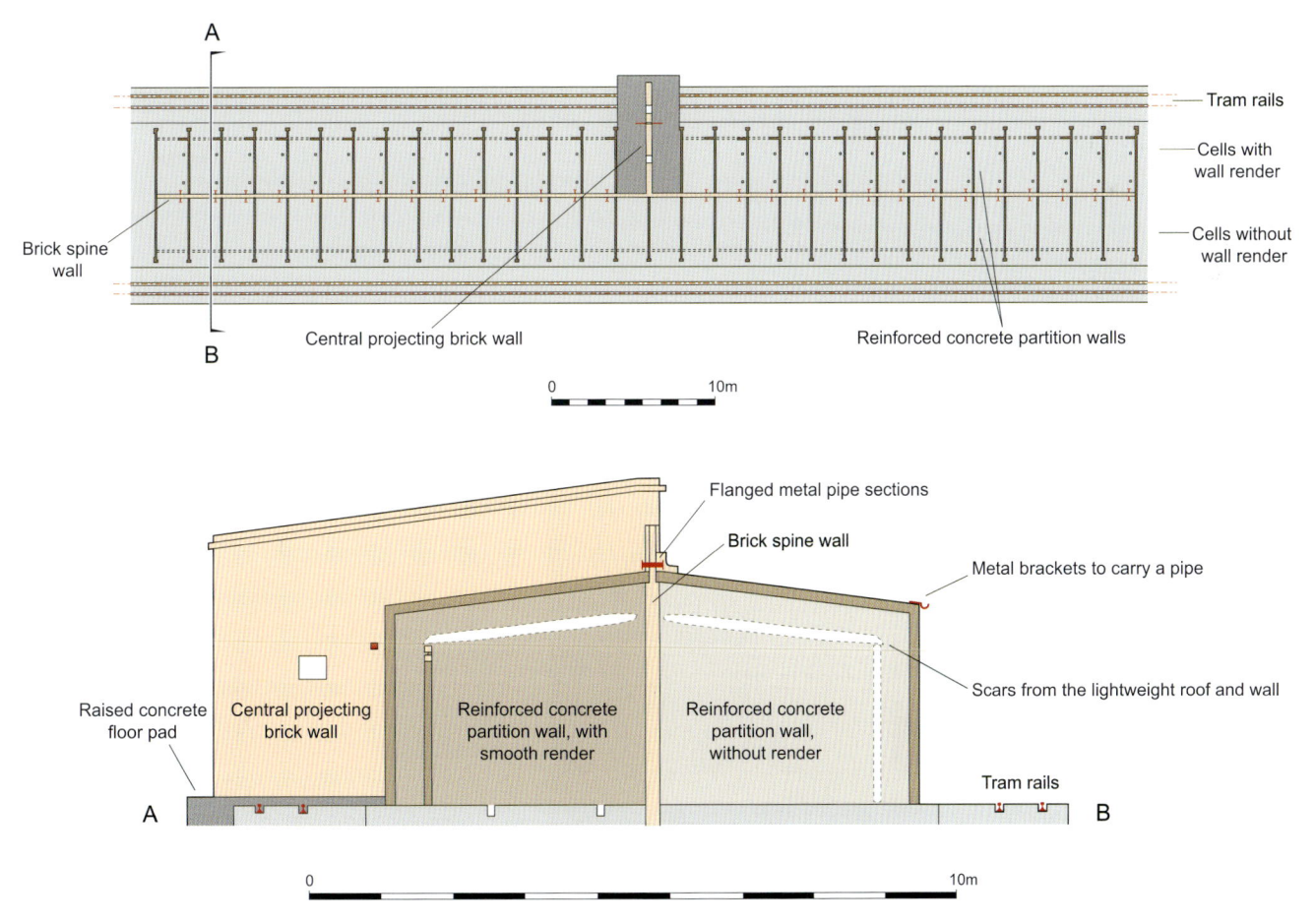

Fig 6.12 (below)
Cliffe, Medway. Floor plan and section through the acetone recovery stoves.

Fig 6.13 (right)
Cliffe, Medway. Floor plan and section of a reinforced cordite drying stove.

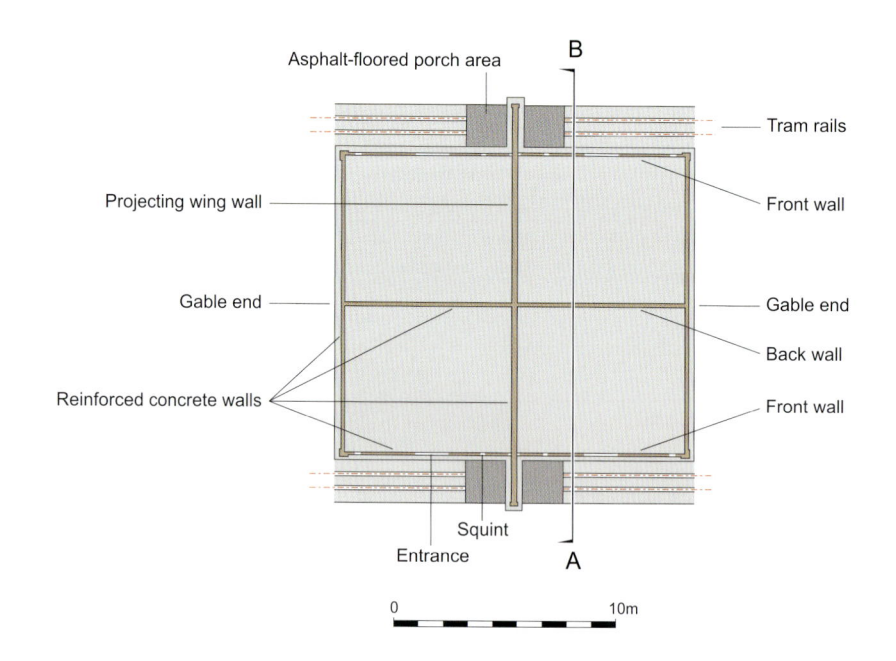

Fig 6.14 (below)
Cliffe, Medway. Detail of a cordite drying stove showing the footings for the porch; lines in the concrete mark the position of the removed tramway. Also visible are a small observation window and the widely spaced reinforcing rods.
[DP141705]

fire reddened possibly from an accidental fire in 1918, or from later fires during demolition.[20] The presence of these acetone recovery facilities suggests that most of the output was for consumption by the navy, as it continued to prefer cordite prepared with acetone due to its stable storage characteristics and known ballistic properties. From the recovery stove the cordite was taken to the batching houses, where cordite from different lots was mixed together to ensure a consistent product. It was then moved by tramway to a bank of 17 drying stoves (Figs 6.13 and 6.14), where the final drying took place before the cordite was moved off-site to the filling factories. Unusually, the stove walls were constructed from reinforced concrete, with widely spaced reinforcing rods.

Acetone

In an attempt to reduce the reliance on foreign acetone supplies, prior to the war the Office of Woods and Forests had built a wood distillation plant at Coleford, Gloucestershire; a handful of other plants followed.[21] At the same time scientists were exploring how agricultural produce might be synthesised into industrial chemicals. Prominent among these pioneers was Chaim Weizmann, a Zionist and first president of Israel, who was driven by a desire to develop an industrial base for a future Jewish state in Palestine. While a reader in biochemistry at the University of Manchester he identified a bacterium *Clostridium acetobutylicum* that was able to produce acetone from a variety of starchy foodstuffs.[22] In August 1914 he made this discovery available to the British government and in early 1916 was approached by the Nobel's Explosives Company. This came to nothing, and in March of the same year he was summoned to the Admiralty. There he met with Winston Churchill, who demanded 30,000 tons of acetone. To take a laboratory phenomenon to full industrial production a pilot fermentation plant was built at Nicholson's gin distillery, Bromley-by-Bow, east London.[23] This was then scaled up to construct an industrial-size plant, which was operational at Holton Heath by 1917 (Fig 6.15).[24] Remains of this include the boiler house, where the starchy liquor was produced prior to fermentation, and six out of the eight reinforced concrete fermentation vessels. At first maize was used as the starch source, but when this supply was threatened by U-boat attacks, schoolchildren were urged to collect acorns and conkers for the war effort, although the precise purpose remained secret (*see* p 177).[25]

Fig 6.15 Royal Naval Cordite Factory, Holton Heath, Dorset. The acetone fermentation plant, whose remains are seen here, may be regarded as the precursor of the modern biotechnology industry. The remains have additional significance through their connections to Winston Churchill and Chaim Weizmann. [BB94/16939]

The Royal Naval Cordite Factory, Holton Heath

The Edwardian royal dockyards were vast manufacturing enterprises that were capable of producing virtually all the requirements of the Royal Navy, apart from explosives. Shortly before the outbreak of war in January 1914, Winston Churchill, then First Lord of the Admiralty, confirmed the decision to build an Admiralty cordite factory at Holton Heath, Dorset.[26] This was to produce cordite of the highest ballistic uniformity (*see* Fig 6.36). It was constructed on open heathland which allowed the production units to be laid out in the most efficient manner; the gentle rolling landscape also allowed liquids in the nitroglycerine plant to be moved safely by gravity. The factory was largely self-sufficient and included a self-contained acid factory with a pyrites plant used in the production of sulphuric acid. It also included a guncotton factory and later an innovative acetone plant.

His Majesty's Factory Gretna

It soon became apparent that extensions to existing works would be unable to supply the vast quantities of cordite required by the army. By June 1915 a large tract of land straddling the English–Scottish border close to Gretna had been identified as the site for a new factory (Fig 6.16). It developed into the largest explosives factory in the Empire, covering 8995 acres (3,640ha) and stretching for 7½ miles (12km), and employing nearly 20,000 people.[27] It was effectively a series of factories including an acids section, glycerine distillery, ether plant, guncotton factory, and mixing and drying

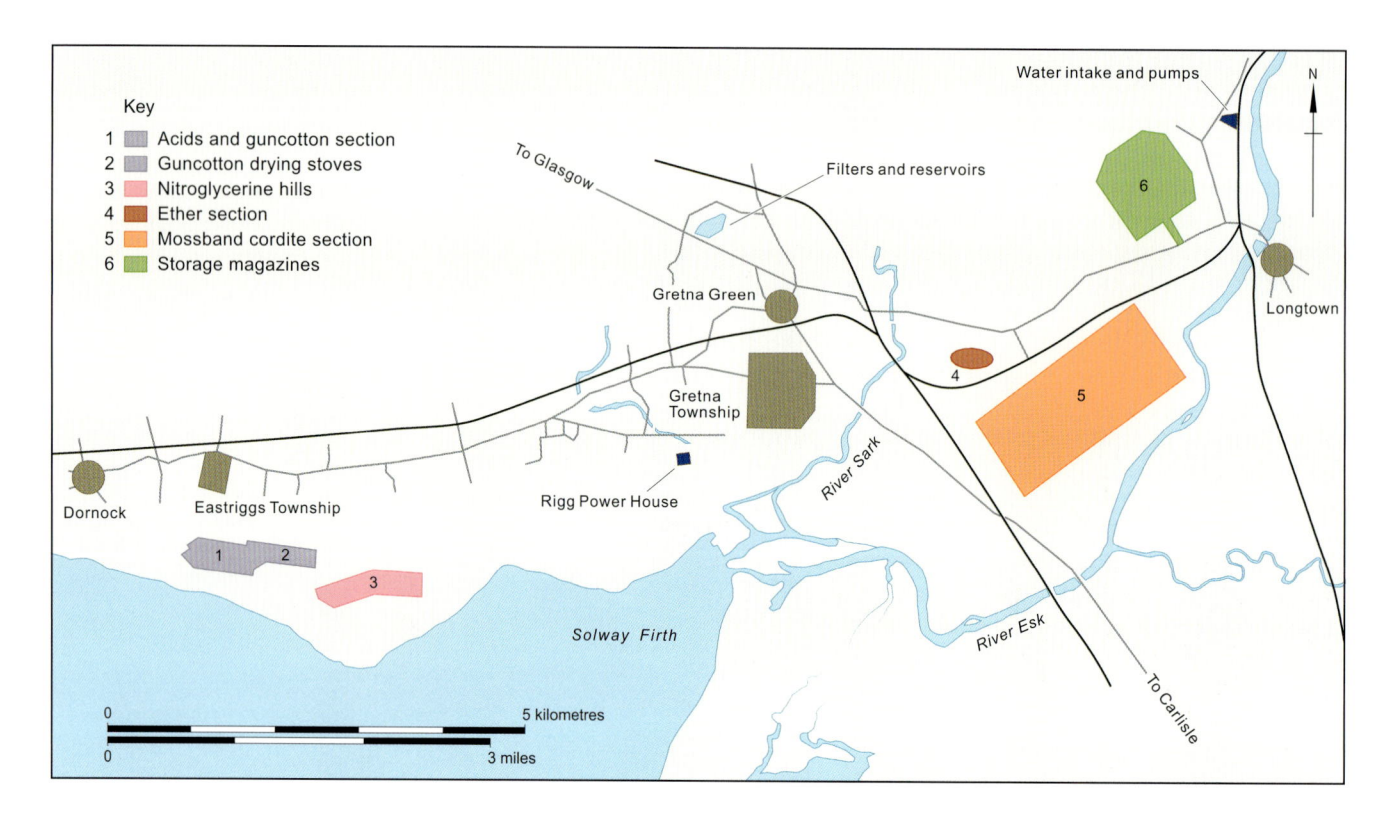

Fig 6.16
His Majesty's Factory Gretna, Dumfriesshire. [Redrawn from TNA/SUPPLY 10/15]

sections. Nitrocellulose, or guncotton, was also supplied by another huge government factory at Queensferry which could produce 250 tons (254 tonnes) per week.[28] It had a maximum production capacity of 1,000 tons (1,016 tonnes) of the new Cordite RDB per week, and because of the economies of scale was able to produce cordite at around 25 per cent lower than the pre-war price.[29]

The project was overseen by Kenneth B Quinan, an American chemical engineer, previously employed by the Cape Explosives Works, South Africa. In designing Gretna and other works he made an enormous contribution to the war effort by introducing innovative chemical technology. He was not alone, and chemists and munitions workers also came from across the Empire to aid the war effort. One of Quinan's introductions was the manufacture of sulphuric acid by the contact process developed by continental acid producers; he also constructed a similar plant at Queensferry.[30] He also built his patent guncotton drying houses, which combined the twin advantages of a faster drying time with improved safety, as there was less guncotton in a stove at a given time compared to the older design. A number of these still survive, although altered to new uses. At the end of the war the projected demand for cordite was low, and the Gretna works was closed in favour of the obsolescent works at Waltham Abbey.[31] Most of the site was cleared, but it was later occupied by an ammunition depot, where a number of modified wartime cordite factory buildings survive.

Shell manufacture

A quick-firing artillery round typically comprised a brass shell case containing the explosive propellant, usually cordite, and a machined steel projectile that might be filled with high explosive, shrapnel balls or poison gas. More sensitive explosives were required to ignite the propellant and detonate the projectile's bursting charge. Detonation was usually initiated by a finely machined brass fuse. Each component of the shell required a specific set of skills for its manufacture, all of which were brought together in the filling factories for final assembly.

In the early months of the war many owners of local engineering concerns joined together to form munitions committees, and engineering works were adapted to manufacture shells. In Liverpool, for instance, the Cunard Steamship Company converted and extended a recently acquired warehouse to manufacture shells (Fig 6.17).[32] Shell works, and projectile works where large-calibre shells were manufactured, would usually be supplied with rough steel billets which would be pressed and machined on a lathe to produce the correct profile (Fig 6.18). A groove would also be cut around the base of the shell to accept the copper driving band, which imparted spin to the projectile by gripping the rifled bore of artillery pieces. All aspects of the machining process were carefully controlled and monitored with special gauges. Finally, prior to dispatch the shells were painted before being moved to the filling factories.

*Fig 6.17
Cunard's Shellworks, Liverpool. In the rear yard steel castings wait for machining and waste swarf is tipped. Unusually, Cunard's works lacked rail sidings and all materials were moved by road. Boys below enlistment age were employed to tidy the yard.
[BL24001/003]*

*Fig 6.18
Cunard's Shellworks, Liverpool. Female lathe operators and a forewoman. Although the wearing of trousers by women became more commonplace, here they continued to favour skirts. Rare surviving uniforms suggest that coloured cuffs, collars and hats might have been used to denote status and roles. Also noticeable are the lack of health and safety precautions, including machine guards, and hand and eye protection.
[BL24001/021]*

Fig 6.19
National Filling Factory No 6, Chilwell. A factory identity disc, the impressed inscription on which may be a later addition made as a souvenir of service at the factory.
[Courtesy Alan Johnson]

Filling factories

To ensure a steady supply of shells for the front, one of the most pressing needs was for filling factories where the various components and explosives were brought together for assembly. Ideally these were placed between the manufacturing centres that produced the inert metal components, the explosives works and the embarkation ports. Good railway connections were a key requirement, as were large open sites and access to a labour supply. The first National Filling Factory was planned in association with the Leeds local munitions committee at Barnbow, concentrating on filling quick-firing rounds. At the end of the war the factory site reverted to farmland, and today the production flow may be traced in its earthwork remains.

The early months of fighting on the Western Front quickly revealed the need for heavy high-explosive shells to batter down German fortifications. With the adoption of TNT as the main British explosive, new shell-filling methods needed to be devised. In particular, to conserve TNT stocks, methods for filling shells with amatol, a mixture of ammonium nitrate and TNT, were required. At Chilwell, Nottinghamshire, Viscount Godfrey Chetwynd, a former car company manager with no previous experience of handling explosives, took a novel approach to the design of a factory to fill shells with amatol. After visiting a number of French explosives factories, and unimpeded by convention, he adapted coal-crushing, stone-pulverising, sugar-drying, paint-making and sugar-sifting machinery, and used porcelain rollers usually found in flour mills to grind TNT. Contrary to usual practice, he built multistorey mills similar to those used for milling flour. Construction began in September 1915 and the factory was in operation by the following March, and it was boasted that nearly every big shell fired during the Somme offensive was filled there.[33] Despite the factory being state-financed, Chetwynd so closely identified with the works that a monogram of crossed Cs was applied to lampposts and the ironwork of buildings' balconies (Fig 6.19). The factory filled prodigious quantities of munitions, including over 19 million shells, 25,000 sea mines, and 2,500 aerial bombs.[34] This represented just over half of all the large-calibre shells handled by the national filling factories. It also had the unfortunate distinction of being the scene of the worst accidental explosion of the war, when 134 people were killed in September 1918.

The design of a filling factory was generally the responsibility of a local committee, company, or their local agent or manager, although the Office of Works might provide advice, and in some cases undertook the provision of light, heat and water supply.[35] This policy, while ensuring the speedy construction of new plant, led to a multitude of factory designs, often resulting in works that were closely designed around a specific production process with little flexibility for adaptation.

One such filling factory, though named Banbury, was located just within Northamptonshire. Construction, under the supervision of its future manager Mr Bing, probably began in late 1915, and shell filling was under way by April 1916. Its main function was the filling of high-explosive Lyddite shells. One of the factory units survives nearly intact as an earthwork, and together with contemporary drawings helps our understanding of the production process (Figs 6.20, 6.21 and 6.22). Empty shells were brought into stores to either side of the production unit

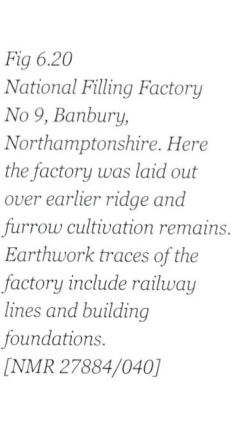

Fig 6.20
National Filling Factory No 9, Banbury, Northamptonshire. Here the factory was laid out over earlier ridge and furrow cultivation remains. Earthwork traces of the factory include railway lines and building foundations.
[NMR 27884/040]

The workshop of the world goes to war

Key
- Empty shell store
- Paint shop
- Melt and filling house
- Filled shell store
- Picric acid store
- Earth bund

Fig 6.21
National Filling Factory No 9, Banbury, Northamptonshire.
[Redrawn from 1:2500 OS Northamptonshire 1922]

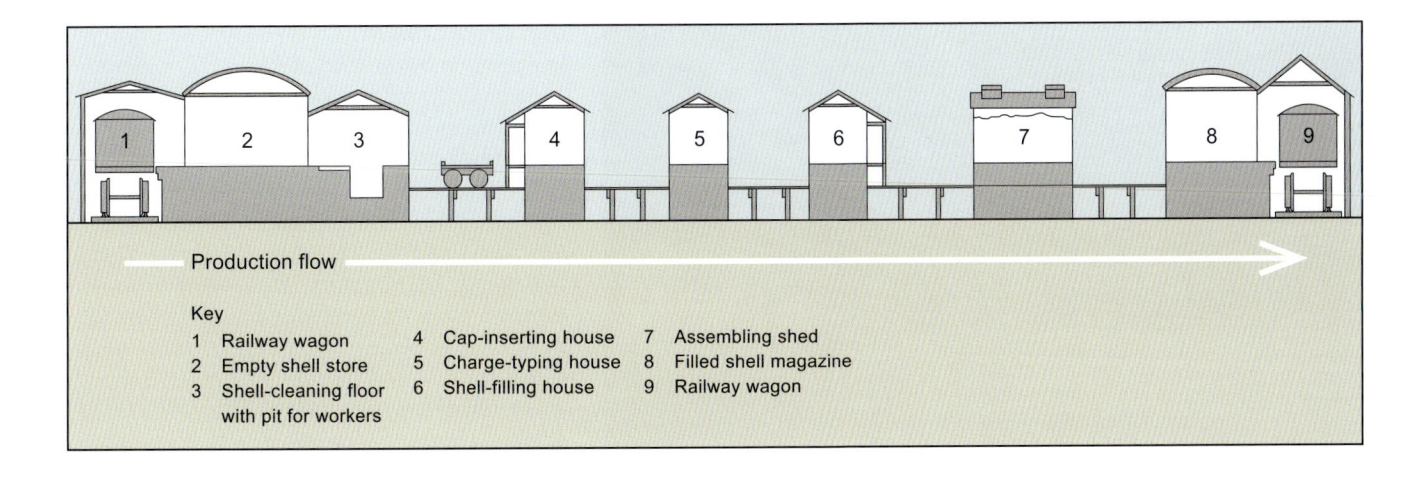

Fig 6.22 (below)
National Filling Factory No 9, Banbury, Northamptonshire. Diagrammatic representation of the filling process.
[Redrawn from TNA, MUN 5/155/122.3/51]

Production flow

Key
1. Railway wagon
2. Empty shell store
3. Shell-cleaning floor with pit for workers
4. Cap-inserting house
5. Charge-typing house
6. Shell-filling house
7. Assembling shed
8. Filled shell magazine
9. Railway wagon

133

*Fig 6.23 (below)
National Filling Factory No 14, Hereford, Rotherwas, Herefordshire. A bonded store for picric acid.
[DP195193]*

*Fig 6.24 (bottom)
National Filling Factory No 14, Hereford, Rotherwas, Herefordshire. A shell store with a wide-span steel roof incorporating runner beams for shell cranes.
[DP195162]*

and were then brought into small central sheds, where they were filled with molten Lyddite; an exploder and fuse were then inserted into the top of the shell. They were then moved to a filled-shell store, and after a quality inspection passed from the civil Ministry of Munitions to the Army Ordnance Department for onward shipment to France. This one factory produced huge quantities, and in one week in March 1917 it filled 7,000 9.2in shells, 10,000 60-pounders and 15,000 6in shells. Another Lyddite filling factory was built at Rotherwas, Herefordshire, where today a handful of First World War buildings survive, including bonded picric acid stores and a shell store (Figs 6.23 and 6.24), among structures from the 1930s.

Salvage was an important part of the wartime economy, and brass shell cases were returned from the front for repair and refilling. Re-forming a case, which could be done up to four times, cost about 4d, whereas a new case was around 7s.[36] Stamps on their bases document journeys to and from the Front.

By 1918, in addition to 22 national filling factories, the Trench Warfare Department operated seven factories producing grenades, mortar shells, lachrymatory grenades and some chemical munitions. Typically these works were built adjacent to existing premises, although at the Ministry sites in Watford purpose-built factories were constructed.

Poison gas

In April 1915, having used it against Russian troops a few months earlier, the Germans released the 'ghastly dew' of chlorine gas on the Western Front. The Allies rapidly began to manufacture war gases themselves, and to provide some protection for their troops by manufacturing increasingly sophisticated gas masks, or respirators.

Facilities were also required to fill cylinders, grenades and shells with war gases. These included lachrymatory agents to induce streaming eyes and vomiting, as well as more deadly and persistent agents. In spring 1918 the under-used filling factories at Banbury and Hereford were identified for conversion to mustard gas, or Hun Stuff, filling. At Banbury a local engineering firm stepped in to refine machinery for this novel manufacturing process. Initially, rough sketches were acquired of a French machine and a prototype was manufactured by the Lennox Foundry Company, London. This in turn provided information for Messrs Samuelson & Co of Banbury to produce drawings for an improved machine, in operation by the start of August. The Banbury vacuum charging machine was also supplied to the factories at Hereford and Chittening, Bristol, and to the Italian government.[37] Banbury was the most prolific gas filling factory, and by September 1918 it had filled 60,000 18-pounder gas shells and 12,000 4.5in gas shells. On 30 September 1918 many of these were expended during a six-hour bombardment of the Hindenburg Line, critically disrupting resistance to the Allied assault. Had the war continued, Banbury was estimated to be capable of filling 100,000 gas shells per week.[38] Some capacity to fill gas shells was also created at the filling factory at Morecambe, Lancashire.[39] Phosgene was even more lethal, and a former edible oil manufacturer at Selby, North Yorkshire, was acquired to produce and fill gas shells of this type. Mustard gas shells were filled at a new factory at Chittening; the last buildings at both works were demolished about 2005 (Fig 6.25). Other types of chemical shells were filled at Greenford, Greater London (Fig 6.26), and lachrymatory shells were filled at a works in Blackhorse Lane, Walthamstow, London.[40]

Fig 6.25
National Filling Factory Chittening, Bristol. A specialist mustard gas filling factory.
[EPW019262]

Fig 6.26 (below)
Greenford, Greater London. A chemical shell assembling station.
[Redrawn from Wootton and Lowry 1919]

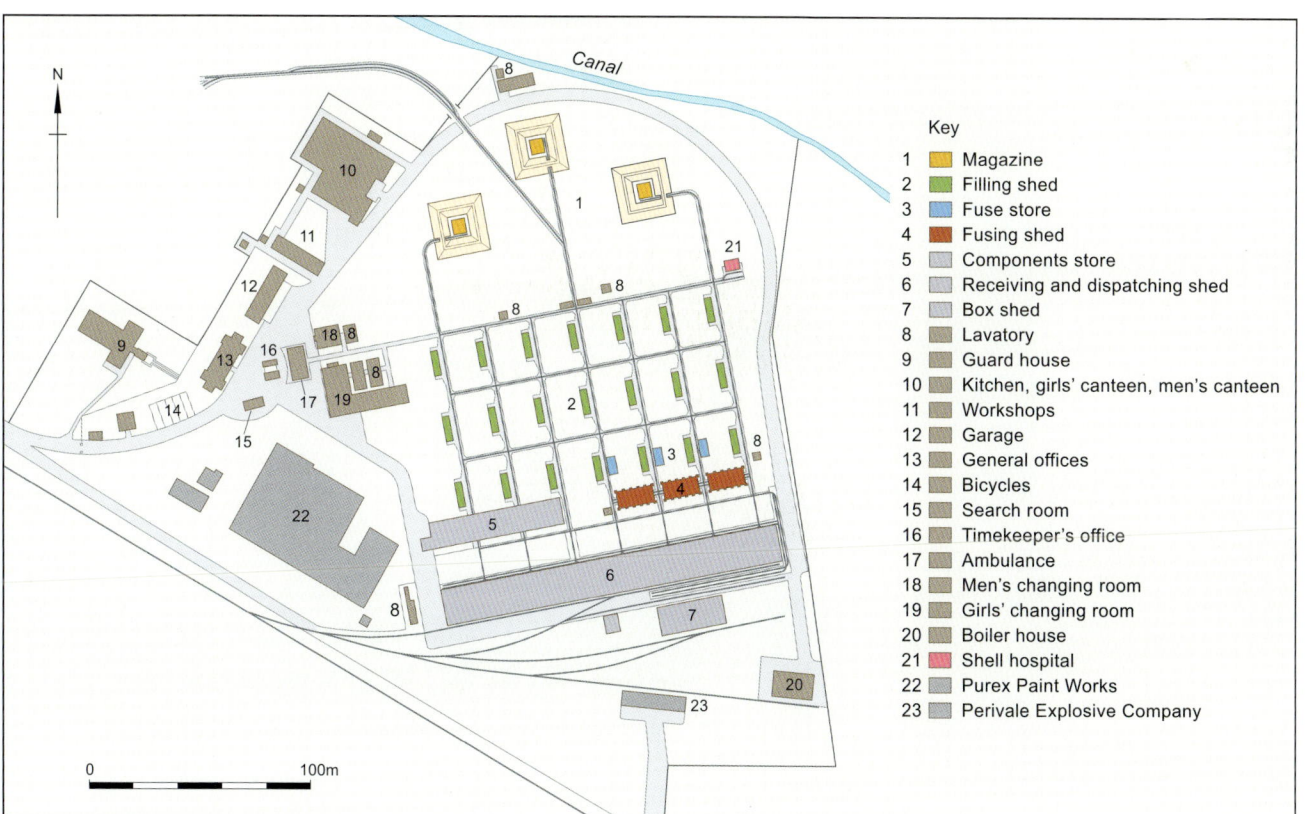

Key

1		Magazine
2		Filling shed
3		Fuse store
4		Fusing shed
5		Components store
6		Receiving and dispatching shed
7		Box shed
8		Lavatory
9		Guard house
10		Kitchen, girls' canteen, men's canteen
11		Workshops
12		Garage
13		General offices
14		Bicycles
15		Search room
16		Timekeeper's office
17		Ambulance
18		Men's changing room
19		Girls' changing room
20		Boiler house
21		Shell hospital
22		Purex Paint Works
23		Perivale Explosive Company

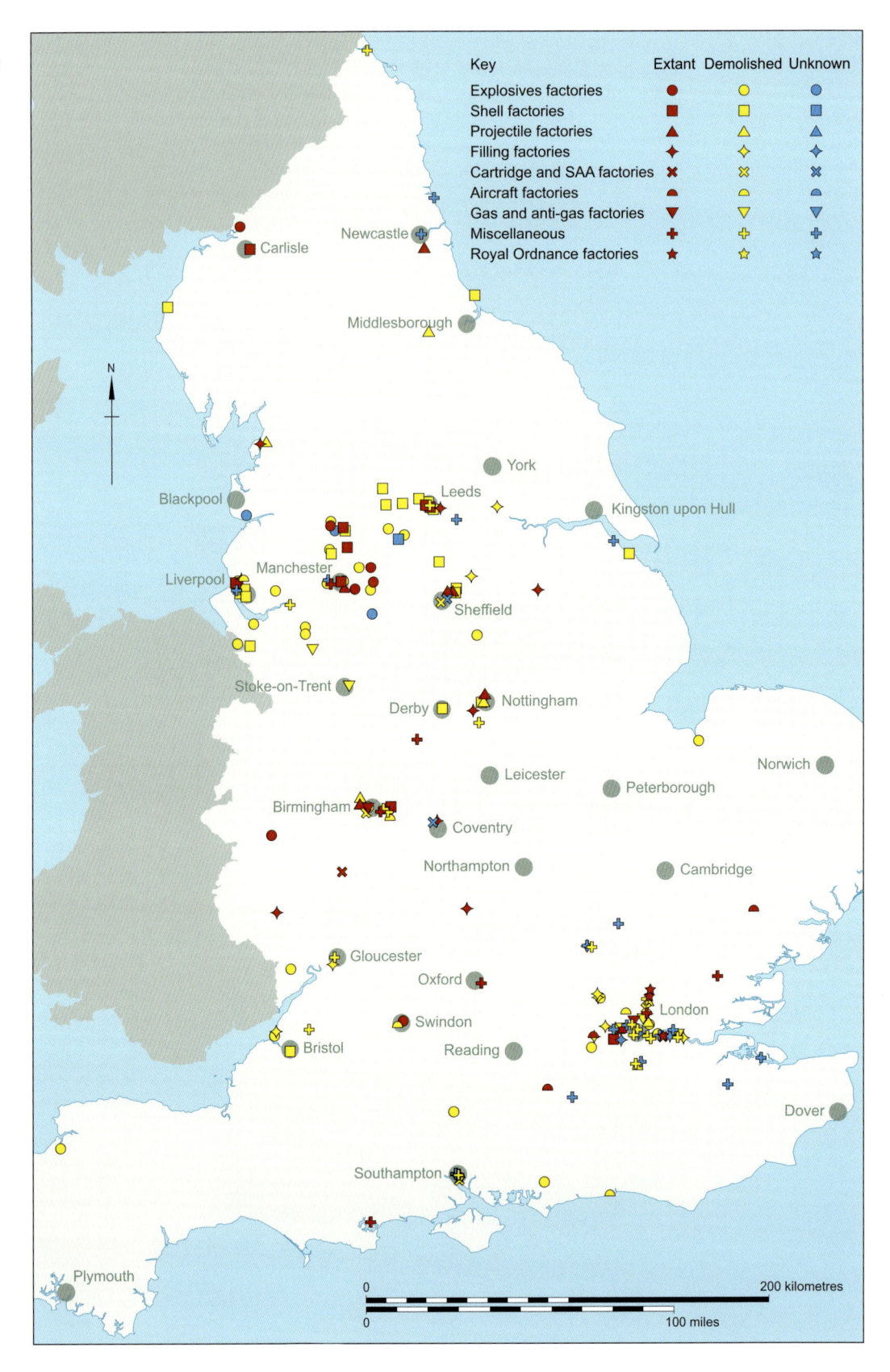

Legacies of the First World War

Fig 6.27
Map of national factories in England.

National factories

The ineffectiveness of the ammunition supply came to a head in spring 1915, when no more than 8 per cent of the shells being sent to the front contained high explosives.[41] This shortage culminated in May 1915 in the 'shells scandal', when it was claimed in *The Times* that the shortage of high explosives and shells had contributed to the lack of progress on the Western Front and heavy loss of life. It was also argued that the shortage of heavy artillery pieces was an additional factor, although contemporary and later arguments have focused on the lack of shells.[42]

Partly in response to this criticism, in June 1915 the newly formed coalition government under Herbert Asquith created the Ministry of Munitions, responsible for all areas of munitions supply and manufacture. Under the new ministry, directed by David Lloyd George, a system of national factories was planned (Fig 6.27).

To supplement the munitions produced by the state establishments and private contractors, the Ministry of Munitions created a network of around 200 directly managed national factories. They produced virtually all the materials required by the armed forces, including aircraft, boxes, concrete slabs, chemicals, explosives,

National Machine Gun Factory

The machine gun, invented in the late 19th century, was used to devastating effect in the fixed lines of the Western Front. By 1914 the Maxim machine gun was obsolescent and was being replaced by one designed by the Vickers company. Large orders were placed for this gun, which was manufactured at its Crayford and Erith plants, the latter being extended to meet demand. Production was, however, beset by many problems, including a shortage of skilled labour, industrial disputes and the supply of raw materials. By 1917 the projected demand for machine guns became even greater with the need to arm increasing numbers of tanks and aircraft, and an expectation the war would continue into 1919. Both Vickers works also lay in areas vulnerable to air raids, and so it was proposed to build a new National Machine Gun Factory at Burton-on-Trent, Staffordshire. Work was under way by early 1918, but remained unfinished by the November armistice.[43] Even at this late stage of the war, architectural standards were maintained and the imposing three-storey administrative building was finished in the neo-Georgian style reminiscent of a country house, although steel-framing, concrete and slab filling were used to speed up construction (Figs 6.28 and 6.29). The expenditure suggests an intention to retain it as a state factory; however, by May 1919, with huge numbers of machine guns in store, the factory was closed.

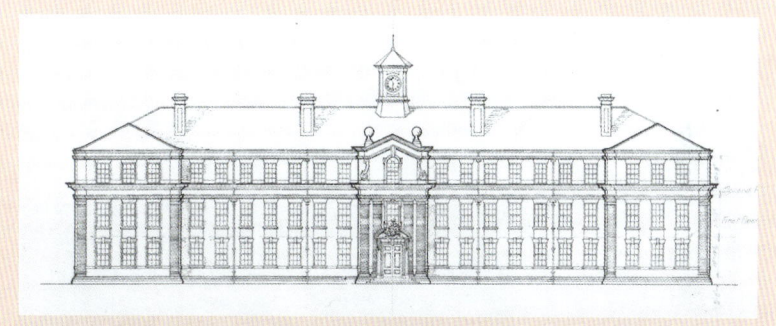

Fig 6.28 (top)
National Machine Gun Factory, Burton-on-Trent, Staffordshire. Elevation drawing of the administration building.
[MD95/09210]

Fig 6.29 (above)
National Machine Gun Factory, Burton-on-Trent, Staffordshire. Built by Thomas Lowe and Sons, 1917/18.
[DP188189]

shells, small arms ammunition and protective equipment against poison gas.[44] Some factories were established in existing premises, while new factories hastened the introduction of the principles of scientific management to factory layouts and improved organisation of the workforce. To utilise new and relatively unskilled labour, through a process known as 'dilution', production was broken down into a number of individual and repetitive tasks, so whereas previously a single skilled worker may have carried out a number of tasks, each now carried out only a limited range of tasks. The National Projectile Factory at Lancaster, where there was a single shed with long production lines, exemplified this with its logical manufacturing lines. The innovations in factory designs and associated welfare facilities were widely reported in the professional and architectural journals, although often locations were omitted.

By spring 1916 the first of the new national factories were in production and ready to equip Kitchener's New Armies for that summer's Somme offensive, and most were working by 1917. In addition to the directly managed national factories, nearly 6,000 factories deemed essential for the prosecution of the war were designated as 'controlled establishments'. This status imposed labour controls, and the liberty of workers to move jobs was strictly regulated. This loss of freedom was partly compensated for by improvements in working conditions, backed up by inspections by the Ministry. The physical remains of the controlled establishments and their products remain a poorly studied aspect of the wartime industrial effort.

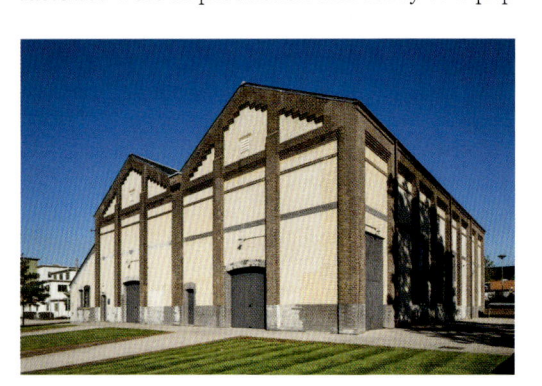

Aircraft factories

By the end of the 19th century the army had recognised the role that aerial reconnaissance might play in any future conflict, and observation balloons were deployed in the Boer War (1899–1902). In the winter of 1904–5 the government's Balloon Factory, established at Aldershot in 1897, was moved to a greenfield site at Farnborough which also became the centre for experiments with manned kites and later powered aircraft. In 1911 it was renamed the Army Aircraft Factory, and later the Royal Aircraft Factory (Figs 6.30 and 6.31).[45] Its products included balloons, airship gondolas, aircraft engines and aircraft. It also became the government's foremost aeronautical research

Fig 6.30 (right)
The Royal Aircraft Factory, Farnborough, Hampshire. Building R52, designed in 1916 by the Office of Works under the supervision of Frank Baines, is finished in red facing bricks from Dane's Hill brickworks with panels of Crowborough brick. It housed one 4ft (1.2m) diameter and two 7ft (2.1m) diameter wind tunnels, and is the oldest surviving wind tunnel building in England.
[DP184123]

Fig 6.31 (below)
The Royal Aircraft Factory, Farnborough, Hampshire. Building Q27, built from 1905 (now demolished), whose products included airship gondolas and later aircraft assembly.
[BB98/26770]

establishment; the first wind tunnel in England was installed here in 1906, and in 1913 a large whirling arm for testing propellers was built.[46]

At the outbreak of war, powered flight in heavier than air machines was just over a decade old, and the use of aircraft by the British army had only begun in 1909. In 1914 just 158 aircraft were available for military purposes, a figure that would rise to over 22,000 by October 1918. By late 1916, aircraft were no longer regarded as a novelty competing for roles with airships, and were recognised as vital war-winning machines. This was reflected in the projected expansion of the RFC from 67 to 200 squadrons, which in turn led to the demand for more airfields, and a need for increased aircraft production.

Besides the Royal Aircraft Factory at Farnborough, the new aircraft industry was generally housed at first in existing factories, and production was shared between a number of manufacturers and component suppliers. Typically, most early aircraft were small, wooden framed and covered in linen hardened with dope. The skills needed to construct these early airframes were found with furniture manufacturers such as Waring and Gillow, who turned over their factories in Hammersmith, London, and Lancaster to airframe production. Similarly, early propellers were carefully hand-fashioned from wood; again furniture manufacturers, including Hampton & Sons, Lambeth, London, were ideally placed to undertake this work (Fig 6.32).[47] By late 1916 it was recognised that greater efficiencies in production could be achieved by concentrating it in larger factories and on fewer aircraft types, and in January 1917 the Ministry of Munitions assumed responsibility for the supply of aircraft.[48] Three national factories were created: two in existing factories in Croydon, Greater London, and Heaton Chapel, Stockport, with a third purpose-built at Aintree, Liverpool, and managed by the Cunard Steamship Company (Fig 6.33). This had steel-framed workshops, electric lighting, heating from overhead pipes, belt-driven machinery and large open assembly

Fig 6.32
Hampton & Sons, Lambeth, London. A pre-war furniture works converted to the production of wooden propellers.
[BL23561/042]

Fig 6.33
National Aircraft Factory No 3, Aintree, Liverpool. By the time this photograph was taken in 1928, the works had been converted to silk production.
[EPW020354]

areas, while the adjacent race course was used for flight testing. It was also proposed to designate the Sopwith Company's factory at Richmond, Surrey, as the fourth national aircraft factory, but it remained under the management of the company, and in December 1918 a couple of works at Oldham, Lancashire, used for the assembly of American aircraft were designated as a national factory. In the event none of the national factories met expectations and very few aircraft were produced due to materials shortages, labour disputes and a lack of skilled staff.

The production of vital aircraft components was also brought under state control. Ash was the principal wood used for air frames, as it was in most railway carriages. Accordingly additional timber-drying capacity was created adjacent to the railway works at Swindon, Wiltshire, and Lancing, Sussex.[49] Mitchell, Shaw and Company's engine factory in a former printing machinery works at Hayes, Middlesex, was designated as a national aero-engine factory, and the Clément-Talbot automobile works at Ladbroke Grove, London, was converted for engine repair work. As demand grew later in the war for larger engines to power bombers, the Motor Radiator Manufacturing Company's works at Greet, Birmingham, and Sudbury, Suffolk (the latter sited in Radiator Road), were brought under state control.

Notwithstanding the increased use of aircraft for artillery spotting, balloons found a new role as anti-aircraft barrages. Additional balloon production capacity was provided by the acquisition of the Bohemia picture palace in Finchley, London.[50]

Local engineering works

Alongside the huge industrial enterprises represented by the naval dockyards, private shipyards, state arsenals and private armaments firms, Britain was able to draw on the resources, skills and expertise of many local manufacturers to supply war materiel. Most local communities were served by blacksmiths, some of whom had diversified to repair bicycles, cars and lorries. Many large market towns had engineering works manufacturing heavy agricultural equipment, including steam traction engines. The entrepreneurial engineers who owned or managed these works proved to be critical in responding with novel solutions to the challenges presented by the unforeseen conditions on the Western Front. Among the other belligerent nations this depth of industrialisation was unmatched, especially among the largely agrarian economies of Central and Eastern Europe.[51]

A measure of the contribution of civilian engineers and serving officers, many Royal Engineers, to the war effort is how their names quickly became synonymous with particular weapons: the Mills bomb, the Stokes mortar, the Livens projector and the enciphered Fullerphone.

Wireless communication, pioneered by Marconi in the last years of the 19th century, was quickly adopted by the leading navies, and networks of stations were established by the colonial powers to supplement the fixed telegraph cable communications. Largely through his Admiralty contracts, Marconi's business blossomed, and in 1912 he built an impressive new factory in New Street, Chelmsford, with a neo-baroque frontage and north-light production shops to the rear, an investment that would serve the company well during the war.

While many small workshops lacked the skills to assemble compete articles, they nevertheless often formed a vital part of the component supply chain. Some public schools even turned their engineering workshops over to war production. At Oundle, Northamptonshire, boys worked in shifts on its workshop lathes, producing 12,376 brass parts for torpedo gear for Messrs Peter Brotherhood in nearby Peterborough, as well as 32,008 steel tools for the Royal Arsenal and 1,393 horseshoes for the Munitions Board. Others made wooden screens for Duston Hospital.[52]

Steel helmets

In August 1914 the soldiers of most European armies wore cloth, felt, hardened leather or thin pressed metal helmets. It soon became clear these offered little protection against a hail of shrapnel and shell splinters. By early 1915 the French had begun to issue the Adrian helmet made from four steel stampings. The British followed suit, and by the summer production of a simpler helmet created by one pressing from a single piece of mild steel sheet was under way. In early 1916 the Germans introduced a *Stahlhelm* based on a medieval sallet helmet, a complex shape that required nine pressings.[53] By the end of the war the profile of each nation's helmet would become a distinctive identifier of allegiances, with British and American troops distinguished by a simple bowl-shaped helmet known as the 'Brodie helmet' after its inventor, John L Brodie of London, or more popularly the 'tin hat' or (when worn by officers) the 'battle bowler'.

The eminent Sheffield metallurgist Sir Charles Hadfield suggested tin hats might be more effective if they were made using harder manganese steel.[54] This alloy was only produced by Thomas Firth & Sons of Sheffield, and to increase its supply they shared their knowledge with the engineering firm William Beardmore, Glasgow, which in conjunction with a local rolling mill was able to produce the required type of steel. Pressing was undertaken by firms in Wolverhampton and Glasgow, and in Sheffield the munitions committee arranged for tableware presses to be converted to helmet production. Manufacture started in November 1915, and between them these works had the capacity to turn out around 100,000 helmets per week. It was soon noted that among troops equipped with helmets head wounds had been reduced by three-quarters. By the end of the war output had reached 7¼ million, including about 1½ million 'Doughboy helmets' supplied for American troops.[55]

Tanks

The invention of the internal combustion engine transformed warfare: it enabled the development of powered flight, the mechanisation of supply transport and, most significantly during the war, the development of self-propelled armoured vehicles – tanks. To disguise their true role, while they were in development the cover story was that they were 'water carriers for Mesopotamia', which was quickly abbreviated to 'tanks'. During the Boer War the British army had experimented with steam traction engines, but in the following years there were few attempts to mechanise military transport. In the months following the outbreak of war, trials were conducted with armoured cars, lorries and even buses; Rolls-Royce armoured cars went on to have some success, especially in the Middle East. To investigate machines that might be able to cross the pockmarked terrain of the Western Front and its barbed wire entanglements, Winston Churchill, First Lord of the Admiralty, established the Landships Committee in early 1915. Under its sponsorship, and after a number of false starts, William Tritton, managing director of an agricultural engineering firm, William Foster Company, Lincoln, working with Walter Wilson, a naval officer, developed the distinctive rhomboid-shaped tank with caterpillar tracks circling its hull (*see* Fig 2.28).[56] These features enabled it to meet the War Office's requirements of a machine that could mount a 1.37m parapet and cross a 2.5m wide trench. After successful demonstrations at Hatfield Park, Hertfordshire, initial orders were placed for 150 tanks; 25 were built by Fosters and the remainder by the railway workshops of the Metropolitan Carriage, Wagon and Finance Company, Oldbury, Birmingham. Further orders were later given to other established engineering works.[57]

Architecture and factory design

Frank Baines, an architect at the Office of Works with a distinguished pre-war career in the conservation of historic buildings, commented after the war that, despite having the resources of a great empire to draw on, speed and economy were the driving forces behind wartime factory construction.[58] In many industries and factories the initial response to the demands of increased production was to build ad hoc extensions to existing plant. As it became clear that the war would endure for some years and consume vast quantities of munitions, purpose-built factories were also required. Standards of construction depended on whether facilities were conceived as permanent establishments that would remain after the war, or semi-permanent or temporary structures built for the duration. Some factories, particularly for heavy engineering and the chemical industry, required robust structures and were unable to skimp on their needs for steel, concrete and bricks.

During the first year of the war the need for the strong state direction of the war effort gradually became clear. In some areas of factory design, especially relating to explosives manufacture, government officials were acknowledged experts, while in other aspects of industrial design expertise lay with the manufacturers. Most government building projects were managed by the Office of Works, and after the formation of the Ministry of Munitions it oversaw the design of many of the new national factories. While these departments designed factories directly funded and managed by the government, they do not appear to have offered generic plant designs to contractors. Instead, local managers or companies were appointed to design and manage factories, which resulted in a wide variety of layouts and building designs. New factories followed up-to-date principles of logically arranged mass production lines as espoused by Henry Ford in the United States (*see also* p 138). One such works was the Associated Equipment Company, Walthamstow, which was awarded an urgent contract to build motor lorries for the Russian government in anticipation of a major offensive in spring 1917. To hasten construction of the factory it was timber framed with hollow terracotta-block walls and an experimental corrugated asbestos roof. The production line comprised a moving platform (276ft long and 8ft wide [84.12m by 2.44m]) along which the lorries were built up as they moved along.[59]

In common with temporary army camps, cheap and quickly erected, single-storey timber-framed buildings were preferred that might be clad in corrugated iron or asbestos cement sheets, or timber weather boarding. Surprisingly, given its comparative cheapness and ease of use, concrete was seldom employed, and the buildings at Cliffe are rare examples (*see* Fig 6.14). At Holton Heath discarded pieces of cement with wire impressions testify to the use of cement rendering over steel mesh, while other buildings were constructed from concrete block (Fig 6.3 shows an example of such blockwork).[60] At White and Poppe's works in Coventry, a novel solution was employed to work around material and labour shortages. Four standard ranges for fuse filling were constructed using different methods and materials. The first had brick walls and piers rendered externally in cement, the second was formed of hollow brick walling with brick piers and an external render, the third was a concrete block with brick piers, an external render and internal hard plaster, and the fourth had a brick base with a timber frame and a weather

Fig 6.34
National Filling Factory No 14, Hereford, Rotherwas, Herefordshire. The headquarters building in neo-Georgian style was designed by Frank Baines.
[DP195747]

boarding covered in felt and lined internally with asbestos sheet; all had identical timber roofs.[61] A variety of industrial roofing styles were used, with the north-light roofs common in buildings sensitive to heat gain. Elsewhere, to reduce the consumption of steel and good quality timber, Belfast-truss roofs were preferred, employing standard cut timber fixed with nails and bolts. These roofs were generally curved, although pitched examples are also encountered. This was a flexible design that could be used to span a variety of building widths of up to about 50ft (15.24m), although the design made the introduction of roof lighting and driveshafts difficult.

In factories that were conceived as permanent or semi-permanent their official authority was often pronounced by impressive neo-Georgian-style administrative buildings. For instance, at Rotherwas, Baines designed a single-storey, brick office block with a central decorative portico featuring an ocular window surmounted by a clock tower and cupola (Fig 6.34). A similar feature was used at the main double-storey offices of His Majesty's Factory, Gretna. At Avonmouth the offices of the picric acid factory were housed in a grand two-storey building with dormers, wide projecting eaves and tall chimneys (Fig 6.35). The composition of the buildings might also be used to enhance the status of the entrance. At the ammonium nitrate factory, Stratton St Margaret (see Fig 6.5), the works was approached along a 30ft (9.14m) wide road that led to a rectangular courtyard, with the administrative offices to the east mirrored by a canteen to the west. To the south were cycle sheds and to the north a time office and garage stood either side of the main gate.[62] A similar scheme was used at Holton Heath, where the site was entered through impressive gate piers that gave access to a square with flag pole bounded on one side by an austere, double-storey, neo-Georgian-style administrative building, and on the other sides by single-storey laboratory buildings (Fig 6.36).

Welfare

Over the course of the Victorian era there had been a gradual improvement in industrial working conditions through various Factory Acts, philanthropic employers and the rise of trades unions. In the new century, in a drive to increase productivity within the munitions industry, theories of scientific management expounded by the American Frederick Taylor were increasingly applied. These included breaking down production into individual tasks which could be undertaken by relatively unskilled labour, a process known as dilution, as noted. Analysis was also undertaken of the health and well-being of the workforce and of how, for instance, better welfare and social facilities might contribute to higher productivity. This became an especial concern of the Ministry of Munitions as large numbers of women and boys entered industry.

The welfare cause was also supported by influential politicians, such as David Lloyd George, who were vocal advocates of the prohibition campaign against alcohol. As described elsewhere, in key munitions producing areas controls were placed on the sale of alcohol, and

Fig 6.35 (top)
His Majesty's Explosives Factory Avonmouth, Bristol. Headquarters of the picric acid factory.
[BB97/00117]

Fig 6.36 (above)
The Royal Naval Cordite Factory, Holton Heath, Dorset. The headquarters was designed by Sir Douglas Fox & Partners of London in 1916.
[BB94/16969]

greater provision was made in public houses for food preparation (*see* p 155). In smaller works, canteens might be no more than a mess room to warm up and consume food, while in large factories purpose-built canteens became commonplace. By the end of 1917 there were 700 canteens in the dockyards, national factories and controlled establishments.[63] Where new canteens were built they were light and well-ventilated, with some also doubling as places of entertainment with dance floors, a stage and piano (Fig 6.37). Within canteens the factory hierarchy was maintained with specific sections set aside for clerks, supervisors and the workforce, with further subdivisions according to gender. Food – meat, pies, fish, vegetables, potatoes and a sweet[64] – was prepared on an industrial scale, sometimes for up to 1,000 workers. To supplement food supplies at a number of factories, such as at White & Poppe's, virtually all the greengrocery required here by its three 2,500-seat canteens was grown on the premises, while at the Barnbow filling factory a herd of 120 cows was kept.[65] Out of working hours the well-being of the workforce was also catered for, and at Banbury, which was typical of many, there was a recreation club with a billiards table, and facilities for tennis, football and cricket.[66]

Even by the usual standards of Edwardian industry, munitions production was especially hazardous and the toxic effects of some chemicals were poorly understood. The tendency of picric acid and TNT to dye the skin and hair yellow, hence munitioneers' nickname 'canaries', was well known. A report in *The Lancet* in summer 1916 by two women doctors employed in munitions factories drew attention to the irritative and toxic symptoms of handling TNT.

Fig 6.37
Cunard's Shellworks, Liverpool, on 30 September 1917. One of the shells displayed on the canteen shelf survives in the Imperial War Museum's collection, with a note that it was the first 8in shell made by female operators.
[BL24001/032]

The exact causes were as yet obscure, but it was observed that good nutrition, including a 10-minute morning break for a 'snack', well-ventilated buildings and protective clothing all helped to maintain the health of the workforce.[67] These concerns were reflected in the provision of changing rooms, especially in explosives works, to prevent the introduction of contraband and contaminated clothing; they might also include washing facilities and baths. At the National Machine Gun Factory, the surviving welfare building includes male and female canteens, surgeries and a social club with an adjacent bowling green (Fig 6.38). First aid and medical centres were also provided at some of the larger factories. At Waltham Abbey a purpose-built Y-shaped, two-storey women's hospital (Fig 6.39) was constructed, and at Chilwell a dedicated medical centre with crosses picked out in brick on its gable and central tower.

The introduction of improved welfare measures wasn't met with universal approval. Workers often regarded the welfare supervisors with suspicion, seeing them as prying into their lives and undermining the role of trades unions to negotiate collective agreements. Some also preferred to continue eating their food at their machines, free from the gaze of their fellow workers.[68] Similarly, some employers resented the imposition by the Ministry of controlled working hours and the expense of welfare facilities, including the employment of unproductive labour in canteens.[69]

Housing

Many of the new factories employed hundreds, sometimes thousands, of people. Factories close to urban areas were able to draw on the local workforce, while those in less accessible locations needed to provide dedicated accommodation. One of the earliest estates was at Well Hall, Eltham, London, where 1,200 houses were completed by the end of 1915 to house workers

Fig 6.38
The National Machine Gun Factory, Burton-on-Trent, Staffordshire, 1917/18. Welfare building.
[DP188195]

Fig 6.39
Royal Gunpowder Factory Waltham Abbey, Essex. The Women's Hospital, quickly constructed with a timber frame and lightweight red asbestos roof tiles. To the rear was an operating room and two wards.
[BB92/26040]

from the Royal Arsenal (see Fig 7.6). Despite the pressures of wartime, the view was taken that the estate should be of a permanent character for continuing use after the war. Its design was overseen by Frank Baines of the Office of Works and was heavily influenced by London County Council's garden suburbs and contemporary Arts and Crafts Movement ideals. It featured curving roads, a central 'village green', and houses constructed in historically inspired designs in a variety of materials and styles. In 1916 Baines was also commissioned to design a similar garden village at Roe Green, Brent, north-west London, for the workers of the Aircraft Manufacturing Company. These pre-war ideals were challenged by Thomas Bennett, also of the Office of Works, who argued publicly in The Builder that with temporary wartime buildings the focus should be on the strictly necessary and functional, and accordingly housing should be planned on rectangular layouts, and curves and angles avoided. He did acknowledge some latitude might be required in the design of accommodation for more senior staff.[70]

A far more ambitious scheme was undertaken for the workers at Gretna where two new 'model' settlements were built at Gretna and Eastriggs. Construction was supervised by Raymond Unwin, who had previously worked on Letchworth Garden City and Hampstead Garden Suburb. Charles Voysey, a noted Arts and Crafts architect, was also involved. Gretna comprised 287 new houses and 29 hostels, as well as civic amenities including churches, police stations, a bank, post office and cinema. Architecturally it followed a restrained neo-Georgian style and was laid out on a rectilinear grid, with a central tree-lined avenue and generously wide side roads with grass verges.[71]

While many workers were accommodated in architect-designed permanent homes, many more were housed in temporary wooden huts. At Woolwich these included a novel A-framed, or triangular section, form of 'cottage bungalow' designed by H E Pritchard. One of the largest temporary settlements served the National Projectile Factory at Birtley, Durham. This factory was staffed by Belgian refugees, and accommodation was required for about 6,000 people. A new town named Elizabethville, after the Belgian queen, followed a rectangular grid and comprised almost entirely timber huts. Facilities included village offices, police and fire station, church, schools for 700 children, provision and meat market, 22 sleeping hutments, 24 sleeping hostels, 3 dining halls, laundry and baths, hospital with laundry, isolation ward, nurses' pavilion, disinfector and mortuary, staff hostel, 6 bungalows for officials, 2 presbyteries, 532 three-bedroom cottages, 342 two-bedroom cottages, sewage disposal works, 17 foremen's cottages and cemetery (Fig 6.40). Despite its frontier town appearance, it attracted some jealousy from locals who complained about apparent favourable allocations of rationed foodstuffs and the provision of indoor toilets and hot and cold running water, facilities missing from many local working-class homes.[72]

Conclusions

In August 1914 few anticipated the eventual scale of the unfolding conflict. The initial responses to the supply of munitions were ad hoc and pragmatic; existing factories were extended and other works adapted to war production. In 1915 the supply of armaments was brought under the centralised management of the Ministry of Munitions, which directed about 200 National Factories and 6,000 Controlled Establishments. Despite the watchwords of 'speed and economy' in wartime factory design, many were laid out to the most modern principles; administrative buildings, in particular, maintained some architectural pretension. Through government investment new technologies such as powered flight and wireless communications advanced rapidly; the tank was one of the most significant innovations. Most importantly the country learnt the lessons of how to provision its armed forces to fight a modern industrialised war, and 20 years later an efficient system of standardised factories and production processes were ready to meet new challenges.

Fig 6.40
Birtley, Durham. Two of the last surviving buildings from Elizabethville, built to house Belgian munitions workers.
[DP174530]

7

Civic and civilian architecture

Katie Carmichael

The perception that civilian and civic building stopped during the First World War is erroneous – while construction declined, a surprising number of new civil buildings were erected between 1914 and 1918. Some were started before the outbreak of war, others were halted and finished when peace returned, but still more were planned, begun and finished all within that period – including some significant and sizeable examples. In addition to new buildings, the war left other physical traces of its presence in the historic environment – changes that would have been felt in almost every town and village across the country. Historic properties were damaged, others were adapted, parks and common spaces were turned over to the war effort, and repairs and alterations were made that reflected the concerns and regulations of the day.

The building trade was in an unusual position during the war. Although 'building is one of the first trades to suffer in a great war'[1] due to reduced general construction levels coupled with increased material and labour costs, what work there was gave plentiful employment for the workforce that remained – so much so that restrictions were enforced to ensure that labour and materials were available for the most important government schemes. Some construction projects struggled to attract the necessary labour, particularly following the introduction of conscription in March 1916, and for the first time it became necessary to advertise for workers – one contractor used cinemas to implore: 'ARTIZANS AND LABOURERS! Come and help your country by building huts for housing the Army.'[2] Although unpopular, the use of female labour (Fig 7.1) was seen as necessary and criticism was mitigated by 'paying them the same rates as the men, which the men regard as a safeguard against their employment in slacker times'.[3] As well as problems attracting and paying labourers, builders also had to contend with rising material costs – how should they allow for these in contracts and tenders at a time when private investment in construction was decreasing and the value of property dropping? All materials rose in price from late 1914 but some, such as downpipes and gutters, had risen by more than 200 per cent by the end of 1916.[4] Meanwhile, the public were encouraged to invest any spare capital in war loans which offered a high – guaranteed – rate of return, thus diverting funds which would otherwise have been available for speculative developments.

The impact of the outbreak of war on the property market was immediate, and investment in existing building stock fell: sales at the London Auction Mart for 1914 totalled over £1.7m in the first seven months of 1914, and

Fig 7.1
Female bricklayers at work on a site in Lancashire during the First World War. Women worked alongside male labourers for the first time during the war.
[© IWM Q 028190]

just £148,000 in the five months following the outbreak of war.[5] Despite statements such as 'from the time when the magnitude of the issues at stake was recognised, who could dream of launching out into new undertakings?',[6] the lists of proposed new buildings and contracts for tender in *The Builder* do not noticeably diminish until late August 1915. By the second quarter of 1915 the estimated value of building plans submitted to councils (outside London) was down 51 per cent on the same period in 1914, with a 64 per cent decrease in dwellings.[7] By 1917 the situation was more pronounced, with a 96 per cent decrease in the number of churches, schools and public buildings being built and a 93 per cent reduction in the number of houses. Even after accounting for the 43 per cent or so increase in factories and warehouses, the overall reduction in the number of construction projects was still around 56 per cent.[8]

Materials and regulations

From such dire statistics it would be reasonable to assume that almost all non-war-related building work stopped, but while some schemes were necessarily postponed or suspended, there was a strong argument in favour of continuing to build as normal during the war, where costs allowed. Given that a successful outcome of the war was seen as assured,[9] it was argued that not only did construction provide employment, but 'public money will be saved, for contracts made after the war will be based on higher rates'.[10] Builders were obliged to stand by their original quotes, despite rising wages and costs, so many councils and individuals preferred to carry on with construction projects while they could – presumably seeing the risk of damage from air raids as insignificant when compared to the money that might be saved. Indeed, shortly after the outbreak of war the Local Government Board 'urged those communities which were considering housing and other utilitarian schemes to expedite them',[11] which resulted in the number of applications dealt with in the seven months ending in January 1915 being higher than in any equivalent period, and the Office of Works expanded to meet demand.[12]

The number, type and styles of buildings constructed during the war changed in line with regulations. The most significant impact on the building trade followed an order issued by the Ministry of Munitions on 20 July 1916 – no building or construction work exceeding £500 in cost (Fig 7.2) or using any structural steel was to commence or continue without licence from the Minister, but work could continue until a licence was refused. At the time it was not possible to say what the impact on the building trade would be – whether most building applications would be refused, or if it was simply a measure to allow the Ministry to track where labour and materials were, should they be needed. Indeed, the enforcement of the order was somewhat variable. In April 1917 contractors working on 1 Wardour Street in London, having been refused permission for the original estimated cost of works (around £3000), were found guilty of altering the plans to show the cost as only £450 and handed fines and costs totalling over £350.[13] Just one month later, in May 1917, the Western Packing Case Company built a factory and sawmills in Bootle, Liverpool (Fig 7.3), using structural steel and at an estimated cost of over £11,000, but were fined just £50.[14] Given the value of the building, such a small fine was unlikely to be a deterrent – it seems likely that leniency was given in this case because the company was providing boxes exclusively to the British American Tobacco Company, which primarily provided goods to the army and navy.

One consequence of the war and the resulting restrictions on building materials was that two very distinct forms of buildings became commonplace – temporary buildings, often in the form of wooden hutments, and fireproof buildings with reinforced concrete floors. Temporary buildings met the need for rapidly erected buildings intended for a specific purpose for the duration of the war only, with prefabricated, standardised

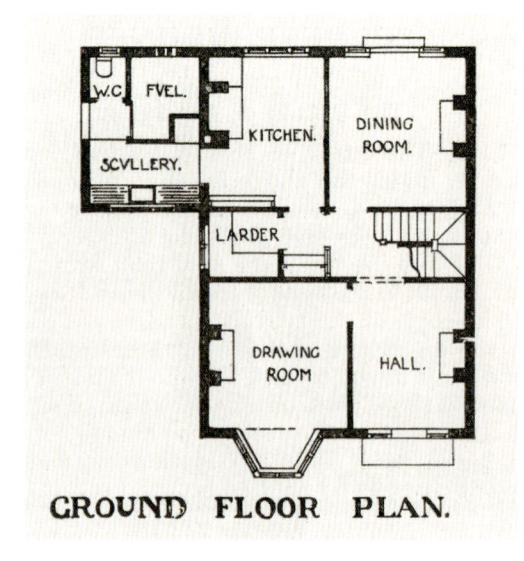

Fig 7.2
Eastcote, 36 St Pauls West, Dorking, Surrey. Built in 1915 at a cost of £749, this relatively modest house has four bedrooms and a simple plan to a design by A C Morris Edwards, showing that very little would have been possible for £500.
[The Builder, CXIII 14 September 1917, 154]

Fig 7.3
Sawmill, Sea View Road, Bootle, Merseyside. Built at a cost of over £11,000 for the Western Packing Case Company; the company was fined for the unsanctioned use of structural steel.
[DP174547]

wooden huts the preferred option. While generally utilitarian these buildings were not without merit. *The Builder* ran an article saying:

> Londoners hardly realise what a transformation scene is springing up in their midst through the large numbers of temporary structures being erected in the parks and gardens and amongst our crowded City thoroughfares ... the result in many cases is far from unpleasing, and does something to ameliorate the austerities of stone and brickwork ... An element of very agreeable picturesqueness and relief has, at all events, been added to our city views in all directions.[15]

Not all temporary buildings were simple and cheap to make, however, and the cost of two notable examples rose from around 4.5d/ft on average to 11d and 12.3d respectively. The first was the erection of buildings on the roof of an existing house in Whitehall Place, London; the other, a small building in the garden of 10 Downing Street for the Prime Minister's secretaries – the excessive cost was due to the work being completed in seven days, which meant working overnight.[16] Some of the most celebrated temporary buildings of the war were the Young Men's Christian Association huts which sprang up across London to provide a place of rest and refreshment for servicemen. Eagle Hut in Aldwych was designed for American and Allied servicemen and operated from mid-August 1917. The hut served around 2 million meals in the two years it operated and was run by 800 volunteers – most of them women. It included 410 beds for servicemen staying overnight and also had a billiard/recreation room and a concert hall. Other notable YMCA huts included Beaver Hut on the Strand, opened by Queen Alexandra in 1916 for the use of Canadian soldiers,[17] and Washington Inn on St James's Square (Fig 7.4). Opened on 24 June 1918 for American Army and Navy Officers, the Washington Inn's distinctive layout followed the plan of the existing octagonal gardens. It contained a lounge, dining hall, bathrooms with slipper baths, bedrooms, kitchen and a quiet room all radiating from a covered corridor and 'rustic' pergola.[18]

Conversely, and as a direct result of the use of such large quantities of timber, the war forced the use of relatively new materials and methods:

> The period of dear timber will drive architects to the use of substitutes, such as concrete, iron, plaster, etc., and fire-resisting buildings will thus possibly become the rule instead of the exception.[19]

- Victor boiler
- Shower
- WC
- Bath
- Basin
- Water tank

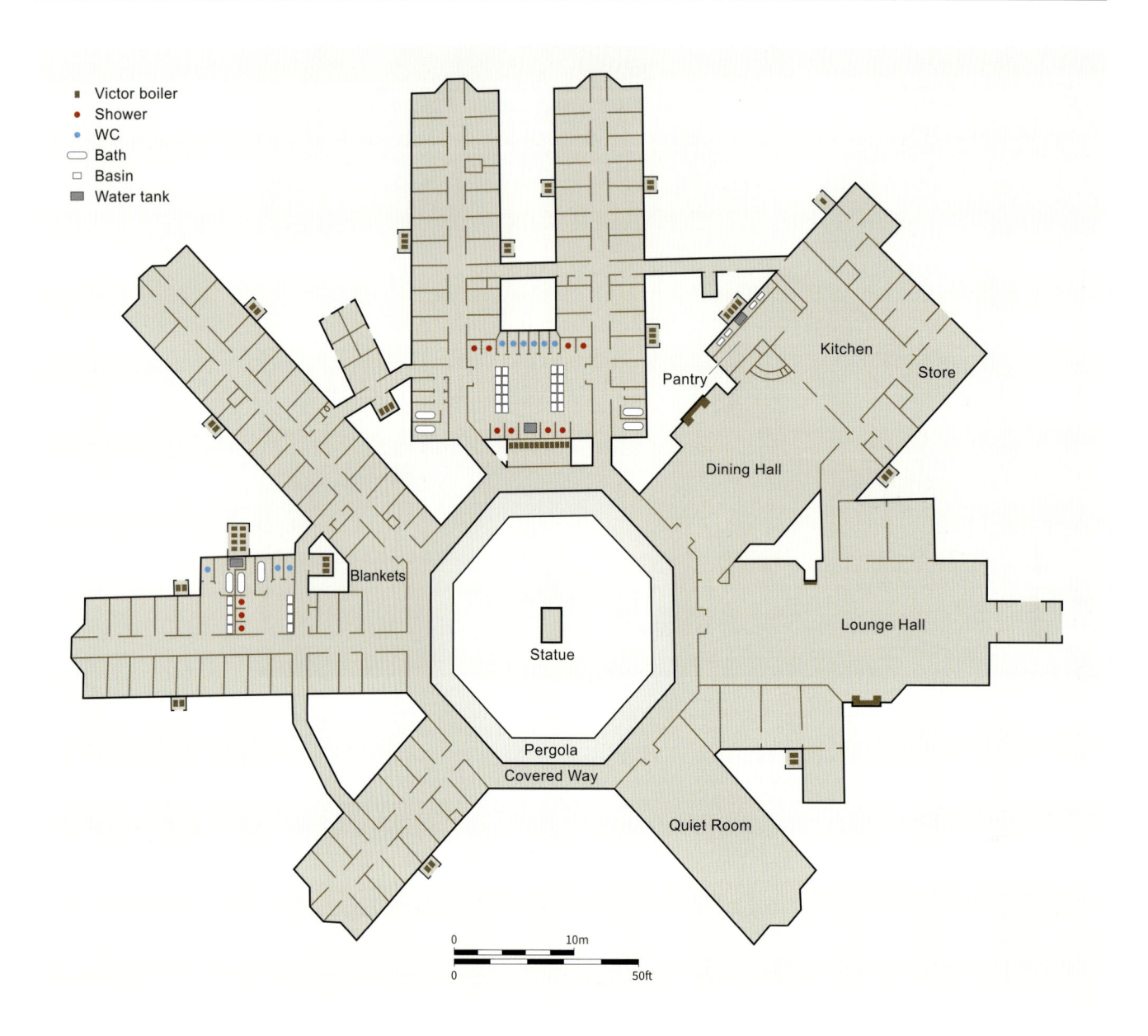

Fig 7.4
The Washington Inn, St James's Square, London. One of London's YMCA huts, it owed its unusual plan-form to the existing layout of the gardens and was designed around the equestrian statue of William III.
[Redrawn from The Builder, *19 July 1918, 40]*

As predicted, this led to new styles of buildings with larger, more open spaces thanks to steel frames and concrete floors. Reinforced concrete had the added benefit of resisting the new threat of exploding and incendiary bombs better than brick buildings, but was found to be of little protection against penetration from unexploded bombs. Consideration was given to a possible requirement for buildings to be bomb-resistant, but the costs of doing so would have far outweighed the cost of rebuilding damaged structures, and it was feared their design would 'adversely affect the architectural features and aspects of our magnificent buildings and towns, and for that reason alone is to be unhesitatingly condemned';[20] notably no mention was made of the potential to save lives. As well as structural innovation, improvements in sanitation, heating and ventilation were continuous – no doubt helped by the capturing of enemy patents, lists of which were published in *The Builder* from January to June 1915.

The use and treatment of timber, much of it imported by sea and prioritised for use on the Western Front, became the focus of orders by the Ministry of Munitions throughout 1917. From 1 April all stocks of soft wood were to be returned to the Director of Timber Supplies and only 1 per cent of the stock was to be sold in any given month, unless required for government contracts or work of national importance.[21] In June all powered machinery for cutting or work-

Civic and civilian architecture

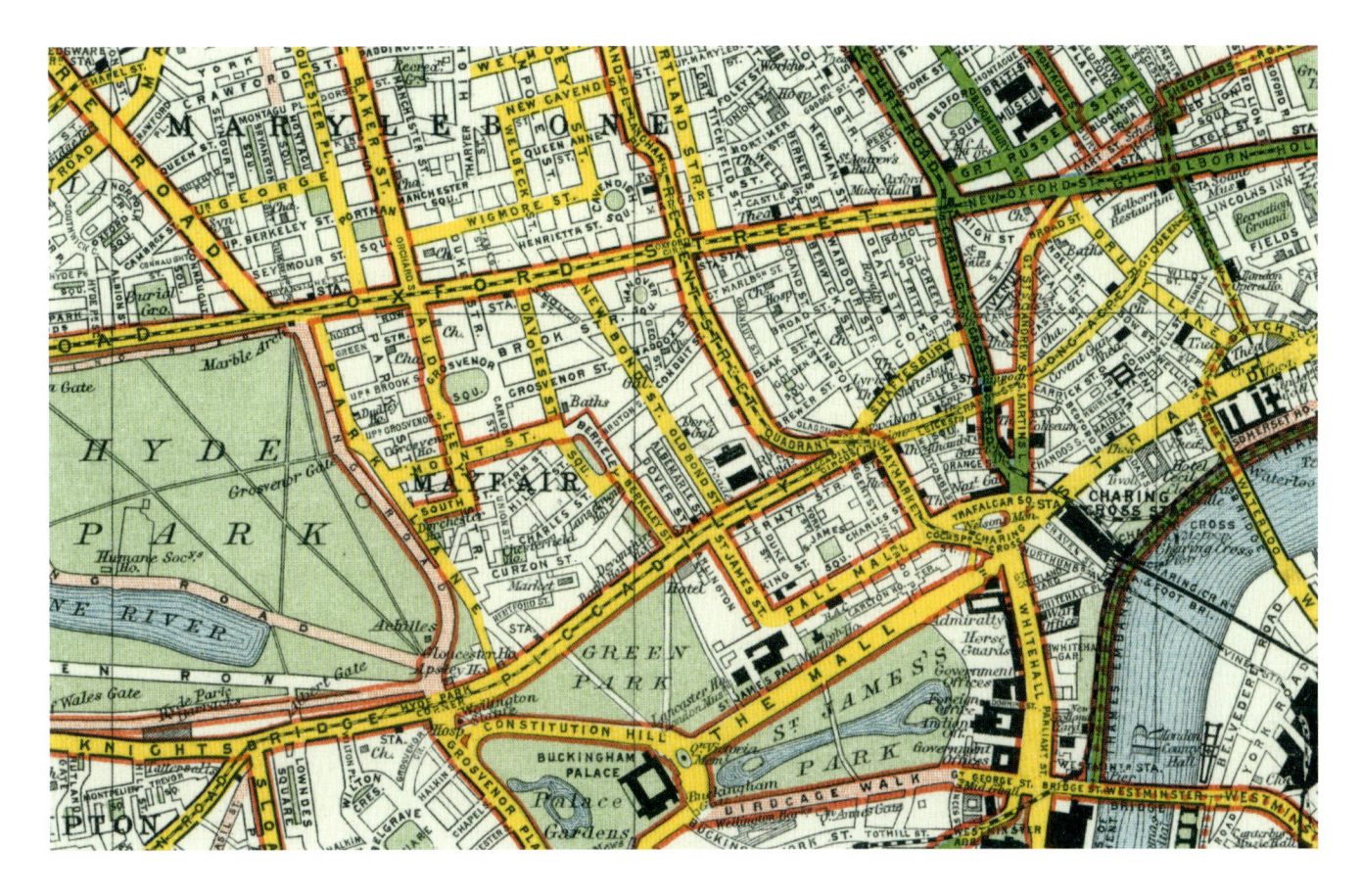

ing wood, and all accessory machines for their maintenance, were classed as war materials, the purchase of which required express permission.[22] In July came an order prohibiting use of creosote without a licence.[23] The severity of the timber shortage by July 1917 also led to a circular to local authorities urging that timber should only be used 'for the most essential needs' and that the replacement of wooden paving setts on roads should be delayed. If unavoidable then the resurfacing of roads should be carried out in asphalt, or by replacing sound wooden paving with stone setts and using the paving for repairing worn-out sections.[24] Timber setts had been widely used for road surfaces and many of London's primary roads were paved in this way (Fig 7.5). The dangers of roads paved with highly flammable creosoted timber became all too apparent early in the war: following a Zeppelin raid in London on 1 June 1915, *The Globe* newspaper reported 'another bomb dropped in a neighbouring thoroughfare and set fire to the wooden paving blocks in the roadway'.[25]

By April 1918 the Ministry of Munitions had issued the Building Bricks Control Order 1918, preventing the sale or delivery of bricks without a permit.[26] This was followed in July by the cement order.[27] In October 1918 it was reported that:

> The War cabinet has recently ordered that the War Priorities Committee should issue instructions that no new works should be started except such as are immediately necessary for winning the war, and that any exceptions to this rule shall be ... only on the personal authority of the Minister of the Department in question.[28]

Housing

Despite increasingly restrictive regulations, buildings of almost every type and style were built, with the construction of houses given particular importance. There was an acknowledged acute lack of housing before the outbreak of war, brought about largely by the 'crushing blow' of the Finance Act of 1909.[29] The war and consequent need for workers' housing further exacerbated the issue – in Barnsley, for instance, home of two National Shell Factories, only seven houses were built in 1916.[30] A report in *The Architect* in November 1915 estimated that

Fig 7.5
Bartholomew's Road Surface Map of London, 1922. Wooden roads are shown in yellow, asphalt in green and macadam in pink.
[© National Library of Scotland]

151

'there is to-day a shortage of 400,000 houses in this country, and that this shortage is increasing at the rate of 90,000 houses a year'.[31] The problems were threefold: the influx of large numbers of workers to certain locations; the demolition, where necessary, of existing housing to make way for war-related building; and the lack of speculative building brought about by the shortage of materials and labour available for non-war-related construction. In most areas demand far outstripped supply and houses were spoken for as soon as their construction was announced, with desperate workers even offering a monetary reward to anyone who found them suitable accommodation at the right price.[32]

A number of speculative developments and private houses were built, but often it fell to the government and employers to provide the mass housing required. The government tried to address the crisis by building housing estates specifically for munitions workers – including the Well Hall (originally Progress) Estate in Eltham, for workers at the Royal Arsenal in Woolwich (Fig 7.6). Designed by Frank Baines, it is a very fine early example of garden suburb townscape design; in 1915 over 1,000 houses were constructed in just 10 months. The work ran over budget and involved the labour of more than 5,000 men, with at one point houses being completed at the rate of one every two hours.[33]

Clearly work on such a scale was not sustainable or affordable, and later estates were simpler and less ambitious in design. Given the pressures involved, it is perhaps unsurprising that certain compromises were made – in the case of Well Hall some of the roads are only 30ft (9m) wide, a contravention of the London Building Act of 1844, while the Coventry Corporation scheme for 600 houses for munitions workers was passed despite the fact 'they were not strictly in accordance with the by-laws'.[34] Roe Green Village in Hendon, north London (1916–18), is a later garden village by Frank Baines, designed for the workers of the nearby aircraft factory and described as 'a standard which is good without being extravagant'.[35] In Longbridge, Birmingham, Austin Village consisted of 200 prefabricated houses shipped over from America and erected alongside 50 brick-built houses in 1917 for workers at the Austin Motor Company. Other developments for individual companies, both in 1915, included over 200 houses for Horden Collieries at Blackhall Colliery, Hartlepool,[36] and the second phase of Vickerstown on Walney Island, Barrow-in-Furness, for employees of the Vickers shipyards.[37]

Houses of every class were built during the war, and occasional references to identifiable 'normal' housing can be found, including the development of Engayne Gardens, Upminster, west London, in 1918, and a private housing development at Brook Street Hill, Brentwood, Essex, in 1915. Generally, however, larger and more unusual houses tend to be the best documented and identifiable. These include:

Fig 7.6
Well Hall Estate, Eltham, London. Designed for munitions workers, the estate was laid out to pre-war garden city principles, reflecting Baines's Arts and Crafts background. It was conceived as an 'old English village' with weather-boarded and tile-hung housing with roughcast finishes set on winding roads.
[BB96/00227]

Fig 7.7 (left)
Hindhead Court, Haslemere, Surrey, by John H Howard, 1916. Now part of the Royal Junior School.
[BL23406A]

Fig 7.8 (below)
No 19 Weymouth Street, London, by Wills, Anderson and Kaula, 1916. A typical large neoclassical house in Portland stone with rusticated banding.
[BL23847]

Hindhead Court, Haslemere, Surrey (Fig 7.7); 42–4 Hertford Street, London; 8 Queen Anne Street, Westminster; 19 Weymouth Street, London (Fig 7.8); Herons House, Ongar, Essex (Fig 7.9); and Gates House, Wyldes Close, London (Fig 7.10).

Despite calls for restraint in spending, dress and general consumption of goods, it is clear that much non-essential work was carried out during the war and interior redecoration work continued, for, as an article in *The Builder* rationalised: 'Some interior decoration must also be carried out, on the principle that, although in wartime we are content to wear old clothes, there is a limit to shabbiness.'[38] Many houses were thus extended or otherwise improved, including 78 Derngate in Northampton – a Georgian house which was extended and redecorated by Charles Rennie Mackintosh in 1916–17 (Fig 7.11). The order books for the Oxford Street decorating company Cowtan & Sons offer a fascinating insight into the life of the upper classes at this time. An entry for July 1915 shows that Mrs Asquith, the Prime Minister's wife, ordered 36 yds (33m) of gold silk for the drawing room of 10 Downing Street, and another 30 yds (27m) of fabric for their country residence at Sutton Courtenay, Oxfordshire, in March 1916. Other entries show that in many cases whole residences were being redecorated and refurbished, a number by individuals fleeing Germany.

Fig 7.9
Herons House, Ongar, Essex, by Courtenay Constantine, 1914. Now called Folyats, Herons House was highly unusual in being constructed from timber panels set within a steel frame.
[DP217135]

Fig 7.10
Gates House, Wyldes Close, Barnet, London, by T Laurence Dale, 1915, with a hipped clerestory lookout and first-storey balcony. The entrance porch has a stone panel inscribed 'Hark Hark to the Lark as Heaven's Gate Sings / Gates House 1915'.
[DP177798]

Civic and civilian architecture

Fig 7.11
No 78 Derngate, Northampton, Northamptonshire. The extension of 1916–17 is thought to be a joint design by Charles Rennie Mackintosh, W J Bassett-Lowke (the homeowner) and the local architect Alexander Ellis Anderson. [Courtesy of the 78 Derngate Northampton Trust]

Leisure

Although ostentatious or frivolous spending did continue to some extent, the vast majority of buildings constructed or extended during the war were necessary in some way, meeting the requirements for a licence where necessary. Leisure facilities continued to be important during the war – in addition to the YMCA huts built specifically for soldiers, a number of public houses, restaurants, theatres and cinemas were erected for the benefit of munitions workers and the general public. The Charter House Hotel in Coventry opened in 1915 and was designed in the popular pre-war Tudor Revival style,[39] while in Carlisle the government bought *c* 340 licensed premises between 1916 and 1918 in what became known as the State Management Scheme, which also ran in the vicinity of the Royal Small Arms Factory in Enfield. Its aim was to reduce the levels of alcohol consumption by introducing seating and removing external advertising – unsuitable premises were closed and, occasionally, new ones built.

Private restaurants and cafes continued to open in the early years of the war, one of the most celebrated being Deller's Café in Exeter (Fig 7.12), while Lyons opened a number of new tea rooms across London in 1915–16, including Avon House on Oxford Street and 211–13 Regent Street.[40] By 1917, however, a very different type of restaurant emerged in response to rationing and dwindling imports, National Kitchens (or Restaurants) (Fig 7.13), which sold healthy and nourishing food which was cheaply priced and eaten communally; by the end of the war some 363 were officially registered.[41] New cinemas erected in 1915–16 included examples in Accrington, Rishton (Fig 7.14) and Irlam in Lancashire; Chelmsford in Essex; Wardour Street in London; and Withernsea in Yorkshire. In Dover, cinemas were granted permission to open on Sunday evenings for the benefit of soldiers,[42] and many screened official propaganda and recruitment films. Official confirmation that films were being created for propaganda purposes came with the creation of the War Office Cinematograph Committee in November 1916, but many films distributed before that date had clear messages encouraging people to enlist or to take up jobs in munitions factories.

Cultural enrichment through access to art galleries, libraries and museums remained a priority. The Westbourne Carnegie library in Bournemouth opened in 1915,[43] and Shipley's neoclassical art gallery in Gateshead in 1917 (Fig 7.15).[44] In London the South Library on Essex Road, Islington, was built in 1915,[45] as was a combined library and museum in Barrow-in-Furness. Localised pressure on educational

Fig 7.12 (right) Deller's Café, Bedford Street, Exeter, Devon. Designed by Hyam and Hobgen and opened in December 1916, this had a Jacobean revival exterior with a grand baroque interior, boasting a ballroom and ornately decorated balconies around the main atria. Referenced in Agatha Christie's The Sittaford Mystery *(1931), it was destroyed by bombing in 1942.*
[OP31439]

Fig 7.13 (below) Nos 33–8 New Bridge Street, London. The first National Restaurant opened in 1918 under the auspices of the Ministry of Food. It was developed out of charitable soup kitchens, with food self-service and prepared in sight of diners.
[BL24272]

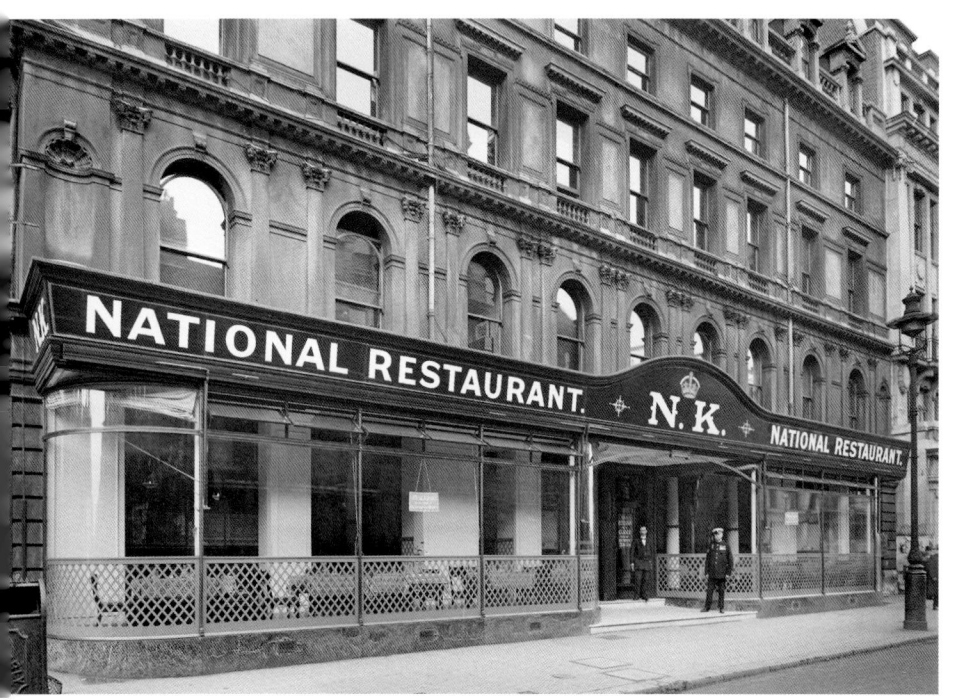

establishments meant that new facilities were required. One of the smallest and most unusual built during the war was the Strike School in Burston, Norfolk (Fig 7.16), which opened in May 1917 to enable the continued teaching of local pupils following the dismissal of their teachers in 1914 and an ensuing strike in their support.[46] Larger examples included Wimborne Infant and Junior School, Portsmouth (1914–16),[47] the Francis Holland School, Marylebone, London (1915), and St Hugh's College, Oxford (1914–16).[48]

Before the war Blackpool, Lancashire, was one of the premier holiday destinations for people from northern industrial towns. Its position on the west coast meant it was seen as safe – it even dared to continue displaying its famous Illuminations despite an Admiralty request for coastal towns to reduce seafront lighting, a fact that shocked many visitors.[49] Throughout the war the town continued to enjoy economic prosperity. Its fortunes were further bolstered

Civic and civilian architecture

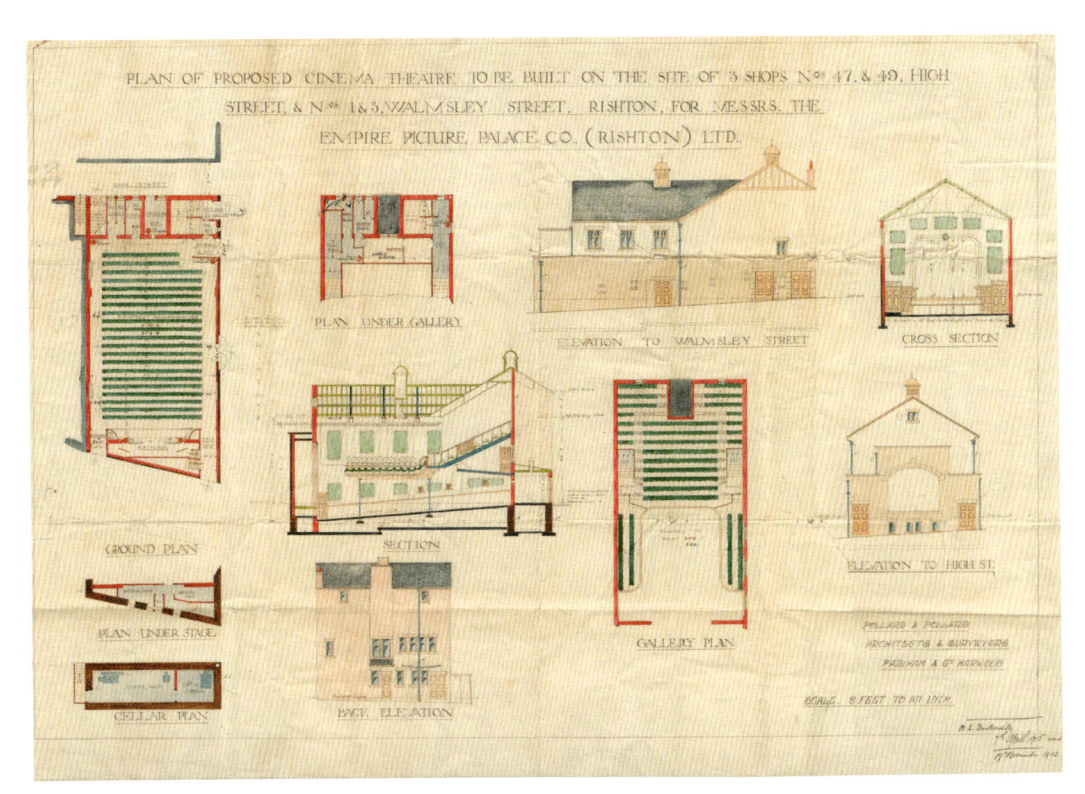

Fig 7.14
Nos 47–9 High Street, Rishton, Lancashire. Plans and amendments for Rishton cinema (later known as the Regal Picture Palace) by W E Bickerdike were approved on 7 April and 17 November 1915.
[Lancashire Record Office]

Fig 7.15
Prince Consort Road, Shipley, Gateshead. Shipley's Grade II listed art gallery was designed by Arthur Stockwell. The two main sculptures by W Birnie Rhind depict the Sciences and Arts.
[DP174573]

by government allowances for sheltering 2,000 Belgian refugees and over 10,000 troops from the winter of 1914–15 onwards. Despite all predictions to the contrary, the August bank holiday of 1918 was one of the busiest seasons on record, with the resort full beyond capacity, visitors forced to sleep outdoors and 30 military bakers brought in to help feed the swollen populace.[50] The war was never far away, and in 1916 a system of practice trenches was dug just off the promenade in Watson Road Park; it was opened as a tourist attraction by recuperating soldiers, with money raised going to help fund treatment of injured troops.

Fig 7.16
Church Green, Burston, Norfolk. The Strike School opened in 1917. The front wall contains stones inscribed with the names of the 83 subscribers from across the world who funded the building, including Leo Tolstoy the younger.
[DP217149]

157

Legacies of the First World War

Religion

Fig 7.17 Horsell Common, Woking, Surrey. A man in traditional Indian dress stands inside the newly completed Muslim Burial Ground. [BL23738/006]

Religion remained for many an important focus of everyday life and various religious institutions were built or extended. Examples completed in 1915 alone include: St Wilfred's Catholic Church in Newington, London;[51] the Gardiner Memorial Hall in Burwell, Cambridgeshire;[52] the Lifford Memorial Hall in Broadway, Worcestershire;[53] St Cuthbert's Church in Portsmouth;[54] and St Barnabas Vicarage in Newcastle upon Tyne.[55] Building work on Liverpool's Grade I listed Anglican Cathedral by Giles Gilbert Scott continued, with the chancel and chapter house described as almost complete in May 1915, and work on the transepts/central crossing under way.[56] Other notable examples include St Mary's Church in Hull by Temple Moore (1915–16)[57] and St Germain's Church in Edgbaston, Birmingham, by Edwin Francis Reynolds (1915–17).[58] In addition to churches, a number of synagogues were built, including the Western Synagogue in Alfred Place, Camden, London, of 1915.[59] To meet the cultural needs of Indian soldiers (see Fig 9.10) who died of their wounds, a purpose-built Muslim Burial Ground, designed by T Herbert Winney, India Office Surveyor, was completed at Woking, Surrey, in 1917 (Fig 7.17). Special crematoria for Hindu and Sikh troops were established at Netley and Brockenhurst, Hampshire, and at Patcham, Sussex. At the latter a memorial Chattri (a domed pavilion), designed by E C Henriques of Mumbai, was completed in 1921, incorporating the concrete slab on which the cremations had taken place.

Commerce

Commerce continued to drive the economy, and companies invested accordingly; consequently, many of the grandest buildings constructed during the war were offices and shops. In major cities these were overwhelmingly built from steel frames with Portland stone facings and favoured neoclassical designs. Perhaps the most famous is one of Liverpool's 'Three Graces' on George's Pier Head – the Cunard Building, intended to house the offices and passenger facilities for the Cunard line. Although building work began in 1912, construction continued after the outbreak of war and the building opened officially on 12 June 1916. The war is referenced in the shields on the Pier Head elevation (Fig 7.18), which contain the arms of the Allies. Examples in London include 70–1 New Bond Street (1915), decorated with figures of Science, Commerce and Art (Fig 7.19); 74 Coleman Street (1916); and the original central section of Heal's department store on Tottenham Court Road (1914–17). The famous spiral staircase at Heal's is not in fact wooden: the treads and risers are all of concrete, disguised by moulding the soffit of the steps in the concrete and using oak on the treads and risers.

Blackfriars House, New Bridge Street (1915–16), is more unusual for having a white majolica façade, rather than the pervasive Portland stone, while the showrooms and offices for the Continental Tyre and Rubber Company on Thurloe Place in Chelsea (1915–18) favoured red brick with stone detailing, in a florid free-baroque style. One of the most striking examples of a commercial premise is Radiant House on Mortimer Street, Westminster (1914–15), with its glazed turquoise tiles and white faience (Fig 7.20).[60] Outside London, classical influences

158

Civic and civilian architecture

Fig 7.18
George's Pier Head, Liverpool, Merseyside. One of Liverpool's famous 'Three Graces', the Cunard Building was built between 1912 and 1916, with the Allied Arms incorporated into the Pier Head façade.
[DP174550]

Fig 7.19
Nos 70–1 New Bond Street, London, by F P Palgrave, as photographed in 1920. The final design was an amendment of the proposed plan of January 1915.
[BL25069]

continued to dominate steel-framed structures. In Leicestershire the 1915 premises for Coalville Working Men's Co-operative Society (Fig 7.21) was built from red brick with stone detailing, Ionic pilasters and Diocletian windows. Another Co-operative Society store, in Upper Parliament Street, Nottingham (1916), was designed in a Renaissance style with terracotta facings. The Sheffield Telegraph and Star building (1916) on Sheffield's High Street is an elaborate baroque-revival-style edifice with a faience-covered façade, topped by a lantern and dome (Fig 7.22).

One of the most important steel-framed buildings constructed during the war was Holland House on Bury Street, in the City of London (Fig 7.23). Grade II* listed, it was built between 1914 and 1916 from designs by Hendrik Petrus Berlage, a prominent Dutch architect. It was commissioned and built for W H Müller, a Dutch company with shipping interests which, being neutral, had the capital and means to invest in such a large project. The Delft bricks on the façade were sent to London on the firm's ships in the middle of the war, and even given priority over other cargoes.

Another building which demonstrated the confidence of a number of firms at this time was the Woolworths on Ramsgate High Street, Kent (Fig 7.24). Despite the inevitable disruption

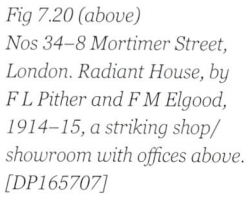

*Fig 7.20 (above)
Nos 34–8 Mortimer Street, London. Radiant House, by F L Pither and F M Elgood, 1914–15, a striking shop/showroom with offices above.
[DP165707]*

*Fig 7.21 (right)
Nos 75–81 Belvoir Road, Coalville, Leicestershire. Coalville Working Men's Co-operative Society, designed by Thomas Ignatius McCarthy of Coalville. The date stone was carved from Rowsley stone by Thomas Bambury of Leicester.
[Courtesy of NW Leicestershire District Council]*

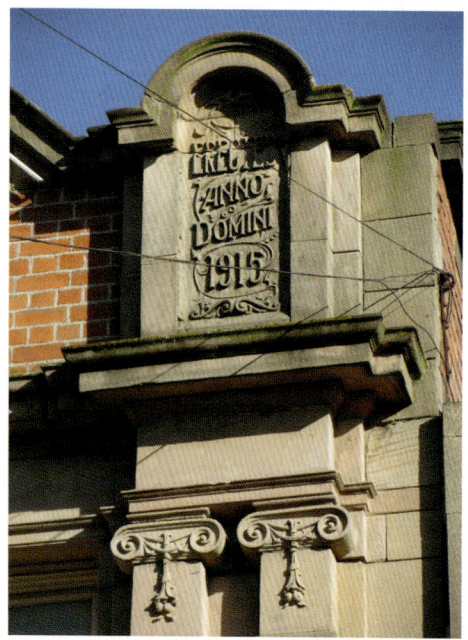

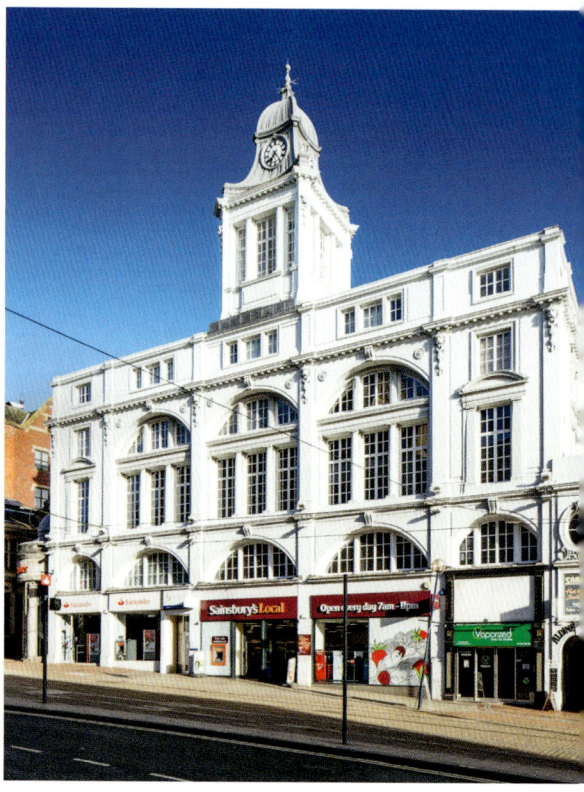

suffered by building trades, this was one of several new-build Woolworths stores completed in the first two years of the war – plans for the Putney store are dated 13 October 1914, just two months after the declaration of war[61] – and Woolworths more than doubled its number of stores in the UK during the course of the war. Unusually, the Ramsgate store was being built in 1916 on the site of a hotel which had been damaged by a Zeppelin raid in 1915.[62] Boots the Chemist similarly saw the war as a time to invest in new or improved building stock, including stores in Bristol, Eastbourne, Evesham, Tiverton, Luton and Torquay.

Statements such as 'The Great War forced a lull in both bank amalgamations and building activity'[63] have gone widely unchallenged. While the number of banks built during the war did decrease, banking and insurance firms were well placed to invest in construction. Phoenix House on King William Street, London, was begun in 1914 for the Phoenix Assurance Company (Fig 7.25). Designed in the ubiquitous classical Renaissance style from Portland stone, the building cost £533,000 and boasted lavish interiors. However, when it opened in 1915 the columns and pilasters in the main rooms, including the banking hall of the National Bank of Egypt, which occupied one corner of the building, were

Civic and civilian architecture

Fig 7.22 (far left)
Nos 13–23 High Street, Sheffield. The Sheffield Telegraph and Star building of 1916 is an unusual example of the baroque-revival- style.
[DP174553]

Fig 7.23 (left)
Nos 1–4 Bury Street, London. Holland House, a steel-framed building constructed between 1914 and 1916, is the only English commission by Hendrik Petrus Berlage.
[DP177795]

Fig 7.24 (below)
Nos 12–14 High Street, Ramsgate, Kent. A Woolworth's store built in the space created by the destruction of an existing building by a Zeppelin raid in May 1915.
[FWW01/01/0072/001]

Fig 7.25
Phoenix House, King William Street, London, by J McVicar Anderson and H L Anderson, 1914–15. The columns of the main hall were given a temporary finish of plaster. [BL23326]

given a temporary finish of plaster, as the marble for them was being worked near Mons in Belgium, which was made inaccessible by the war.[64] The headquarters of the Ocean Marine Insurance Company on Old Broad Street, London, was ten storeys tall and built in a Stripped Classical style between 1915 and 1916. The Prudential Assurance Company, Leicester (1915), with façades to both Grey Friars and Hotel Street, was decorated in the baroque revival and Greek revival styles respectively. In Cirencester an Edwardian baroque-style bank (1915–16) in Portland stone opened on a prominent corner site just off the market, complete with a circular turret over its entrance, while 1917 saw the construction of a substantial six-storey bank and office on Colmore Row, Birmingham, designed with blinds and casement curtains to comply with the lighting restrictions.[65] Not all work was allowed to continue, however. Kinnaird House on London's Pall Mall East, for instance, was designed for Barclays Bank with offices above, but construction was halted at second-floor level in 1918 when it was commandeered by the Ministry of Munitions;[66] it was not completed until 1922.

Civic and civilian architecture

Public buildings

Public buildings were seen as important symbols of optimism and pride, and their ability to provide much-needed administrative space was often cited as an economic reason favouring completion – renting additional space during the war was expensive. Two of London's public buildings in particular, the Port of London Offices in Tower Hamlets and the Australian High Commission building in Westminster (Fig 7.26), were seen as highly symbolic of Britain's aspirations for the future. Permitting construction to continue during the war 'shows the world that we are confident of our great future and determined to provide for it', stated *The Builder*.[67] Pragmatically, however, their near completion and affordable scale probably played a large part in securing their completion, as work on two equally symbolic but more ambitious buildings, London's new County Hall and the Water Board Offices, was halted. Other public buildings completed during the war included British Columbia House on Regent Street, London (1914–15);[68] Marylebone Town Hall (1914–16);[69] West London Police Court (1914–15);[70] and post offices in Bolton, Carlisle and Northampton (all 1916 in a neoclassical or neo-Georgian style).

Cultural heritage

In contrast to the destruction suffered by the villages and cities, and then largely unrecognised archaeological remains of northern France and Flanders, England's cultural heritage was relatively unscathed. Following a comparatively minor attack on Great Yarmouth on 3 November, the war came firmly to Britain's shores on the night of 16 December 1914 when the German navy shelled Scarborough, Hartlepool and Whitby, which resulted in around 150 dead and 500 wounded – primarily civilians. In the course of the attack Whitby Abbey (*see* Fig 3.1), then in private ownership, was shelled, which led to the arch of the west doorway and arcade to either side collapsing, with further damage to the great west window and stair. Scarborough

Fig 7.26
Australia House, Strand, London. The Australian High Commission building by A Marshall Mackenzie and Son, 1913–18. Built from Portland stone on a steel frame in a monumental beaux arts/ imperial baroque style; all the interior timbers and marbles were imported from Australia.
[BL23797]

Physical legacies of war

Faint traces of the war may be seen in unexpected places. In 1915, fearing the possibility of a coastal invasion by German troops, the government oversaw the creation of an evacuation plan for civilians from Essex to Oxfordshire via Hertfordshire which avoided main roads. Certain towns were designated as rest stations and the routes were marked with white arrows on walls and gates – including two which have survived in Saffron Walden, Essex (Fig 7.27), while the location of another was commemorated after the war by a stone plaque (Fig 7.28). Elsewhere, individual soldiers left their mark – such as the graffiti on the side of 6 Albert Terrace, Beverley, Yorkshire (Fig 7.29). An outcrop of rock near Broughton-in-Furness, Cumbria, was scheduled in 2016. The rock, which may have acted as a vantage point for the men to look out for police searches, is inscribed with the date '1916' and the text 'CONs OBJECTORS', along with the name 'A BOOSEY' and six sets of initials of men on the run from the authorities. A better-known collection of graffiti made by imprisoned conscientious objectors survives in the cell block of Richmond Castle (Fig 7.30).

Fig 7.27 (right)
Victoria Avenue, Saffron Walden, Essex. A rare surviving evacuation arrow marking the route inland, from the Essex coast, to Oxfordshire.
[DP182427]

Fig 7.28 (below)
Pound Lane, Ugley, Essex. A plaque commemorating the location of an evacuation route arrow. The routes ran along back roads leaving main roads to troops.
[DP186226]

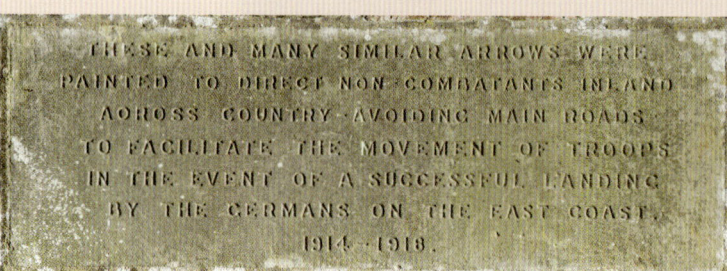

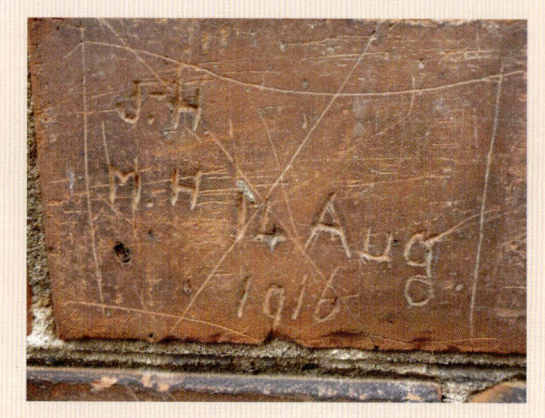

Fig 7.29 (above)
No 6 Albert Terrace, Beverley, East Yorkshire. The alley to the side of the house leads to a large patch of formerly open ground which was probably used as a parade ground by troops training at the drill hall opposite (a converted building with limited space). A number of men carved their initials into the wall, probably before deployment to Europe.
[© Darren Williamson]

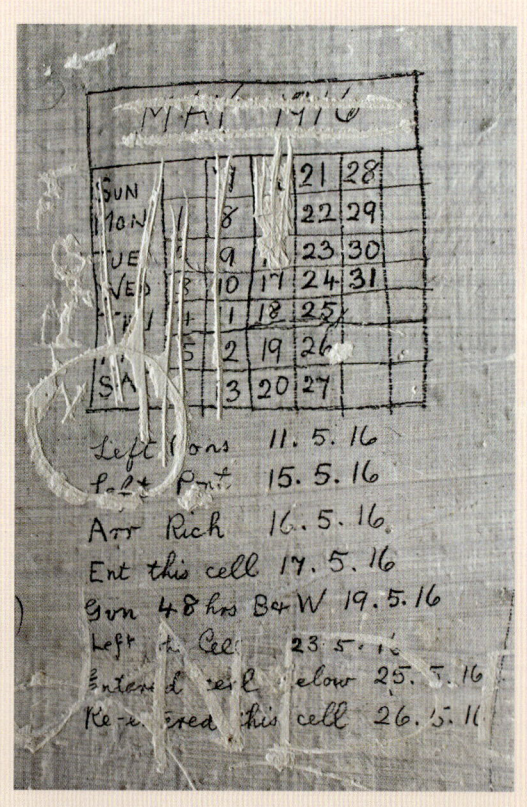

Fig 7.30 (above)
Richmond Castle, Tower Street, Richmond, North Yorkshire. An example of graffiti by a group of conscientious objectors, known as the Richmond Sixteen, who were imprisoned in Richmond Castle in May 1916 before being sent to stand trial in France later that month.
[DP164199]

Castle came under heavy fire, with extensive damage to the castle walls and the barracks. Throughout the war London was a primary target, the River Thames acting as a convenient navigation aid from the air. Lincoln's Inn Chapel still bears the shrapnel marks from a Zeppelin raid, while Cleopatra's Needle on the Embankment has those from a Gotha bomber raid, and many memorial plaques in the city bear witness to both victims and bombardments. Attacks on cultural heritage often invoked more outrage than attacks on military or economic targets, being seen as 'iconoclastic attempts to alter or erase a nation's cultural memory'.[71]

The digging of practice trenches seemed likely to threaten archaeological remains, although a report in *The Builder* stated that no news of damage to ancient earthworks or archaeological sites had been reported as being caused by the construction of trenches, huts and other wartime construction projects.[72] This has, however, been contradicted by archaeological survey where traces of training trenches dug by men at Park Hall Camp were found within Old Oswestry hill fort, Shropshire.[73] The war saw most archaeological work in England suspended, and despite having previously been tasked with recording monuments damaged by air raids, the Royal Commission on Historical Monuments (England) found itself much depleted due to the number of men on active service, with the Treasury ceasing all payments to the remaining staff on 31 March 1916, forcing the Commission to suspend work for the duration of the war.[74] Staff from the Ministry of Works who had been employed on the conservation of ancient monuments were moved on to war work, most notably Frank Baines, who went on to design munitions works and housing estates.[75] Despite everything, the Office of Works made a number of acquisitions during the war, most notably Rievaulx Abbey, North Yorkshire, which was taken into guardianship in May 1917 following the death of the owner, Lord Feversham, at the Somme in September 1916.[76]

In addition to the light restrictions, active measures were taken where possible to reduce the likelihood of damage to key historic or cultural sites – primarily by disguising their position or protecting the most vulnerable elements. The stained-glass windows of York Minster were removed as a precaution against damage from air raids,[77] while large portions of the glass dome of the Royal Albert Hall were removed and replaced by fireproof plaster.[78] The British Museum, along with other museums in London, took special precautions to protect its collections in the event of air raids – portable objects of special value were moved to safes or a specially constructed strong room in the basement and replaced by objects of lesser value or by facsimiles. The Parthenon frieze was protected by sandbags and anti-combustion material.[79] During an air raid on 31 January 1915, the reservoirs of Stowe and Minster Pool in Lichfield happened to be empty for repair and cleaning. Zeppelins passed over Lichfield, and it was suggested that, as the pools were dry, the navigators in the aircraft were thrown off course, and thereby the Cathedral was saved.[80] Similarly, the lake in St James's Park was drained in an attempt to protect Buckingham Palace, the site being utilised for temporary Government offices (*see* Fig 1.6).

Conclusions

The architectural legacy of the First World War on the civil realm of England may be modest compared to the preceding decades, but it is far from insignificant. Temporary or permanent in design, the impact on the country's towns and countryside was dramatic and affected almost every aspect of civilian life. Restrictions on materials and labour, technological developments, international influences, social change and a desire to look to the future all resulted in permanent changes to building styles, materials and the historic environment alike.

8

Feeding the nation

Paul Stamper

Introduction

In the later 1870s what became known as the great depression settled on British agriculture as cheap imports of wheat and meat – on which the country was heavily reliant – depressed the price of foodstuffs.[1] Over the following 40 years huge swathes of arable land went down to grass, ditches were left uncleared and hedges uncut, and weeds, scrub and secondary woodland encroached on land which it was uneconomic to manage. All manner of vermin proliferated. By 1914 the situation had worsened, and critically two-thirds of what the country consumed came from overseas. For wheat and flour, the key staples, as much as 80 per cent was imported. Astute observers questioned if the country could feed itself during a protracted European war.

In fact, during the first two years of the war bumper harvests and a continued flow of imported foodstuffs meant that food was plentiful. However, there were no government restrictions to limit the number of skilled farm-workers who rushed to join the colours, lured by better wages and the prospect of adventure; something like a third of the 816,000 men employed on the land joined up.[2] As early as June 1915 the Army Council had to agree that furlough – home leave to help with the harvest – be granted to a limited number of men, and that for the time being no further skilled workers would be recruited.

The food crisis

By the end of 1916 food was becoming scarcer, with a poor cereal harvest, the failure of the potato crop and increased shipping losses from U-boat attacks. Retail prices were markedly higher as a consequence, up 60 per cent on 1914. Then, in February 1917, after two years

Fig 8.1
Reading, Berkshire. A food queue.
[© IWM Q 056276]

of restraint in deference to neutral countries, Germany introduced unrestricted U-boat warfare and the blockade of British ports began: the Kaiser threatened to starve Britain into submission. That month 230 ships were sunk, and losses rose steadily thereafter: 875,000 tons (794,000 tonnes) of Allied shipping were sunk in April, three times what it had been the previous autumn. And as less food was reaching the country, home production was declining, in part due to a shortage of labour: manpower was down by about 12 per cent. By April 1917 only six weeks' supply of wheat remained in the country. Soon long queues were forming at shops for all manner of foodstuffs: meat, sugar, tea, margarine, bread and vegetables, especially potatoes (Fig 8.1). Fuel, too, was in short supply, and in April 1917 (the winter of 1916/17 being one of the coldest on record) the *Observer* reported long queues of women and children waiting to buy coal in south London railway sidings from soon after seven in the morning.[3]

On 1 January 1917, after the formation of David Lloyd George's coalition government, a Food Production Department was established by the Board of Agriculture to raise production, and to obtain and distribute farm machinery, labour, fertiliser and foodstuffs. The policy of 'Back to the [eighteen-] seventies and better!' recalled the high point of Victorian farming, before the onset of the agricultural depression, and especially the need to plough up grassland, which had increased by 3.4m acres (1.4m ha) over the intervening 40 years. The War Agricultural Executive Committees, established in each county in 1915 but initially ineffectual, were given far-reaching powers: to inspect land, issue directions on what was to be ploughed and even take possession of badly run farms.

A new labour force

By 1917 the shortage of labour was acute as so many skilled agricultural workers had joined up, and food shortages were worsening: as noted above, even potatoes were in short supply. Some of the substitute labourers directed onto farms were not always to a farmer's liking. One in Shropshire, having been sent a piano tuner, complained, 'I could knock nothing in to him!'[4] Generally more satisfactory was the contribution of soldiers on furlough, village women, Land Army Girls and prisoners of war. Schoolchildren, too, played a part.

Arrangements for furlough, introduced in 1915, were also put in place in later years; in 1916 ploughmen were released from the forces to help with the spring cultivation, farmers were allowed to hire horses from military camps and further men were sent home to help with the harvest. Some 17,000 soldiers were employed on farms in the UK in the summer of 1916, and by March 1917, after the formation of the Labour Corps, the number had more than doubled to 36,000, and their training was better.[5] However, most of these were men from the lower medical categories, many with no agricultural experience and, at least to begin with, of little use.[6] By November 1918 there were 84,000 soldiers at work just on farms in England and Wales.[7]

In the first two years of the war, notwithstanding a government scheme to train them in milking and in light farm work, relatively few women joined the agricultural labour force. Of these, most were characterised as 'better educated', as opposed to the 'village women' who had traditionally done gang work (Fig 8.2). Numbers grew from 1916 with the formation of Women's War Agricultural Committees, which registered women willing to work in agriculture: by mid-May Shropshire had 800 signed up, and by mid-October Wiltshire claimed 3,154 and Durham, the highest number, 4,938. Accurate figures are hard to come by, but something like 29,000 women may have been at work on the land in August 1916.[8] By then women were being enrolled in the Women's National Land Service Corps (based on the Women's Farm and Garden Union). This formed an interim stage between the early voluntary initiatives and the formation of the government-backed Women's Land Army (WLA), set up in March 1917.[9]

Fig 8.2
Pudsey, West Yorkshire. Village women helping with the turnip crop. A long-handled mallet is being used to break up heavy clods.
[Courtesy Paul Stamper]

It was anticipated that only women 'of the better sort', 'sufficiently high in character to make it safe to send out to live alone on farms or in cottages', would be accepted into the WLA, and between 1917 and 1919 nearly half the 43,000 applicants were rejected.[10] Organised by county-based Women's War Agricultural Committees, the WLA assisted in all aspects of work on the land, including cultivation – many of the newly imported tractors were driven by women – dairying, carting horticulture and forestry (Fig 8.3).[11] It reached its maximum strength of 16,000 in September 1918,[12] by when its members came from a much wider range of social, economic and educational backgrounds than at first. In March 1918, for instance, an experiment began in taking girls from munitions factories 'who are breaking down' – many were anaemic – and transferring them to 'land work', where, after being well fed and spending time in the open air helping with gentle gardening, they would move on to be trained for farm work.[13] By the war's end, farmers' and male labourers' initial scepticism about women's abilities (if not the fact they wore trousers)[14] had often been replaced by admiration for their expertise and perseverance,[15] although such a generalised conclusion hides a very wide range of experiences and perceptions, on the part both of farmers and of Land Girls.[16]

On the outbreak of war some 10,000 Germans classified as enemy aliens were interned, soon to be joined by a relatively small number of captured soldiers and sailors: roughly 7,000 by February 1915. Numbers of both civilian and military prisoners increased over the year, notably after the internment of all enemy aliens of military age, although it was only after the German spring offensive of 1917 that large numbers of military prisoners were held in Britain. By 20 November 1917, 79,329 people were interned in British camps, and by the war's end 115,950, of whom 89,937 had been serving in the German army (including 5,005 officers), together with 1,491 naval personnel.[17]

In terms of working on the land, a small number of selected civilian internees were employed in agriculture in spring 1915, but it was only from February 1916 that POWs were more widely used for labour outside their camps, and in agriculture from the end of that year (Fig 8.4). While a minimum wage was paid, the main incentive – understandably – seems to have been to get out of camp. Agricultural work was favoured; many prisoners came from a farming background and, one way or another, it offered the chance to get a little more to eat. As well as on general farm work, POWs were used for land clearance projects; in January 1917, for instance, 17 Hungarians were sent to the Forest of Dean – a prohibited area – to break up rough common ground for cultivation.[18] POW employment in farming increased markedly in 1918, fuelled by fears that the harvest could not be gathered due to a shortage of labour. Some stayed in working camps (such as the workhouse in Oundle, Northamptonshire) to which they returned at night, while others found employment in 'migratory gangs' that lived on the farms where they worked or in the stables of country houses – the horses having been taken for the war effort. While POWs and Land Girls often worked alongside each other, especially that summer, the official policy was to limit social fraternisation. At the war's end there were about 30,000 POWs engaged in farm work.[19]

The conscientious objectors were a fourth category of substitute labour. Between the introduction of conscription in 1916 and the end

Fig 8.3
Rawtenstall, Lancashire. The Grade II* listed war memorial. The figures shown on its bronze reliefs (by L F Roslyn) include, one behind the other, members of the Women's Land Army and the Women's Forestry Corps.
[DP168816]

of the war, about 20,000 men refused to fight on moral or religious grounds. Of these, about half were deemed to be engaged in essential war work, or were directed to work of national importance in industry or on the land. However, Lord Ernle reckoned that due to the strength of public hostility, only around 200 were at work on farms at any one time; the only precise figure is from June 1918, when 214 were employed in agriculture. More seem to have been used in out-of-the-way land reclamation schemes and the like. In 1918 around 500 of the 1,200 conscientious objectors housed in Dartmoor Prison (the criminal inmates having been moved elsewhere) were participating in the Tor Royal (or Tor Park) intake, the reclamation of some 1,200 acres (500ha) of granite-strewn moorland.[20]

Finally, widespread use was made on the land of schoolboys aged 12 and over, their farmer-employers being granted school exemption certificates.[21] In January 1916 exemption was extended to girls who could look after younger children, thereby allowing their mothers to work.[22] Public schoolboys, too, were drafted in to help with the harvest: 5,000 for the 1917 corn harvest, 15,000 for that in 1918 (Fig 8.5). Uppingham School (Rutland), for instance, sent 50 boys to help with the corn harvest in Cumberland.[23] It was not always a great success: whether in the case of 50 boys from Westminster, deployed for three periods of three weeks, this was down to the boys or to 'a lack of co-operation or organising skill on the part of the farmers' seems uncertain.[24] Also seen more often in the harvest field in the last years of the war were the 'Blue Boys', convalescent soldiers in their distinctive blue jackets and bright red ties (Fig 8.6).

Fig 8.4
German POWs, happy and healthy, apparently engaged in gardening work in October 1917.
[© IWM Q 054200]

Fig 8.5
Eton College, Berkshire. A gardener shows boys how to dig potatoes.
[© IWM Q 030857]

Fig 8.6
Great Dixter, East Sussex. Convalescent soldiers helping the women and children with haymaking in summer 1916. This was the home of the author and photographer Nathaniel Lloyd, and was in use as a military hospital.
[CC002585]

The Women's Institute

The Women's Institute movement was founded in Ontario, Canada, in 1897. As concerns grew over food supply, Madge Watt, secretary of the WI Advisory Board for British Columbia, was employed to set up WIs in Britain, the first being at Llanfairpwll in Wales in September 1915 and the first in England, for Singleton and East Dean (West Sussex), in November 1915 (Fig 8.7). The aim was to encourage countrywomen to get more involved in cultivating and preserving food. By 1917 there were 137 WIs and by the end of 1919, when the WI was independent of the Food Production Department, there were 1,405 across the UK as a whole.[25]

Fig 8.7
Charlton, West Sussex. The Fox Goes Free pub, where the first ever English WI was founded in November 1915. It was relisted at Grade II in November 2015, in acknowledgement of this aspect of its history.
[DP218063]

The ploughing-up campaign

The necessity under the 'plough policy' to get more land under arable cultivation when there were markedly fewer horses available to do the work promoted the more widespread adoption of tractors on British farms, 15 years or so after they first appeared. British manufacturers like Ivels of Biggleswade could not meet the demand as military engineering contracts took priority, and so government purchasing agencies looked to the USA for supplies. Best equipped to supply the large numbers of tractors required was Henry Ford, which used its car manufacturing skills to rush through a new design, the Fordson. The British government ordered 6,000 of these in 1917, despite the fact it was only at prototype stage.[26] Over the course of the war, tractor numbers rose from perhaps 1,000 to 5,000 in late 1917 and perhaps 6,000 by the war's end (Fig 8.8). That said, they were little beyond the experimental stage and prone to breaking down (often lying idle while spares were awaited from America), and while the Food Production Department recommended their use for breaking up pasture laid down since the 1870s, it said they should not be used on older pasture land or 'very high backed land' – that is, particularly pronounced ridge-and-furrow.

Gradually lessons were learnt about how best to deploy tractors. At Swaffham Prior, Cambridgeshire, tractors ploughed the fields but horses finished off the headlands.[27] Mowers, reapers and smaller numbers of ploughs and cultivators also arrived from the States.[28] John Allen, owner of a leading steam ploughing business,[29] persuaded the government that steam, too, had a part to play, and, as honorary adviser to the Food Production Committee, located some of the double-engined steam ploughing sets which had been left idle since the demand for their use had declined in the 1880s. These were set to breaking up land, especially on heavy soils before wheat and potatoes were planted, or where land was 'too banky or too steep for tractor work'.[30] Soon Allen had a workforce of a hundred, with four cars to keep in contact with the six-man ploughing teams which worked seven days a week. For his efforts he was appointed OBE at the war's end.[31] By January 1917 there were 500 steam sets in Britain, although nearly half of those were out of service, lacking a driver or needing repair. Action was taken, and by June all but 40 obsolete sets were at work.[32] Overall, it was estimated 1.2m acres (0.5m ha) were steam-ploughed in England and Wales in 1917–18, about three times the area normally tilled in peacetime.[33] Just how radical the deployment of new machinery was is suggested by the conclusion of a member of the government in 1919: it was 'magnificent, but not agriculture'.[34]

While some land that was returned to cultivation after a long period as pasture was rich and productive, elsewhere (for instance in the

Fig 8.8
Members of the Army Service Corps instructing farmers in tractor ploughing on the Welsh/Shropshire border. Training is overseen by two bowler-hatted members of the local War Agricultural Committee.
[© D J T Evans]

uplands) the soil was thin and poor, needing hard-to-come-by fertiliser, with supplies from abroad again restricted by the U-boat blockade. Enrichment was also needed on land which had reverted to woodland and scrub, such as that noted on Langton Wold, on the Wolds of East Yorkshire, in 1917: 'it ... has lain a long time in grass and is partly covered with whins and thorns, which will require to be stubbed up before it can be ploughed; if possible, the rough grass should also be burnt off'.[35] Limekilns dating to the 18th and 19th centuries, often disused for 40 years or more, were brought back into production to sweeten or neutralise acid soils. At Halton Quay on the River Tamar, Cornwall, lime was carried by wagon 2½ miles (4km) uphill from riverside kilns to Viverdon Down, ploughed up as part of the war effort.[36]

Especially during the last two years of the war there was considerable investment in improving drainage, notably in areas, often coastal, where there were either extensive areas of low-lying land, or large catchments drained by major rivers, such as the Norfolk Ouse. Insofar as surviving records show, the counties most concerned with flooding were Cheshire and Lancashire, followed by Cumberland, the West Riding of Yorkshire, Norfolk, East Suffolk, Essex and Lindsey. In Lindsey, in the Caistor district, 3,000 acres (1,215ha) of warp land were said to be inundated each year by the Ancholme River and Caistor Canal, while drains installed in the 19th century lay so deep they were useless and had to be replaced by shallower ones. Attempts were made to recall skilled drainers from the army and munitions factories, and to revive small brickyards to supply pipes and tiles. Much use was made of POWs, who were available in large numbers in 1918. In Cheshire 635 were deployed, alongside soldiers, with the biggest scheme involving 250 POWs being the cleaning of 19 miles of the rivers Birkett, Fender and Arrow. Overall it was estimated that a total of 405,000 acres (182,000ha) in England and Wales benefited from wartime drainage.[37]

A notable government initiative, in response to evidence that the quality of Britain's seed stocks was declining, was the setting up in 1917 of the Seed Testing Station (Fig 8.9). A leading figure in the establishment and success of the STS – despite having no background in agriculture or science – was Lawrence Weaver (1876–1930), until 1916 the architectural editor of *Country Life*, one of those men of 'push and go' so crucial to the war effort. Working with traders and bureaucrats, Weaver introduced the Testing of Seeds Order 1917, which required that a sample of all seeds (essentially agricultural crops) offered for sale in the UK had to be tested and issued with a certificate of quality. Initially the STS operated from offices within the Food Production Department, set up earlier in 1917, at 70 Victoria Street in the City of Westminster. Apart from the Director and his assistant, all the staff of the STS were 'bright and intelligent young women and cockney girls', at first two botanical assistants, a clerk and eight messenger girls, although by the end of the war there were three female assistants, each with a degree in science.[38]

The reason for the ploughing-up campaign was, of course, that land used as arable, growing cereals and vegetables, could feed far more people than when it was used as pasture for milk and meat. While necessary and successful, the acreage put down to the plough was fairly modest, especially when compared with the equivalent campaign in the Second World War, when roughly six times as much land was turned over to cereal production.[39] Initiated late in 1916, the campaign came too late to have much effect on the 1917 harvest, although ploughing that spring did add 174,000 acres (70,400ha) of oats and 128,000 acres (51,800ha) of barley. The acreage under plough then increased further (farmers were given guaranteed minimum prices for wheat and oats early in 1917), and in 1918 – when national food rationing was introduced – the area sown with wheat had increased by 645,000 acres (261,000ha) over 1916 and oats by 695,000 acres (281,000ha). The potato

Fig 8.9
'The Official Seed Testing Station: the main laboratory showing some of the germinators.'
[J Board Agriculture 1917, 941; Courtesy of Dr Dominic Berry]

crop expanded too, to 206,000 acres (83,000ha), up almost 50 per cent on 1916. As a consequence the area of permanent grass in England fell over the two years by about 1,400,000 acres (567,000ha or about 9 per cent) and that of temporary grass by 500,000 acres (202,000ha or 20 per cent). Inevitably there was less milk and meat to be had, but thanks in part to these emergency measures, the country survived.[40] However, ploughing up was not the sole factor, nor by any means the most significant. Over the course of the war, home food production rose only from 38 per cent to 40 per cent, with imports still accounting for 53 per cent of food in 1918. In reality it was other measures, notably price controls, rationing (voluntary rationing was introduced in 1917, formal rationing in July 1918)[41] and the introduction of the convoy system for merchant shipping on the north Atlantic route, which kept the country from starvation.[42]

The impact of the ploughing-up policy varied widely across the country, with the upland areas of western and northern Britain – the dividing line running from the western boundary of Dorset to the mouth of the Humber – seeing the greatest expansion in arable. Leaving aside Monmouthshire, then officially part of Wales, where the increase was 103.5 per cent, Westmoreland had the highest figure at 65.4 per cent, with Derbyshire and Leicestershire (much of which had gone down to grass since the 1870s) also seeing an increase of over 50 per cent. In southern England the Sussex Downs saw some of the most extensive ploughing (fatally for prehistoric earthworks), accounting for much of the 30 per cent increase in tillage in East Sussex. Overall about 68 per cent of the new land was planted with oats, 16 per cent wheat and 6 per cent barley.[43] The remainder was accounted for by potatoes, pulses and minor corn crops. The area given over to market gardens also increased noticeably, in Kent, for instance, taking over land traditionally used for hop growing.[44]

Wartime contingencies sometimes had unforeseen mid- and long-term consequences. On the East Yorkshire Sledmere estate, the ploughing out of grassland on the thin chalk soils of the Wolds and the reduction of sheep, turnips and clover upset the delicate crop-rotation balance, leaving much land 'poverty stricken'.[45] Equally damaging, at least in the short term, were military camps and training activities. A Wiltshire farm bailiff seems to have had a particularly trying time.[46] In August 1917 he complained that an aircraft from the RFC's Training Squadron at Yatesbury had damaged 32 acres (13ha) of barley, and claimed £15 compensation. In October he complained about Australians from Codford camp digging trenches, 'great holes … on some of the best land', and in November he expressed a concern about the extension of rifle ranges onto the farm's only area of roots where 320 sheep were to be 'lambed down'. The proximity of camps brought other problems, with pigs killed by kitchen slops, and concerns that stable manure would be contaminated with disease. Not all farmers were worried about the latter, and in 1915 Henry Young of Bulford took 20,000 tons (18,143 tonnes) of manure from the camps to spread on his 1,500 acres (607ha) of arable.

In general, farmers did well out of the war financially. A G Street, the writer and broadcaster who farmed at Ditchampton Farm, Wilton, Wiltshire, thought it was impossible to lose money during the war, making £2,000 a year from his 300 acres/121ha (just over half of which was arable),[47] while *Country Life* recorded a farmer who made £20,000 from potatoes.[48]

Horses

Especially after the formation of the New Armies, the army had an almost insatiable demand for horses and mules. The latter could be evil-tempered, but became tractable when treated well; moreover, they ate less and were harder working and far less prone to illness (notable skin diseases) than horses.[49] Their principal roles were in transport and artillery hauling, especially on the Western Front: animals coped better than lorries in the mud of Flanders. In response, specialist remount depots were set up in England where animals were gathered in and trained for their new roles (Fig 8.10). As it was thought to be a war where cavalry would play a vital role, the stables of country houses and hunts were heavily impressed: 'How many will ever again hear the sound of the horn?' plaintively asked *Country Life*.[50] That said, most of the 468,000 horses bought later in the UK probably came from towns and industry. However, at first most horses were drawn from the land, and as a consequence the number on farms fell from some 927,000 in 1914 to 858,000 in 1915. While this was a small drop in percentage terms, this still meant there were too few horses to meet the requirements of the ploughing-up campaign of 1916.

Fig 8.10
A government poster from 1915 advertising for suitably experienced men to work at remount depots.
[© IWM PST 007678]

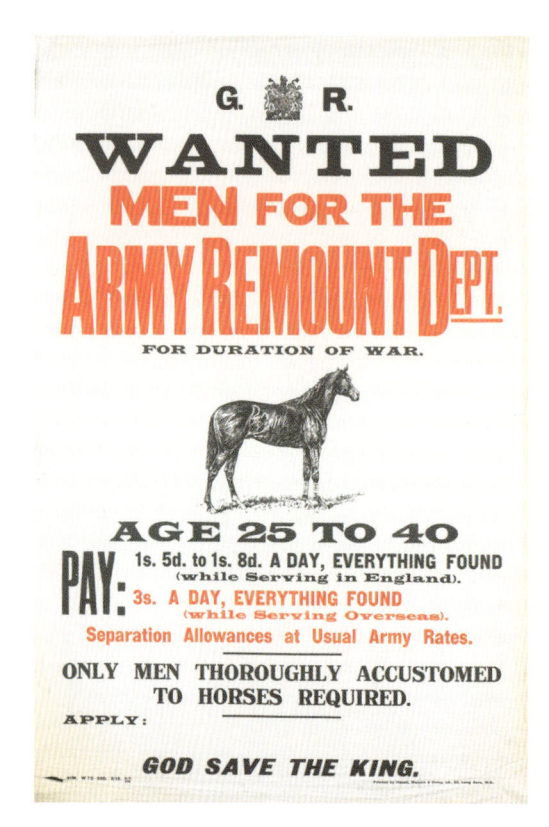

Fig 8.11 (below) Arborfield, Berkshire. The surviving stables from its remount depot.
[Courtesy W D Cocroft]

Remount depots were run by the Army Service Corps. One such depot had already been set up in 1891 at Woolwich, London, and a further one in Lusk, just north of Dublin, prior to the Boer War (1899–1902). Two more remount depots were opened a little later at Arborfield Cross, Berkshire (1904) and Melton Mowbray, Leicestershire (1911); these comprised a few stables and agricultural buildings, along with grazing land, where the horses could be kept.

However, it soon became evident that the scale of horse mobilisation in the event of a European war had been underestimated, and from 1914 to 1915 further large reception remount depots were set up to take in imported horses at Lathom Park, near Ormskirk, Lancashire, to serve Liverpool docks, and Shirehampton, Bristol, for taking animals (primarily the 618,000 horses and mules – twice as many of the former as the latter – imported from the Unites States and Canada) arriving by sea at Avonmouth. At first Shirehampton comprised 35 paddocks, each designed to accommodate a 100-horse troop and equipped with two stable blocks. For every five troops there was a blacksmith's forge and a shoeing shed, and the depot had three forage barns for feed. Later the depot roughly doubled in size to ten 500-horse squadrons, each with a staff of 150 men.[51] Two further large depots were established: Romsey, Hampshire, was primarily a training and conditioning depot, while Swaythling, near Southampton, was responsible for collecting horses from reserve units and training depots and forwarding them on to France.

Physical remains of the remount depots are limited. At the end of the war, as with so much of the military estate, they were apparently rapidly dismantled and disposed of. One of the few survivals is the Infirmary stables of 1911–12 at Arborfield (Fig 8.11). Shirehampton closed in October 1919, and its buildings were dismantled and sold, with 70 of the men's barracks being bought by Bristol City Council for conversion into 140 temporary homes.[52]

Wherever they were drawn from (over 400,000 horses were also purchased abroad), the army's horses and mules required feeding, and new systems had to be set up to gather and transport fodder and bedding, principally to the Western Front. In November 1915 a Forage Committee was set up, with six English Forage Department Companies and others in Scotland and Ireland. The Forage Corps was some 6,000 strong; after March 1917 a 4,200-strong women's section provided the majority of its labour force as men were released for front-line service. Teams equipped with steam engines, threshers and balers (all often newly built by firms including Rustons and Fowlers) toured the country processing hay and straw on farms – compression into bales was essential – and carrying them to rail depots from where they would be transported to military depots or camps (Fig 8.12). The baling was especially

Fig 8.12
Women from the Forage Corps, and an Army Service Corps sergeant, baling hay.
[© IWM Q 030691]

important, given the distance the hay and straw had to travel, often across the Channel. A scheme to bring in hydraulic presses was introduced in 1916, and by 1918 there were a hundred. In March 1917, 70,000 tons of hay per month was being shipped across the Channel, four-fifths of it hydraulically pressed, and in bulk terms more fodder was taken to France than munitions.[53] For a firm of ropemakers in Bridport, Dorset, it brought a massive boost in business: a million hay-nets were supplied for the wartime army, whose official regulations required that 'every animal should have a nose-bag and hay net'.[54]

Smallholdings

Smallholding numbers had increased markedly from the 1880s, notably after the Small Holdings and Allotments Act of 1907. Between 1908 and 1914 over 205,000 acres (83,000ha) were acquired by English county councils, and 14,045 smallholders were settled on the land.[55] However, while this may have led to it being more intensively cultivated, this was land which was already in productive use, and in any case the outbreak of war saw a general end to the acquisition of smallholdings. Presumably many smallholders, like farmworkers, rushed to join up, and so it seems unlikely that smallholdings' yield would have increased during the war years.

Parks

By 1914, after a generation of falling prices and rents, most country house estates faced financial difficulties; many had either been sold or were being offered for sale. The war only compounded matters with the deaths of owners and heirs. In 1917 the number of estate sales began to rise, and at the end of 1918 *Country Life* published a roll call of recent or impending sales, including 7,000 acres (2,800ha) of the Alton estate in Staffordshire, 3,000 acres (1,200ha) at Panshanger in Hertfordshire and 2,000 acres (810ha) of the Oakley estate near Bedford.[56] Even where owners hung on, their houses might have been requisitioned by the military (or perhaps voluntarily offered up for use as hospitals), and their parks taken over for camps and training facilities of all kinds, or ploughed up with their avenues and trees felled for timber.

Most agricultural intensification in country parks followed the 1917 Corn Production Act which guaranteed the minimum price of wheat and oats for six years. Most owners probably complied fairly willingly, like the Cecils at Great Wigsell, East Sussex, where the lawns were grazed by lambs and the flower borders were given over to vegetables. There were, however, some families who saw the legislation as part of Lloyd George's attack on the landowning classes, and Gerald Gliddon suggests an unofficial

Allotments

While the impact of the plough campaign has been much discussed, far less attention has been paid to the very considerable contribution which private allotments made to feeding the country, especially in the latter stages of the war.

Fig 8.13
D J Coke, War Allotments in a London Suburb, *1919. A mixed group of allotmenteers, including women and wounded soldiers in 'hospital blues', tend their vegetables. In the background is the London County Council school at Norbury, used as a military hospital. During the First World War, Dorothy J Coke (1897–1979) was a pupil at the Slade, and during the Second World War she worked as an official war artist.*
[© IWM ART 002366]

Fig 8.14
Girl Guides working on an allotment. The conical shrubs behind them to the right strongly suggests this is in a park.
[© IWM Q 027919]

Arguably, this was at least equal to the ploughing-up campaign (Fig 8.13). In 1914 there were between 450,000 and 600,000 allotments in England, many created as a result of successive Allotment Acts of 1887 and later. While from the outbreak of war owners of large gardens had been encouraged to donate seeds and stock to existing allotment holders, it was only in December 1916 – put off until then, like food rationing, as it was feared the measures would be bad for morale by revealing the losses to U-boats – that there was a concerted effort to increase the area under cultivation, and local authorities were empowered to take over any uncultivated land and turn it into allotments. Notwithstanding the resistance met in some places to such provision – in Lincoln 'middle class Aldermen and councillors' initially objected to allotmenteers (as they became known) entering in to their neighbourhood – by the end of 1917, 1,500,000 plots were under cultivation, producing an estimated 2 million tons (1,800,000 tonnes) of vegetables.[57]

To give but two examples: first, in Hornchurch, Essex, the number of permanent allotments rose to 254, to which 256 temporary 10-rod wartime plots were added. The council also supplied in all 5,760 glass jars for preserving fruit for the winter.[58] Second, in Bristol, the number of council allotments grew from 2,500 in 1914 to around 20,000 by 1919, when there was also an unknown number of privately rented 'war plots' scattered across the city.[59] Schools, from the smallest village school to Eton College and the other public schools, hospitals, reformatories and workhouses all had ground brought into cultivation by the 'short-sleeve army', while allotments provided by railway companies had grown from 27,683 in 1914 to 93,473 in 1918 (Fig 8.14). Where space allowed, government factories for munitions and the like had vegetable plots to supply works' canteens, whose waste swill was fed to pigs. Even in Lincoln the number of council plots had risen by the war's end from 84 to 406, and a schedule had been prepared to identify every last scrap of uncultivated land.[60] By late in the war the county War Agricultural Committees had become involved, giving out seed potatoes to cottagers and small cultivators, and (like Hornchurch council) distributing preserving sugar and glass jars for fruit bottling.[61]

propaganda machine set out to discredit such 'grumblers' as 'betrayers of their country'. Mrs Humphry Ward, popular novelist, patriot and war correspondent, for instance, published a story called *The War and Elizabeth* (1918). In this a bad-tempered country gentleman not only tries to stop his son going to war but also takes on the government over corn production. His defeat is humiliating, with his gates torn down and his parkland ploughed up.[62]

Municipal parks, too, were similarly surrendered to military uses, or food production. In 1918 the first *Blue Guide to London* described how many of its parks were utterly transformed during the war. In Regent's Park the Army Postal Service put up supposedly the world's biggest wooden building to handle post to and from the front, while the lake in St James's Park was drained and Ministry of Shipping buildings were erected on the lakebed (*see* Fig 1.6). In others, hospitals, camps, training grounds and anti-aircraft batteries were set up, or they were ploughed up or divided into allotments.[63]

Other crops

After the appointment of a Food Controller in December 1916, the planting of relatively new crops like sugar beet was encouraged, while at the same time 'Half-forgotten crops became familiar again'.[64] For instance, in 1917 the Ministry of Munitions bought up the entire British flax crop (supplies from Russia and Italy having been cut off), much from along the Norfolk/Suffolk border, to supply (among other things) the army with tents and kitbags and the RFC with nets for balloons and linen shirts for airmen.[65] Gathering it in was a holiday task for hundreds from the towns, mainly women and girls (Fig 8.15).[66] Blackberries, whortleberries and even wild flowers were collected (often by children) for dyes and drugs; some individuals planted them as crops.[67] In the autumn of 1917, schoolchildren were encouraged (there was a cash bounty) to gather sackfuls of conkers and acorns to be used in the manufacture of acetone, a key component of cordite – the smokeless propellant for shells and bullets (*see* p 129). While this process was supposedly kept secret lest Germany copied the method, the enterprise was widely advertised and reported, for example the note carried by the local paper on 27 December 1917 of the collection by Poole Secondary School in Dorset of 'four tons of acorns for munition making'.[68]

Nutshells and fruit stones were converted into the charcoal used in gas masks, bracken tops were used as vegetables, seaweed was used for gelatin and diseased potatoes were used to make alcohol.[69] Perhaps the most important enterprise was the gathering of large quantities of sphagnum moss for wound dressings; it was extraordinarily absorbent, and unlike inert cotton – needed anyway in the manufacture of

Fig 8.15
Photograph of 'college girls' gathering and processing flax in Somerset, probably taken at Barwick, near Yeovil. Here in the summer of 1918 a 600-strong Women's Land Army camp became a local curiosity. The flax was processed (again by the WLA) in the nearby government Bunford Flax Factory, whence the linen was sent to the Westlands Works aircraft manufactory (also in Yeovil) to cover aircraft frames.
[© IWM Q 030896]

explosives – promoted antisepsis. Dartmoor, Devon, was one of the main sources, with members of the Mothers' Union and children gathering, cleaning and drying moss, which was then carried by a donkey cart to two collection depots. In 1918 the Tavistock depot dispatched 25,476 dressings, along with many hampers of moss, to the Auxiliary Military Hospital at Exeter, while Princetown, staffed by 40 women ('clad and capped in spotless white') and 2 men, sent out 21,476 dressings.[70]

Vermin control

As the need to increase food production rose in the last years of the war, there was an increased emphasis on the control of vermin. In 1917 the Board of Agriculture initiated action against rabbits and rooks, authorising action by the counties' War Agricultural Executive Committees. Rabbits were perhaps the main concern, and in 1917 the Food Production Department stressed the need to safeguard crops from them on the newly reclaimed wheatlands of St Leonards Forest in East Sussex. The Lancashire committee was in contact with a large number of rookery owners, and in 17 cases took action to destroy birds when the owners failed to do so. Woodpigeon shoots were organised, and in 1918 the Board of Agriculture encouraged the formation of Rat and Sparrow Clubs (notwithstanding concerns that the destruction of birds would lead to a plague of insects). In Lancashire bounties of one shilling a dozen for rats' tails and threepence for a dozen sparrows' heads were paid, while in Hertfordshire the totals destroyed in 1917–18 were 103,512 rats, 40,586 mature sparrows and 8,670 unfledged ones, plus 19,216 sparrows' eggs.[71]

Traditional crafts and industries

The exceptional wartime conditions and demands supported traditional industries and crafts, many of which had been waning for a long time. Writing in 1922 Ernest Pulbrook noted, 'One rural industry after another was recalled to life or started into full activity after having almost ceased to exist … in fact, most of the country arts and crafts of bygone eras were reborn.'[72] The 'braiders' or net makers of Bridport and the villages around it produced all manner of rope, twine, sacking and nets, including the hay-nets noted above, with Belgian refugees taken on in place of the hundreds of workers who had joined up.[73] Disabled soldiers made shell-carrying cases of cane and osiers, and perhaps the protective wicker carriers for the army and navy's omnipresent rum jars.[74]

Timber

Perhaps an even greater impact on the countryside than the ploughing up of grassland came with the felling of British woodlands.[75] As with food, Britain had long been a heavy importer of timber, from Russia, Scandinavia and North America, and the reduction in the supply of softwood from abroad due to U-boat action (at first down to 75 per cent, and by 1916 to about 65 per cent) coincided with much greater demands from the military for materials for camps and the like, although the British Expeditionary Force on the Western Front was supplied from the French forests. Timber was also needed for pit props by the coal mining industry: both the navy and industry were principally steam-powered and reliant on coal, in vast quantities. So acute was the need for timber and wood that ancient woods, hedgerows, and parkland trees and ornamental avenues all fell to axe and saw. In Gloucestershire, Lord Wemyss reportedly remarked 'My heart is broken for Lidcombe' as woodland was felled near his home at Stanway, while in 1923 a visitor commented how depressing it was to see the Wolds around Sledmere, East Yorkshire, so denuded of trees by the necessity of wartime.[76] In all, it is estimated that 450,000 acres (182,000ha) of woodlands in Britain were felled over the course of the war.[77]

As with farmworkers, the outbreak of war saw large numbers of woodmen leaving to serve in the forces, notwithstanding the increased demand for wood and timber.[78] Nor were the country's sawmills able to meet demand. In response, a new labour force entered the woods, including POWs, Portuguese woodmen and the Canadian Forestry Corps (CFC, an administrative branch of the Canadian Army), which arrived in England in 1916, with 3,000 of its troops based at 'Hut Town' in Windsor Great Park.[79] This was supplemented in August 1917 when the Women's Forestry Corps (WFC) was separated from the WLA, initially employing 25 timber measurers and 20 cutters, the latter trained in camps in Nottinghamshire and

The blockade of Germany

From the start of the war, the Allies adopted the same policy as Germany: a blockade to cut off imports of raw materials and foodstuffs to the enemy homeland (see Chapter 3).[80] The four-year blockade was important, but whether it was a decisive factor in Germany's defeat (as is sometimes claimed) is debatable. For instance, the fact that the United States only became an active belligerent in 1917 meant that the blockade could not be enforced as fully before that date as it was thereafter, while the need to appease neutral opinion was a constraint on the implementation of economic warfare.[81] Be that as it may, turnips became the mainstay of many Germans' diet during the hard winter of 1916/17, and by October 1918, when several hundred thousand people (the scale of the death toll is much disputed) had already died of starvation, large-scale famine threatened Germany. Together with the hopeless situation on the Western Front, this sapped morale and the will to fight on. Within a fortnight there had been a naval mutiny and working-class insurrections. Threatened by the prospect of a Soviet Germany, its generals removed the Kaiser, withdrew troops from France and Belgium and sought an armistice. While food was reaching Germany by the spring of 1919, the blockade was only fully lifted on the eve of the peace in June 1919.

Suffolk. The WFC expanded only slowly, but in January 1918, 400 women were working as foresters, and by the war's end the WFC had employed some 2,000 women; an additional 1,000, although not officially registered with the organisation, had worked in forests and sawmills (Fig 8.16).[82] Few physical traces are thought to remain of this important activity. Stanton Moor, in Derbyshire, which by the early 19th century was almost entirely planted with fir, larch, oak and Spanish chestnut, was clear-felled towards the end of the war using local female labour under the supervision of a CFC unit. The timber was extracted to a temporary sawmill using an animal-hauled narrow-gauge light railway, earthwork traces of which still remain.[83] In Northwood, on the Slindon estate in West Sussex, a brick incinerator used to burn waste wood by the CFC survives, and rails are sometimes found from the narrow-gauge railway which took timber out of the wood.[84] Charcoal production was increased,[85] in part through its use in gas masks.

Conclusions

England's heavy reliance on imported goods, especially foodstuffs, presented enormous challenges for the authorities the longer the war progressed, and especially in the face of submarine attacks. This was not only in terms of keeping the home population fed, but also in supporting the armed forces, and their horses and mules. In the event the country muddled through with a mixture of government initiatives, not least the ploughing-up campaign, rationing, and myriad local and private enterprises perhaps most especially the drive to create more allotments. Equally important was the fact that lessons were learnt, and when war threatened again just twenty years later, planning was in place, and the response far more effective.

Fig 8.16
The Women's Forestry Corps stripping bark from trees destined to be sent to the Western Front as telegraph poles.
[© IWM Q 030704]

9

Back to Blighty: British war hospitals, 1914–18

Kathryn A Morrison

Introduction

The First World War created appalling casualties: hundreds of thousands of soldiers were wounded in conflict, were gassed on the battlefield or suffered from trauma ('shell shock'). Many sailors and airmen also received horrific injuries. Furthermore, filthy conditions in trenches spread infection and dysentery; trench foot and scabies were common, and venereal disease rife.[1]

Under the circumstances, medical facilities had to be provided on an unprecedented scale. In France and Belgium, casualties might pass through a regimental aid post, a field ambulance and an advanced dressing station before reaching a casualty clearing station, which usually comprised tents or huts. After an uncomfortable and dangerous journey, wounded men might be treated at a base hospital – that is, a general or stationary hospital run by the Royal Army Medical Corps (RAMC) – perhaps occupying a converted hotel or a château. Many of these base hospitals were concentrated by the coast, for example at Étaples, Boulogne and Calais. In addition, several continental hospitals were set up by wealthy and well-connected women. In October 1914, for example, with the approval of the Army Medical Service (AMS), the Duchess of Westminster opened a hospital in Le Touquet Casino, while the Duchess of Sutherland set up in the Hotel Belle Vue, near Dunkirk. A great many casualties, however, were sent home in hospital ships for further treatment or recuperation (Fig 9.1).

Around 2.6 million sick and wounded were sent home between 1914 and 1919, the majority from the Western Front.[2] Despite being protected by the Hague Convention (1907) and flying the red cross, 11 British (among 16 Allied) hospital ships were sunk in the course of the war. In the aftermath of these events, horrified

Fig 9.1
The Carisbrooke Castle *was typical of many vessels requisitioned as hospital ships. She was originally built in 1894 as a Royal Mail steamer and saw war service as a cross-Channel hospital ship before being used as a troop ship; she survived the war.*
[BL14861]

Back to Blighty: British war hospitals, 1914–18

seamen witnessed the floating corpses of nurses, their dried skirts billowing like sails in the wind.[3] When the *Anglia* (a steamship built in 1900 and used in peacetime as a ferry on the Holyhead–Kingston route) hit a mine off Folkestone in 1915, 160 lives were lost, including amputees from Loos who had been strapped to their beds (*see* Fig 3.16).

Back in Blighty, properly equipped and staffed hospitals were needed to cope with the influx of casualties. Following the sinking of the SS *Königin Luise* and HMS *Amphion* on 5–6 August 1914 – the first naval losses of the war – many injured men were taken to Shotley Hospital, Suffolk, and to Harwich, Essex, where, it was reported on 7 August, the red cross flew over the Great Eastern Hotel.[4] Thirty wounded men from Mons (fought on 23–24 August 1914) arrived at Folkestone on 27 August, and within days hundreds were disembarking at Southampton Docks. In the course of the war, many thousands were admitted from a reception station there to the nearby Royal Victoria Hospital at Netley overlooking Southampton Water (Figs 9.2 and 9.3). Erected in the aftermath of the Crimean War, this was the most capacious military hospital in the country, with 955 beds. Despite this, Netley was far from able to admit all casualties of the First World War, and patients had to be transported in large numbers by hospital trains from Southampton or Dover – which was, from January 1915, an alternative disembarkation point for hospital ships – to institutions throughout the country.[5]

At the start of August 1914, in addition to Netley, Britain's armed services were equipped with several large general hospitals, isolation hospitals and mental hospitals, as well as numerous smaller barracks hospitals.[6] Most of the military general hospitals were imposing establishments, built in the 18th and 19th centuries, with a concentration in southern England. They included the naval hospitals at Haslar, Hampshire (1746–61), Plymouth (1758–62), Great Yarmouth, Norfolk (1809–11), Shotley (HMS *Ganges*, 1900–2), Portland, Dorset (1901), and Chatham, Kent (1899–1905). Large army hospitals existed at Plymouth (1797), Woolwich (the Herbert Hospital, 1865), Aldershot (the Cambridge Hospital, 1875–9; the Connaught Hospital, 1895–8), Colchester (1893–8), Cosham, Hampshire (Queen Alexandra Hospital, 1904–7), and London (Queen Alexandra's Hospital, Millbank, 1903–5). Taken together, when war broke out the existing military hospitals provided around 7,000 equipped beds; during the war they expanded to hold 26,982 beds.

Fig 9.2
An aerial view of Netley, Hampshire, showing the extensive hutted hospital built to the rear of the Royal Victoria Hospital in 1914–18. The huts – originally portable in design, with the intention of sending them for service overseas – had been removed by 1923. The main hospital was demolished in 1956, leaving a handful of standing structures, including the chapel and mental hospital (Block D; 1866).
[AA93/06075]

Fig 9.3
Patients with gas burns undergoing salt-water bath treatment at Netley during the war.
[© IWM Q 114057]

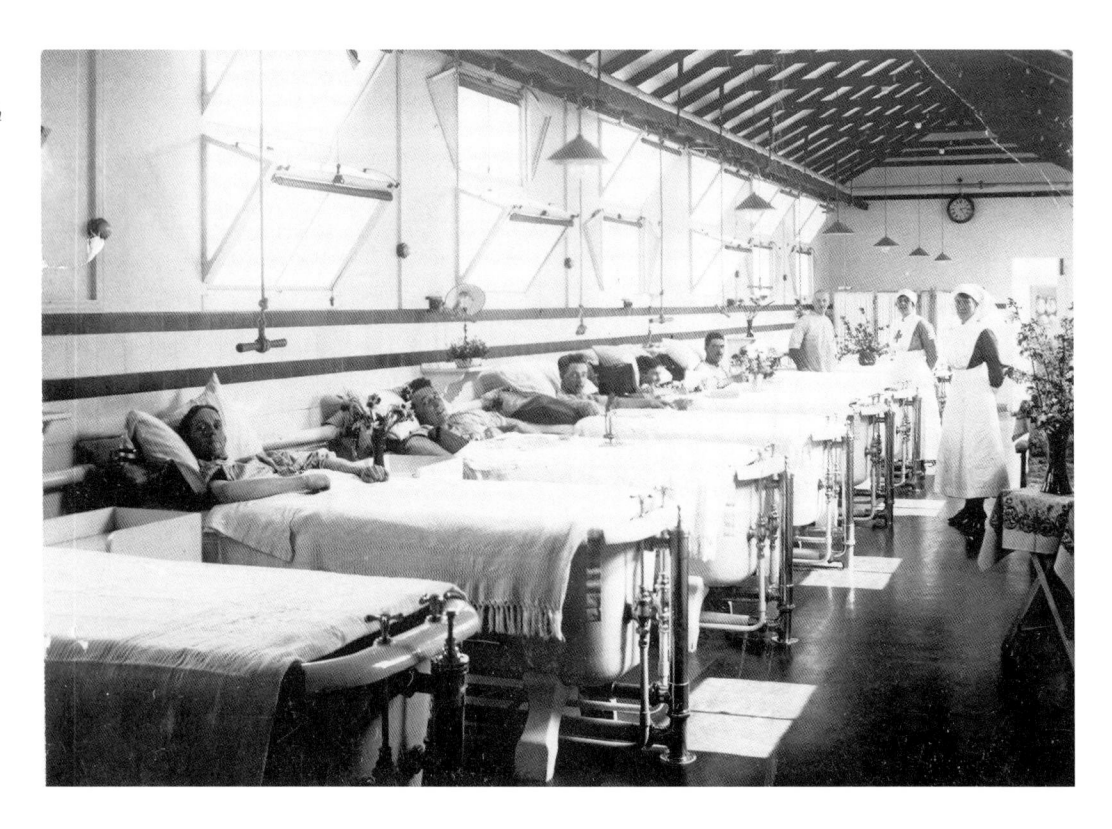

By the armistice the total number of hospital beds provided at home for sick and wounded servicemen had risen to 364,133 (including 18,378 for officers).[7] This remarkable feat was achieved in numerous different ways, some anticipated before the war, and others contrived in the face of necessity.

The RAMC had begun its preparations for large-scale conflict as early as 1907. Following a scheme devised by Sir Alfred Keogh, it laid down plans for 23 Territorial Force hospitals which, once mobilised, would augment the permanent military hospitals. These would be established with 520 beds in converted buildings, principally schools, colleges or workhouses.[8] Eventually, as the conflict intensified, the Territorial hospitals expanded by taking over many more educational and poor-law premises. Two completely new Territorial hospitals were created, and numerous additional asylums and workhouses were handed over to the military as 'war hospitals'. Thus the daily life of many institutions was rudely interrupted, with children dispatched to new schools, paupers ousted from poor-law institutions and the mentally ill evicted from asylums. This had inevitable repercussions. Paupers, for example, were boarded out at institutions far from families and friends, and poor-law authorities had to resort increasingly to outdoor relief.[9]

As the initial trickle of wounded men quickened into a flood in winter 1914–15, it became clear that existing military and Territorial hospitals would not suffice. Although there was no centralised Emergency Medical Service, like that set up in advance of the Second World War, voluntary hospitals set aside thousands of staffed beds (16,000 in all, which might be compared with the 26,853 beds provided in converted schools) for sick and wounded sailors and soldiers, receiving a daily fee of around 4s per patient (6s in infectious diseases hospitals) from the Admiralty or War Office. Even this failed to meet requirements, however, and civilians rose magnificently to the challenge. In the first weeks of the war the authorities were swamped with offers of private houses and other buildings for use as hospitals. Before long, responsibility for converting and equipping selected premises as Auxiliary Home Hospitals had devolved to the Joint War Committee of the British Red Cross Society and the Order of St John of Jerusalem (better known as the St John's Ambulance Association).[10] Some members of the upper classes ran hospitals in their own homes, independent of the Joint War Committee.

There were precedents for such generous gestures. During the Boer War (1899–1902), for example, Agnes and Fanny Keyser had converted their Belgravia home into the King

Edward VII Hospital for Officers, an institution which acquired permanent status and expanded hugely during the First World War. In fact, many private houses were converted specifically for the reception of wounded officers in 1914–18, including Jamnagar (demolished) in Staines, Surrey, the home of the Maharajah of Nawanagar, which became the Prince of Wales Hospital in 1915.[11] The 'most fashionable' officers' hospital was deemed to be Lady Ridley's Hospital at 10 Carlton House Terrace in London, today home to the British Academy.[12] Yachts and motor vehicles were also offered for medical purposes: Lord Tredegar's steam yacht, *Liberty*, for example, was fitted up as a hospital ship, and the delivery vans of Messrs Lyons & Co were commandeered as ambulances. People banded together to sponsor wards, beds, medical facilities and comforts, such as tobacco, for patients. Many general practitioners and other trained medical personnel assumed temporary commissions in the RAMC, while unqualified civilians joined Voluntary Aid Detachments (VADs). These had been organised on a county basis under the auspices of the Red Cross since 1909, and delivered training in first aid and other skills which would help in setting up and running temporary hospitals. In wartime, members of VADs were primed to assume valuable jobs, for example as nurses, stretcher-bearers or hospital cooks. Indeed, numerous middle- and upper-class women joined VADs to train in nursing. Many of the auxiliary hospital schemes put into operation in the course of the war were prepared and staffed by VADs.

Physically, the hospitals of the Great War may be categorised as follows: existing purpose-built military hospitals; existing purpose-built civilian hospitals; complete new hutted hospitals; hutted hospital extensions; converted institutional buildings (for example, schools, colleges, asylums, workhouses) and converted non-institutional buildings, such as houses, hotels (Fig 9.4), warehouses or church halls. The focus here is on hutted hospitals and conversions, since these left the most tangible – if, ultimately, ephemeral – material legacy after 1918.

Hutted hospitals

For 50 years prior to the First World War, the army and the navy had built hospital wards on the pavilion principles endorsed by Florence Nightingale, one of the most recent examples being an extension to the military hospital at Fort Pitt, Chatham, which opened in January 1914.[13] Just one new hospital had been built for casualties of the Boer War, the hutted Princess Louise Hospital at Alton in Hampshire, which was not completed in time and never used for military purposes.[14] Reflecting the influence of modern sanatoria, Alton originally comprised three semicircular groups of 10 wooden ward blocks radiating from the south side of a curved veranda, to maximise sunlight.[15]

Fig 9.4
The Palace Hotel, Southend-on-Sea, Essex, was transformed into HM Queen Mary's Royal Naval Hospital in 1914.
[AA92/02066]

Although the layout of Alton was never exactly replicated, the idea of the hutted hospital was adopted widely during the First World War, and the influence of sanatoria – with an emphasis on fresh air and sunlight – remained pervasive. It was recognised in advance that hospitals might need to be extended quickly in an emergency, and so the War Office drew up model plans for hutted hospitals, comprising four parallel blocks of 25-bed wards (Fig 9.5).[16] This basic official design, by Major Armstrong, was modified by civilian architects in the course of the war, chiefly to implement what was called 'open-air treatment'.

Hutted hospitals could be erected quickly and economically: they could cost as little as £20 per bed (though the standard Armstrong hospital bed cost £80), much less than a well-finished civilian hospital, which might cost £200 a bed, rising to £400 in central London. Some were built as stand-alone hospitals – which inevitably put the cost up – but the majority were erected in the grounds of permanent hospitals, converted houses or other institutions, making use of existing centralised facilities. The single-storey ward blocks were usually built with wooden frames on brick or concrete foundations, with flat or A-frame roofs. They could be clad in corrugated iron, asbestos sheet,[17] timber or, less commonly, brick. Wooden floors were laid with linoleum and metal windows included inward-opening hoppers for optimum ventilation (see Fig 9.3). Heating could be by means of radiators or upright cylindrical slow-combustion stoves, which stood on sheet-iron hearths and had iron flue pipes carried up through the roofs. Electric lighting was standard. The wards were usually arranged in pairs, to either side of a covered way that connected them with central services. These included a recreation room, mess rooms, nurses' quarters, orderlies' accommodation, administrative offices, stores, kitchen, laboratories, operating theatre, X-ray room and mortuary.

One of the first hutted hospitals to be completed was the corrugated-iron 100-bed Welsh War Hospital, assembled on land behind the Royal Victoria Hospital at Netley (see Fig 9.2) in October 1914.[18] Designed by the established hospital architects Edwin T and E Stanley Hall and constructed by Humphreys of Knightsbridge, the huts were initially intended to be sent overseas, but this never happened. Not only did the Welsh War Hospital stay put, but it doubled in size. Humphreys was also responsible for the Queen Mary and Princess Christian base hospital erected at South Queensferry in Scotland in 1914.[19]

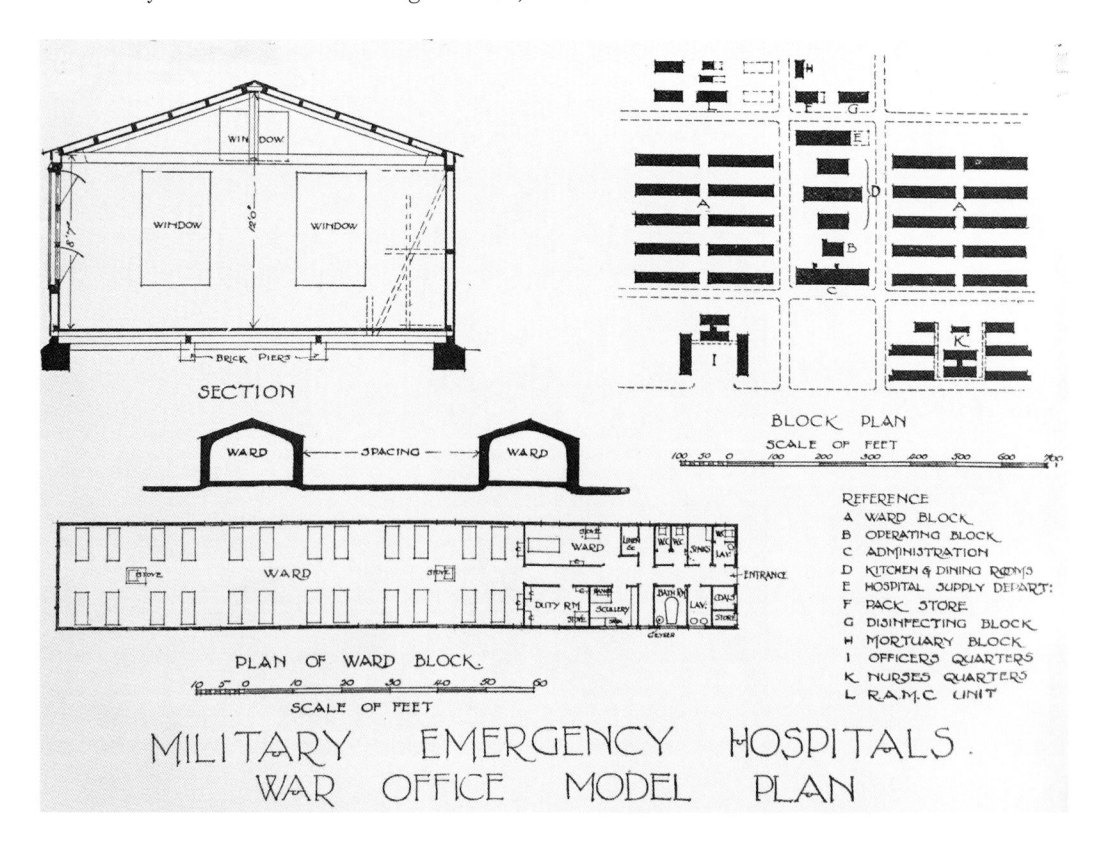

Fig 9.5
The War Office model plan for a Military Emergency Hospital.
[Building News, 17 November 1915, 552]

Before long the hutted hospital complex at Netley was augmented by a Red Cross hospital.[20] The initial section was a 'portable barrack hospital', on the so-called Furley-Fieldhouse pattern, for 500 patients. Sir John Furley was a founder of the British Red Cross and, with William J Fieldhouse, specialised in ambulance trains and stretchers. The Furley-Fieldhouse hospital design appears to have been fairly widely adopted by the Red Cross in the course of the First World War.[21] At Netley it included an operating theatre designed by Fieldhouse himself. Among later additions were a 200-bed 'Irish Hospital' funded by Lord Iveagh, completed in March 1915; non-portable huts on concrete bases; brick-built open-air shelters for tuberculosis cases; orthopaedic workshops; and a convalescent section in marquees. Between 1914 and 1919 the Welsh War Hospital cared for 9,616 patients, while the Red Cross Hospital treated 20,400. In all, Netley is estimated to have processed at least 50,000 casualties.

The highly influential hutted First Eastern General Hospital in Cambridge (Figs 9.6 and 9.7) was begun in late September 1914 and completed eight weeks later.[22] It occupied a perfectly level site, a cricket ground shared by King's and Clare Colleges, today occupied by

Fig 9.6 (above)
The ward huts of the First Eastern General Hospital, built on the cricket fields of King's and Clare Colleges, Cambridge, now the site of the University Library. Note the open south-facing fronts of the ward blocks.
[Courtesy Wellcome Collection / Museum of Military Medicine]

Fig 9.7 (left)
The interior of one of the open-air hutted wards of the First Eastern General Hospital. The men in the foreground are wearing 'hospital blues'.
[Courtesy K A Morrison]

Fig 9.8
The Ontario Military Hospital in Orpington, Kent, built by Canadian engineers to designs by Charles F Skipper. It accepted men from all Allied forces. It opened in February 1916 and received its first casualties in June 1916. When it was extended in 1917 it was renamed the 16th Canadian General Hospital. One of the last hutted hospitals to survive from the First World War, it was photographed in 1996, shortly before the last huts were demolished and houses built on the site. [BB96/00912]

Giles Gilbert Scott's towering Cambridge University Library of 1931–4. It comprised 1,200 beds (later enlarged to 1,700) in 60-bed wards: much larger than the usual civilian complement of 20–25 beds per ward. The overall scheme had been thought out some years previously by Dr Joseph Griffith, head of the Red Cross at Cambridge, following experience with open-air treatment at the city's Addenbrooke's Hospital, and the buildings were designed by Charles F Skipper, architect to the Cambridgeshire and Isle of Ely Territorial Force Association. The buildings incorporated principles that had been tried and tested in the treatment of tuberculosis, pneumonia and bronchitis, in the belief that these would also be beneficial for the healing of wounds. The south sides of the wards were completely open, except for a low railing and canvas sun blinds that flapped noisily, while the north walls incorporated louvred openings close to the roof. It was claimed that 'at the First Eastern Hospital, Cambridge … in spite of the closely drawn blinds over the open south fronts the rain blew into the wards, and even on to the patients' beds in the south row on each ward'.[23] Nevertheless, the patients 'looked upon the hospital as a paradise after life in the trenches'. The nurses, on the other hand, were adversely affected by changes in temperature and became prone to colds.[24]

His expertise established, Skipper went on to design at least 14 other hutted war hospitals, including the Duchess of Connaught's Canadian Red Cross Hospital at Taplow, Buckinghamshire, located by a covered tennis court in the woods near Waldorf Astor's home at Cliveden in Buckinghamshire.[25] The butterfly plan of this hospital optimised sunlight, while window glass was replaced with fine gauze to exclude draughts and dust. Radiators were turned on only when patients were preparing for bed. Skipper also designed the Ontario Military Hospital at Orpington in Kent (Fig 9.8) and the Scottish National Red Cross Hospital in Glasgow.[26]

Architects extending smaller auxiliary hospitals took inspiration from Skipper's ideas, but often modified the open-air concept to allow for bad weather. A symmetrical asbestos-clad hut with two 30-bed wards, designed by local architects Edward Boardman & Son and erected in the grounds of the Norfolk and Norwich Hospital in winter 1914–15, resembled a sanatorium, having a long veranda on which beds were placed (except in inclement weather) along its south side.[27] Other huts described as 'open-air wards' were erected at Royds Hall Hospital in Huddersfield (by Kenneth F Campbell, the Borough Surveyor), at Victoria Park Red Cross Hospital, Newbury, 80 Daisy Bank Road, Manchester (by the Manchester Corporation Architect, Henry Price),[28] and at Hammerton House, 4 Gray Road, Sunderland (by John Hall).[29] A timber hut added to Hammerton House in 1917 illustrated a 'modified form of the open-air principle', having one side which could be closed by a folding Esavian screen. A 16-bed ward for gas poisoning and septic wounds at the Brookdale Auxiliary Home Hospital at Alderley Edge, Cheshire, in 1915, also claimed to be suitable for all weathers. It had:

> an ingenious arrangement of weather-proof shutters travelling upon and dependent from a runway or overhead monorail, running uninterruptedly around the ward outside it. The shutters are of light construction, consisting of a wooden framework panelled with asbestos sheeting, with a suitable number of windows.[30]

The opening of the St John's VAD Hospital, The Woodlands, Southport, Merseyside, in September 1915, is documented in a British Pathé film which shows the open-air Hartley Ward: this was a true open-air ward, typically with the feet of the front row of beds facing the open south front of the hut.[31]

One of the main arguments in favour of open-air treatment in hutted hospitals was that it promoted a quick recovery, with men less likely to require a lengthy stay in a convalescent home. This is a reminder that the primary task of war hospitals was to return soldiers to the front as quickly as possible.

Territorial and war hospitals

The names of the 23 Territorial hospitals planned in 1907 corresponded to the regional army command centres, of which there were 6 in England, 1 in Scotland and 1 in Ireland. The First London General Hospital (Fig 9.9), for example, occupied St Gabriel's College, Camberwell, while the Second Scottish General Hospital was set up in Craigleith Poorhouse (later the Western General), Edinburgh.

Within days of the declaration of war, the Territorial hospitals were mobilised. Their commanders notified the proprietors of buildings earmarked for hospital use, compelling them to vacate the premises. Thus, on 4 August 1914, the Second Eastern General Hospital took possession of the New Grammar School in Brighton and equipped it with 260 beds.[32] Shortly afterwards, a council school nearby was requisitioned to increase capacity. Similarly, on 7 August the Manchester Municipal Secondary School for Boys (or Central High School) on Whitworth Street was taken over by the Second Western General Hospital.[33] To speed up the necessary alterations – bathrooms, beds and telephone lines, costing around £30,000 – a detachment of Royal Engineers was sent from Chester to oversee the work. Since there was little vacant surrounding land, the Second Western expanded through the acquisition of separate sites scattered throughout the Manchester area, rather than by the addition of huts. By August 1917 the hospital had 6,700 beds in 34 different premises, mostly converted schools.[34] The experience was similar in Cardiff, where five schools had been transformed for the Third Western by November 1914.[35]

The five large Territorial hospitals established in London – like most of their ilk throughout the country – were centred on existing institutions, with huts as appendages. Only two were based at civilian hospitals: the Fourth London at King's College Hospital, Denmark Hill, and the Fifth London at St Thomas's Hospital, Lambeth Palace Road. The Third London was set up in the Royal Victoria Patriotic Asylum at Wandsworth Common, built in 1857–9 as an orphanage for dependents of servicemen lost in the Crimean War.[36] As was typical, the children's infirmary was devoted to officers, while the dormitories in the main building (their windows replaced with hopper sashes; baths and lavatories installed) were adapted as wards for 250 men.[37] By October 1915, extensive hutting had been erected in the grounds to the north, and on a portion of the common to the east, providing an additional 1,300 beds. This massive complex was the work of the architect John Pain Clark. The first huts were on the War Office (probably Armstrong) pattern; the remainder had continuous hopper glazing.

In summer 1916 the interior designer Howard Kemp Prosser offered to paint the walls of London's military hospitals in 'peace' colours, preferring yellow 'with violet, mauve, sapphire,

Fig 9.9
A school next door to St Gabriel's College, Cormont Road, Camberwell, taken over by the First London General Hospital during the Great War and flying the red cross.
[AA92/2071]

and green for accessory relief'.[38] According to Kemp Prosser, soldiers were averse to red colours, 'which greatly affect them'. The 'Kemp Prosser "Colour Cure"' even found its way into wartime advertisements for paint.[39]

Another Territorial hospital based in an existing building and enlarged by huts was the Fifth Northern in Leicester. It cost £10,000 to convert the Leicester and Rutland County Asylum (now the Fielding Johnson Building, University of Leicester), a large institution which had been unoccupied for several years, plus an additional £5,000 to equip it as a military hospital.[40] The biggest expenses included overhauling the drains and adding sanitary facilities. Furthermore, in order to make use of the single cells – a standard feature of Victorian lunatic asylums – their doors were removed and windows enlarged. Some saving was made, however, by reusing old materials, obtained by demolishing the walls of the airing yards and redundant ancillary structures. A hutted extension, designed by the local architect S Perkins Pick in 1915, included flat-roofed open-air wards.[41]

By the end of 1917 the Territorial hospitals held 48,234 beds. They were augmented by numerous so-called 'war hospitals', as the military gradually took over the best and most up-to-date asylums (for example, the Edinburgh War Hospital, Bangour), poor-law institutions (for example, the Military Orthopaedic Hospital, Shepherd's Bush, London) and Metropolitan Asylums Board (MAB) fever hospitals (for example Dartford War Hospital).[42] These war hospitals provided 58,000 beds by the armistice. In addition, several new hutted military hospitals were built, ranging from the Princess Christian Military (until 1917 Red Cross) Hospital, Englefield Green, Surrey, with 120 beds, to the Oswestry Military Hospital, Shropshire, with 3,116 beds. Over and above this, hospital provision at hutted camps – constructed for recruits from October 1914 – expanded greatly as the war progressed: initially these camps had little more than sick bays in marquees, but as they grew, so did their medical provisions.[43] The largest camp hospitals were located on and around Salisbury Plain (for example, Chiseldon Camp Military Hospital, with 1,120 beds), and comprised hutting augmented by tents. A separate hospital, surrounded by barbed wire, for soldiers suffering from venereal disease was set up at Chiseldon in 1917. This had over 1,000 beds and was known locally as the 'Bad Boys' Camp'.

Hospitals for the Allied forces and prisoners of war

Although British military hospitals did not discriminate by nationality, several hospitals were operated by and for Britain's allies, including those from Belgium, India, Canada, New Zealand, Australia, South Africa and America. It was thought that men would benefit from the care and company of their compatriots.

It was originally planned that Indian troops would be sent to a hospital in Alexandria, but it proved more convenient to bring them to England. Eventually three hospitals in Brighton provided 3,300 beds for Indian soldiers under the control of the Indian Medical Service. These included one of the most extraordinary hospital conversions of the war, the Royal Pavilion (Fig 9.10), as well as the Secondary Council School on York Place and Brighton Poor Law Institution on Elm Grove, which was renamed the Kitchener Indian Hospital. The Kitchener had

Fig 9.10
Indian soldiers under the exotic dome of the Royal Pavilion, Brighton, painted by Douglas Fox-Pitt in 1919.
[IWM ART 000323 A]

over 2,000 beds and was staffed entirely by men. Every block had three kitchens: 'one for Mahomedans, one for vegetarian Hindus and one for meat-eating Hindus', and provided six alternative diets.[44] A floor of the Royal Victoria Hospital at Netley was also given over to Indian soldiers, and a ghat (crematorium) built by a stream in the grounds. Those who died in the Brighton hospitals were cremated on a funeral pyre at Patcham.

At least 15 general hospitals and numerous convalescent homes were devoted to Canadian troops. By October 1914 Sir Arthur Markham's house, Beachborough Park near Shorncliffe in Kent – a strategic position close to Folkestone – had been transformed into the Queen's Canadian Military Hospital and was equipped with wards, X-ray machinery and an operating theatre.[45] Its first intake of patients came from Antwerp, which had fallen after a prolonged bombardment. By November 1915 a hutted hospital had been added to the site following designs by the architect W Henry White (Fig 9.11). As well as the Canadian Hospital at Taplow and the Ontario Hospital in Orpington (see p 186), the King's Canadian Red Cross Special Hospital at Bushy Park, London, was a notable establishment. It steadily expanded between 1915 and 1919, from 30 to 300 beds. After a spell as an open-air school, in 1944 the site became the Supreme Headquarters of the Allied Expeditionary Force under General Eisenhower.

The first hospital devoted to New Zealand troops (later named the No 2 New Zealand General Hospital) occupied an Italianate villa, Mount Felix (demolished), at Walton-on-Thames, Surrey. This had originally been requisitioned for billeting British troops, but was offered to the New Zealand War Contingent Association by the War Office in June 1915, and was quickly converted into a large hospital. Within two days of opening in August 1915, it began to receive casualties from Gallipoli. Typically, huts were later added, increasing the capacity of the hospital to over 1,000. In July 1916 a convalescent hospital opened for New Zealand troops at Grey Towers (demolished), Hornchurch, in the London Borough of Havering, and a month later another hospital (the No 1 New Zealand General Hospital) opened at Brockenhurst in Hampshire. This received men who disembarked at Southampton, while Mount Felix took men from Dover.

From 1915, the primary Australian establishment was Harefield Park, Middlesex, offered by its Australian owner, Charles Billyard-Leake, as a convalescent home and, following the usual pattern, soon greatly extended by hutting. The principal convalescent establishments for Australians were the base depot at Weymouth, Dorset, and an intermediate depot at Bostall Heath in Greenwich.

America joined the war in April 1917. US servicemen were given the use of two large Victorian hospitals, originally built by the MAB as fever hospitals, while several houses dotted around London (such as St Katherine's Lodge in Regent's Park, which took orthopaedic cases) provided more comfortable quarters for the recuperation of American officers. In May 1918 the Joint War Committee decided to gift a fully equipped 500-bed Red Cross hospital to American troops, as an expression of gratitude for their involvement in the war. The King gave land in Windsor Great Park, and plans were laid for 'the finest example of a hut hospital which can be built in the light of the experience gained since war broke out'.[46] This was to be set out in a semicircle. In July 1918, however, a site with better drainage was chosen in Richmond Park, where there was already an extensive hutted hospital for South African troops.[47] Like the established South African hospital, the American hospital was to include a theatre for 'cinematograph shows'.[48] The design, by the Office of Works architect R J Allison, was progressing well in

Fig 9.11
Plan of the hutted extension to the Queen's Canadian Military Hospital (Beachborough Park), Shorncliffe, Kent.
[Building News, 17 November 1915, 552]

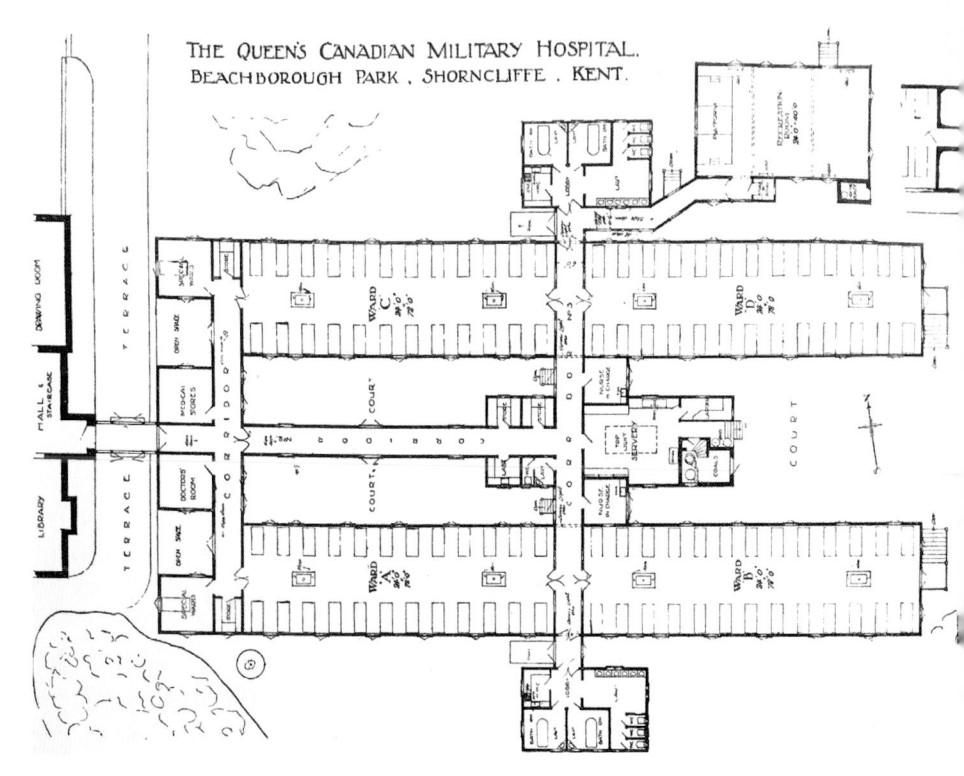

November 1918, when the war ended. Almost immediately it was decided to demolish the partially complete huts and reinstate the site. No doubt some foundations from this short-lived complex lurk beneath the surface of Richmond Park, ready to confuse the archaeologists of the future. The financial loss, borne by the Red Cross, was computed at £38,460.

Another important American hospital under construction in the closing years of the war, but again never completed, was Sarisbury Court near Southampton. Trees on the estate were felled to provide timber for ward huts, which were to be steam heated; meanwhile, 'Bessonneau' tents – with windows in the sides and double roofs – were erected for use as wards.[49] Surprisingly, over half of the deaths of American servicemen in Britain were caused not by wounds, but by influenza.[50] The global pandemic of 1918 was probably exacerbated by wartime conditions and placed a great strain on medical resources in the UK in the closing months of the war.

At first, prisoners of war were distributed to the military hospitals in the same manner as Allied sick and wounded. In autumn 1914 those in Netley received a high-profile visit from the King, which was reported in German newspapers.[51] In 1917 separate hospitals were established for imprisoned German combatants at Belmont (a former workhouse in Surrey) and Brocton, a hutted complex attached to a camp in Staffordshire (Fig 9.12).[52] Otherwise large numbers were received in separate divisions of the Dartford War Hospital, Oswestry Military Hospital, Fargo Camp Military Hospital on Salisbury Plain, Nell Lane Military Hospital in West Didsbury (Manchester) and elsewhere. Conditions in prisoner-of-war hospitals were monitored by a Swiss delegation whose reports are invaluable to historians.[53]

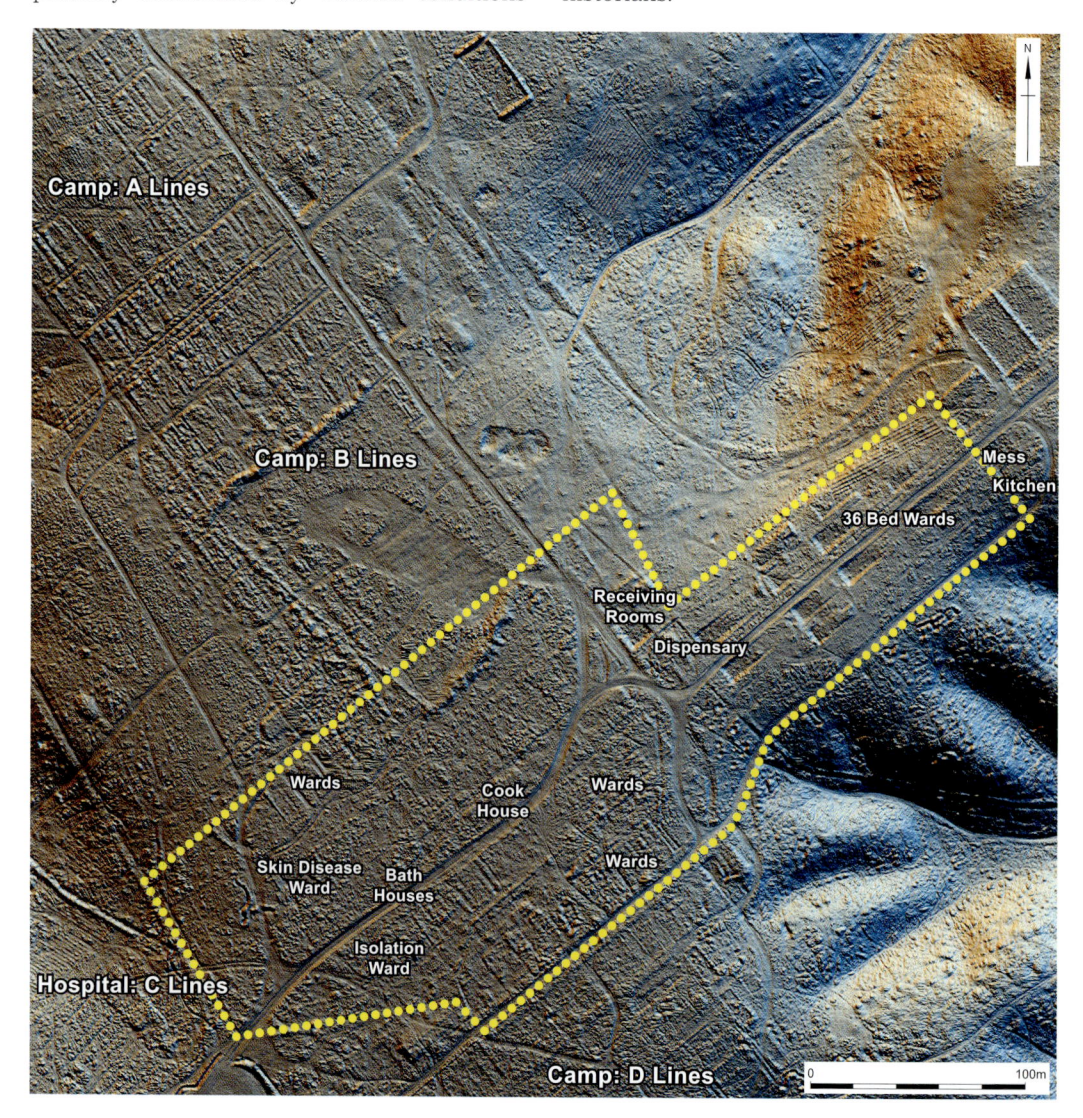

Fig 9.12
Overgrown earthworks revealed through lidar. These are all that remain of the 1,000-bed prisoner-of-war hospital at Brocton in Staffordshire.
[Chase Through Time 2016 lidar. Source Staffordshire CC/Fugro Geospatial BV 2016]

Auxiliary hospitals and convalescent homes

In August 1914 the Duke of Sutherland began to organise the registration of country houses as temporary hospitals, and himself offered Dunrobin Castle, Sutherland, as a surgical base for the North Sea Fleet.[54] Soon the Duke's appeal had elicited 250 responses, including golf clubs and a bishop's palace, as well as country houses.[55] At the same time, however, it was the duty of the Incorporated Soldiers' and Sailors' Help Society to organise temporary convalescent homes for wounded and disabled men in time of war, and they, too, issued a call for the donation of properties.[56] Eventually these two initiatives collaborated to create a Central Convalescent Home Registry, with the intention of placing men on sick furlough close to their own homes. In the first months of the war, it was considered beneficial for men to recuperate at home, with their family and friends, before returning to the front, but it was found that home circumstances were not always ideal for this purpose.

Auxiliary hospitals, including convalescent homes, received less severe cases than the military hospitals; they had milder discipline and suffered fewer fatalities. Between 1914 and 1918 the Joint War Committee operated approximately 1,000 auxiliary hospitals (353 in London alone) of wildly varying sizes in England and Wales.[57] From September 1915 these were divided into Class A (essentially overflows for the military and Territorial hospitals, though some did receive patients direct from overseas) and Class B (previously referred to as convalescent homes). They received considerable government grants (70 per cent of their costs; the remaining 30 per cent was raised by voluntary subscription and fundraising) and were attached administratively to the principal military hospitals. Lady Ridley's Hospital, for example, was affiliated with Queen Alexandra's Hospital, Millbank. It was calculated that the auxiliary hospitals provided 11,730 beds by November 1914, 32,582 by August 1915, 43,445 by August 1916 and 59,706 by September 1917.[58]

Most of the auxiliary hospitals occupied non-institutional buildings which required a greater degree of adaptation than, for example, workhouses or asylums. This generally involved the addition of sanitary facilities, an operating theatre and X-ray equipment. Some extraordinary conversions took place. In 1914, for example, the Duchess of Bedford turned the Riding School at Woburn Abbey, Bedfordshire, into a hospital by removing the ground-floor windows and adding a veranda. In country houses, valuable items were stowed away for safety and architectural features were protected. This was the case at Dunham Massey, Cheshire – Stamford Military Hospital – which treated 281 cases between April 1917 and January 1919. Several of the hospital's principal rooms were recreated in 2014 by its present owner, the National Trust, to mark the centenary of the war.[59] As in 1917, items of furniture were stored in the Great Gallery. Visitors could see the main ward named 'Bagdad' (the Saloon, with its columns boxed in), the recreation/mess room (the Great Hall), the operating theatre (tucked under the Great Stair) and the nurses' station (the Billiard Room). Each room was furnished with original artefacts that had survived in the house since 1919.

The single most important conversion was probably the 1,650-bed King George V Military Hospital in London. This Red Cross hospital opened (for surgical cases) on 26 May 1915 in a six-storey reinforced-concrete warehouse (1912–14; R J Allison) at Waterloo, built for His Majesty's Stationery Office.[60] The building's open floors were supported by rows of columns, three or four bays wide, and lit by three central 'open areas'. This was far from ideal for the purpose of a hospital, but by erecting light asbestos-sheet partitions the architect Edwin T Hall managed to create individual wards to either side of central corridors.[61] Lighting and ventilation remained inadequate, but the hospital had distinct advantages, including its airy roof garden and its proximity to Waterloo Station. On a much smaller scale, and much less suited to hospital use, was St Matthew's Church Institute in Willesden, north London. This was transformed by the architect J H Fry into a 30-bed hospital with three rows of beds in the hall, and an operating theatre in the committee room. Other buildings unexpectedly turned to hospital use included the village hall in Shepreth, Cambridgeshire; swimming baths in Swindon; the Grand Stand at Epsom; the cricket pavilion at Trent Bridge, Nottingham; and a Masonic Hall in West Hartlepool, which was shelled during the bombardment of the town in December 1914.

Some military and auxiliary hospitals were exclusively for officers, but the majority accepted both officers and men, though always segregated in separate wards. Greater distinctions were applied to the handling of convalescents. In November 1914 the Central Convalescent

Wrest Park Hospital

Andrew Hann

Wrest Park, the Bedfordshire seat of Lord Lucas, was probably the first country house to take in wounded soldiers during the Great War. On 5 August 1914, the day after war was declared, Lord Lucas (always known as Bron) wrote to Winston Churchill offering up Wrest as a hospital for naval ratings (Fig 9.13).[62] The offer was accepted, and work started immediately to convert the house into a hospital, supervised by his sister, Nan Herbert, later 9th Baroness Lucas: furniture was cleared and moved to the basement, 130 hospital beds were acquired, temporary electric lighting was installed and 20 nurses were recruited (Fig 9.14). Dr Sydney Beauchamp, a family friend, agreed to act as resident surgeon. Another friend, J M Barrie, author of *Peter Pan*, gave £1,000 to support the venture. He would later be a regular visitor to the hospital, organising games and entertainment for the convalescents.

By September, however, it was thought that the hospital at Wrest would not be needed, and Lord Knutsford, chairman of the London Hospital House Committee, asked if it could instead be used as a convalescent home. The first 66 convalescents arrived from the General Hospital, Whitechapel, on 7 September 1914, just two weeks after the first major engagement involving British troops, at the Battle of Mons. Their arrival was widely reported in the local press, and welcomed by a large crowd of villagers as they disembarked from a fleet of motorcars and omnibuses.[63]

By early October the last of the convalescents had been discharged, and with no new arrivals in prospect the home closed. However, with casualties on the Western Front continuing to mount, Wrest was reopened a month later as a base hospital. It was run jointly with nearby Woburn Abbey, receiving wounded soldiers by ambulance train directly from the front line. The first 100 patients arrived on 20 November, brought from Ampthill station.[64]

Conversion from convalescent home to hospital had been achieved in little more than a week. The enfilade of ground-floor reception rooms became A-Ward, housing the most serious cases. B-Ward was in the large first-floor bedrooms on the south side of the house overlooking the gardens, while C-Ward was hidden away in the Bachelors' Wing on the east side of the house. Rooms for the medical officer, X-ray equipment and operating theatre were provided on the north side of the first floor, and a stripping room for delousing in the former billiard room (Fig 9.15). The 24 nurses occupied servants' rooms on the attic floor. Nan took over the more generously proportioned housekeeper's suite at the west end of the attic corridor.

Fig 9.13 Auberon Herbert, 8th Baron Lucas, in uniform as a captain in the Royal Flying Corps. He enlisted in June 1915, trained as an observer at Fort George, Gosport, Hampshire, and was deployed to Egypt with 14 Squadron, 5th Wing, then to the Western Front with 48 Squadron. [Private Collection]

Fig 9.14 Wrest House library after conversion to a hospital ward, September 1914. Note the bookshelves covered over with sheeting, and temporary electric lighting suspended from the ceiling. [Private Collection]

We know a good deal about the running of the hospital because of a detailed diary kept by Nan (Fig 9.16) and the scrapbooks she compiled after the war, bringing together letters, photographs and other ephemera. She wrote on 1 October 1915, a typical day in the life of the hospital: 'Early morning round and hard work at nurses' register and correspondence. Mr Ewart [the surgeon] arrived at 1.54 for eleven operations. I attended four, and did swabs for the appendix case.' Some of the entries capture the full horrors of war. For instance, on 17 July 1916: 'Hectic day. Long round in C-Ward. At 12.15 emergency operation; Kirkwood took off man's arm… Have never seen anything like it – up to the elbow the arm was rotten and blue (gas gangrene).'

In February 1915, following an intensive course of training at the Metropolitan Hospital in London, Nan took over as matron from the ineffectual Sister Martin. Over the next two years this formidable woman ran the hospital with military efficiency, ably assisted by the Medical Officer, firstly Dr Sydney Beauchamp, then Dr William Kirkwood, and Army Surgeon Major Churton. She recruited the nurses, arranged provisions and managed the throughput of patients. When beds were vacated a telegram was sent to the War Office stating how many spaces were available, and a few days later new cases arrived by ambulance train. Officially Wrest had 150 beds, though on occasion there were 200 patients in residence. Once well enough they were moved on to a ring of smaller convalescent homes that had been set up in the vicinity, such as Bromham Hall, Hinwick House and Old Warden Park, freeing up space for new arrivals.[65] In all 1,600 men passed through the hospital's wards. By the summer of 1916 Wrest had a deserved reputation as one of the best country-house base hospitals.

Conditions were more relaxed at Wrest than in most military and Red Cross hospitals. Convalescents had full use of the grounds, and photographs show them playing football and tennis, fishing and boating on the lakes. A full programme of social activities was laid on to keep up morale, including outings, cricket matches, concerts and theatricals in the staircase hall (Fig 9.17). Fraternising between staff and patients was tolerated too, although in May 1915 a former NCO, Sergeant Major Kingsley, was brought in to improve discipline.[66] Unlike most auxiliary hospitals, Wrest was run and

Fig 9.15
Wrest House stripping room in the former billiard room used for delousing patients arriving. The 'louse room' was installed in November 1914 with 'arrangements made for the inexhaustible supply of hot water to supply the line of baths'. [London Metropolitan Archives, City of London; Courtesy Royal Sun Alliance]

Fig 9.16
Nan Herbert dressed in her matron's uniform, 1915. Her first experience of nursing came as a volunteer with the Red Cross in Montenegro in the First Balkan War in the winter of 1912–13. [Private Collection]

Fig 9.17
Convalescents watching a concert in the staircase hall, September 1914. Nan wrote in her journal: 'Summers, the little Cockney from the London Hospital unearthed the old costume box, and from that time, evening concerts were in steady demand, especially as extra beer was served.' Scrapbook, September 1914. [Private Collection]

Fig 9.18
The north front of Wrest House after the fire with rescued hospital furniture in the foreground, 15 September 1916. The fire started when sparks from a defective boiler flue at the east end of the house set roof timbers alight and spread rapidly along the roof space, destroying much of the attic storey as far as the central dome.
[Private Collection]

Fig 9.19
Convalescents manning Wrest House's manual fire engine during a fire drill in November 1915. The manual engine, rather old-fashioned by then, drew water from hydrants located around the curtilage of the mansion. The estate also had a more modern Merryweather steam fire engine (current whereabouts unknown).
[Private Collection]

financed independently by the Lucas family and their friends. Surviving hospital accounts for August 1914 to February 1915 reveal expenditure of £8,163, including £1,216 on hospital equipment, £856 on groceries and £555 on nurses' wages. Nan confessed that in the early days of the hospital they had been rather reckless financially. Land agent Cecil Argles, who kept the accounts, calculated that during May and June 1915 37,888 meals were served in the hospital at a cost of 11s 7d per person per week.

The end of the hospital came abruptly on 14 September 1916 when a chimney fire at the east end of the house caused serious damage to the upper storey (Fig 9.18).[67] All the patients were safely evacuated, thanks in part to the regular fire drills that Nan had instituted (Fig 9.19). The most serious cases were transferred to Woburn and the walking wounded to Ampthill Training Depot[68] along with the nurses, who had lost most of their possessions in the fire. The staff were keen to continue, but the damage was such that reopening was not a practical option. Moreover, with AMS now better resourced, there was less need for a privately run hospital such as Wrest.[69] Indeed, Lord Lucas had already made plans for the sale of Wrest and its contents when he was killed in action on 3 November, having joined the RFC. The house was quickly patched up and sold in September 1917 to John George Murray, an industrialist from north-east England.

Today little physical evidence of the hospital remains, due to the extensive renovation after the fire by Mr Murray, and further work when Wrest was used as an agricultural research institute after the Second World War. Brick inserts in the library fireplaces, later tiled, are from this period,[70] as probably are some modifications to the engine house associated with the introduction of electricity.[71] Evidence of the fire is scanty: a few scorched door frames on the attic storey and some blackening of roof timbers within the central dome.[72] The archival record is, however, outstanding, providing a detailed and evocative picture of the hospital in operation, and enabling the use of many of the rooms within the mansion to be identified.

Home Registry was abandoned, and separate registers were set up for officers (a central register held by the War Office) and for the rank and file (registers in the separate command centres, designed to tighten supervision over those on sick furlough). Class B auxiliary hospitals, dotted throughout the country, were now largely restricted to officers.[73] The Joint War Committee even provided funding to enable officers to be housed with their families and a servant for the period of their convalescence. Meanwhile, in contrast, 'Tommies' were sent to large military convalescent hospitals (Fig 9.20).[74] The first of these opened at Eastbourne on 8 April 1915, with accommodation for 3,840 men (Fig 9.21). At least 10 similar establishments had opened by the end of 1917, including a Dysentery Convalescent Depot which opened at Barton on Sea, Hampshire, in April 1916.[75] These establishments were for men likely to be fit for duty within six weeks. Those requiring longer to build up their strength were summoned to a Command Depot. Established in late 1915, these provided exercise, therapeutic gymnastics and massage rather than medical treatment. Twenty existed by April 1918.

Disabling Injuries

Of course, many men were unable to rejoin their comrades at the front. Wartime hospitals dealt with horrifically disabling injuries, mental and physical, which few doctors had encountered before. Despite the stressful and often makeshift conditions in wartime hospitals, important medical advances were pioneered, notably in the fields of psychiatry, orthopaedics and plastic surgery. Even in specialist hospitals, however, men were segregated from officers.

In the first years of the war, the government failed to cope with the needs of disabled men. The War Pensions Statutory Committee was formed in 1915 to coordinate medical treatment, training and employment for men who had left the services through disability, but it was insufficiently resourced. The Ministry of Pensions was formed in 1916, uniting the pensions systems of the War Office and Admiralty, and in 1917 it formed a subcommittee on Institutional Treatment, concentrating on paraplegics, neurasthenics, epileptics and advanced cases of tuberculosis. From 1917 further funding for institutions for these cases came from the Joint War Committee, and a number of new institutions were created to deliver the specialist care and training which disabled servicemen required.

Fig 9.20
A large ward of the King George V Military Hospital, Stamford Street, London, painted by J Hodgson Lobley in 1918. The patients wear 'hospital blues'.
[© IWM ART 003821]

Fig 9.21
Eastbourne, Sussex. A convalescent camp.
[BB90/09277]

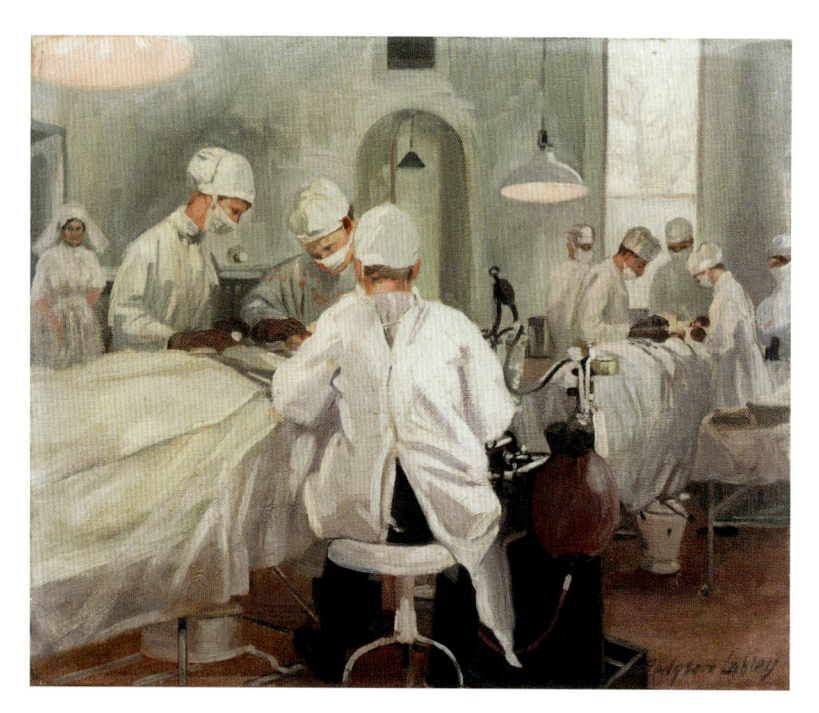

Fig 9.22
The operating theatre of the Queen's Hospital for Facial Injuries, Frognal, Sidcup, Kent, painted by J Hodgson Lobley in 1918. Two operations are in progress.
[© IWM ART 003659]

Much has been written about the treatment the war poets Siegfried Sassoon and Wilfred Owen received for shell shock from Dr W H R Rivers at Slateford Military Hospital, a hospital for officers at Craiglockhart, Edinburgh. By 1918 the country was equipped with six special hospitals for officers with shell shock, and 16 for other ranks, many of whom ended up in the asylum (Block D) at Netley. Treatment was experimental and variable: Rivers favoured a 'talking cure', but others practised combinations of psychotherapy, massage, electric-shock treatment, isolation or light work.

As well as admitting cases of shell shock, the 1,000-bed Canadian Special Hospital in the Granville Hotel, Ramsgate,[76] treated injuries to bones and joints. Many servicemen suffered severe injuries to their limbs and underwent amputations. A year or two into the war it was realised that such men were being discharged too soon from the general military hospitals, and that further specialist treatment and rehabilitation was desirable. In 1915 Queen Mary's Convalescent Auxiliary Hospital for the Limbless opened in Roehampton House, south-west London, and did much beneficial work in fitting, and eventually manufacturing, artificial limbs.[77] In 1916 a Department of Military Orthopaedics was established within the British army, headed by the surgeon Robert Jones.[78] One of the first dedicated military orthopaedic hospitals opened in London in February 1916 in the Hammersmith Workhouse Infirmary, next to Wormwood Scrubs. This was an up-to-date poor-law hospital, built in 1903–5. Here Jones set up a hospital which served as a model for other orthopaedic centres, providing massage, electrical treatment, hydrotherapy and, crucially, training workshops to promote rehabilitation. All kinds of training were provided, from making surgical boots to photographic work. By this stage of the war, vocational training was available for disabled men at most of the large military hospitals, including Netley.

The principal military hospital for injuries to the face and jaw was the Queen's Hospital for Facial Injuries, which opened in August 1917 in Frognal House, Sidcup (Fig 9.22). The ward huts in the grounds were arranged radially.[79] This specialist hospital, with six attached auxiliary hospitals, became renowned, but maxillofacial surgery was undertaken at many other hospitals, for example the Cambridge Military Hospital, Aldershot. The Third London (see p 187) had a special centre where surgeons and artists cooperated to manufacture lifelike masks for servicemen with disfigured faces.[80] Furthermore, every military hospital had a dental department.

Many other specialist hospitals existed for military cases, including those repatriated with malaria. Isolating those with dysentery was of vital importance, to prevent them spreading the disease. Many blind cases were sent to the Second London or St Dunstan's (see below). Venereal cases were generally not returned to Britain until after the armistice, but special hospitals for venereal disease did exist in each command area. In March 1919 the country had over 8,000 beds for servicemen with venereal disease.

Aftermath

Britain was bound to care for large numbers of disabled servicemen for decades to come. An early initiative was the purchase in 1915 of the Star and Garter Hotel, Richmond, for permanently disabled soldiers and sailors. An annexe containing the banqueting hall and ballroom was retained for immediate use while the main building was pulled down and work commenced on a new building designed by Edwin Cooper, following plans drawn up by Giles Gilbert Scott.[81] This project, however, was defeated by wartime shortages of labour and materials, and had to be suspended. The home was eventually built in 1921–4, and opened as the women of the Empire's memorial to the Great War.

Another early initiative, started in March 1915, was St Dunstan's, a villa in Regent's Park which – together with several other houses and annexes – rehabilitated blinded servicemen. It has been estimated that 95 per cent of the men blinded by war service lived at one time, or were trained, at St Dunstan's. The original villa, by Decimus Burton, was demolished in the 1930s and replaced by a new house for Barbara Woolworth.

Village centres, or colonies, were set up to house disabled men and train them in appropriate work, examples being Enham in Hampshire (set up by the Village Centres Council with grants from various bodies, such as the British Red Cross) and Shrivenham in Berkshire (set up by Lady Barrington, who raised funds through charitable endeavours).

In 1919 the Ministry of Pensions assumed responsibility from the War Office for wounded and disabled soldiers. It acquired many wartime hospitals, for example buying the Canadian Hospital at Orpington for £80,000. Many of these institutions continued to care for the disabled and shell-shocked for decades. Other war hospitals became specialist orthopaedic centres, caring for the civilian population. One example was the Shropshire Orthopaedic Hospital (later renamed the Robert Jones and Agnes Hunt Orthopaedic Hospital) near Oswestry.[82] Although some of these sites have continued to function as hospitals to the present day, their original buildings have long been superseded by more permanent structures. Typically, the huts at Oswestry were replaced by new buildings in 1931–3.

Most wartime hospitals closed in the course of 1919. In London some hospital huts continued to occupy public spaces for years after the war. Those of the Fourth London (Fig 9.23) in Ruskin Park, Denmark Hill, were still in use in 1921, despite the availability of beds in the nearby main building of King's College Hospital and a local demand for recreation space.[83] These

Fig 9.23
Interior of a ward hut, at the Fourth London General Hospital, 1918. Note the stove and the piano. A full set of photographs of this hospital, showing treatment and wounded soldiers in the grounds, was taken in 1918 by George P Lewis.
[© IWM Q 027808]

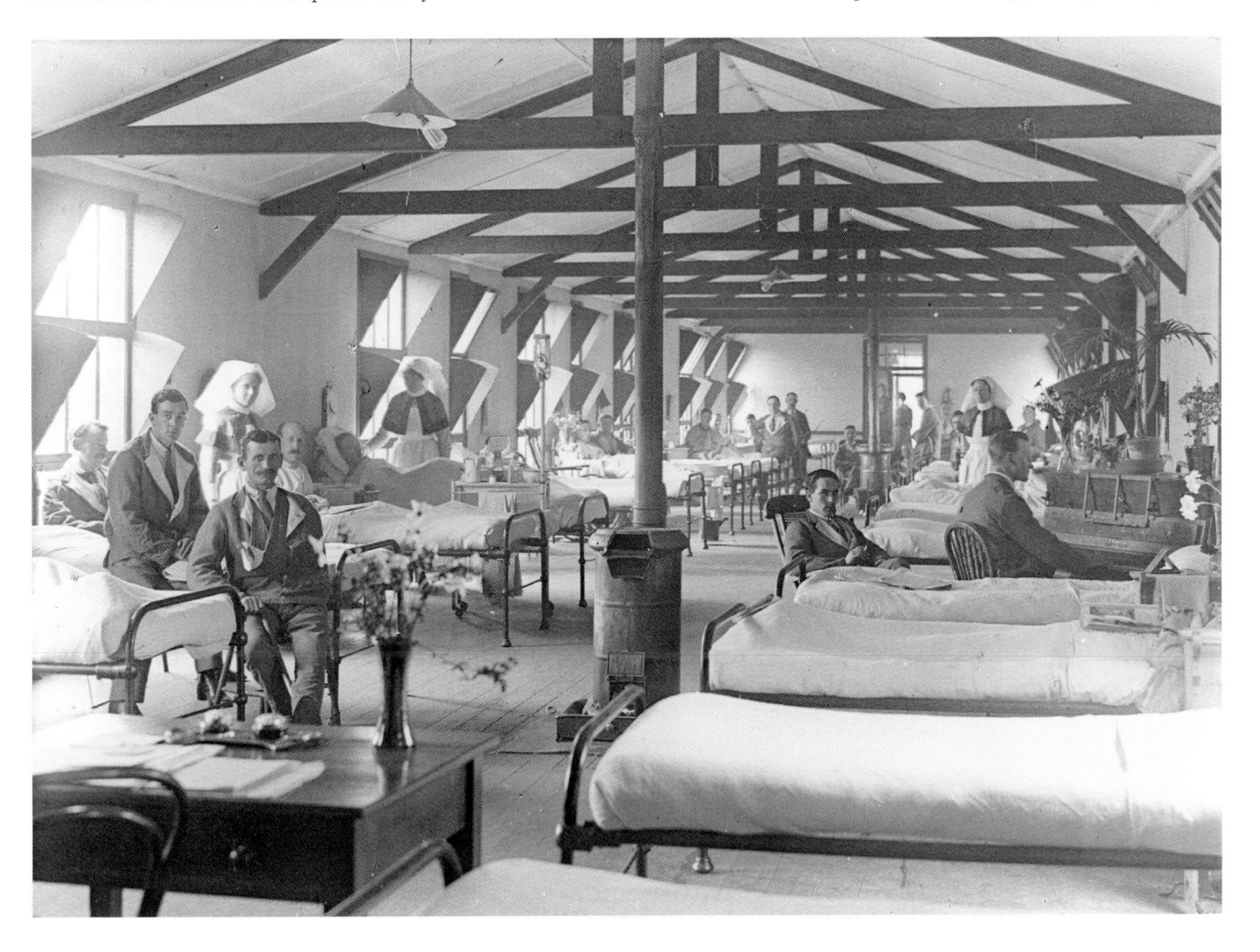

huts were eventually sold at auction in 1924.[84] Indeed, most temporary hospital buildings had been sold off by 1925, often through the Surplus Government Property Disposals Board. When the New Zealand government advertised the buildings of the Second New Zealand Hospital, Mount Felix, Walton-on-Thames, in September 1919, it suggested that they might be suitable for conversion into bungalows.[85] Certainly, hospital huts in northern France seem to have been recycled as housing in war-torn villages. Others in Britain became village halls. The Memorial Hall at Wellington Heath near Ledbury in Herefordshire, for example, comprised a 'hospital hut' and two circular steel tents, purchased in 1923 from George Blay, a contractor to the War Office.[86] The 'hospital hut' was a Nissen hut, with a semicircular profile clad in corrugated iron, and with a continuous roof lantern rather than the more typical dormers. Nissen huts had been designed by Captain Peter Norman Nissen and entered production in 1916. Their chief benefit was portability, and they were mainly used for barracks. Although widely used for hospitals in the Second World War, no hospital huts of this form are known to have been erected in Britain in 1916–18, though they were certainly used on the continent, as can be seen in archive photographs of the Fourth Station Hospital, Longueness,[87] and at Hesdin.[88]

As early as October 1914, *The Hospital* predicted the fate of the hutted hospitals of the Great War:

> it must not be forgotten that these institutions sooner or later are destined to disappear as rapidly as they arose, and can necessarily leave little to recall their value beyond the memories of those who were personally engaged in working them.[89]

No First World War hospital ward huts are known to survive today – one of the last complexes, at Orpington (*see* Fig 9.8), was demolished in 1996 – and the redevelopment of sites means that they have left few permanent marks on the landscape.[90] Most poignantly, the hospitals of the First World War have now also passed beyond living memory.

Though the hospital wards have gone at Orpington, the Clock Tower from the Reception Block was saved when the building was demolished and was set up in its present location in 1993 (Fig 9.24). Other rare fragments of wartime hospitals may survive elsewhere, possibly unrecognised or *ex situ*. Traces of the medical history of the war may linger in the hundreds of houses and other buildings converted into temporary hospitals, though in most cases their pre-war condition was quickly reinstated after 1918. In general, the most tangible evidence of the hospitals of the First World War is commemorative, taking the form of memorial plaques, street names or artworks. The University of Leicester, for example – established in the former Fifth Northern General Hospital in 1921 – was conceived as a war memorial and adopted the apt motto *ut vitam habeant* ('so that they have life').

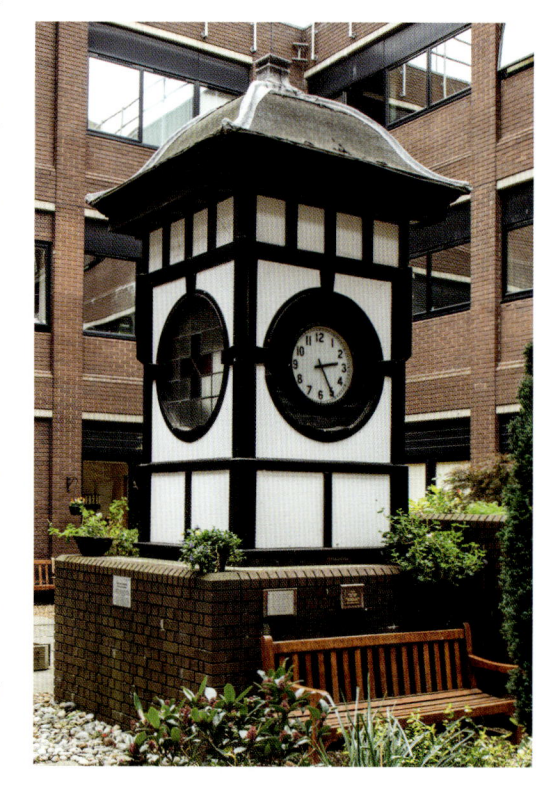

Fig 9.24
Clock Tower from the Reception Block, the only surviving part of Ontario Military Hospital, Orpington. Dating from 1916, it was recovered when the building was demolished and is now located in the internal courtyard of the Canada Wing (1983) of Orpington Hospital.
[DP217122]

10

Remembering the dead

Roger Bowdler

Expressions of loss: the English war memorial

War memorials of the Great War represent the greatest wave of commemoration ever experienced in Britain. Tens of thousands – we do not yet know just how many – were raised by communities during and after the war, ranging from mighty monuments of bronze to plain crosses, and from modest cottages for district nurses to football grounds.[1] Today, they constitute the most enduring tangible legacy of that conflict. Nor are they slipping from public consciousness: indeed, quite the reverse is happening.[2] The late A A Gill described them as:

> the great blessing of the English. Culturally, they are their finest creation ... Over time war memorials grow in stature, they don't grow old as other art grows old. Their simplicity and honesty, their grave purpose and their heavy mordant elegance grows into the age. They seem to anticipate the look of things to come, the brutal, minimal stark lines and planes, the emptiness of the post-war world.[3]

Others came to criticise them as inadequate responses to world catastrophe.

Writer J B Priestley had served at the front and had lost many of his companions. As recounted in his 1934 travelogue *English Journey*, he returned to Bradford for a reunion of the Duke of Wellington's Regiment. Amid the bonhomie was much underlying sadness:

> the men who were boys when I was a boy are dead. Indeed, they never even grew to be men. They were slaughtered in youth; and the parents of them have gone lonely, the girls they would have married have grown grey in spinsterhood, and the work they would have done has remained undone. It is an old worn topic: the choicer spirits begin to yawn at the sight of it; those of us who are left of that generation are, it seems, rapidly becoming mumbling old bores.[4]

Priestley was not quite 40 when he wrote this. Memorials, respectful and humane as they might be, could not help but trigger bitter thoughts towards the futility of the war. One such memorial glimpsed on his travels ('a fine obelisk, carefully flood-lit after dark') led him to a devastating conclusion: 'The same old muddle, you see: reaching down to the very grave, the mouldering bones.'[5] A similar mood is conjured up in Alan Sorrell's 1936 *A Land Fit for Heroes* (Fig 10.1). The apogee of a memorial's purpose was to serve as the backdrop to annual services of remembrance, but Sorrell's dark scene provided mordant commentary on such events, as a veteran grandee is ushered along a file of broken men, their wheelchairs and litters drawn up in pathetic parade-ground fashion. While there is a danger of this preoccupation with death veiling our understanding of the conflict,[6] war memorials retain an immediacy and local relevance one hundred years on. Of all the reminders of the Great War today, war memorials are surely the most poignant.

Origins and emergence

Such commemoration had clear antecedents, but the quantity of the monuments erected in the years after 1918 was wholly unprecedented. Public memorials to the dead of the Napoleonic Wars tended to be reserved for officers receiving monuments in churches.[7] The first stirrings of commemoration of all ranks can be sensed in the 1840s, upon regimental memorials to the casualties of imperial conflicts such as the Sikh Wars (1845–6 and 1848–9); the Crimean War (1854–6) increased their number further. The Boer War (1899–1902) showed how Edwardian

Fig 10.1
Alan Sorrell, A Land Fit for Heroes, 1936. Ink and gouache on paper.
[The Artist's Estate, courtesy of Liss Llewellyn Fine Art]

England had succumbed to 'statue-mania' – a Europe- and America-wide phenomenon in which public memorials proliferated in the urban public realm. While at 20,000 the numbers of fatalities in that war were relatively low, compared with the 722,000 fatalities (some 12 per cent of servicemen) the United Kingdom endured in the Great War, the Boer conflict struck at the chords of the imperial national heart. The status of soldiers was rising; there was stronger local identification with county-based regiments of foot; and citizen-members of the young Territorial Forces were fighting (and dying) alongside Regulars. Imposing Boer War memorials arose in Newcastle upon Tyne, Liverpool, Bristol and elsewhere. Within 20 years they would be wholly eclipsed by a new wave of monuments, and, for some writers, the memorials of the Boer War[8] showed just how the nation should *not* commemorate the dead, in their pith-helmeted bombast.[9]

Given the vast numbers erected to honour the dead of the First World War, only a brisk survey is possible here. Rather than studying the great set-piece memorials, this chapter will concentrate on the range and diversity of locally raised memorials, and consider prevailing ideas about memorialisation. Any study of England's monuments to the dead needs to stand alongside the remarkable programme of battlefield commemoration raised abroad by the Imperial (now Commonwealth) War Graves Commission at the actual resting places of the fallen.[10] Most of the dead lie overseas, remembered through a remarkable programme of state-led memorialisation which emphasised equality in death, and harmonised design of great dignity. Back home in England, however, their names were perpetuated in a great variety of ways, in an unsurpassed movement of domestic remembrance, emerging from myriad and diverse civic, community, congregation and family initiatives.

This movement began almost as soon as the war did: rolls of honour of those serving were displayed in public places, and once casualties were reported back to these local places, more permanent tributes began to be erected.[11] Rawtenstall, Lancashire, raised a granite cross in June 1915, to which names were steadily added. One of the earliest permanent memorials was raised in the churchyard at St Botolph without Bishopsgate, City of London (Fig 10.2), bearing the name of the two most famous fatalities of 1916 – Field Marshal Earl Kitchener and Boy (First Class) Jack Cornwell VC. At St George's church in Deal, Kent, a granite cross was raised in 1916 to the vicar's heroic son, Sub-Lieutenant Arthur Tisdall VC, killed at Gallipoli in May 1915, and which was subsequently adapted to serve as the parish memorial (and to mark the loss of another son). Temporary shrines arose in churches and streets alike, listing the names of serving men and marking out the fatalities: these were encouraged by Anglo-Catholic clergy, eager to promote prayers for the living. Church memorials proliferated: at Chilham, Kent, photographs of the fallen were framed together and hung in the church; at Ardeley, Hertfordshire, individual prayer cards for the village's fighting men were similarly displayed. Tensions between churchmen and servicemen could lead to the duplication of memorials: Albert Richardson designed two in Ampthill, Bedfordshire – a column in the Alameda walk and a churchyard cross, both of 1921 – because factions could not agree.[12] As Alex King's *Memorials of the Great War in Britain* (1995) has shown, the local circumstances of memorialisation were key determinants in their erection. Each was local, and the names recorded had an immediacy of recall to the contemporary viewer that is hard to imagine today. Memorials in churches proliferated: rood screens, windows, tablets and rolls of honour were installed in very considerable numbers and explored the theme of Christian sacrifice. Wholly exceptional was the sequence of stained-glass windows in St Mary's church, Swaffham Prior, Cambridgeshire, which connected scenes of fighting and the war effort with apposite biblical verses, designed by the squire and his daughter (Fig 10.3). Wooden street shrines were sometimes recreated in more permanent stone and bronze: in Cyprus Street, Bethnal Green, London Borough of Tower Hamlets, an arched tablet was erected upon the long terrace to name the street's fatalities; another was installed at the blocks of artisan dwellings at New Court, Hampstead, London Borough of Camden, listing the same. At St Albans, Hertfordshire, there is a unique series of 10 stone street plaques, promoted by Canon George Glossop of St Alban's Abbey. Each of these, beneath small crucifixes, lists the names of the town's fatalities on the streets where they had lived.[13] In general, however, street shrines

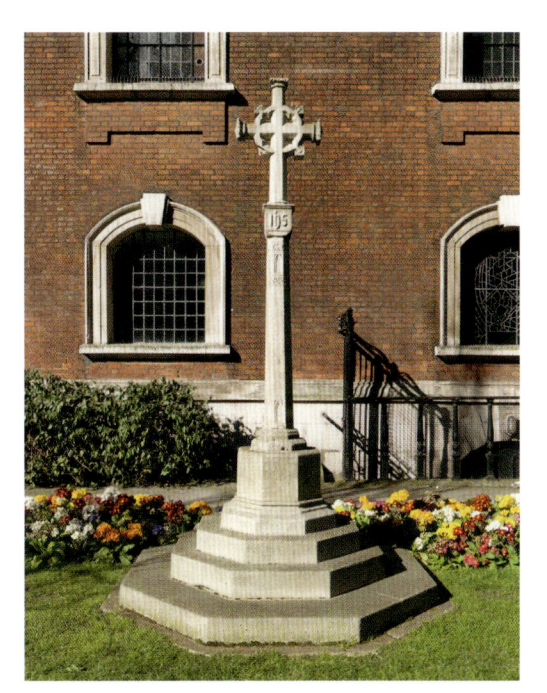

Fig 10.2 (left)
St Botolph without Bishopsgate war memorial, City of London. This memorial of 1916 was among the earliest to be erected, and named the two most celebrated fatalities of that year: Earl Kitchener and Jack Cornwell.
[DP183273]

Fig 10.3 (below)
The unique series of war-related stained-glass windows at St Mary's, Swaffham Prior, Cambridgeshire. These were commissioned by the squire C P Allix, designed with the help of his daughter Cecily and executed by Curtis, Ward & Hughes in 1919.
[BB96/02773]

were taken down once permanent memorials were erected.

The best-known of all war memorials, the Cenotaph in Whitehall (Fig 10.4), also started as a temporary structure made of wood and plaster: as a marker on the route of the Victory March in July 1919, where the memory of the dead could be saluted by the passing parade.[14] The word, from the Greek, means 'empty tomb' and thus was highly appropriate as a homeland memorial for the absent dead. Ordered (in a hurry) by Prime Minister Lloyd George, Sir Edwin Lutyens's striking classical shaft, carefully proportioned and austerely furnished with funeral wreaths and spare inscriptions ('The Glorious Dead'), was recreated in stone in 1920 in time to be present for the procession bearing the Unknown Soldier to Westminster Abbey in November 1920. Lutyens's design was taken up for other memorials, both at home (Southampton and Manchester, besides others) and abroad (Bermuda and Hong Kong included); some carried carved effigies of dead soldiers on top.[15] Lutyens was one of the first three principal architects employed by the Imperial War Graves Commission: the others, Sir Herbert Baker and Sir Reginald Blomfield, also designed local memorials. The Commission raised headstones, 'Stones of Sacrifice', memorial screens and 'Crosses of Sacrifice' (the latter designed by Blomfield) wherever a certain number of servicemen were buried, and these official monuments, designed to standard templates and still carefully tended, stand alongside the far more diverse legacy of local memorials erected at home.

Fig 10.4
The Cenotaph, Whitehall, City of Westminster. Designed by Sir Edwin Lutyens, this was erected in stone in 1920 as the focus of British and Empire commemoration.
[© Jerry Young]

Raising war memorials

For most communities, discussions about memorialising only commenced with the signing of the armistice on 11 November 1918, and once the forces began to be demobilised. Renowned soldier-poet Robert Graves (with Alan Hodge) wrote in 1940 of these challenges:

> The war had now to be solidly commemorated by public subscriptions. Plans were made for the organization of vast war cemeteries in France, and in every village in England the problem of the local war memorial was raging – where should it be placed? What form should it take – statue, obelisk or cross? Could the names of all the dead be inscribed on it? Or would it not be more sensible to use the money collected for a recreation ground and engrave the names on an inexpensive plaque in the church? So great was the demand for war memorial designs and so puzzled were committees as to where they should go for them that the Medici Society inserted a full-page disclaimer in the weekly journals: 'In view of the daily enquiries for price lists, catalogues, etc. of War Memorials, the Medici Society begs to repeat that it does *not* supply "stock designs", *nor* issue price-lists or catalogues of Memorials.'[16]

What guidance was there for these patrons of war memorials? The publishing house B T Batsford released several titles on commemorative art in the early years of the war, anticipating a renewed interest in the monumental arts. The Civic Arts Association, an offshoot of the Art Workers' Guild set up expressly early in 1916 to ensure quality of design in war memorials, set out its aims in a letter from the architect W R Lethaby to *The Spectator*. This drew attention to an exhibition it was mounting on the subject at the Royal Institute of British Architects in July 1916:

> The members of the Association are anxious that all the memorials called for by the terrible war may be, each of its kind, as fine and worthy as possible, for all these things are parts of the civilization of which they will be records; they are memorials not only of individuals whom we wish to honour, but also of this age and of the people who set them up.[17]

The Association issued a booklet *On War Memorials* by Arthur Clutton-Brock, art critic of *The Times,* later that year. The Victoria & Albert Museum held an exhibition on war memorial designs in 1919.[18] For most communities, however, the artistic memorial was beyond their means. Tributes to the dead often comprised modest and conventional crosses and obelisks, supplied by monumental masons, and as such in the long-established mode of the commercial cemetery monument. Tradition was a deeply important element: Sir Herbert Baker, writing in *The Times* in January 1919, saw the purpose of commemoration as 'to express the heritage of unbroken history and beauty of England which the sacrifices of our soldiers have kept inviolate'.[19] In late 1919 the *Architectural Review* reported a Royal Academy discussion on the ideal war memorial: 'while they speak to future generations of the courage and patriotism of those who have died, they do not sacrifice any of that older beauty which is England's legacy from an immemorial past'.[20] Modernity and the memorial were generally kept apart, which is what makes the sculptures of Charles Sargeant Jagger, or the singular Belgian Gratitude Memorial on London's Embankment by Victor Rousseau, just so arresting.[21] Far more often, memorials sought the comfort of the past: by replicating the churchyard or wayside cross, or drawing on the iconography of chivalry.

Utilitarian memorials

The discussion over whether to pay tribute to the dead through a monument or a more utilitarian foundation was a particularly widespread one: some communities managed to afford both. Thus Wiveliscombe, Somerset, both erected a conventional stone cross in the churchyard and laid out a recreation ground with commemorative obelisk; a swimming pool, tennis court and grandstand were added later (Fig 10.5). Feelings could run high on this topic. At Chipping Campden, Gloucestershire, epicentre of the Arts and Crafts Movement, the artist Frederick Grigg's proposal for an elegant medievalising cross, designed gratis (Fig 10.6), was resisted by the local doctor, solicitor and headmaster, who were all in favour of practicality over art.[22] In Islington there was a strong preference for a practical memorial, so a large wing (with archway of inscriptions of the dead) was added to the Royal Northern Hospital, leaving this populous London borough with just a plain 1918 concrete structure on Islington Green as its ceremonial monument.[23] Hospital

Fig 10.5
The roadside obelisk on the memorial recreation ground at Wiveliscombe, Somerset.
[© Paul Stamper]

Fig 10.6
F L Griggs's war memorial cross, Chipping Campden, Gloucestershire, unveiled 1921.
[BB79/04747]

Legacies of the First World War

wings, memorial homes for the wounded, cottage hospitals and district nurses' cottages: all were built as tributes. Stockport, Greater Manchester, raised a particularly unusual memorial to its 2,200 dead: it built an art gallery, designed by J Theo Halliday, with a memorial hall featuring a top-lit statue of Britannia and a dying soldier by Gilbert Ledward.[24] More common still were memorial halls, almost all in villages.[25] These would provide social facilities and foster community spirit through entertainment and events: Chawton, Hampshire, has one particularly good example (Fig 10.7), built (as were so many) in an Arts and Crafts manner in 1924; Owlerton, South Yorkshire, has another. At the most modest end of the commemorative range were four memorial benches at Cropton, North Yorkshire, each embellished with the names of the fallen. Sporting facilities were particularly apt ways of remembering the lost young men: Bristol Rugby Club gained a new venue in 1920, named the Memorial Ground (later shared with Bristol Rovers Football Club, and at the time of writing facing an uncertain future), while the dead of the Royal Grammar School, Colchester, Essex, were remembered through a swimming baths, opened in 1923. Animals had played a vital part in the fighting and were not forgotten: in Kilburn (London Borough of Brent) Daisy, Countess of Warwick, opened an animal dispensary (Fig 10.8).

The most important mid-century book on commemoration, Arnold Whittick's *War Memorials* (1946), cited a Mass Observation survey of citizen commentators, which found that 'practically no-one wanted the memorials of this [Second] world war to take the form they often did after the last – that is, costly erections in stone'.[26] Whittick drew the inevitable conclusion, while regretting the decline of the true monument: 'These numerous failures in expression and beauty which are familiar all over the country have, therefore, prompted the wish that their repetition should be avoided, and have driven many to the advocacy of the utilitarian memorial which is really a pseudo memorial.'[27] And while war memorials continue to be at the heart of remembrance services, the utilitarian versions have often become defunct and redeveloped, as health and welfare provision has changed. Memorial hospitals and housing schemes for disabled ex-soldiers, such as the Haig Homes scheme established in 1928, could, however, combine utility and dignity.[28]

'Costly erections in stone': the words 'war memorial' tend to be synonymous with sculpted angels and bronze Tommies. Before looking at the types of memorial sculpture, another way of remembering needs consideration – the landscape memorial.[29] The City of Carlisle, Cumbria, purchased a park and erected a memorial bridge to reach it.[30] Padiham, Lancashire, also opened a memorial park, while Gheluvelt Park in Worcester is an explicit tribute to the gallant stand of the Worcesters in 1914 at the First Battle of Ypres, and was embellished with water features and recreational spaces.[31] Some large areas could be given for public enjoyment, in memory of the dead: Scafell Pike in the Lake District was acquired by the National Trust in 1920,[32] while Piel Island was given to Barrow-in-Furness for the same reason. At the other end of the spectrum, individual trees could themselves constitute memorials. At Dowdeswell, Gloucestershire, popular topographer Arthur Mee was very struck by this approach: 'In the churchyard a charming idea has been carried

*Fig 10.7 (below)
Chawton, Hampshire: the village war memorial hall, opened in 1924. A characteristic example of the utilitarian approach to remembrance.
[© Roger Bowdler]*

*Fig 10.8 (right)
Plaque within the Animal War Memorial Dispensary, 10 Cambridge Avenue, Kilburn, London Borough of Brent. Opened in 1931, with sculpture by Fred Hitch. The plaque relates that 484,143 horses, mules, camels and bullocks died in active service with the British forces.
[Courtesy RSPCA]*

204

out, every name on the village roll of honour being inscribed on a brass tablet attached to standard rose trees on each side of the path.'[33] In a rare tribute to the heroism of French allies, a smart suburban development of 1922 in Purley, London Borough of Croydon, included a 'Promenade de Verdun' (Fig 10.9), with an avenue of poplars planted in soil specially brought from the Western Front, from a battlefield at Armentières on which both British and French armies had fought; the soil had to be carefully sieved to remove the many projectiles it still contained.[34] 'Verdun oaks' were planted from French acorns across England in memory of the bitter battles of 1916, and in 1931 at Whipsnade, Bedfordshire, a 'Tree Cathedral' was planted by Edmund Blyth across nearly 4 hectares, in memory of fallen friends. Landscape-scale memorials included the large cross cut into the chalk of the North Downs in 1922 at Lenham, Kent (Fig 10.10). If – in Rupert Brooke's words – some corners of foreign fields had been made forever England, then corners of England were also dedicated to the memory of the departed too. Prominent hilltop monuments, such as the tall granite chip concrete shaft of 1927 at Bradgate Park to the Leicestershire Yeomanry (Fig 10.11), followed the post-Waterloo tradition in creating powerful statements visible from far and wide, so the dead would never be forgotten.

Fig 10.9 (above left) Promenade de Verdun, Purley, London Borough of Croydon. This suburban avenue was lined with poplars, planted in soil brought from the battlefields of France. [DP183199]

Fig 10.10 (above) Lenham, Kent. An aerial view of 1947 showing the memorial cross of 1922, cut into the chalk of the North Downs along the Pilgrims' Way. [EAW011822]

Fig 10.11 (left) The Leicestershire Yeomanry memorial, Bradgate Park, Leicestershire. Unveiled in 1927, this tall shaft dominates the landscape of the Charnwood Forest. [DP219712]

Monumental memorials

Far more common than trees or towers were the free-standing war memorials: the crosses, columns, obelisks, urn-topped plinths which are so familiar today. Attention has tended to be directed towards war memorial sculpture: this is wholly understandable, given its frequent high quality and the eloquence of its symbolism, but this has had the effect of presenting an unbalanced view of the war memorial heritage in its fullest sense. Writing about the unusually progressive monument to the 24th Division in Battersea Park by Eric Kennington (Fig 10.12), the *Daily Mail* concluded it would be a 'controversial war memorial', but at least it avoided resembling the 'majority of war memorials which generally take the shape of a village cross, or a soldier with a fixed bayonet, or an amply dressed lady with wings growing out of her dress and a laurel wreath held aloft'.[35] These allegorical figures became one of the commoner sorts of sculpted memorial. Writing of the Uxbridge war memorial, London Borough of Hillingdon, Captain Adrian Jones wrote:

> I was asked to submit a sketch design and I made a symbolical figure of Peace to be placed on a twenty-six feet granite column with some emblems of war at the foot of the column. I thought we had quite enough memorials that seemed to revive the war spirit rather than to consider peace which is, after all, the aim and end of every great struggle.[36]

Winged allegories of Victory and Peace were easily confused, and could be mistaken for angelic figures of the after-life; the age-old tradition of sculpted symbolism was in decline.

Given the thousands of examples across England to consider, a regional sample is one useful way to look at this range. The Midland county of Leicestershire has been thoroughly surveyed by the County Council's war memorials project, and its combination of industrial and rural districts makes it representative of the country at large. Out of 180 free-standing monuments from all periods, 150 were raised after 1918. Of these, 96 were crosses; 15 were lychgates; 12 were obelisks; and 11 were memorials attached to churchyard walls. Only 25 of the 180 memorials included figural sculpture. In addition, there are 50 war memorial buildings, 18 gardens, fields and parks, and 15 trees or avenues. There are 90 further memorials which are utilitarian, ranging from sundials to almshouses. And there are over 50 stained-glass windows in places of worship too.[37] Categories can be identified: but it is the ubiquity and cumulative variety which are the truly striking factors.

The cross, with its clear echoes of chivalry and the Crusades, beside its Christian form, was an obvious memorial type to select. Many are wholly conventional. Others sometimes attained special distinction through sculptural enhancement – none more so than Eric Gill's wayside cross at Trumpington, Cambridgeshire, of 1920, with its reliefs fusing soldiers with scenes of Christ. Gothic shrines, like that at Solihull, West Midlands, were much rarer, and presented a more intense form of medievalising, comparable to the statues of armoured knights and St George.[38] None surpassed the Eleanor Cross at Sledmere, East Yorkshire, a fine 1890s version of a 13th-century original by Temple Moore, to which no fewer than 22 brasses of fallen soldiers, each in uniform, were added from 1918 (Fig 10.13).[39] Some chivalric statues, such as

Fig 10.12
War memorial to the 24th Division, Battersea Park, London Borough of Wandsworth. Designed and sculpted by Eric Kennington and unveiled in 1924, this was an unusually progressive form of memorial. One of the figures was modelled on Robert Graves.
[CC73/03040]

the dramatic equestrian group of St George and the dragon by Charles Hartwell in St John's Wood, City of Westminster (and repeated in 1923 for Eldon Square, Newcastle upon Tyne), constitute some of the finest late romantic public sculptures anywhere.[40] Relic-like fragments of materiel from the fighting were occasionally worked into the fabric of war memorials: at Leckhampstead, Berkshire, is an obelisk with a clock face, the hands wrought from bayonets and the hour markers from bullets; the chain fence, suspended from shells, is from an unspecified Royal Naval vessel present at Jutland. At Westwell, Oxfordshire, a brass Gothic numeral taken from the clock face of the badly damaged Cloth Hall at Ypres was incorporated into a rough-worked slab of local stone as a memorial to two brothers.[41] Other reminders of the fighting were depictions of the enemy. These are rare, ranging from a dead pickelhaube-wearing fallen enemy on the Blackpool war memorial by Ledward, to the souvenir enemy helmet on the Cambridge war memorial.[42] Even rarer are memorials to dead Germans: the relief at the former prisoner-of-war camp at Fordington, Dorset, showing a kneeling *Landser* at prayer, was carved by Josef Walter, and raised in 1919.[43] The foe was more commonly depicted as a vanquished dragon, than represented in a factual guise.

Regiment, business and school: institutional memorials

Regiments were keen to prolong the camaraderie of service, and many erected their own memorials. Some of these emphasised the historic lineage of fighting forces by placing Tommies from the Great War alongside martial figures from the past: at Royston, Hertfordshire, the 1922 memorial by Percy Morley Horder included reliefs by Benjamin Clemens (teacher of both Jagger and Ledward at the Royal College of Art) of a medieval bowman, a Cromwellian Ironside and a Napoleonic fusilier in ghostly white stone behind the modern bronze soldier.[44] The contrast between past and present was even starker on Francis Derwent Wood's misunderstood memorial to the Machine Gun Corps at Hyde Park Corner, City of Westminster, which combined an exquisite classical nude with the hardware of mass killing: two addorsed Vickers machine guns, minutely depicted (Fig 10.14).[45]

Representations of servicemen fell into two categories: the active soldier, often vividly depicted,[46] and the elegiac. Captain Adrian Jones sculpted the vigorous 1922 Bridgnorth war memorial, 'having designed it to pay tribute

Fig 10.13 (far left) The Eleanor Cross at Sledmere, East Yorkshire. Originally erected in 1896, it was adapted in 1918 by Sir Mark Sykes to honour the dead of the war. Brasses were added of men in uniform: a fusion of the medieval and the modern. [© R J C Thomas]

Fig 10.14 (left) The Machine Gun Corps Memorial, Hyde Park Corner, City of Westminster. A deceptively aesthetic memorial, unveiled in 1925. Its sculptor, Francis Derwent Wood, knew just what the impact of warfare was on the human body through his hospital work on facial reconstruction. [© Jerry Young]

to the undaunted courage of a Shropshire lad. It will not be forgotten that the Shropshire Regiment received from the French Government the *croix de guerre* for distinguished service in the field … the unveiling was performed by Private Eli Jones who lost both his legs in the Great War' (Fig 10.15).[47] The decorated officer-sculptor Lindsey Clark sought to express 'dogged determination and unconquerable spirit' in his advancing Tommy in Borough High Street, London Borough of Southwark.[48] Some showed fighting: Jagger's Royal Artillery Memorial (also at Hyde Park Corner) was unsurpassed in its stylised realism, its reliefs – now sadly losing their legibility – showing the different ways in which Gunners fought this war, a war in which artillery had played such a devastatingly important role (Fig 10.16).[49] Jagger's draped corpse remains the best-known memorial depiction of the war dead. The Macclesfield memorial of 1921 by John Millard was equally controversial in depicting modern forms of killing: a dead soldier, his hand still groping for his gas mask, was shown receiving a tribute from Britannia.[50] On the 1921 churchyard memorial at St Anne's Limehouse, London Borough of Tower Hamlets, the unusual figure of Jesus Christ stands over a relief by A G Walker of a devastated trench, with dead bodies clearly visible.[51] Such grimness was wholly exceptional.

Ferdinand Blundstone's Prudential Assurance Company memorial, unveiled at its Holborn headquarters (London Borough of Camden) in March 1922, consisted of a fatally wounded soldier, lying amid the detritus of modern warfare, being ministered to by elegant females, while the bare-breasted corner sentinels, as graceful as any

Fig 10.15 (right)
Bridgnorth's war memorial, Shropshire, by Captain Adrian Jones. Completed in 1920, it features a grenade-throwing infantryman and is one of the more dynamic depictions of the fighting Tommy.
[© Paul Stamper]

Fig 10.16 (below)
The Royal Artillery Memorial, Hyde Park Corner, by Charles Sargeant Jagger. One of the greatest war memorials of all. The stone howitzer is guarded by bronze figures of the highest quality; unusually, these include a recumbent corpse.
[© Jerry Young]

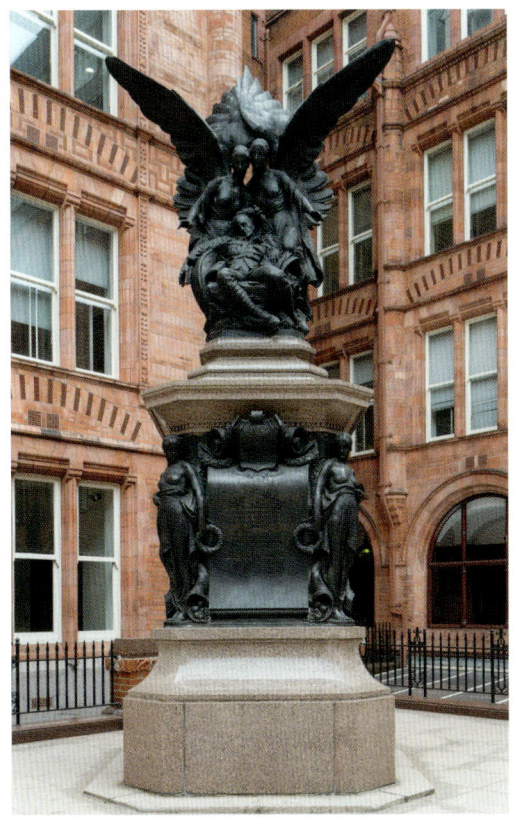

Fig 10.17 (far left)
The Prudential Assurance Company war memorial, 1922, at the company headquarters on Holborn, London Borough of Camden, by Ferdinand Victor Blundstone. Ascension to a very feminine heaven, expressed in a striking late romantic manner.
[© Jerry Young]

Fig 10.18 (left)
Bevan's Cement Works war memorial, Northfleet, Kent, by Francis Doyle-Jones. Suitably enough, the figure of Britannia is executed in cement.
[© Jerry Young]

Fig 10.19
Winchester College cloister, Hampshire. By Sir Herbert Baker and dedicated in 1924, the largest private institutional war memorial anywhere in Europe.
[DP189171]

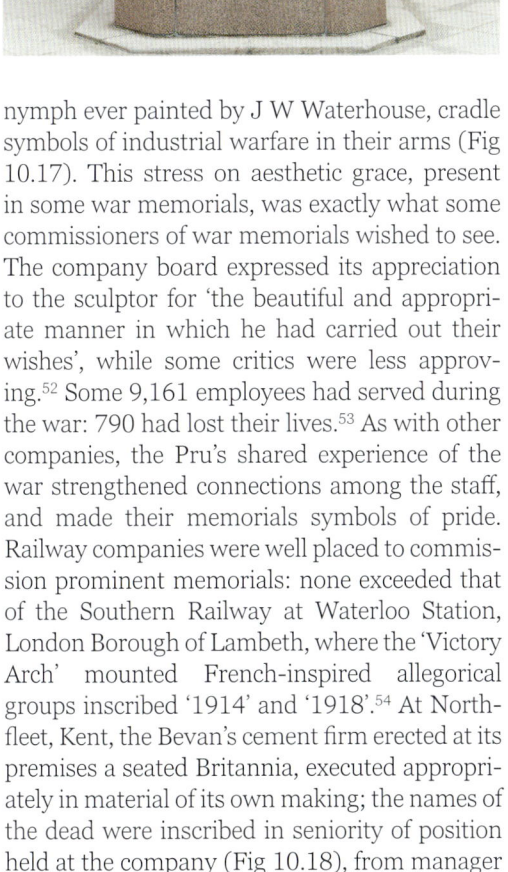

nymph ever painted by J W Waterhouse, cradle symbols of industrial warfare in their arms (Fig 10.17). This stress on aesthetic grace, present in some war memorials, was exactly what some commissioners of war memorials wished to see. The company board expressed its appreciation to the sculptor for 'the beautiful and appropriate manner in which he had carried out their wishes', while some critics were less approving.[52] Some 9,161 employees had served during the war: 790 had lost their lives.[53] As with other companies, the Pru's shared experience of the war strengthened connections among the staff, and made their memorials symbols of pride. Railway companies were well placed to commission prominent memorials: none exceeded that of the Southern Railway at Waterloo Station, London Borough of Lambeth, where the 'Victory Arch' mounted French-inspired allegorical groups inscribed '1914' and '1918'.[54] At Northfleet, Kent, the Bevan's cement firm erected at its premises a seated Britannia, executed appropriately in material of its own making; the names of the dead were inscribed in seniority of position held at the company (Fig 10.18), from manager downwards.

Of all community memorials, those at schools were among the most poignant.[55] They embodied the ethos of duty and sacrifice, and when schools possessed the space and the resources to honour their dead, the results could be spectacular. Sir Herbert Baker's war memorial cloister at Winchester College, Hampshire (Fig 10.19), the largest private war memorial in Europe,

209

Legacies of the First World War

Fig 10.20 (above) Nottingham Memorial Gardens. Given to the city by Sir Jesse Boot in 1920, and one of the grandest of all commemorative landscapes. [EPW021047]

Fig 10.21 (right) Sir Walter Tapper's Loughborough Carillon, Leicestershire. This sonic memorial was opened in 1923 with music for the bells especially composed by Sir Edward Elgar. [DP219701]

was dedicated in 1924 in honour of 500 fallen Wykehamists. Marlborough College in Wiltshire lost 749 alumni: its semicircular memorial hall (designed by W G Newton, and based on the Greek theatre model)[56] bore an internal frieze inscribed seven-deep with names. Such grandeur was unaffordable for most schools: responses ranged from complete rebuilding (as at Holy Trinity Primary School in Bury, Greater Manchester, in 1920) to a single clock at the Lowestoft County Grammar School, Suffolk. Many set up scholarship schemes too.

Architectural memorials could vary from elemental assemblages of local stones to sophisticated Beaux Arts ensembles. At Lelant, Cornwall, massive blocks of local granite created a trilithon-like arch with a wheel-head cross above; this design was copied for the memorial at Crewkerne, Somerset, by Hubert Worthington.[57] Comparable is the memorial cairn of Purbeck stone at Swanage, Dorset. At the other end of the spectrum were architectural set-pieces like the archway and screen at Nottingham's Memorial Garden, given to the city by chemist Sir Jesse Boot in 1920 and unveiled in 1927 (Fig 10.20). While there is nothing in England with quite the total effect and setting of Sir Robert Lorimer's

Scottish National War Memorial on Castle Rock, Edinburgh, some English set-pieces attain a sustained dignity and intensity. Individual buildings like Birmingham's Hall of Memory, opened in 1925, created immersive shrines in the heart of the city: with its relief depiction of crippled veterans returning home, this one did not overlook the human consequences of war.[58] Different again was Loughborough's carillon, or bell tower (Fig 10.21). Designed by the ecclesiastical architect Sir Walter Tapper, and standing at over 45m high, it is an imposing and costly structure containing 47 bells cast by the local foundry, John Taylor. In 1923 Sir Edward Elgar composed a piece of music to be played at the unveiling service: here was sonic remembrance, to carry across the Soar valley.[59] Utterly contrasting was the hut-sized 'Temple of the Brave' at Hedge End, Botley, Southampton, a private garden chamber of remembrance now known only from postcards (Fig 10.22); just how many of these private spaces were actually created is now impossible to determine.

Memorials of private grief

Alongside the grandeur of public memorials were the private ones. These could range in scale from the monumental to the domestic, suited more for the mantelpiece in scale. One of the very oddest of all memorials was the miniature biplane, executed in concrete, in memory of Captain the Hon Eric Lubbock MC at High Elms, Farnborough, London Borough of Bromley. The son of the 1st Lord Avebury, Lubbock had been fatally shot down in 1917. The family already had a private burial enclosure on their estate, and this may have encouraged such a singular departure from the commemorative norm on the part of his heartbroken mother.[60] Sometimes, family members themselves might create these sculptures: in the churchyard of Holy Trinity, Guildford, Surrey, Major Geoffrey Parnell was remembered by his sister Edith Farmiloe, who portrayed him as a bronze angel (Fig 10.23), raised in his memory and that of his comrades in the Queen's Regiment who fell at High Wood on the Somme in July 1916.[61] Many churches contain effigies and cartouches of fighting men (almost always officers) which generally revived the medieval tradition of the recumbent effigy:[62] the grandest was William Reid Dick's marble effigy in St Paul's Cathedral to Kitchener; one of the latest, and most memorable, was Eric Kennington's recumbent likeness at Wimborne, Dorset, of Lawrence of Arabia.[63] There were also private family gravestones which mentioned the fallen: one in St Dunstan's churchyard, Canterbury, Kent, remembers the two husbands of Gladys Goldsack, both of whom were killed. Sometimes families would incorporate the bronze memorial plaques – the 'Dead Man's Pennies' by E Carter Preston given to them by the nation in remembrance of their dead – into family graves.[64] Few private memorials can have been stranger than the blacksmith's tribute at Stow, a metal cylindrical roll of honour with revolving colour-coded indicators to show the fate of the village's men.[65]

Fig 10.22 (above)
The 'Temple of the Brave', a private chamber of remembrance in Botley, Southampton, Hampshire, now known only from postcards.
[Courtesy of Roger Bowdler]

Fig 10.23 (left)
Edith Farmiloe's memorial to her brother, Major Geoffrey Parnell (d 1916), at Holy Trinity Church, Guildford, Surrey. This unusual churchyard memorial depicts Parnell, but remembers all of his fallen comrades as well.
[© Roger Bowdler]

Conclusions

The English war memorial is ubiquitous, extremely varied and often surprising. Thanks to bodies like the War Memorials Trust and Civic Voice, and local initiatives like the North East War Memorials Project, they were in receipt of ongoing care and attention in the approach to the centenaries of their erection. 'Why was it that death continued to overwhelm victory in the popular conception of the First World War?' asks Dan Todman.[66] Modern emphases on the commemorative, sorrowful aspects of war memorials reflect a society which places great emphasis on the human price of conflict, and which, through the revived interest in family history, can continue to connect with the names of the dead. But war memorials tell other stories as well. They marked a hard-fought war, in which the nation, mobilised as never before, responded to a military situation of great peril and found the means and techniques to secure victory. In their legion forms, memorials reflect how the country saw its own martial identity through an unsurpassed and ubiquitous programme of commemorative endeavour. Perhaps none display this duality as clearly as the Liverpool Cenotaph (Fig 10.24), with its frieze of marching men offset on the other side by a poignant scene of grieving civilians in front of a sea of Imperial War Graves Commission headstones.[67] Their historical value continues to rise: and so too does their eloquence.

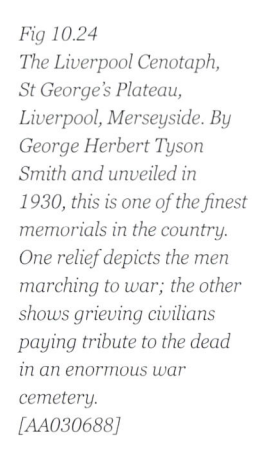

Fig 10.24
The Liverpool Cenotaph, St George's Plateau, Liverpool, Merseyside. By George Herbert Tyson Smith and unveiled in 1930, this is one of the finest memorials in the country. One relief depicts the men marching to war; the other shows grieving civilians paying tribute to the dead in an enormous war cemetery.
[AA030688]

11

Epilogue

Wayne Cocroft and Paul Stamper

Few came home to the 'land fit for heroes' promised by David Lloyd George. While most servicemen had been demobbed by the end of 1919, far from all slotted straight back into a pre-war job (Fig 11.1). Across Europe mass unemployment and social unrest characterised the interwar period. In Britain a short-lived economic boom in 1919 ended in 1920 and unemployment began to increase, reaching 2.5 million by 1922. And even when a man came home to a job, family life could be very difficult: he had to adjust as best he could to life on civvy street, while his wife returned to a subservient domestic role after months or years as head of the house and often in financially gainful war-work. Many came home physically or mentally damaged: in 1929, a decade after the conflict's end, there were still 65,000 ex-servicemen in British mental hospitals, while in the same year the ongoing need for amputations saw 5,205 artificial legs and 1,106 prosthetic arms issued for the first time.[1] Housing conditions for many remained dire; local authorities were slow to provide 'Homes fit for heroes', with council house building in many parts of the country only starting to accelerate, alongside slum clearance, after 1930.[2] While most of the new houses were in towns and cities, some were built on the edge of villages and along the roads into the countryside. Their impact on the landscape was among the concerns of the Council for the Protection of Rural England, founded in 1926 as a new chapter in conservation and planning opened.[3]

Once demobilisation was largely complete, land taken up by the government for war purposes could begin to be released. However, the scale of the country's massive wartime infrastructure meant that dismantlement and disposal was often a protracted business. While key sites such as Bovington, Catterick and Porton Down were retained for military purposes, the Disposals Board soon got to work selling off the thousands of huts erected for the forces and to house prisoners of war, along with all manner of military paraphernalia (Fig 11.2). For instance, 15 army huts were purchased by Norfolk County Council in August 1919 for conversion to houses on county council smallholdings, with a further 100 in 1920,[4] while many others found a new life as village halls. Airfields were perhaps the easiest sites to deal with: expansive, yet with few if any permanent buildings. Of some 300 sites

Fig 11.1
Offices of the Royal Institute of Architects, 9 Conduit Street, London, 1919, decorated to celebrate the end of the war while looking forward to a return to 'business as usual'.
[BL24653]

Fig 11.2
Frog Island, Rainham Marshes, Essex, 1921. T W Ward shipbreakers at work scrapping surplus destroyers.
[EPW006567]

in Britain, it is reckoned 271 had been disposed of by March 1920; meanwhile RAF manpower shrank from just over 300,000 in late 1918 to 29,500 in 1920.[5] The hutted hospitals of the First World War were similarly cleared as soon as they were no longer needed, and while huts on some sites remained in use until after the Second World War, today only fragments – often of unverified origin – survive. Alterations made to other buildings, such as country houses, to make them suitable for hospital use in 1914–18 were mostly reversed soon after the war ended, although commemorative plaques (as at Kings Weston House, Gloucestershire) can often be found.

In the countryside as a whole, land which had gone down to plough generally went back to grass as soon as government support for agriculture was removed and the renewal of grain imports depressed prices. The Forestry Commission, established in 1919, set about making good losses of trees. As it grew to become one of the greater landowners of Britain, its impact was one of the most lasting legacies of the war. The war's impact on the hereditary landowners was considerable, and by the armistice their real income from rents had been roughly halved. Heavier death duties further shook the old order, as in many cases did the death of heirs in the conflict. Ever more estates were split up for sale, to tenants if they could be persuaded to buy: owner-occupation of farmland in England rose from about 12 per cent in 1914 to 36 per cent in 1927, accelerating change in the countryside.[6]

Control of armaments production was quickly relinquished by the government at the war's end. The Cessation Act of 1921 wound up the Ministry of Munitions, and explosives production and research retreated to Waltham Abbey, Holton Heath and the Royal Arsenal. Small arms production was concentrated at Enfield, while larger guns remained the domain of the Royal Arsenal. Nearly all national factories were closed; some sites, but not all, were soon cleared and returned to agricultural use. There were similar closures among the trade factories, and by 1920 most explosives firms had amalgamated to form Nobel Industries Ltd, itself absorbed into Imperial Chemical Industries (ICI) in 1926. Specialist explosives plants offered few opportunities for conversion to peaceful purposes, but other types of munitions works, such as filling and projectile factories and some engineering concerns – all with large, flexible, covered, open spaces – were put to new uses. The emerging automotive industry in particular benefited from the legacy of newly built munitions factories; elsewhere the orderly layouts of wartime factories were easily adapted to trading estates (Fig 11.3). Of more enduring worth have been many of the residential estates built to house the munitions workers.

The most tangible legacy of the naval war lies in the remains 'littering' the sea, as described

*Fig 11.3 (left)
Slough Trading Estate, 1920. Rows of War Department vehicles await repair and sale to civilian owners.
[EPW000022]*

*Fig 11.4 (below)
U-118 washed ashore at Hastings (East Sussex) in April 1919, having broken free while under tow to be scrapped. It immediately became a tourist attraction, and the town clerk was authorised to charge a small fee to those who wished to climb on deck. It was finally broken up on the beach in late 1919.
[BB88/07120]*

on a post-war fishing chart,[7] and there are more identified wreck sites in English waters from the First World War than for any other period, including the Second World War. Just in terms of submarines, research has identified 48 First World War wrecks in English territorial waters; the exact locations of some are known and detailed reports have been prepared, while others remain unidentified or unlocated.[8] This is true of many hundreds of wartime wrecks of all sorts, where further work is often required to map or name lost vessels. There is also a notable subset of post-armistice losses, the consequence of peacetime vessels striking stray mines and of redundant and surrendered vessels succumbing to the weather or (like several submarines) being lost under tow – albeit typically after their recyclable components had been stripped to service British industrial output (Fig 11.4).

Research in the future

The centennial period has seen a great reawakening of interest in the First World War by academic historians, archaeologists and community researchers. Even so, many questions remain about the material legacy of the home front. In many instances the precise location of many sites has yet to be discovered, including wireless stations, munitions factories, training trenches, prisoner-of-war camps and anti-aircraft gun sites. And there is much more to be learnt about individual places through documentary research alongside fieldwork. Professional archaeological excavation techniques employed on the Western Front since the turn of the century are now being applied to training trenches in England.[9] The academic study of early 20th-century artefact assemblages is still

Fig 11.5 (opposite) Trafalgar Square, London. Crowds gather to celebrate the armistice on 11 November 1918. [© IWM Q 069032]

in its infancy, but has the potential to enhance understanding of camp economies and wartime consumption.[10] Similarly, future research will undoubtedly throw light on how the fabric of villages, towns and cities – as well as life within them – was changed by the war.

This book has explored the British experience, as exemplified mainly by England, of a country transformed to fight total war and the changes made manifest through their physical remains.[11] Elsewhere across Europe – and indeed in all the theatres across the world where the war was fought – there is similarly the potential for understanding of the war to be deepened through the identification and study of its physical remains. Virtually all European countries at national and local level have taken the opportunity to review the effect of the war through museum exhibitions. However, for many the catastrophe of the Second World War and communist domination until the end of the Cold War has overshadowed the First World War in their nation's stories. In France, the battles of the Western Front resonate particularly strongly, and archaeological work, including air photographic plotting, remains concentrated on the former front lines. Germany, like Britain, was subject to aerial attack, although the level of destruction was a fraction of that she would later endure. Here a handful of places directly associated with the war have been protected, although primarily for their architectural interest. Exceptionally, to coincide with the centenary of the outbreak of the war, the Rhineland Regional Council commissioned a survey of 20th-century military remains, which included explosives works, destroyed fortifications, border trench lines and an airship station, a project also linking many other cultural activities.[12] In the Harz Mountains a prisoner-of-war camp has been excavated in advance of road works.[13] Neutral countries, such as Denmark and the Netherlands, were profoundly affected by the war, but it has left few physical traces. Across the Dutch border at Dodendraad, Belgium, part of an electrified fence built to contain Belgium refugees, and on which 2,000–3,000 died, has been partly recreated.[14] In Central Europe the centenary has stimulated interest in the traces of the high Alpine trench lines and ones further east facing the Russian Empire.[15] Until recently these remains often lay in closed border regions and in countries where the study of the military exploits of former empires was discouraged by successor regimes intent on nation building and imposing new ideologies.

The end of hostilities with the signing of the armistice on 11 November 1918 had been anticipated for over a month (Fig 11.5). While London saw three days of wild celebrations, elsewhere, not least among those on the front line, reactions were typically more muted. If the overall toll of the first truly global conflict – 9 million soldiers and 6 million civilians killed and 21 million wounded – had yet to be reckoned, few had escaped the loss of family members, friends or comrades. The impact of war on the economy and society had been profound, as the chapters of this book have sought to show. But much greater still was the First World War's emotional impact. Beatrice Webb wrote: 'Every day one meets saddened women with haggard faces … and one dare not ask after husband or son.'[16] That continues to be its most remembered legacy.

Epilogue

Notes

Preface

1. RCHM(E) 1916, xvi–xx.
2. Thurley 2013, 86.
3. RCHM(E) 1916, xvii.
4. Marwick 1965.
5. Thurley 2013, 164–5.
6. Listed at Grade II in 2017: NHLE 1444381.

1 Introduction

1. Hansard, House of Commons Debates LXV (3 August 1914), columns 1809–32.
2. Howard 1972 is still the best short introduction to these points.
3. Lambert 2012 makes this point most forcefully but also selectively.
4. Sumida 1989.
5. Gooch 1974 remains the fullest account of British military planning, but Williamson 1969 places it in a broader political context.
6. Carmichael 2015.
7. Beckett 1991, 228.
8. Winter 1985, 71.
9. Morrow 1993, 107–10, 220–2, 296.
10. 'Estimated strength of the forces abroad and at home by months since November 1916', War Office 1922, 31–7.
11. Dewey 1984; Simkins 1988.

2 The army

1. War Office 1922.
2. The National Archives [TNA], RECO 1/759 and 760.
3. Douet 1998, chapter 8.
4. TNA, WO 107/263.
5. Douet 1998, 168, map.
6. See Carmichael 2015.
7. See Crawford 2012.
8. Kelly 2014, 17–22.
9. See Jessop forthcoming.
10. See www.greatwarhuts.org [accessed January 2017].
11. See Skinner 2011.
12. See Wessex Archaeology 2013 or CgMs 2016.
13. Jones 2011, 22; Panayi 2012, 43.
14. Hague Convention 1907.
15. Paterson 2012, 101.
16. Anon nd [Bathurst 1917?], 2.
17. Smith 1986.
18. Panayi 2012, 84.
19. Anon nd [Bathurst 1917?].
20. Newell *et al* 2016, 159.
21. RCHME 1991.
22. Paterson 2012, 113.
23. Foley 2015, 19, 23.
24. Chapman and Moss 2012, 6.
25. Ibid, 19.
26. Ibid, 12, 15.
27. Yarnall 2011, 146.
28. Cocroft and Tuck 2005, 231.
29. *Derby Daily Telegraph*, 26 October 1914, 3.
30. *Architect & Contract Reporter*, 19 February 1915, 6.
31. *Leeds Mercury*, 8 October 1914.
32. *Nottingham Evening Post*, 3 November 1914, 3.
33. Jones 2011, 24.
34. Prisoners of War Information Bureau nd [*c* 1919].
35. Holt 2015, 81.
36. TNA, WO 293/2, War Office Instruction No. 108 (L 47/549 MT2).
37. www.britishpathe.com [accessed January 2017].
38. Brown and Nichol 2014.
39. Hay 1916, chapter 7.
40. Brown 2017, 17.
41. Institution of the Royal Engineers 1952, vol V.
42. Barton *et al* 2004.
43. Carter 1992, 7.
44. Canadian War Museum, object 197110261-0772, Gas Chamber at Seaford.
45. Carter 1992, 1–26.
46. See Wessex Archaeology 2013.
47. Pugh 2014.
48. See Lanning 1970.
49. See TNA, WO 153/978.
50. See www.eastsussexww1.org.uk [accessed January 2017].
51. See www.stepshort.co.uk [accessed January 2017].
52. Pratt 1921.
53. Kinsey 1981, 28–9.

3 The naval war

1. Friel 2003, 233.
2. Memorandum to War Cabinet on trade blockade. January 1917. TNA, CAB 1/22, fols 1–2.
3. TNA 2016.
4. Dunkley 2013, 26.
5. Francis and Crisp 2008, 6.
6. Ibid.
7. Coad 2013, 50–2.
8. Dittmar and Colledge 1972, 13; Evans 2015.
9. McCartney 2016, 253.
10. Firth 2015, 438.
11. Ibid, 440.
12. National Heritage List for England (NHLE), 1356947: https://historicengland.org.uk/listing/the-list/list-entry/1356947 [accessed 16 March 2017].
13. Sales particulars for the auction on 31 July 1917, with the hammer price of £60,200 recorded on the front cover in a contemporary hand. Historic England Archive, SC00686.
14. *Hansard*, HL (series 5) vol 5, cols 69–70 (7 March 1910): http://hansard.millbanksystems.com/lords/1910/mar/07/naval-mine-sweeping#S5LV0005P0_19100307_HOL_22 [accessed 12 January 2018]; ibid, vol 8, cols 995–1003 (30 May 1911): http://hansard.millbanksystems.com/lords/1911/may/30/trawling-section-of-the-naval-reserve#S5LV0008P0_19110530_HOL_51 [accessed 12 January 2018].
15. Cant 2013a, 83–4.
16. Ibid, 85.
17. National Heritage List for England (NHLE), 1432595: https://historicengland.org.uk/listing/the-list/list-entry/1432595 [accessed 17 October 2016].
18. Since the early years of this century, many First World War vessels have been correctly identified, as revealed by droits declared to the Receiver of Wreck since 2000.
19. Gribble and Scott 2017.
20. The Q-Ship *Baralong* sank *U-27* in the act of attempting to sink the *Nicosian* on 19 August 1915. The shooting of escaping German submariners as reprisal for the sinking of the British passenger liner *Lusitania* on 7 May 1915 caused as much international comment as the *Lusitania* had done.
21. Tarrant 1989, 12.

22 *Hansard*, HC (series 5) vol 90, cols 1359–98 (21 February 1917): http://hansard.millbanksystems.com/commons/1917/feb/21/sir-e-carsons-statement [accessed 12 January 2018].
23 Cant 2013a, 86, supplemented by National Record for the Historic Environment data, November 2016.
24 *Hansard*, HC (series 5) vol 90, cols 1359–98 (21 February 1917): http://hansard.millbanksystems.com/commons/1917/feb/21/sir-e-carsons-statement [accessed 12 January 2018].
25 Cant 2013a, 92–7.
26 Dunkley 2014, 151.
27 Source: National Record of the Historic Environment, November 2016.
28 Cant 2016.
29 Cant 2013a, 86.
30 Goschen: *Hansard*, HC (series 4) vol 81, col 1402 (6 April 1900): http://hansard.millbanksystems.com/commons/1900/apr/06/submarine-torpedo-boats [accessed 12 January 2018]; Selborne, Memorandum on Shipbuilding 17 January 1901, Navy Estimates 1901–2, TNA, CAB 37/56/8. The tradition that submarines were regarded as 'damned unEnglish' is apocryphal: Dash 1990, 88; Hore 2013, 313.
31 Hall 2001, 19.
32 Wessex Archaeology 2015a.
33 Source: Helgason nd.
34 Walker 2014.
35 Hall 2001, 19.
36 Wessex Archaeology 2015b.
37 Dunkley 2013, 26.
38 Terraine 1990, 127–8.
39 Board of Trade 1921; Lloyd's 1990.
40 Ferris 1989, 432–57.
41 Faulkner and Durrani 2008, 77.
42 Gannon 2010, 12.
43 Sockett 1981, 51–60.
44 Faulkner and Durrani 2008, 79.
45 West 1987, 61–4; Hartcup 1988, 124; Faulkner and Durrani 2008, 73–84.
46 Faulkner and Durrani 2008, 74.
47 Strachan 2003, 422.
48 West 1987, 99–107.
49 Whaley *et al* 2008, 15–16.
50 Phimester 2015, 43, 50–2.
51 Prince 1920, 377–90; Hartcup 1988, 154–6.
52 Phimester 2015, 45–6.
53 Round 1920, 224–57.
54 West 1987, 56.
55 Ibid 60; Gannon 2010, 233.
56 Faulkner and Durrani 2008, 73–84; Newland 2012, 118–27.
57 Gannon 2010, 246. At the end of the war most War Office intelligence files were burnt.
58 Round 1920, 247–8.
59 Lloyd's of London 1990.

60 *Hermes* was lost at sea early in the war, sunk by *U-27* on 31 October 1914 with the loss of 22 of her crew, some 22 miles east of Dover, where her remains have been identified at a depth of 30m.
61 Finnis 2000, 31.
62 The *Campania* sank following a storm in the Firth of Forth in November 1918 and is now designated a Historic Marine Protected Area.
63 Finnis 2000, 40.
64 English Heritage, 2002.
65 Keble Chatterton 1923, 114.
66 Bowden and Brodie 2011, 65.
67 Francis 2011.
68 Rossano 2010, 150.
69 Sockett 1989, 181.
70 Maritime Archaeology Trust 2016, 16–18.
71 Cant 2013b, 29–30.
72 Lloyd's of London 1990, 375–81.
73 *Derby Daily Telegraph*, 25 February 1920, 2; *Strathord* has been reported in various positions, one 30 miles due east of Runswick Bay, consistent with the position of 37 miles ENE of Scarborough reported at the time of loss, but there are also reports of this vessel being located in the vicinity of Robin Hood's Bay, North Yorkshire. (Source: National Record of the Historic Environment.)
74 *Dundee Evening Telegraph*, 4 May 1920, 6.
75 Bruton 2016.

4 Defending the coast

1 Saunders 1989, 209.
2 TNA, CAB 3/2/46, fols 27–9, 'Home Ports Defence Committee: Constitution, functions, and procedure', 1 July 1909.
3 For example, TNA, WO 33/39, 'Report of Committee on defences of mercantile ports of the United Kingdom', 1882; WO 33/47, 'Report of a Consultative Committee on plans proposed for fortifications and armament of our military and mercantile ports, and the importance and approximate cost of the works and armaments necessary for the defence of these stations', 1887; CAB 16/1, 'Armaments of defended ports at home and abroad', 1905.
4 TNA, Supp 6/645, 'Report of Committee on armaments of home ports', 1905.
5 Ibid, 66; not including 70 old rifled muzzle-loaders, which were all reduced.
6 TNA, CAB 13/1, fols 1–12, 'Fixed defences at British Defended Ports. Standard of primary armament. Memorandum by a Joint Committee of the Colonial Defence Committee and Home Ports Defence Committee', 22 December 1909.
7 TNA, CAB 13/1, 'Harwich fixed defences. Memorandum by the Home Ports Defence Committee', 15 April 1910.
8 TNA, WO 33/581, 'List of Defended Ports at home etc.', 1 March 1912.
9 The Dover Defence Plan, for example, was circulated to 37 individuals.
10 For example, TNA, WO 33/697, 'Manual of coast fortress defences', 1914; WO 33/711, 'Coast defence rangefinding', 1915.
11 Maurice-Jones 1959.
12 War Office, 'The organization and fighting of the fixed armaments of a coast fortress or defended port (provisional)', London, 1911.
13 TNA, Supp 6/645, 'Report of Committee on armaments of home ports', 1905. Dover was therefore considered subject to potential attacks of middling size.
14 *Dover and the European War, 1914–18*. Dover: Dover Express and East Kent News, 1919 [reprint], 40.
15 Pattison 2010.
16 TNA, WO 33/602, 'Defence scheme. South East Defended Ports. Dover', revised to August 1912, 15.
17 *Dover and the European War*, 5.
18 TNA, WO 78/4424, 'Dover land defences', March 1915.
19 *Dover and the European War*, 5.
20 TNA, WO 33/697, 'Manual of coast fortress defences', 1914; Maurice-Jones 1959.
21 TNA, plans and drawings, WO 78/3998, 4207, 4860, 4862, 4978, 5213.
22 War Office, 'Coast artillery drills and general information', London, 1924; War Office, 'Gun drills for B.L. & Q.F. guns and movable armaments', Isle of Wight, 1909.
23 Hogg and Thurston 1972.
24 TNA, WO 78/4978.
25 TNA, plans and drawings, WO 78/4321, 78/4968, 79/4969, 78/5152, 78/4111, 78/4218.
26 TNA, plans and drawings, WO 78/4862; WO 192/86, 'Fortress record book', 1914–19.
27 TNA, plans and drawings, WO 78/4219, 4262, 4312, 4856, 4858, 4860; WO 192/231, 235, 'Fortress record book', 1939–55; WO 199/1170, 'Fixed defences, Humber', 1 February 1943 – 30 April 1945; WO 199/1440, 'Spurn defences', 1 August 1940 – 30 April 1942; WO 33/944, 'Chain of artillery command', 1919.
28 TNA, WO 33/944, 'Chain of artillery command', 1919; Hogg 1984; Clarke and Rudd 1989.
29 J Monson, 'Guy Maunsell', www.engineering-timelines.com/who/Maunsell_G/maunsellGuy3.asp [accessed 15 January 2018].
30 Maurice-Jones 1959.
31 TNA, CAB 24/36/41, 'Troops available for home defence'. Copy of letter from the Field-Marshal Commander-in-Chief Home

Notes

Forces, to Secretary, War Cabinet, 25 March 1918.
32 TNA, CAB 38/16, no 20, 'Home defence. Memorandum on the principles governing defence of the United Kingdom', 4 October 1910.
33 Summarised in TNA, CAB 3/3, 'Home defence. Memorandum by the Secretary (Committee of Imperial Defence)', 5 July 1915.
34 Ibid, 14–18.
35 Ibid, 10–14.
36 TNA, CAB 23/1/40, War Cabinet, 40, 'Minutes of a meeting of the War Cabinet held at 10, Downing Street, S.W., on Monday, January 22, 1917, at 11.30 a.m.'
37 TNA, CAB 3/3, 'Troops required for home defence. Memorandum by the Chief of the Imperial General Staff', 15 January 1918; CAB 23/13/55, War Cabinet, 316 A, 'Minutes of a meeting of the War Cabinet held at 10 Downing Street, on Monday, January 7th 1918, at 12:00 noon'; CAB 24/38/12, 'Troops required for home defence', March 1917.
38 War Office, *Military Engineering: (Part 1) Field Defences*. HMSO, 1908, 85–6.
39 Ibid, 62.
40 TNA, WO 78/4856.
41 TNA, WO 78/4968.
42 Kent 1988, 167.
43 Ibid, 185–6; Bird 2014, 5.
44 North Norfolk District Council, *The North Norfolk World War 1 Pillbox Trail* [leaflet; nd].
45 Bird 2014, 9.
46 Ibid, 7.
47 Bringham 2014.
48 Ibid, 146–50 and 156–7.
49 Hamilton-Bailey 2003, 6; Beanse and Gill 1998.
50 Smith 2016.
51 Anstee 2011.
52 Smith 2016, 72–81.
53 In the Royal Engineers Museum and Library, Brompton, Kent.
54 TNA, WO 78/4400, 6in (152mm) OS map sheet showing defences at Chattenden and Lodge Hill, 6 Sept 1913.

5 The aerial war

1 Barber 2014 for Stonehenge; Dobinson 1998, 16.
2 Raleigh 1922, 411; Edgerton 1991, 10.
3 Hamilton-Paterson 2015, 9.
4 Edgerton 1991, 10.
5 For the formation of the short-lived Air Battalion, see Driver 1997, 259–71.
6 The building, with its attached balloon equipment store, supported the training and instruction of men in handling kites, balloons and aeroplanes. For Farnborough in this period, see Lee 2009, 105–9.
7 Raleigh 1922, 142–3; South Parker 1982; White 1995.
8 Ashworth 1985, 88–90; Croydon 1998.
9 Raleigh 1922, 127, 125. For a summary of Eastchurch's growth to 1913, see Grey 1913b. The development of the hangars at Eastchurch is well documented in *Flight*, the Aero Club's own journal: 30 April 1910, 330–1; 11 June 1910, 449; 17 June 1911, 422, for panoramic view.
10 Driver 1997, 113, and Croydon 1998, 25–8. Driver 1997, 68–72, for the origins of Eastchurch.
11 Jones 1931, 73.
12 *Flight*, 26 June 1914, 3 July 1914; Grey 1914.
13 As the official historian of the air war commented, it was 'Not by "doing", but by "being" they saved many vessels' (Jones 1934, 60). Aircraft accounted for far more sightings and attacks than airships and balloons: ibid, 76.
14 See Layman 1996 for a full account of the RNAS's involvement in the development of air power as a strategic weapon.
15 For more on this, see Jones 1931, 151–7; Cole and Cheeseman 1984, 41–3.
16 General report on East Fortune, RNAS, January 1916, TNA, AIR 17/122/41.
17 Abbatielo 2004, 138–41. Sturtivant and Page 1992, 121–5, provides a chronology and typology of sites. Gordon Leith's 2015 article on the RAF Museum website (*Flying Boats over the Western Approaches*) provides a useful introduction to the western seaplane stations: see www.rafmuseum.org.uk/blog/flying-boats-over-the-westrn-approaches/ [accessed 4 June 2017].
18 Hamilton-Paterson 2015, 259.
19 Cole and Cheeseman 1984, 18–28.
20 The memorial in Brompton Cemetery to Flight Sub-Lieuenant Reginald Warneford, VC, depicts the downing of the airship, along with a carved relief portrait of Warneford.
21 Cole and Cheeseman 1984, 207, 232–8.
22 For example the destruction of the newest navy Zeppelin, L48, by aircraft from Orfordness on 16–17 June (Cole and Cheeseman 1984, 250–5).
23 Hamilton-Paterson 2015, 270.
24 More than 300, 000 people used tube stations between May 1917 and May 1918, far greater in number than during the London Blitz in 1940. For air raid precautions see Cole and Cheeseman 1984, 134–5, 164–5.
25 Steel and Hart 1997, 260–85.
26 Dobinson 2001, 10–14; Kendall 2012, 143–4.
27 For Monkham's Hall, see Faulkner and Duranni 2008, 93–112.
28 Delve 2007, 163–4. Significant survivals at Hendon are also Graham-White's architect Herbert Matthews's neo-Georgian factory along Aerodrome Road and housing for its employees at Aeroville (*see* Cherry and Pevsner 1998, 166–7).
29 One of these was Roderick Ward Maclennan, a Canadian who documented the day-to-day life of a flying training cadet and who was later killed over the Western Front (Maclennan 2009).
30 Winter 1982, 36.
31 Hamilton-Paterson 2015, 123, 127.
32 A general introduction to the development of aerial photography from the mid-19th century to the end of the First World War can be found in Barber 2011. A more detailed account examining the place of aerial photography within the context of First World War survey and cartography can be found in Chasseaud 1999. Finnegan 2011 also contains considerable detail.
33 See Wickstead and Barber 2012.
34 For a summary of Smith-Barry, see Hamilton-Paterson 2015, 142–8. Alverbank in Stokes Bay is now a hotel. It is listed at Grade II.
35 For the military development of Orfordness, see Kinsey 1981. It housed 612 personnel in 1918 (TNA, AIR 1/453/15/312/26).
36 The Small Tunnels (as the tunnels in R52 were known) were used for aero-elasticity experiments, the testing of Mitchell's Supermarine 'S' series of high-speed aircraft, for streamlining bomb shapes and their release characteristics, and for the first supersonic tests (with high-speed aerofoils) in 1928. Between 1918 and 1958 the aerodynamics team was led by the internationally recognised Miss Fanny Bradfield, who became Head of the Small Tunnels Division in 1942.
37 Most are listed in Sturtivant *et al* 1997, 46–7.
38 Grey 1913a.
39 Belfast-truss lattice girders became the standard form of truss used for the General Service Sheds of the Training Depot Stations of 1917–18. In England its use outside the military sphere – including the Ministry of Munitions – seems to have been restricted to a small number of dock warehouse buildings (Peter Guillery, pers comm).
40 Douet 1998, 169–70, 183–8.
41 See Francis 1996, 81–90, for the development of hangars to 1918.
42 For Manston, see Lee 2009, 206–8.
43 See for example Whittaker 1912a, 1912b and 1913.
44 Dobinson 1998.
45 Subsequently many of the pilots who qualified at Duxford proceeded for further bombing practice to 3 Flight Group's

46 Francis 2001.
47 Jones 1937, 333.
48 TNA, AIR 1/631/17/122/45. My thanks to Martin Hayes and friends in Goodwick for information on the seaplane station, which was located to the north of the railway station at Fishguard harbour. The slipway survives.
49 Escott 1989, 25–7; Cooksley 2000, 165–75.
50 RAF Museum drawings 1332/18. They evolved from the pre-war standard site plans for infantry with covered ways to enable walking between barracks and dining rooms (Douet 1998, 186–94).
51 TNA, AIR 1/452/15/312/26, 1/453/15/312/26.
52 Wantage Hall, by the architect Charles Steward Smith, is listed at Grade II. Ashworth 1985, 245; *see also Great War Forum* at http://1914-1918.invisionzone.com/forums/index.php?/topic/231881-no1-technical-training-school-reading-1917/ [accessed 4 June 1917].
53 This is an under-researched topic. For example, for the drafting of a Chinese labour battalion for the construction of sea defences for Orfordness, *see* Cocroft and Alexander 2009, 12.
54 *See* TNA, AIR 2/7, for the 1919 Report of the Treasury Committee on Aerodrome Construction Accounts.
55 TNA, AIR 2/A7691/72/45/7.
56 Blake 1969.
57 For a summary of survival in an international context, *see* Lake 2004 and C Czymay, 'Military aviation sites in Berlin-Brandenburg', 50–8, *in* J Lake, C Dobinson and P Francis, 'The evaluation of military aviation sites and structures in England', 23–34, and P Smith, 'Monuments of aviation in France', 41–9, all in Hawkins *et al* 2005. For the management of a Wright landscape, *see* McEnaney 2000.
58 One of many around Salisbury Plain, now next to English Heritage's new Stonehenge visitor centre, commemorates a Major Hewetson, who was killed in July 1913 while flying from nearby Larkhill.
59 Lake 2003.
60 Spencer 2013, 11–12.
61 Henlow retains four paired Belfast-truss hangars and two 100ft span hangars for general testing and to store planes with greater wing spans, the latter built by Dorman Long in late 1918 representing the first move from wood to metal trusses in RAF hangar design.
62 For surviving sites in Wales and Scotland, *see* Barclay 2013; for Scapa Flow, *see* Stell 2011, 151–4.
63 Donibristle, in industrial use since the 1950s, was a repair depot for fleet aircraft, a store for reserves and a landing ground for aeroplanes returning from ships. For Catfirth, *see* 'Cat Firth, seaplane base', https://canmore.org.uk/site/105814/cat-firth-seaplane-base [accessed 5 February 2018].
64 Rossano 2010, 149–85.
65 Dobinson 2001, 54.
66 Lake and Schofield 2000.
67 *Shenley in Word War 1: A Record of a Village in War Time*: https://shenleyww1.wordpress.com/royal-flying-corps-at-shenley/ [accessed 4 June 2017]. Albert Ball's diary in the Nottinghamshire Archives (DD/682) details life at London Colney.
68 For Manston, *see* Lee 2009, 207–8. Cole and Cheeseman 1984 offer an excellent day-by-day account of air attacks on Britain in the First World War, with details of the targets and stations involved.
69 Halfpenny 1982, 45–53.
70 Chorlton 2012, 132.
71 Cole and Cheeseman 1984, 46–7; Dobinson 2010, 4–15 and 15–19 for later wartime experimentation in sound detection.
72 www.abct.org.uk [accessed 2 July 2018].
73 www.airfieldresearchgroup.org.uk [accessed 2 July 2018].
74 For the 1918 survey, *see* AIR 1/452/15/312/26 and 1/453/15/312/26. *See also* Davis and Morgan 2010 for an alphabetical list which includes the gazetteers dating from 1916.
75 The concept of 'aviation archaeology' as its own discipline has developed since the 1970s: *see* Robertson 1977 and Holyoak 2001.
76 www.stowmaries.org.uk [accessed 2 July 2018].
77 Atkins Heritage 2006.
78 Archaeological Surveys, *WWI German Prisoner of War Camp, Yatesbury, Wiltshire: Magnetometer Survey Report*. Archaeology Data Service, 2011, https://doi.org/10.5284/1016752 [accessed 2 July 2018].
79 Quoted in Cooper 1986, 103.
80 For a useful summary of Trenchard's independent force, *see* Cooper 1986, 128–40.

6 The workshop of the world goes to war

1 Lloyd George 1938, 83.
2 HMSO 1920–2.
3 Putnam and Weinbren 1992, 90.
4 Ibid, 154.
5 Cocroft 2000, 121–2.
6 Robertson 1920, 710–12, 743–5.
7 Edgeworth 2013.
8 Lewes 1915, 821.
9 Picric acid when used as a shell filling in British service was known as Lyddite, after Lydd in Kent, where it was first tested. In other countries it was variously called Melinite, Shimose, Pertite and Picrinit.
10 Smith nd [*c* 1920], 5–11.
11 Hill and Bloch 2003.
12 Billings and Copland 1992.
13 Earnshaw 1990, 28.
14 Levy 1920, 92; TNA, MUN 5/239, Photographs of H M Factories at Queensferry, Gretna, and Langwith under construction and in operation.
15 Watts 1923, 55–6.
16 Baines 1919a, 230–1; Irvine 1958, 23–4; Freeth 1964; Dick 1973, 36.
17 TNA, MUN 7/555, Reduction in output at Royal Gunpowder Factory Waltham Abbey and question of future of factory, 1918–19; HMSO 1920–2, vol X, part IV, 28.
18 Trebilcock 1966.
19 Pullen *et al* 2011, 240–2.
20 Ibid, 219–27.
21 HMSO 1920–2, vol X, part IV, 28.
22 Lloyd George 1938, 347; Cocroft 2000, 157–9.
23 Bunch 2014, 218.
24 Weizmann 1949, 219–22.
25 Bunch 2014, 220.
26 Bud 1994, 37–45.
27 HMSO 1920–2, vol X, part IV, 3.
28 Levy 1920, 92.
29 TNA, MUN 7/555, 1918–19.
30 Hardie and Davidson Pratt 1966, 99.
31 Command Paper 667 1920.
32 Cocroft and Leith 1996.
33 Haslam 1982, 22.
34 Ibid, 1–70.
35 HMSO 1920–2, vol X, part V, ch 3, 'The establishment of the National Filling Factories, 1915–16', 21.
36 Hansard, 28 June 1917, **95** 558–674.
37 Bing 1919, 1.
38 Ibid, 3; Wootton and Lowry 1919, 1; Lester 1983.
39 HMSO 1920–2, vol X, part V, ch 4, 'Administrative problems, 1916–18', 43.
40 Kenyon 2015, 79.
41 Lloyd George 1938, 119–21.
42 Strachan 2003, 1077.
43 HMSO 1920–2, vol XI, part V, 'Machine guns', 9–13.
44 TNA, MUN 5/146/1122/8, Factories operated by the Ministry of Munitions, 31 October 1918.
45 Cooper 1996, 10, 24.
46 Ibid, 13, 29.
47 Historic England Archive, BL23561/039.
48 HMSO 1920–2, vol VIII, part I, 'Review of state manufacture', 56.

49 Kenyon 2015, 91–6.
50 HMSO 1920–2, vol VIII, part 1, 'Review of state manufacture', 56, 197–213.
51 Vocelka 2014, 138.
52 Walker 1956, 540–1.
53 Deutsches Historisches Museum, Berlin, display.
54 Tweedale 1985, 71.
55 HMSO 1920–2, vol XI, part I, 'Trench supplies', 100–2.
56 Fletcher 1984, 1–4.
57 Ibid, 14.
58 Baines 1919a, 230; 1919b, 258.
59 Baines 1919b, 256.
60 Bennett 1916a, 71.
61 Baines 1919a, 236–7.
62 Ibid, 230.
63 *Engineer* 1917b.
64 *Engineer* 1917a, 1917b.
65 *Engineer* 1918, 289; Cocroft 2000, 189.
66 Lester 1983.
67 Livingstone-Learmonth and Cunningham 1916, 262–3.
68 HMSO 1920–2, vol V, part III, ch 2, 'Welfare in factories', 26.
69 Whiteside 1980, 320–1.
70 Bennett 1916a, 1916b.
71 Cocroft 2000, 190–3; Kenyon 2015, 32–5.
72 TNA, MUN 5/157, History of the National Projectile Factory, Birtley, 57–9.

7 Civic and civilian architecture

1 *The Builder*, 28 January 1916, 92.
2 *The Builder*, 21 January 1916, 70.
3 *The Builder*, 28 January 1916, 83.
4 *The Builder*, 15 December 1916, 371.
5 *The Architect & Contract Reporter*, 29 October 1915, 351.
6 Ibid.
7 *The Builder*, 28 July 1916, 43.
8 *The Builder*, 1 March 1918, 136.
9 'The present war will end by bringing home to the most ignorant the greatness of the British Empire … We do not know what lies before us, and cannot tell how long the struggle may last; but we most of us feel confidence and faith that we are working towards a known and inevitable result.' *The Builder*, 8 January 1915, 23.
10 *The Builder*, 19 January 1917, 49.
11 *The Builder*, 23 July 1915, 62.
12 *The Builder*, 8 January 1915, 23.
13 *The Builder*, 16 March 1917, 177.
14 *The Builder*, 6 April 1917, 223.
15 *The Builder*, 29 June 1917, 409.
16 *The Builder*, 5 July 1918, 14.
17 *Lichfield Mercury*, 30 June 1916, 2.
18 *The Builder*, 19 July 1918, 40.
19 *The Builder*, 22 January 1915, 77.
20 *The Builder*, 14 September 1917, 151.
21 *The Builder*, 1 June 1917, 348.
22 *The Builder*, 8 June 1917, 365.
23 *The Builder*, 20 July 1917, 35.
24 Ibid.
25 *The Globe and Traveller*, 2 June 1915, evening edn.
26 *The Builder*, 12 April 1918, 227.
27 *The Builder*, 19 July 1918, 48.
28 *The Builder*, 18 October 1918, 241.
29 *The Builder*, 1 June 1917, 347.
30 *The Builder*, 16 February 1917, 122.
31 *The Architect & Contract Reporter*, 19 November 1915, 395.
32 *The Builder*, 5 November 1915, 334a.
33 'Progress Estate Conservation Area: Character appraisal', Greenwich Council, www.royalgreenwich.gov.uk/download/downloads/id/17/progress_estate_character_appraisal_adopted_dec_2007 [accessed 19 January 2018].
34 *The Builder*, 10 December 1915, 438.
35 *The Builder*, 4 January 1918, 5–8.
36 *The Architect*, 5 March 1915, 223.
37 *The Architect*, 22 January 1915, 87.
38 *The Builder*, 23 February 1917, 139.
39 *The Architect*, 15 October 1915, 315.
40 *The Architectural Review*, **40**, no 239, October 1916, 86; *The Builder*, 2 July 1915, 16.
41 B Evans, 'National kitchens: Communal dining in wartime', *The Gazette*, www.thegazette.co.uk/all-notices/content/100292 [accessed 5 January 2017].
42 *The Newcastle Daily Journal*, 16 January 1915, 7.
43 *The Western Gazette*, 20 August 1915, 2.
44 'The Shipley bequest', *The Newcastle Daily Journal*, 29 November 1917, 6.
45 *The Builder*, 21 May 1915, 497.
46 *Diss Express*, 18 May 1917, 5.
47 *The Builder*, 19 January 1917, 54.
48 *The Builder*, 7 May 1915.
49 Walton 1996, 608.
50 Walton 1996, 612.
51 *The Builder*, 8 January 1915, 43.
52 'Burwell Public Hall', *The Cambridge Independent Press*, 25 June 1915, 5.
53 Grade II listed, by A N Prentice.
54 *The Architect*, 7 May 1915, 400.
55 *The Architect*, 18 June 1915, 521.
56 *The Builder*, 14 May 1915, 473; 19 November 1915, 367.
57 *The Hull Daily Mail*, 20 June 1916, 2.
58 Foster 2007, 293–5.
59 *The Builder*, 4 June 1915, 530. Destroyed by an air raid in 1941.
60 Cherry and Pevsner 1999, 645.
61 London Metropolitan Archives, GLC/AR/BR/13/186142, architectural drawing for shop at 45–7 High Street, Putney. In 1925 the store spread into nos. 51–3 High Street, which were rebuilt in matching style in 1934. The store, which was damaged during the Second World War, was rebuilt in 1970.
62 Morrison 2015, 28.
63 Burton 2016, 110.
64 *The Architectural Review* **39**, no 233, April 1916, 80.
65 *The Architectural Review* **43**, no 259, January–June 1918, 96.
66 *The Builder*, 17 May 1918, 300.
67 *The Builder*, 5 January 1917, 1.
68 *The Builder*, 18 June 1915, 569.
69 *The Builder*, 5 January 1917, 1.
70 *The Builder*, 22 January 1915, 93.
71 Malvern 2001, 50.
72 *The Builder*, 8 October 1915, 260.
73 Smith 2010, 7.
74 RCHME 1916, xvii.
75 Thurley 2013, 99.
76 Ibid 100.
77 *The Builder*, 6 July 1917, 6.
78 *The Builder*, 10 December 1915, 430.
79 *The Builder*, 8 October 1915, 260.
80 Van Leerzem and Williams 2007, 146–7.

8 Feeding the nation

1 For overviews of the agricultural background before and during the war, drawn on later in the chapter, *see* Brown 1987, Dewey 1989 and Perren 1995.
2 While it is widely accepted, Dewey disputes this figure, putting the proportion at nearer a tenth: Dewey 1989, 46.
3 Hughes-Wilson 2014, 336.
4 Hill and Stamper 1993, 123.
5 Brown 1987, 65–6.
6 Crawford 2012, 121.
7 Brown 1987, 65–6.
8 Dewey 1989, 52–3.
9 Ibid, 53–5, 131–6; White 2014.
10 Adie (2013, 268) offers an even lower figure, saying that of the first 48,000 women who applied, fewer than a quarter were accepted.
11 Hill and Stamper 1993, 122–6.
12 Brown 1987, 65.
13 TNA, IWM LAND 6/101.
14 Adie 2013, 266.
15 King 1999, 97.
16 White 2014, 80–6.
17 Panayi, P, 'Prisoners of war and internees (Great Britain)', *in* Daniel, U, Gatrell, P, Janz, O, Jones, H, Keene, J, Kramer, A and Nasson, B (eds) *1914–1918-online: International Encyclopedia of the First World War*, Berlin: Freie Universität Berlin, 2014. DOI: http://dx.doi.org/10.15463/ie1418.10296 [accessed 2 July 2018].
18 Paterson 2012, 105–6.
19 Brown 1987, 65; Dewey 1989, 120–7.
20 Appleby *et al* 2015, 84–5; Dewey 1989, 138.
21 Dewey 1989, 48; Appleby *et al* 2015, 76.
22 Gliddon 1988, 75.
23 Dewey 1989, 137.
24 Parker 1987, 264.
25 Verdon 2015.

26 Brown 1989, 78–9.
27 Sheail 1976, 116–17.
28 Dewey 1989, 63, 148–63.
29 And coincidentally father of the pioneer archaeological aerial photographer Major George Allen.
30 Brown 2014, 44; Sheail 1976, 114.
31 Morris 2012, 97–8.
32 Dewey 1989, 150–1.
33 Sheail 1976, 114.
34 Ibid, 117.
35 Ibid, 115.
36 Wainwright 2007, 46–7.
37 Paragraph based on Dewey 1989, 190–1, and Sheail 1976, 119–21.
38 Paragraph based on Berry 2015.
39 Dewey 1989, 202.
40 Brown 1987, 72–5
41 Hughes-Wilson 2014, 336–9.
42 Perren 1995, 35–6.
43 For the figures, *see* Dewey 1989, 202–3.
44 Le Lievre 1986, 180.
45 *VCH East Yorks* VIII 2008, 47.
46 For this and following, *see* Crawford 2012, 122.
47 Ibid, 122. That said, with the changed post-war circumstances, Street's farm income fell to almost nothing in 1921: ibid.
48 Strong 1996, 77. Landowners failed to share in the bounty as the government held down rents for the duration of the conflict: Cannadine 1990, 455.
49 For horses and remount depots, *see* War Office 1922, 861; Bosanquet 2014, 38–9; Appleby *et al* 2015, 78–9.
50 Strong 1996, 76–7.
51 Kelly 2014, 36–7.
52 Ibid, 38–9.
53 Pratt 1921, 873–4; War Office 1922, 844–5.
54 Adie 2013, 246.
55 Wade Martins and Williamson 2008, 57.
56 Strong 1996, 79–80.
57 Way 2008, 12.
58 Perfect 1920, 220.
59 Byrne and Burlton 2014, 102. For another local study, *see* Allison 2000, 284–6.
60 Crouch and Ward 1988, 70–2; Cocroft 2000, 189; Tann 2008, 12; Way 2008, 17–18.
61 Dewey 1989, 193.
62 Gliddon 2002, xi.
63 Seifalian 2014 and 2016.
64 Pulbrook 1922, 223.
65 Gliddon 1988, 76; Adie 2013, 251.
66 Pulbrook 1922, 227.
67 Ibid.
68 J England, 'Manufacture of acetone', *The Story of the Royal Naval Cordite Factory, Holton Heath, Dorset, UK*, www.greenacre.info/RNCF/page12.html [accessed 20 January 2018].
69 Le Lievre 1986, 180; Laws 2016, 125.
70 Richardson 1919, 10–16; Ayres 2013.

71 For this paragraph: Sheail 1976, 121–2; Dewey 1989, 191–2.
72 Pulbrook 1922, 223; David 2014. While 3,000 tonnes were collected, yields proved disappointing and acetone production using conkers ceased after three months.
73 Adie 2013, 250.
74 Pulbrook 1922, 227.
75 Apart from where noted, this paragraph is based on James 1981, 207–9.
76 Felling was encouraged by the high prices offered. On the Lamport estate in Northamptonshire the agent reported in November 1915: 'I have sold 111 trees (90 ash, 5 oak, 13 elm, 3 sycamore) on Mr Robinson's farm at Scaldwell for £500. The ash sold particularly well as the government is buying rather largely and prices are fully 50 per cent above pre-war prices.' Northants RO, Isham papers 76, 3 November 1915.
77 Brown 2014, 44; Appleby *et al* 2015, 80.
78 Anon 1918.
79 Smith 2004, 240–3.
80 Strachan 2003, 214–21.
81 I am grateful to Sir Hew Strachan for his tempering views on the blockade's effectiveness.
82 Vickers 2011, 103.
83 Appleby *et al* 2015, 80.
84 Epsom 2014.
85 Pulbrook 1922, 227.

9 Back to Blighty: British war hospitals, 1914–18

1 After the first winter of war, trench foot was treated effectively (information from Nick Bosanquet; *see* Bosanquet 1996).
2 Macpherson and Mitchell 1921, 100. For information on hospital ships, *see* ibid, 109–13.
3 Porter and Wynn 2015, 98.
4 *Manchester Guardian*, 7 August 1914, 5. Men injured in this incident (including German prisoners of war) were also treated in the Royal Naval Hospital and Fort Pitt Hospital in Chatham.
5 In August 1914, 12 new hospital trains were ordered, to supplement one surviving from the Boer War, still in use at that time at Netley.
6 In total there were around 150 military hospitals in 1914.
7 Macpherson and Mitchell 1921, 71. The total number of beds in 1914, including those unequipped, was 9,000. Of these, just 2,000 were occupied at the outbreak of war.
8 'Territorial hospitals: The guiding principles of the scheme', *The Hospital*, 10 October 1914, 33–4. For a list of Territorial hospitals, *see* Macpherson and Mitchell 1921, 74–6.
9 Deaths among the aged, and from tuberculosis, seem to have peaked in 1914–18, but these statistics must be treated with caution since military personnel (that is, large numbers of healthy young men) were excluded from the base population. *See* Griffiths and Brock 2003.
10 The Joint War Committee was formed on 20 October 1914 and operated from headquarters provided by the Royal Automobile Club at 83 Pall Mall, London. *See* Reports by the Joint War Committee 1921. For a summary (and contemporary) account of the role of the Red Cross, *see The Times*, 27 September 1917, 8. The Joint War Committee received grants from the War Office and raised its own funds through individual donations, the *Times* newspaper (the 'Times Fund'), street and church collections, flag days, auctions and other enterprises.
11 *The Times*, 19 June 1915, 5.
12 Quoted from contemporary press clippings, cited in a panel of an exhibition mounted at 10 Carlton House Terrace, autumn 2014. Huts were built on the terrace in 1915. For their post-war disposal, *see The Times* 1 May 1919, 18.
13 Historic England Archive (HEA) NBR: 100722.
14 HEA NBR: 100101.
15 *British Med J*, 18 July 1903, 163; HEA NBR: 100101.
16 *Building News*, 17 November 1915, 552–5; Scott-Moncrieff 1924, esp pp 374–5. The plans were finalised in mid-October 1914. Each ward held 24 ordinary cases and one special case, and included a nurse's duty room, store and sanitary facilities. Covered ways connected them to one another and to other hospital buildings: the administration block, operating theatre, nurses' quarters and mess rooms for medical officers and the RAMC. Later in the war Major Armstrong devised a 100-bed ward with a clerestory over the central area. In Britain, Armstrong hospitals were mostly built at hutted camps, and generally had a maximum of 600 beds, but in France they could be much larger, for example at Étaples.
17 It was reported that 'the tobacco-smoke grey of asbestos walls was soothing to the eye', though – alarming in retrospect – the material 'snapped under a sharp blow' (*Building News*, 10 November 1915, 524).
18 *The Hospital*, 24 October 1914, 95; *Building News*, 17 November 1915, 553.
19 *The Hospital*, 15 August 1914, 539, and 6 March 1915, 521.
20 Reports by the Joint War Committee 1921, 695–8.
21 The Princess Christian Red Cross Hospital at Englefield Green, Surrey, of 1915, was an example.

22 Saundby 1914; *Country Life*, 27 March 1915, 393–5; *Building News*, 10 November 1915, 524; *The Builder*, 12 November 1915, 342.
23 *Building News*, 17 Nov 1915, 554.
24 Morrison 1998, 99; *Building News*, 10 November 1915, 524.
25 *Building News*, 17 November 1915, 554–5.
26 *The Builder*, 12 November 1915, 343.
27 *The Hospital*, 27 February 1915, 491.
28 One of the first Red Cross hospitals of the First World War, Neuberg, was fitted up as a hospital for training purposes in June 1914 and, renamed Newbury (no doubt on account of its Germanic name), received its first patients in October 1914 (http://rusholmearchive.org/rusholme-military-hospitals-1914–1918 [accessed 21 January 2018]). See *Manchester Guardian*, 18 June 1915, 6.
29 *The Builder*, 19 January 1917, 54, including plan, elevation and section. The additions had been removed by the time the 25in (635mm) OS map published in 1919 was surveyed.
30 Brockbank 1915. See also *Manchester Guardian*, 8 December 1915, 5 (illustrations) and 14.
31 'Mayor of Southport opens Vad Hospital', www.britishpathe.com/video/mayor-of-southport-opens-vad-hospital-aka-wounded [accessed 21 January 2018].
32 *The Hospital*, 22 August 1914, 567.
33 *Manchester Guardian*, 8 August 1914, 10. The Manchester School of Technology was commandeered at the same time.
34 Macpherson and Mitchell 1921, 73.
35 *The Hospital*, 14 November 1914, 151–2.
36 See http://thirdlondongeneral.blogspot.co.uk/2010_03_01_archive.html [accessed 22 November 2016].
37 See HEA NBR: 101224.
38 *The Builder*, 21 July 1916, 34; *The Times*, 21 March 1916, 6.
39 'WW1 colour therapy for shell-shocked patients: The Kemp-Prossor "colour cure" ward', 19 December 2013, http://blog.maryevans.com/2013/12/ww1-colour-therapy-for-shell-shocked-patients-the-kemp-prossor-colour-cure-ward.html [accessed 21 January 2018].
40 *The Hospital*, 10 October 1914, 36–7.
41 Ibid, 34–9; 23 October 1915, 81–2. The hutted hospital was built in 1915.
42 Macpherson and Mitchell 1921, 79–82, including a list of war hospitals. Two new hutted war hospitals were built, in Bath and Huddersfield.
43 Macpherson and Mitchell 1921, 76.
44 *The Times*, 28 May 1915, 11; 4 September 1915, 3.
45 *The Times*, 19 October 1914, 5.
46 *The Times*, 30 May 1918, 9.
47 *British J Nursing*, 24 August 1918, 124.
48 TNA, WORK 16/4/4.
49 *The Times*, 2 July 1918, 5; *New York Times*, 18 August 1918, np.
50 *The Times*, 29 March 1919, 17.
51 *The Times*, 22 September 1914, 6.
52 Lines A, B, C, E and F at Brocton were built for the 1st and 2nd Infantry Brigade in 1915, but were turned into a POW camp in 1917. The hospital occupied C lines, with B lines incorporated in 1918. See Holt 2015, *passim*.
53 TNA, FO 383/277.
54 For lists of early offers, including Cardiff Castle, Nuneham Park, Welbeck Abbey and Eaton Hall, see *The Times*, 10 August 1914, 3, and 11 August 1914, 3; *The Hospital* 15 August 1914, 540.
55 *The Times*, 13 August 1914, 3. Eventually 5,000 properties were offered to the authorities (Reports by the Joint War Committee 1921, 211).
56 *The Hospital*, 15 August 1914, 541.
57 Not all voluntary hospitals were operated by the Joint War Committee. The grand total nationally of 1,600 included many run by private individuals and organisations, and by the Scottish Red Cross Society.
58 *The Times*, 27 September 1917, 8.
59 Anon 2014; Palmer 2014.
60 *The Times*, 25 May 1915, 3. Today it forms part of King's College, London.
61 HEA NBR: 101173; *Building News*, 6 December 1912, 795; 20 November 1918, 848.
62 At the time Lord Lucas was serving alongside Churchill in Herbert Asquith's Liberal government as Parliamentary Secretary at the Board of Agriculture.
63 'The wounded at Wrest Park', *Bedfordshire Times and Independent*, 11 September 1914, 5.
64 'Wrest House Hospital', *Luton Times and Advertiser*, 27 November 1914, 5.
65 There is a list of properties offered to the Red Cross as temporary hospitals and convalescent homes in August 1914 in the *Luton Times and Advertiser*, 21 August 1914, 6.
66 During the operation of the hospital there were only 11 cases of breaking bounds. Scrapbook, June 1915, private collection.
67 Martin 2016.
68 Ampthill Park was in use as a training camp for the Bedfordshire Regiment, which, along with Royal Engineers from nearby Haynes Park, assisted in fighting the fire.
69 Before deciding to close the hospital, Bron consulted with Surgeon General Keogh, who confirmed that although Wrest had done 'great work', small private hospitals were no longer needed.
70 A photograph of the library taken shortly before the setting up of the hospital shows no inserts in place.
71 The 1917 sales catalogue lists 'additional Stabling' converted into an 'Engine-house' and 'Accumulator Room'. Bedford, Bedfordshire and Luton Archives and Records Service, L23/999/1, Messrs Daniel, Smith, Oakley & Garrard, 'Particulars of Wrest mansion with grounds, park, woodlands and home farms, comprising an area of about 1,668 acres', 17 July 1917.
72 Observations by Pete Smith.
73 As in the Boer War, Lady Dudley raised funds and administered convalescent homes for officers. This initiative was subsumed by the Officers' Convalescent Homes Committee of the Joint War Committee, formed in December 1915 and chaired by Lady Dudley. The military operated a few convalescent hospitals exclusively for officers, and assigned a section of the convalescent hospital in Blackpool for officers.
74 Macpherson and Mitchell 1921, 89.
75 Ibid, 90.
76 *The Times*, 11 October 1916, 11. The hotel was designed by E W Pugin and built in 1869.
77 Set of images: IWM, 33669–89.
78 Thom 1998, 117.
79 Plans were signed by Hayward & Maynard, architects; Liddle 2016, 146–7 and fig 47.
80 A series of photographs in the IWM (Q30449 to Q30460) show facial plate moulding and painting at Third London.
81 Cohen 2001, 139.
82 Thom 1998, 118.
83 *The Times*, 7 June 1921, 7.
84 *The Times*, 11 January 1924, 8.
85 *The Times*, 13 September 1919, 19.
86 Information received from Maggie Goodall, Friends of War Memorials, 5 May 2000. The building was demolished in March 2001 and replaced by a new Memorial Hall with the help of a Heritage Lottery Fund grant (*Hereford Times*, 23 March 2001, np).
87 IWM, Q 7968.
88 IWM, Q 2505.
89 *The Hospital*, 10 October 1914, 34.
90 A surviving hut relocated from an unknown site to the Fortescue Estate on Exmoor in 1920 as a shepherd's hut has been identified as a standard 60ft (18m) hut which might have been used as 'a hospital doctor's or officer's accommodation hut', but does not appear to have any distinctive 'hospital' features. See Dawson 2011.

10 Remembering the dead

1 The literature on British war memorials is growing. Borg (1991) is the key overview of the type. Boorman (1988) remains a very useful pioneering survey. Winter (1995) offers a wide cultural context. King (1998)

looks specifically at the local aspects of commemoration; comparable is Connelly (2002), looking at a narrower London area. Gray (2010) provides a clear county-wide survey for Devon. Archer (2009) looks in depth at symbolism and artistic production. For a clear survey of a wide range of memorial responses, *see* Moreton (2015), while Login (2015) places the English phenomenon in an international context.

2   This interest has been fostered at a national and local level. The Imperial War Museum's *War Memorials Register* was originally founded in 1989 by its Director, Alan Borg. The War Memorials Trust, established in 1997, is devoted to the care of memorials of all periods. Historic England is working on adding 2,500 war memorials to the National Heritage List for England during the centenary period. Local responses such as the exemplary North East War Memorials Project reflect a growing interest in the topic, and its enduring community resonance.
3   Gill 2005, 61.
4   Priestley 1934, 159.
5   Ibid, 160.
6   Sir Hew Strachan, 'First World War anniversary: We must do more than remember', *Daily Telegraph*, 11 January 2013, www.telegraph.co.uk/history/9795881/First-World-War-anniversary-we-must-do-more-than-remember.html [accessed 23 January 2018].
7   Bromley and Bromley 2012–15 provides a gazetteer of identified examples across the world.
8   *See* Parkhouse 2015 for a thematic overview of British and overseas Boer War memorials.
9   Weaver 1915, 1–2.
10 On which, *see* Crane 2013 and Stamp 2006, especially ch 4.
11 On wartime responses to commemoration, *see* King 1998, 44–61.
12 *See* National Heritage List for England (hereafter NHLE), List entry no 1431612, for the Ampthill cross and its background.
13 *See* Cox and Dean 2015.
14 Hanson 2005, 412 ff.
15 Skelton and Gliddon 2008, 36 ff.
16 Graves and Hodge 1940, 30. The Medici Society was a private firm of art publishers.
17 *The Spectator*, 15 July 1916, 12.
18 For background to advice on commissioning memorials, *see* Turner 2015.
19 Sir Herbert Baker, 'War memorials: The ideal of beauty', *The Times*, 9 January 1919, 9.
20 'The Royal Academy War Memorials Committee', *Architectural Review* **45**, 1919, 21.
21 On Jagger, *see* Compton 2004; Rousseau's statue, set within a much more conventional setting by Blomfield, is discussed in Ward-Jackson 2011, 353–5.
22 Moore 1999, 130. The architect W R Lethaby described the cross (which was eventually built) as 'one of the most appropriate and beautiful memorials he had ever seen'.
23 This was replaced in 2007 (amid mild controversy) by a stone loop by John Maine RA.
24 Moriarty 2003, 45–7.
25 *See* Imperial War Museum, www.iwm.org.uk/memorials [accessed 23 February 2017]. On memorial halls, *see* Moreton 2015, 145–8; Lawrence Weaver's *Village Clubs and Halls* was published by Country Life in 1920 to provide inspiration.
26 A Whittick, *War Memorials*, London: Country Life, 1946, 1.
27 Ibid, 3.
28 *See* Hasted 2016.
29 Grieves 2011, 141–5.
30 Carter 2014, 227–8.
31 Lambert 2014.
32 *See* Westaway 2013. The special issue of *Garden History* (**42**, Supplement 1, 2014), *Memorial Gardens and Landscapes: Design, Planting and Conservation*, is also very worthwhile.
33 Mee 1938, 176.
34 NHLE, entry no 1431287; *see* Williams 2009.
35 *Daily Mail*, 2 October 1924, 4. *See* Black 2002, 28–34.
36 Jones 1933, 185.
37 My thanks to Elizabeth Blood, formerly of the Leicestershire County Council War Memorials Project, for this breakdown and for other assistance. The project can be consulted at www.leicestershirewarmemorials.co.uk [accessed 2 July 2018].
38 On this theme, *see* Goebel 2007.
39 NHLE, entry no 1083806.
40 Usherwood *et al* 2000, 99–10.
41 NHLE, entry no 1427472.
42 *See* Moriarty 2003, 46, on Blackpool, and Hussey 1929, ch 15, for the Cambridge memorial, known as 'The Home-coming'.
43 NHLE, entry no 1428334.
44 Archer 2009, 41–2.
45 Crellin 2001, 75–88.
46 Archer 2009, ch 7.
47 Jones 1933, 180.
48 Cavanagh 2007, 212 ff.
49 Ward-Jackson 2011, 96–100.
50 Archer 2009, plates 1, 2, 28, 218 and 234; *see also* Morris and Roberts 2012, 135–8.
51 Illustrated in Moriarty 1991, 74.
52 Prudential Assurance Company Archives, Minute Book no 48 (1921–2), 214. For critical disapproval, *see* Black 2004, 77–8.
53 Prudential Assurance Company Archives, Minute Book no 48 (1921–2), 202.
54 Cavanagh 2007, 107–9.
55 Kernot 1927 offers an overview of designs and related dedication services, while Parker 1987 offers a more detached commentary.
56 Kernot 1927, 108–11.
57 NHLE, entry no 1393513.
58 Noszlopy 1998, 21–4.
59 NHLE, entry no 1074532.
60 Mackersey 2012, 179. For photographs of the memorial, *see* Lubbock, L 2015 'Lubbock family burial ground: A short history', www.farnborough-kent-parish.org.uk/documents/parish_lubbock/Lubbock%20family%20burial%20ground%20-%20history.pdf [accessed 23 January 2018].
61 NHLE, entry no 1438717.
62 *See* Goebel 2007, 268 ff.
63 Black 2002, 57–65.
64 The Dakers family tomb in Hampstead Cemetery, London Borough of Camden, had two such plaques to fallen sons; both have been stolen.
65 Jones and Howell 1972, 175–6, illustration: whether this is the Lincolnshire Stow is not stated.
66 Todman 2005, 61.
67 Cavanagh 1997, 97–102; Archer 2009, 263.

11 Epilogue

1   Greaves 2014, 194.
2   Burnett 1986.
3   Reynolds 2016, 35–41.
4   Wade Martins and Williamson 2008, 60.
5   Clarke 2008, 46.
6   J Brown, 'Feeding the nation', www.landscapethejournal.org/Feeding-the-nation [accessed 5 September 2017]; Perren 1995.
7   Close 1938.
8   Walker 2014.
9   Brown 2017.
10 Licence 2015.
11 For Scotland, *see* Munro 2014.
12 Hoppe *et al* 2014; '1914 – Mitten in Europa', www.lvr.de/de/nav_main/kultur/berdasdezernat_1/1914/1914_1.jsp [accessed 6 September 2017].
13 Demuth 2009, 163–81.
14 H Janssen, 'Twenty questions about the wire of death', trans. M De Laet, www.dodendraad.org/wire-of-death [accessed 5 September 2017].
15 Košir *et al* forthcoming.
16 Hughes-Wilson 2014, 424.

Bibliography

Abbatielo, J 2004 'British naval aviation and the anti-submarine campaign'. Doctoral thesis, Department of War Studies, Kings College, London. Available at http://www.dtic.mil/dtic/tr/fulltext/u2/a425512.pdf [accessed 4 January 2017]

Adams, R J Q 1978 *Arms and the Wizard: Lloyd George and the Ministry of Munitions, 1915–16*. London: Cassell

Adie, K 2013 *Fighting on the Home Front*. London: Hodder

Allison, K J 2000 'The provision of allotment gardens in East Yorkshire'. *Northern Hist* **37**, 275–92

Anon nd [Bathurst, L 1917?] *German Prisoners in Great Britain*. Bolton and London: Tillot [copy held at IWM: www.iwm.org.uk/collections/item/object/1504007022]

Anon 1918 'The organisation and development of the home timber trade during the war'. *Timber Trades J*, 29 June 1918, 919–36

Anon 2014 'Sanctuary from the trenches: A country house at war'. *Western Front Association Bulletin* 98, March 2014, 26–7

Anstee, A R 2011 'The artillery of the Great War anti-invasion defences of the Swale area of Kent'. *J Ordnance Soc* **23**, 55–79

Appleby, C, Cocroft, W and Schofield, J (eds) 2015 *The Home Front in Britain, 1914–18*. London: Council for British Archaeology

Archer, G 2009 *The Glorious Dead: Figurative Sculpture of British First World War Memorials*. Kirstead: Frontier

Ashworth, C 1985 *Action Stations, 9: Military Airfields of the Central South and South-East*. Wellingborough: Patrick Stephens

Atkins Heritage 2006 *Old Sarum Airfield Character Appraisal and Assessment of Eligibility for Conservation Area Designation*

Auten, H 1919 *Q-boat Adventures*. London: Herbert Jenkins

Ayres, P 2013 'Wound dressing in World War I: The kindly *sphagnum moss*'. *Field Bryology* 110, 27–34

Baines, F 1919a 'War factories and sheds: Their construction and adaptation to future needs, part I'. *J R Inst Br Arch* **26**, August 1919, 230–40

Baines, F 1919b 'War factories and sheds: Their construction and adaptation to future needs, part II'. *J R Inst Br Arch* **26**, September 1919, 248–59

Baker-Brown, Brigadier General W 1925 and 1926 'Notes by a chief engineer during the Great War of 1914–18'. *R Engineers J* **39**, 587–602, and **40**, 105–111, 422–436 and 631–644

Barber, L and Russell, J 2015 'Training for war: Plans of the three great divisional camps in Sussex'. *Sussex Archaeological Collections* **153**, 191–201

Barber, M 2011 *A History of Aerial Photography and Archaeology: Mata Hari's Glass Eye and Other Stories*. Swindon: English Heritage

Barber, M 2014 *Stonehenge Aerodrome and the Stonehenge Landscape*. Historic England Research Report 07–2014

Barclay, G J 2013 *The Built Heritage of the First World War in Scotland*. Edinburgh: Historic Scotland and RCAHMS. Available at www.scotlandsfirstworldwar.org

Barnett, C 1970 *Britain and Her Army: A Military, Political and Social History of the British Army, 1509–1970*. London: Penguin

Barton, P, Doyle, P and Vandewalle J 2004 *Beneath Flanders Fields: The Tunnellers' War*. Staplehurst: Spellmount

Beanse, A and Gill, R 1998 'The London mobilisation centres'. *The Redan* (Palmerston Forts Society) **43**, 12–24

Beckett, I F W 1991 *The Amateur Military Tradition, 1558–1945*. Manchester: Manchester University Press

Beckett, I F W 2006 *Home Front, 1914–1918*. Kew: The National Archives

Beckett, I F W and Simpson, K 2014 *A Nation in Arms: The British Army in the First World War*. Barnsley: Pen & Sword Military

Beesly, P 1984 *Room 40: British Naval Intelligence 1914–1918*. Oxford: Oxford University Press

Bennett, G 2001 *Naval Battles of the First World War*. London: Penguin

Bennett, T P 1916a 'Temporary buildings for war purposes'. *The Builder*, 21 January 1916, 69–71

Bennett, T P 1916b 'Temporary buildings for war purposes'. *The Builder*, 18 February 1916, 143–5

Berry, D 2015 'Agricultural modernity as a product of the Great War: The founding of the Official Seed Testing Station for England and Wales, 1917–1921'. *War & Society* **34** (2), 121–39

Billings, J and Copland, D 1992 *The Ashton Munitions Explosion, 1917*. Tameside: Tameside Leisure Services

Bing, H 1919 *Report on the Development of the Vacuum Charging Machine for HS*. London: HMSO

Bird, C 1999 *Silent Sentinels: The Story of Norfolk's Fixed Defences during the Twentieth Century*. Dereham: Larks Press

Black, J 2002 *The Sculpture of Eric Kennington*. Much Hadham: Henry Moore Foundation

Black, J 2004 'Ordeal and re-affirmation: Masculinity and the construction of Scottish and English national identity in Great War memorial sculpture 1919–30' *in* Kidd, W and Murdoch, B (eds) *Memory and Memorials: The Commemorative Century*. Aldershot: Ashgate, 75–91

Blake, R 1969 'The impact of airfields on the British landscape'. *Geographical J* **135**, 508–28

Board of Trade 1921 *Return of Shipping Casualties and Loss of Life for the Period Ended 31st December 1918*. London: HMSO

Boorman, D 1988 *At the Going Down of the Sun: British First World War Memorials*. York: Derek Boorman

Borg, A 1991 *War Memorials from Antiquity to the Present*. London: Leo Cooper

Bosanquet, N 1996 'Health systems in khaki: The British and American medical experience', *in* Cecil, H and Liddle, P *Facing Armageddon*. Barnsley: Pen & Sword

Bosanquet, N 2014 *Our Land at War: Britain's Key First World War Sites*. Stroud: History Press

Bowden, M and Brodie, A 2011 *Defending Scilly*. Swindon: English Heritage

Bringham, T 2014 *Rapid Coastal Zone Assessment Survey Yorkshire and Lincolnshire: Phase 3 Project Overview. Thematic Discussion of Selected Aspects*. Humber Archaeology Report 422

Brockbank, E M 1915 'Open-air construction for war hospitals'. *The Lancet*, 25 December 1915, 1405

Bromley, J and Bromley, D 2012–15 *Wellington's Men Remembered*. 2 vols. Barnsley: Pen & Sword

Brown, J 1987 *Agriculture in England: A Survey of Farming, 1870–1947*. Manchester: Manchester University Press

Brown, J 1989 *Farm Machinery, 1750–1945*. London: B T Batsford

Brown, J 2014 'Feeding the nation'. *Landscape (being the journal of the Landscape Institute)*, 40–5

Brown, M 2017 *First World War Fieldworks in England*. WYG for Historic England

Brown, M and Nichol, K 2014 *Messines Model, Cannock Chase, Staffordshire: Excavation and Survey 2013*. No Man's Land report for Staffordshire County Council

Bruton, L 2016 *The War at Sea*. Available at: www.bl.uk/world-war-one/articles/the-war-at-sea [accessed 16 March 2017]

Buckton, H 2008 *Salisbury Plain: Home of Britain's Military Training*, Chichester: Phillimore

Bud, R 1994 *The Uses of Life: A History of Biotechnology*. Cambridge: Cambridge University Press

Bull, S 2010 *Trench: A History of Trench Warfare on the Western Front*. Oxford: Osprey

Bunch, A W 2014 'How biotechnology helped maintain the supply of acetone for the manufacture of cordite during World War 1'. *Int J Hist Eng & Tech* **84** (2), 211–26

Burk, K (ed) 1982 *War and the State: The Transformation of British Government, 1914–1919*. London: Allen and Unwin

Burnett, J 1986 *A Social History of Housing, 1815–1985*. London: Methuen

Burton, N 2016 'Bankers Georgian', *in* Holder, J and McKeller, E (eds) *Neo-Georgian Architecture 1880–1970: A Reappraisal*. Swindon: Historic England, 109–21

Byrne, E and Burlton, C 2014 *Bravo Bristol! The City at War, 1914–1918*. Bristol: Redcliffe

Cannadine, D 1990 *The Decline and Fall of the British Aristocracy*. London and New Haven: Yale

Cant, S 2013a *England's Shipwreck Heritage: From logboats to U-boats*. Swindon: Historic England

Cant, S 2013b 'Surrendered and sunk: Post-war U-boat losses'. *Conservation Bulletin* **71**, Winter 2013, 29–30

Cant, S 2016 'Diary of the war: September 1916', *Wreck of the Week* blog: https://thewreckoftheweek.wordpress.com/2016/09/02/diary-of-the-war-september-1916/ [accessed 22 November 2016]

Carden-Coyne, A 2014 *The Politics of Wounds: Military Patients and Medical Power in the First World War*. Oxford: Oxford University Press

Carmichael, Katie 2015 *Drill Halls: A National Overview*. English Heritage Research Report 6–2015. London: Historic England. Available at https://historicengland.org.uk

Carter, D 2014 *Carlisle in the Great War*. Barnsley: Pen & Sword

Carter, G B 1992 *Porton Down: 75 Years of Chemical and Biological Research*. HMSO: London

Cavanagh, T 1997 *Public Sculpture of Liverpool*. Liverpool: Liverpool University Press

Cavanagh, T 2007 *Public Sculpture of South London*. Liverpool: Liverpool University Press

CgMs 2016 'A summary of archaeological excavations: Land at St Martin's Plain, Shorncliffe Garrison, Folkestone, Kent'. Unpublished report

Chapman, C and Moss, R 2012 *Detained in England, 1914–1920: Eastcote POW Camp Pattishall, a Brief, Illustrated History*. Dursley: Lochin

Chapman-Huston, Maj D and Rutter, Maj O 1924 *General Sir John Cowans GCB GCM: The Quartermaster General of the Great War*. Vol II. London: Hutchinson

Chasseaud, P 1999 *Artillery's Astrologers: A History of British Survey and Mapping on the Western Front, 1914–1918*. Lewes: Mapbooks

Cherry, B and Pevsner N 1998 *London 4: North*. The Buildings of England. London: Penguin

Cherry, B and Pevsner, N 1999 *London 3: North West*. London: Penguin

Childers, E 1903 *The Riddle of the Sands*. London: Smith Elder

Chorlton, M 2012 *Action Stations Revisited: The Complete History of Britain's Military Airfields*. No 7. *Scotland and Northern Ireland*. Manchester: Crécy

Clarke, B 2008 *The Archaeology of Airfields*. Chalford: Tempus

Clarke D and Rudd A 1989 'Tyneside in the breech loading era'. *Fortress* **3**, pp 33–42

Close, A 1938 *Close's Fishermen's Chart of the North Sea*. London: Edward Stanford

Coad, J 2013 *Support for the Fleet: Architecture and Engineering of the Royal Navy's Bases, 1700–1914*. Swindon: Historic England

Cocroft, W 2000 *Dangerous Energy: The Archaeology of Gunpowder and Military Explosives Manufacture*. London: English Heritage

Cocroft W D and Alexander M 2009 *Atomic Weapons Research Establishment, Orfordness, Suffolk*. Survey Report. English Heritage, Research Department Report Series 10

Cocroft, W D and Leith, I 1996 'Cunard's Shellworks, Liverpool'. *Archive*, **11**, 53–64

Cocroft, W D and Tuck, C 2005 'The development of the Chilworth Gunpowder Works, Surrey, from the mid-19th century'. *Industrial Archaeol Rev* **27** (2), 217–34

Cohen, Deborah 2001 *The War Come Home: Disabled Veterans in Britain and Germany, 1914–1939*. Berkeley: University of California Press

Cole, C and Cheesman, E F 1984 *The Air Defence of Britain, 1914–1918*. London: Putnam

Command Paper 667 1920 *Committee of Inquiry into the Future of His Majesty's Factories at Gretna and Waltham Abbey*. HMSO: London

Compton, A 2004 *The Sculpture of Charles Sargeant Jagger*. Much Hadham: Henry Moore Foundation

Connelly, M 2002 *The Great War, Memory and Ritual: Commemoration in the City and East London, 1916–1939*. Woodbridge: Boydell for the Royal Historical Society

Cooksley, P G 2000 *The RFC/RNAS Handbook, 1914–18*. Stroud: Sutton

Cooper, M 1986 *The Birth of Independent Air Power*. London: Allen and Unwin

Cooper, P J 1996 *Forever Farnborough: Flying the Limits, 1904–1996*. Berwick on Tweed: Hikoki

Copping, J 2013 'The little boat that could …'. *The Sunday Telegraph*, 8 August 2013

Cox, J and Dean, A 2015 *The Street Memorials of St Albans Abbey Parish*. St Albans: St Albans and Hertfordshire Architectural & Archaeological Society

Crane, D 2013 *Empires of the Dead: How One Man's Vision Led to the Creation of WWI's War Graves*. London: William Collins

Bibliography

Crawford, T S 2012 *Wiltshire and the Great War: Training the Empire's Soldiers*. Ramsbury: Crowood

Crellin, S 2001 'Hollow men: Francis Derwent Wood's masks and memorials, 1915–1925'. *Sculpture J* **6**, 75–88

Crossley, J 2011 *The Hidden Threat: The Story of Mines and Minesweeping by the Royal Navy in World War I*. Barnsley: Pen & Sword

Crouch, D and Ward, C 1988 *The Allotment*. London: Faber & Faber

Croydon, B 1998 *Early Birds: A Short History of How Flight Came to Sheppey*. Sheerness: Sheppey Heritage Trust

Dash, M W 1990 'British submarine policy, 1858–1918'. Unpublished PhD thesis, University College London

David, S 2014 'Did conkers help win the First World War?' *BBC Hist Mag*, October 2014, 72–3

Davis, M and Morgan, B 2010 'Gazetteer of flying sites in the UK and Ireland, 1912–1920', *Cross and Cockade Int J: The First World War Aviation Hist Soc* **4** (nos 1–3)

Dawson, L 1935 *Flotillas: A Hard-Lying Story*. London: Rich & Cowan

Dawson, N 2011 *Blackpits Barn: A First World War Building at Blackpits near Simonsbath*. Exmoor National Park Historic Environment Series 5

Delve, K 2007 *The Military Airfields of Britain: Northern Home Counties*. Ramsbury: Crowood

Delve, K 2010 *The Military Airfields of Britain: Scotland and Northern Ireland*. Ramsbury: Crowood

Demuth, V 2009 '"Those who survived the battlefields": Archaeological investigations in a prisoner of war camp near Quedlinburg (Harz/Germany) from the First World War'. *J Conflict Archaeol* **5** (1), 163–81

Dewey, P 1984 'Military recruiting and the British labour force during the First World War'. *Hist J* **27**, 199–223

Dewey, P E 1989 *British Agriculture in the First World War*. London: Routledge

Dick, W F L 1973 *A Hundred Years of Alkali in Cheshire*. Birmingham: ICI

Dittmar, F J and Colledge, J J 1972 *British Warships, 1914–1919*. London: Ian Allan

Dobinson, C 1997 'Twentieth century fortifications in England. Vol. IX: Airfield themes'. Unpublished report by Council for British Archaeology for English Heritage

Dobinson, C 1998 'RAF Netheravon, a short structural history'. Council for British Archaeology: Report for English Heritage

Dobinson, C 2001 *AA Command: Britain's Anti-aircraft Defences of the Second World War*. London: Methuen

Dobinson, C 2010 *Building Radar: Forging Britain's Early-Warning Chain, 1935–45*. London: Methuen

Dorling, T ('Taffrail') 1935 *Swept Channels: Being an Account of the Work of the Minesweepers in the Great War*. London: Hodder and Stoughton

Douet, J 1998 *British Barracks, 1600–1914: Their Architecture and Role in Society*. London: Stationery Office

Driver, H 1997 *The Birth of Military Aviation. Britain, 1903–1914*. Woodbridge: Royal Historical Society and Boydell

Dunkley, M 2013 'Defending the east coast: Investigating England's forgotten war channels'. *Conservation Bulletin* **71**, Winter 2013, 26–27

Dunkley, M 2014 'Understanding and managing modern material remains in England's inshore region', in Guérin, U, et al (eds) *The Underwater Cultural Heritage of World War I: Proceedings of the Scientific Conference on the Occasion of the Centenary of World War I, Bruges, Belgium, 26 & 27 June 2014*, UNESCO, 147–52

Earnshaw, A 1990 *Britain's Railways at War, 1914–1918*. Penryn: Atlantic

Edgerton, D 1991 *England and the Aeroplane: An Essay on a Militant and Technological Nation*. London: Macmillan

Edgeworth, M 2013 *Grain Island Firing Point, Yantlet Creek, Isle of Grain, Medway: Archaeological Desk Based Assessment*. English Heritage Research Report 39–2013

Encyclopaedia Britannica 1922. 12 edn. London

The Engineer 1917a 'Canteens at munitions works'. *The Engineer*, 28 September 1917, 268–69

The Engineer 1917b 'Engineering works canteens'. *The Engineer*, 7 December 1917, 471

The Engineer 1918 'Birmingham and the production of munitions no.II'. *The Engineer*, 5 April 1918, 288–9

English Heritage 2002 *Military Aircraft Crash Sites: Archaeological Guidance on Their Significance and Future Management*. Available at: https://historicengland.org.uk

Epsom, B 2014 'The rise of Northwood: A pre-war restoration'. *Views* **51**

Escott, B E 1989 *Women in Air Force Blue: The Story of Women in the Royal Air Force from 1918 to the Present Day*. Wellingborough: Patrick Stephens

Evans, G 2015 *Dazzle-Painted Ships of World War I*. Portishead: Bernard McCall

Faulkner, N and Durrani, N 2008 *In Search of the Zeppelin War: The Archaeology of the First Blitz*. Stroud: Tempus

Ferris, J 1989 'Before 'Room 40': The British Empire and signals intelligence, 1898–1914'. *J Strategic Stud* **12** (4), 431–457

Finnegan, T J 2011 *Shooting the Front: Allied Aerial Reconnaissance in the First World War*. Stroud: Spellmount

Finnis, B 2000 *The History of the Fleet Air Arm, from Kites to Carriers*. Ramsbury: Airlife

Firth, A 2015 'East coast war channels: A landscape approach to battlefield archaeology in the North Sea'. *Int J Nautical Archaeol* **44** (2), 438–45

Fletcher, D 1984 *Landships: British Tanks in the First World War*. London: HMSO

Fletcher, D 2016 'The first tanks at Elveden'. *Stand To* (The Western Front Association) **104**, 86–90

Foley, M 2015 *Prisoners of the British: Internees and Prisoners of War during the First World War*. Stroud: Fonthill Media

Forbes, Maj Gen A, 1931 *A History of the Army Ordnance Services: The Great War*, 2 edn. London: Medici Society

Foster, Andy 2007 *Pevsner Architectural Guides: Birmingham*. London: Yale University Press

Francis, P 1996 *British Military Airfield Architecture from Airships to the Jet Age*. Sparkford: Patrick Stephens

Francis, P 2001 'RAF Duxford: Historical appraisal'. Unpublished report for Imperial War Museum, Duxford. Ware: Airfield Research

Francis, P 2011 *RN Air Station Howden: An Assessment of Its Buildings*. Airfield Research Group

Francis, P and Crisp, G 2008 'Military command and control organisation. Vol I. The Royal Navy'. Unpublished report for English Heritage

Freeth, F A 1964 'Explosives for the First World War'. *New Scientist* **402**, 274–6

French, D 1986 *British Strategy and War Aims, 1914–1916*. London: Allen and Unwin

French, D 1995 *The Strategy of the Lloyd George Coalition, 1916–1918*. Oxford: Clarendon

Friel, I 2003 *Maritime History of Britain and Ireland*. London: British Museum

Gannon, P 2010 *Inside Room 40: The Codebreakers of World War 1*. Hersham: Ian Allan

Gill, A A 2005 *The Angry Island: Hunting the English*. London: Weidenfeld & Nicolson

Gliddon, G (ed) 1988 *Norfolk & Suffolk in the Great War*. Norwich: Gliddon

Gliddon, G 2002 *The Aristocracy and the Great War*. Norwich: Gliddon

Goebel, S 2007 *The Great War and Medieval Memory*. Cambridge: Cambridge University Press

Gooch, John 1974 *The Plans of War: The General Staff and British Military Strategy, c1900–1916*. London: Routledge and Kegan Paul

Graves, R and Hodge, A 1940 *The Long Weekend: A Social History of Great Britain, 1918–1939*. London: Faber & Faber

Gray, T 2010 *Lest Devon Forgets: Sacrifice and the Creation of Great War Memorials*. Exeter: Mint

Greaves, S 2014 *The Country House at War: Fighting the Great War at Home and in the Trenches*. London: National Trust

Gregory, Adrian 2008 *The Last Great War: British Society and the First World War*. Cambridge: Cambridge University Press

Grey, C 1913a 'Aeronautical nomenclature'. *The Aeroplane* **4**, 6 February 1913, 123–4

Grey, C 1913b 'The growth of Eastchurch'. *The Aeroplane* **4**, 29 May 1913, 622–3

Grey, C 1914 'The concentration camp'. *The Aeroplane* **6**, 11 June 1914, 655

Gribble, J and Scott, G 2017 *We Die Like Brothers: The Sinking of the SS* Mendi. Swindon: Historic England

Grieve, Capt W G and Newman, B 1936 *Tunnellers: The Story of the Tunnelling Companies, Royal Engineers, during the Great War*. London: Herbert Jenkins

Grieves, K 2011 'Remembering the fallen of the Great War in open spaces in the English countryside', in Andrews, M et al (eds) *Lest We Forget: Commemoration and Remembrance*. Stroud: History Press

Grieves, K 1988 *The Politics of Manpower, 1914–18*. Manchester: Manchester University Press

Griffiths, C and Brock, A 2003 'Twentieth century mortality trends in England and Wales'. *Health Statistics Quarterly*, Summer 2003, *passim*

György, M and Schmidt, M (eds) 2014 *Europe's Fraternal War, 1914–1918*. Budapest: Közép-és Kelet-Európai Történelem És Társadalom Kutatásért Közalapítvány

Hague Convention 1907 *Convention (IV) respecting the Laws and Customs of War on Land and Its Annex: Regulations concerning the Laws and Customs of War on Land*. The Hague, 18 October 1907. Available at: www.opbw.org/int_inst/sec_docs/1907HC-TEXT.pdf [accessed 23 August 2016]

Halfpenny, B 1982 *Military Airfields of Yorkshire: Action Stations, 4*. Wellingborough: Patrick Stephens

Hall, K 2001 *HMS Dolphin: Gosport's Submarine Base*. Stroud: Tempus

Hamilton-Bailey, J R E 2003 'A history of fortification in the United Kingdom, 1870 to 1955'. *Fort* **31**, 6–40

Hamilton-Paterson, J 2015 *Marked for Death: The First War in the Air*. London: Head of Zeus

Hanson, N 2005 *The Unknown Soldier*. London: Corgi

Hardie, D and Davidson Pratt, J 1966 *A History of the Modern British Chemical Industry*. Oxford: Pergamon

Harrison, A N 1979 *The Development of HM Submarines from* Holland No. 1 *(1901) to* Porpoise *(1930)*. London: HMSO

Hartcup, G 1988 *The War of Invention: Scientific Developments, 1914–18*. Brassey's: London

Haslam, M 1982 *The Chilwell Story: VC Factory and Ordnance Depot*. Nottingham: Boots

Hasted, R 2016 *Domestic Housing for Disabled Veterans, 1900–2014*. Historic England Introductions to Heritage Assets. Available at: https://historicengland.org.uk

Hawkins B, Lechner G and Smith P (eds) 2005 *Historic Airports: Proceedings of the International 'L'Europe de l'Air' Conferences on Aviation Architecture*. London: English Heritage

Hay, I 1916 *The First Hundred Thousand: Being the Unofficial Chronicle of a Unit of 'K(1)'*. London: William Blackwood

Helgason, G nd 'U-boat fates: U-boat losses, 1914–1918', https://uboat.net/wwi/fates/losses.html [accessed 16 March 2017]

Hill, G and Bloch, H 2003 *The Silvertown Explosion: London, 1917*. Stroud: Tempus

Hill, R and Stamper, P 1993 *The Working Countryside, 1862–1945*. Shrewsbury: Swan Hill

Historic England 2016 *Historic Military Aviation Sites: Conservation Management Guidance*. Historic England

Historic England 2016 *Introductions to Heritage Assets: Ships and Boats, 1840 to 1950*. Available at: https://historicengland.org.uk

Historic England nd *National Heritage List for England (NHLE)*: https://historicengland.org.uk/listing/the-list/ [accessed 16 March 2017]

Historic England nd *National Record of the Historic Environment (NRHE)*: https://www.pastscape.org.uk/ [accessed 16 March 2017]

HMSO 1919 and 1947 *British Vessels Lost at Sea 1914–1918 and 1939–1945*. London: Patrick Stephens (collated facsim edn 1988)

HMSO 1920–2 *The Official History of the Ministry of Munitions*. London: HMSO

Hogg, I V and Thurston, L F 1972 *British Artillery Weapons & Ammunition, 1914–1918*. Shepperton: Ian Allan

Hogg, R 1984 'The Tyne Turrets: Coastal defence in the First World War', *Fort* **84** (Fortress Study Group), 97–104

Holt, B 2015 *A Long Slow Walk from the Station: The Story of Brocton Prisoner of War Camp, 1917–1919*. Stafford: Russell

Holyoak, V 2001 'Airfields as battlefields, aircraft as an archaeological resource: British military aviation in the first half of the C20th' in Freeman, P W M and Pollard, A (eds) *Fields of Conflict: Progress and Prospect in Battlefield Archaeology*. BAR International Series 958. Oxford: Archaeopress, 253–64

Hoppe, W, Wegener, W, Keller, C, Schmidt, C and Weber, C 2014 *Archäologische Kriegsrelikte im Rheinland Führer zu archäologischen Denkmälern im Rheinland*. Essen: Klartext

Hore, I 2013 *The Habit of Victory: The Story of the Royal Navy, 1545–1945*. London: Sidgwick & Jackson

Howard, M 1972 *The Continental Commitment: The Dilemma of British Defence Policy in Two World Wars*. London: Temple Smith

Hughes-Wilson, J 2014 *A History of the First World War in 100 Objects*. London: Cassell

Hurd, A and Castle, H 1913 *German Sea Power: Its Rise, Progress and Economic Base*. London: John Murray

Hussey, C 1929 *Tait McKenzie: A Sculptor of Youth*. London: Country Life
Institution of the Royal Engineers 1952 *History of the Corps of Royal Engineers. Vol V. The Home Front, France, Flanders and Italy in the First World War*. Chatham
Irvine, A S 1958 *A History of the Alkali Division, formerly Brunner, Mond & Co Ltd*. Birmingham: Kynoch
James, N D G 1981 *A History of English Forestry*. Oxford: Basil Blackwell
James, N D G 1983 *Gunners at Larkhill: A History of the Royal School of Artillery*. Henley-on-Thames: Gresham
Jessop, L forthcoming *Catterick Garrison, Near Richmond, North Yorkshire: Historic Area Assessment*. Historic England Research Report
Jones, A 1933 *Memoirs of a Soldier Artist*. London: Stanley Paul
Jones, B and Howell, B 1972 *Popular Arts of the First World War*. London: Studio Vista
Jones, H 1928 *The War in the Air: Being the Story of the Part Played in the Great War by the Royal Air Force*. Vol II. London: Hamish Hamilton (facsim edn 1969)
Jones, H 1931 *The War in the Air: Being the Story of the Part Played in the Great War by the Royal Air Force*. Vol III. London: IWM and Battery (facsim edn 1998)
Jones, H 1934 *The War in the Air: Being the Story of the Part Played in the Great War by the Royal Air Force*. Vol IV. London: IWM and Battery (facsim edn 1998)
Jones, H 1935 *The War in the Air: Being the Story of the Part Played in the Great War by the Royal Air Force*. Vol V. London: IWM and Battery (facsim edn 1998)
Jones, H 1937 *The War in the Air: Being the Story of the Part Played in the Great War by the Royal Air Force*. Vol VI. London: IWM and Battery (facsim edn 1998)
Jones, H 2011 *Violence against Prisoners of War in the First World War: Britain, France and Germany, 1914–1920*. Cambridge: Cambridge University Press
Keble Chatterton, E 1923 *Q-Ships and Their Story*. London: Sidgwick & Jackson
Kelly, M (ed) 2014 *Bristol and the First World War*. Bristol: Bristol Cultural Development Partnership
Kendall, P 2012 *The Royal Engineers at Chatham, 1750–2012*. Swindon: English Heritage
Kenney, J and Hopewell, D 2015 'First World War military sites: Military landscapes'. Report by Gwynedd Archaeological Trust for Cadw. Available at www.heneb.co.uk [accessed 2 July 2018]
Kent, P (1988) *Fortifications of East Anglia*. Terence Dalton
Kenyon, D 2015 *First World War National Factories: An Archaeological, Architectural and Historical Review*. English Heritage Research Report 076-2015
Kernot, C F 1927 *British Public Schools War Memorials*. London: Roberts and Newton
King, A 1998 *Memorials of the Great War in Britain: The Symbolism and Politics of Remembrance*. Oxford: Berg
King, P 1999 *Women Rule the Plot: The Story of the 100 Year Fight to Establish Women's Place in Farm and Garden*. London: Duckworth
Kinsey, G 1981 *Orfordness: Secret Site. A History of the Establishment, 1915–1980*. Lavenham: Terence Dalton
Košir, U, Crešnar, M and Mlekuž, D forthcoming *Forgotten Fronts, Enduring Legacies: Archaeology and the Great War on the Soca and Eastern Fronts*

Lake, J 2003 'Thematic survey of military aviation sites and structures'. Revised unpublished report, English Heritage Thematic Listing Programme
Lake, J 2004 'Historic airfields: Evaluation and conservation', in Schofield, J, Johnson, W G, and Beck, C M (eds) *Matériel Culture: The Archaeology of Twentieth Century Conflict*. London: Routledge, 172–88
Lake, J and Schofield, J 2000 'Conservation and the Battle of Britain', in Addison, P and Crang, J (eds) *The Burning Blue: A New History of the Battle of Britain*. London: Pimlico, 229–42
Lambert, D 2014 *War Memorial Parks and Gardens*. Historic England Introductions to Heritage Assets. Available at: https://historicengland.org.uk
Lambert, N 2012 *Planning Armageddon: British Economic Warfare and the First World War*. Boston, MA: Harvard University Press
Lanning, G E 1970 *From Rifle Range to Garrison: An Essay on Bovington Camp (1899–1925)*. Available at www.forcesbovington.2day.uk
Laws, B 2016 *Herefordshire's Home Front in the First World War*. Logaston: Logaston Press
Layman, R D 1996 *Naval Aviation in the First World War: Its Impact and Influence*. Ebbw Vale: Chatham
Le Lievre, A 1986 'When surpluses were sought after: Wartime gardening, 1914–18'. *Country Life*, 23 Jan 1986, 180–1
Lee, D 2009 *Action Stations Revisited: The Complete History of Britain's Military Airfields. No 3. South East England*. Manchester: Crécy
Lester, E 1983 'The vital role of our gas factory'. *Banbury Guardian*, 13 January 1983
Levy, S I 1920 *Modern Explosives*. London: Pitman
Lewes, V B 1915, 'Modern munitions of War'. *J R Soc Arts* **63**
Licence, T 2015 *What the Victorians Threw Away*. Oxford: Oxbow
Liddle, P H 1987 *The Airman's War, 1914–18*. Poole: Blandford
Liddle, Peter (ed) 2016 *Britain and the Widening War, 1915–1616: From Gallipoli to the Somme*. Barnsley: Pen & Sword
Livingstone-Learmonth, A and Cunningham, B M 1916 'The effects of tri-nitro-toluene on women workers'. *The Lancet*, 12 August 1916, 261–3
Lloyd George, D 1938 *War Memoirs of David Lloyd George*. London: Odhams
Lloyd's of London 1990 *Lloyd's War Losses: The First World War. Casualties to Shipping Through Enemy Causes, 1914–1918*. London: Lloyd's of London Press (facsim edn)
Login, E 2015 *Set in Stone? War Memorialisation as a Long-Term and Continuing Process in the UK, France and the USA*. Oxford: Archaeopress
Long, Long Trail: The British Army in the Great War of 1914–1918, www.1914-1918.net/hospitals_uk.htm [accessed 2 July 2018]
Lost Hospitals of London, http://ezitis.myzen.co.uk/alphabeticallist.html [accessed 2 July 2018]
Mackersey, I 2012 *No Empty Chairs*. London: Weidenfeld & Nicolson
Maclennan, R W 2009 *The Ideals and Training of a Flying Officer*. Manchester: Crécy [1st edn available at https://archive.org/stream/idealstrainingof00macl]
Macpherson, W G and Mitchell, T J 1921 *History of the Great War Based on Official Documents: Medical Services General History*. Vol I. London: HMSO
Malvern, Sue 2001 'War tourisms: 'Englishness', art and the First World War'. *Oxford Art J* **24** (1), 47–66

Marble, W S 2003 *The Infantry Cannot Do with a Gun Less: The Place of the Artillery in the BEF, 1914–1918*. New York: Gutenberg/Columbia University Press

Maritime Archaeology Trust, 2016 *German Destroyers V44 and V82: Archaeological Report*. Available at: www.forgottenwrecks.maritimearchaeologytrust.org/images/forgottenwrecks/Reports/V4482_SiteReport1_February2016.pdf

Martin, C 2016 'Fire at the First World War military hospital at Wrest Park'. *History in Bedfordshire* **7**, 5–9

Marwick, A 1965 *The Deluge: British Society and the First World War*. London: Macmillan

Massie, R K 2007 *Castles of Steel: Britain, Germany and the Winning of the Great War at Sea*. London: Vintage

Maurice-Jones, Col K W 1959 *The History of Coast Artillery in the British Army*. London: Royal Artillery Institution

McCartney, I. 2014 'The "Tin Openers" myth and reality: Intelligence from U-boat wrecks during WW1', *Proceedings of the 24th Annual Historical Diving Conference*. Poole: Historical Diving Society

McCartney, I 2015 *The Maritime Archaeology of a Modern Conflict: Comparing the Archaeology of German Submarine Wrecks to the Historical Text*. New York: Routledge

McCartney, I 2016 *Jutland, 1916: The Archaeology of a Naval Battlefield*. London: Conway

McEnaney, M 2000 'From pasture to runway: Managing the Huffman Prairie flying field', in *American Aviation: The Early Years*. Washington: US National Park Service, 11–13. Available at: www.nps.gov/crmjournal/CRM/v23n2.pdf

Mee, A (ed) 1938 *The King's England: Gloucestershire*. London: Hodder & Stoughton

Messenger, C 2005 *Call to Arms: The British Army, 1914–18*. London: Cassell

Millman, B 2000 *Managing Domestic Dissent in First World War Britain*. London: Frank Cass

Mitchinson, K W 2005 *Defending Albion: Britain's Home Army 1908–1919*. Basingstoke: Palgrave Macmillan

Moore, J N 1999 *F.L. Griggs (1876–1938): The Architecture of Dreams*. Oxford: Clarendon

Moreton, F 2015 'Commemoration', in Appleby *et al* 137–55

Moriarty, C 1991 'Christian iconography and First World War memorials'. *Imperial War Museum Rev* No 6, 63–75

Moriarty, C 2003 *The Sculpture of Gilbert Ledward*. Much Hadham: Henry Moore Foundation

Morris, E and Roberts, E 2012 *Public Sculpture of Cheshire and Merseyside (excluding Liverpool)*. Liverpool: Liverpool University Press

Morris, R 2012 *Time's Anvil: England, Archaeology and the Imagination*. London: Weidenfeld & Nicolson

Morrison, K 1998 'The hospitals of the armed forces', in Richardson, H (ed) *English Hospitals, 1660–1948*. London: RCHME, 76–103

Morrison, K A 2015 *Woolworth's: 100 Years on the High Street*. Swindon: Historic England

Morrow, J H 1993 *The Great War in the Air: Military Aviation from 1909 to 1921*. Shrewsbury: Airlife

Mullay, A J 2014 *Blighty's Railways: Britain's Railways in the First World War*. Stroud: Amberley

Munro, K 2014 *Scotland's First World War*. Edinburgh: Historic Scotland

Napier, G 2005 *Follow the Sapper: An Illustrated History of the Corps of Royal Engineers*. Chatham: Institution of Royal Engineers

National Trust 2014 'Sanctuary from the trenches: A country house at war'. *Western Front Association Bulletin* **98**, March 2014, 26–7

Newell, J, Winser, K and English, J 2016 'The Iron Age enclosure and First World War prisoner of war camp at Felday, Holmbury St Mary, near Dorking'. *Surrey Archaeological Collections* **99**, 148–64

Newland, C 2012 'Mr Hopgood's shed: An archaeology of Bishop's Canning wireless station', in Saunders 116–29

Noszlopy, G 1998 *Public Sculpture of Birmingham including Sutton Coldfield*. Liverpool: Liverpool University Press

Osborne, M 2017 *If the Kaiser Comes: Defence against a German Invasion of Britain in the First World War*. Stroud: Fonthill Media

Palmer, S 2014 'A country house at war'. *National Trust Magazine*, Spring 2014, 37–43

Panayi, P 2012 *Prisoners of Britain: German Civilian and Combatant Internees during the First World War*. Manchester: Manchester University Press

Parker, P 1987 *The Old Lie: The Great War and the Public-School Ethos*. London: Constable

Parkhouse, V 2015 *Memorializing the Anglo-Boer War of 1899–1902*. Kibworth Beauchamp: Matador

Paterson, S 2012 *Tracing Your Prisoner of War Ancestors: The First World War. A Guide for Family Historians*. Barnsley: Pen and Sword

Pattison, P 2010 'Admiralty lookout and the defence of Dover Harbour, 1905–1945'. *English Heritage Hist Rev* **5**, 156–71

Pennycuick, Brig J A C 1965 'Hill 60 and the mines at Messines'. *R Engineers J* **79**, 388–97

Perfect, C T 1920 *Hornchurch in the Great War: An Illustrated Account of Local Activities and Experiences*. Colchester: Benham

Perren, R 1995 *Agriculture in Depression, 1870–1940*. Cambridge: Cambridge University Press

Phimester, J 2015 *First World War Wireless Stations in England*. Oxford Archaeology. English Heritage report. Available at: https://historicengland.org.uk

Porter, K and Wynn, S 2015 *Castle Point in the Great War*. Barnsley: Pen & Sword

Pratt, E 1921 *British Railways and the Great War: Organisation, Efforts, Difficulties and Achievements*. London: Selwyn and Blount

Priestley, J B 1934 *English Journey*. Harmondsworth: Penguin [1981 edn]

Prince, C E 1920 'Wireless telephony on aeroplanes'. *Institution of Electrical Engineers J* **58**, 377–90

Prisoners of War Information Bureau nd *List of Places of Internment*. IWM (facsim edn)

Pugh, R 2014 *The Most Secret Place on Earth: The Story of the East Anglian Village of Elveden and the Birth of the World's First Tanks*. Dereham: Larks

Pulbrook, E C 1922 *English Country Life and Work: An Account of Some Past Aspects and Present Features*. London: B T Batsford

Pullen, R, Newsome, S, Williams, A and Cocroft, W D 2011 *Curtis's and Harvey Ltd Explosives Factory, Cliffe and Cliffewoods, Medway*. English Heritage Research Report 11–2011

Putnam, T and Weinbren, D 1992 *A Short History of the Royal Small Arms Factory, Enfield*. Centre for Applied Historical Studies Middlesex University

Raleigh, W 1922 *The War in the Air: Being the Story of the Part Played in the Great War by the Royal Air Force*. Vol I. London: Hamish Hamilton (facsim edn 1969)

Rawlinson, A 1923 *The Air Defence of London, 1915–1918*. London: Andrew Melrose

Rawson, A 2006 *The British Army, 1914–18*. Stroud: History Press

RCHM(E) 1916 *An Inventory of the Historical Monuments in Essex* **1**. London: HMSO

RCHME 1991 'Old Madeley Manor, Staffordshire Archaeological Survey Report'. Historic England Archive COLL 662327

Reports by the Joint War Committee 1921 *Reports by the Joint War Committee and the Joint War Finance Committee of the British Red Cross Society and the Order of St. John of Jerusalem in England on Voluntary Aid rendered to the Sick and Wounded at Home and Abroad and to British Prisoners of War, 1914–1919*. London: HMSO

Reynolds S 2016 *The Fight for Beauty: Our Path to a Better Future*. London: Oneworld

Richardson, R 1919 *Through War to Peace: Being a Short Account of the Part Played by Tavistock and Neighbourhood in the Great War*. Tavistock

Ride, D 2006 *In Defence of Landscape: An Archaeology of Porton Down*. Stroud: Tempus

Robertson, B 1977 *Aviation Archaeology: A Collector's Guide to Aeronautical Relics*. Cambridge: Patrick Stephens

Robertson, R 1920 'The Research Department at Woolwich'. *Nature* **105** (2649), 710–12 [part 1] and 743–5 [part 2]

Roper, Lt Col R E nd 'The RE Experimental Section, Porton'. Unpublished report at The National Archives, London, WO 142/254

Rossano, G L 2010 *Stalking the U-Boat: US Naval Aviation in Europe during World War I*. Gainesville: University Press of Florida

Rössler, E 1981 *The U-Boat: The Evolution and Technical History of German Submarines*. Annapolis: Naval Institute Press

Round, H J 1920 'Direction and position finding'. *Institution of Electrical Engineers J* **58**, 224–57

Sassoon, S 1941 *Memoirs of an Infantry Officer*. London: Faber & Faber

Saundby R 1914 'An open-air military hospital, the First Eastern Military Hospital (T.F.), Cambridge'. *Br Med J*, **2** (2813), 942–3

Saunders, A 1989 *Fortress Britain*. Oxford: Oxbow

Saunders, N J (ed) 2012 *'Beyond the Dead Horizon': Studies in Modern Conflict Archaeology*. Oxford: Oxbow

Schofield, J 2006 *England's Army Camps* [characterisation report by English Heritage of army camps, 1848–2000], available at Archaeology Data Service: http://archaeologydataservice.ac.uk/

Scott-Moncrieff, Maj Gen Sir G 1924 'The hutting problem in the war'. *R Engineers J* **38**, 361–80

Seifalian, S 2014 'In commemoration of London's parks and their contribution to the home front during the First World War'. *London Landscapes* **44** (1), 115–34

Seifalian, S 2016 'The role of London's royal parks during the First World War with particular reference to Regent's Park'. *Garden Hist* **38**, 15–16

Sheail, J 1976 'Land improvement and reclamation: The experiences of the First World War in England and Wales'. *Agric Hist Rev* **24**, 110–24

Simkins, P 1988 *Kitchener's Army: The Raising of the New Armies, 1914–1916*. Manchester: Manchester University Press

Sinclair, Col H M 1919 'History of the Railways and Roads Training Centre RE Longmoor'. *R Engineers J* **30**, 28–42

Skelton, T and Gliddon, G 2008 *Lutyens and the Great War*. London: Frances Lincoln

Skinner, R. 2011 *Kitchener's Camps at Seaford: A First World War Landscape on Aerial Photographs*. English Heritage Research Report 27–2011

Smith P G A nd [*c* 1920] *The Shell that Hit Germany the Hardest*. London

Smith, C 2004 *The Great Park & Windsor Forest*. New Romney: Bank House

Smith, L 1986 *The German Prisoner of War Camp at Leigh, 1914–1919*. Privately published

Smith, N 2010 *Old Oswestry, Selattyn & Gobowen, Shropshire: Analysis of earthworks. Archaeological Survey Report*. English Heritage Research Report Series 82–2010

Smith, V T C 2014 '"Barbed Wire Island": Sheppey and the defended ports of the Thames and Medway during the First World War'. *Fort* **42**, 141–75

Smith, V T C 2016 'If the Kaiser should come: Defending Kent during the Great War'. *Archaeologia Cantiana* **137**, 63–105

Smith, V, Anstee, A and Mason, S 2014 'Britain's First World War defences'. *After the Battle* **165**, 39–49

Sockett, E W 1981 'Stockton-on-Tees "Y" Station'. *Fortress* **8**, 51–60

Sockett, E W 1989 'Yorkshire's early warning system, 1916–1936'. *Yorkshire Archaeol J* **61**, 181–8

South Parker, N 1982 *Aviation in Wiltshire*. South Wiltshire Industrial Archaeology Society Monograph 5

Spencer, J 2013 'Twentieth-Century Military Project: First World War scoping study'. Clwyd-Powys Archaeological Trust, report for CADW

Stamp, G 2006 *The Memorial to the Missing of the Somme*. London: Profile (rev edn 2016)

Steel, N and Hart, P 1997 *Tumult in the Clouds: The British Experience of the War in the Air, 1914–1918*. London: Hodder and Stoughton

Stell, G 2011 *Orkney at War: Defending Scapa Flow*. Vol I. *World War I*. Kirkwall: Orcadian

Strachan, H 2003 *The First World War*. Vol I. *To Arms*. Oxford: OUP

Strong, R 1996 *Country Life, 1897–1997: The English Arcadia*. Basingstoke and Oxford: Boxtree

Sturtivant, R 1994 'British flying training in World War 1'. *Cross and Cockade Int J* **25** (1), 18–28

Sturtivant, R and Page, G 1992 *Royal Navy Aircraft Serials and Units, 1911–1919*. Tonbridge: Air-Britain

Sturtivant R, Hamlin J and Halley J 1997 *Royal Air Force Flying Training and Support Units*. Tonbridge: Air-Britain

Sumida, J T 1989 *In Defence of Naval Supremacy: Finance, Technology and British Naval Policy, 1899–1914*. Boston, MA: Allen and Unwin

Tann, G 2008 *Lincoln's Allotments: A History*. Lincoln: Survey of Lincoln

Tarrant, V 1989 *The U-Boat Offensive, 1914–1945*. New York: Sterling

Terraine, J 1982 *White Heat: The New Warfare, 1914–18*. London: Guild

Terraine, J 1990 *Business in Great Waters: The U-Boat Wars, 1916–1945*. London: Mandarin

Thom, C 1998 'Specialist hospitals', *in* Richardson, H (ed) *English Hospitals, 1660–1948*. London: RCHME, 104–31

Thurley, S 2013 *Men from the Ministry: How Britain Saved Its Heritage*. Newhaven and London: Yale University Press

TNA, MUN 5/155/122.3/51, Historical note, note with plans and graphs, on No. 9 Factory, Banbury, Oxon

TNA 2016 *The Blockade of Germany*, www.nationalarchives.gov.uk/pathways/firstworldwar/spotlights/blockade.htm [accessed 16 March 2017]

Todman, D 2005 *The Great War: Myth and Memory*. London: Hambledon & London

Trebilcock, R C 1966 'A special relationship: Government, rearmament, and the cordite firms'. *Econ Hist Rev* 2 ser **19**, 364–79

Tunbridge, P 1995 *History of Royal Air Force Halton: No. 1 School of Technical Training*. London: Regency

Turner, A 2010. *Messines, 1917: The Zenith of Siege Warfare*. Oxford: Osprey

Turner, S V 2015 'The poetics of permanence? Inscriptions, memory and memorials of the First World War in Britain', *Sculpture J* **24** (1), 73–96

Tweedale, G 1985 'Sir Charles Abbott Hadfield F.R.S. (1858–1940), and the discovery of manganese steel'. *Notes Rec R Soc Lond* **40** (1), 63–74

Usherwood, P, Beach, J and Morris, C 2000 *Public Sculpture of North-East England*. Liverpool: Liverpool University Press

Van Leerzem, J and Williams, B 2007 *The History of South Staffordshire Waterworks Company, 1853–1989*, www.southstaffswaterarchives.org.uk/SSHISTRY2.pdf [accessed 31 October 2016]

Verdon, N 2015 '100 years of the WI'. *Rural Hist Today* **29**, 1–2

Vickers, E 2011 '"The forgotten army of the woods": The Women's Timber Corps during the Second World War'. *Agric Hist Rev* **59** (1), 101–12

VCH 2008 *Victoria History of the Counties of England*. York: East Riding 8. London: Boydell & Brewer/Institute of Historical Research

Vocelka, K 2014 'The Austro-Hungarian Empire in the First World War: Hopes for the war and reasons for the fall', *in* György and Schmidt 137–148

Wade Martins, S and Williamson, T 2008 *The Countryside of East Anglia: Changing Landscapes, 1870–1950*. Woodbridge: Boydell

Wainwright, M 2007 *Wartime Country Diaries*. London: Guardian

Walker, K 2014 'Strategic assessment of submarines in English waters'. Unpublished report by Cotswold Archaeology for English Heritage, report ref. 6655

Walker, W G 1956 *A History of the Oundle Schools*. London: Grocers' Company

Walton, J K 1996 'Leisure towns in wartime: The impact of the First World War in Blackpool and San Sebastian'. *J Contemp Hist* **31** (4), 603–18

War Office 1922 *Statistics of the Military Effort of the British Empire during the Great War, 1914–1920*. London: HMSO

War Office 1932 *Report of the Committee on the Lessons of the Great War*. London: Imperial War Museum and Naval and Military Press

Ward-Jackson, P 2011 *Public Sculpture of Historic Westminster*. Vol I. Liverpool: Liverpool University Press

Watts, J I 1923 *The First Fifty Years of Brunner, Mond & Co., 1873–1923*. Winnington: Brunner, Mond & Co.

Way, T 2008 *Allotments*. Oxford: Shire

Weaver, L 1915 *Memorials and Monuments: Old and New. Two Hundred Subjects Chosen from Seven Centuries*. London: Country Life

Weizmann, C 1949 *Trial and Error: The Autobiography of Chaim Weizmann*. London: Hamish Hamilton

Wessex Archaeology 2013 *Belton House, Belton, Lincolnshire: Archaeological Evaluation and Assessment of Results*. Project code 85203. Salisbury: Wessex Archaeology for Videotext Communications (Time Team)

Wessex Archaeology 2015a 'HMS D5 Off Lowestoft, Suffolk'. Unpublished report for Historic England, report ref. 108280.19

Wessex Archaeology 2015b 'U8 Off South Varne Buoy, English Channel'. Unpublished report for Historic England, report ref. 108280.14

West, N 1987 *G.C.H.Q.: The Secret Wireless War, 1900–86*. Sevenoaks: Coronet

Westaway, J 2013 'Mountains of memory, landscapes of loss: Scafell Pike and Great Gable as war memorials, 1919–24'. *Landscapes* **14** (2), 174–93

Whaley, R, Morrison, J and Heslop, D 2008 *A Guide to the Archaeology of the Twentieth Century Defence Sites of Tyne and Wear*. Newcastle: Newcastle City Council

White, B 2014 *The Women's Land Army in First World War Britain*. Basingstoke: Palgrave Macmillan

White, C M 1986 *The Gotha Summer: The German Daytime Raids on England, May to August 1917*. London: Hale

White, G 1995 *Tramlines to the Stars: George White of Bristol*. Bristol: Redcliffe

Whitehouse, C J and Whitehouse, G P 1978 *A Town for Four Winters: Great War Camps on Cannock Chase*. Brocton: C and G Whitehouse

Whiteside, N 1980 'Industrial welfare and labour regulation in Britain at the time of the First World War'. *Int Rev Soc Hist* **25** (3), 307–31

Whittaker, W 1912a 'Military aerodromes'. *The Aeroplane* **3**, 5 December 1912, 558–60

Whittaker, W 1912b 'Military aerodromes (continued)'. *The Aeroplane* **3**, 12 December 1912, 584–6

Whittaker, W 1913 'Aerodromes'. *The Aeroplane* **4**, 20 March 1913, 334–6

Wickstead, H and Barber, M 2012 'A spectacular history of survey by flying machine'. *Cambridge Archaeol J* **21** (3), 71–88

Williams, S 2009 '"Some appendages to the city": A look at three of London's less well-known garden suburbs', *Lond Gardener* **14**, 59–66

Williamson, S R 1969 *The Politics of Grand Strategy: Britain and France Prepare for War, 1904–1914*. Cambridge, MA: Harvard University Press

Wilson, Trevor 1986 *The Myriad Faces of War: Britain and the Great War, 1914–1918*. Cambridge: Polity

Winter, D 1982 *The First of the Few: Fighter Pilots of the First World War*. London: Viking

Winter, J M 1985 *The Great War and the British People*. London: Macmillan

Winter, J 1995 *Sites of Memory, Sites of Mourning: The Great War in European Cultural History*. Cambridge: Cambridge University Press

Wootton, H A and Lowry, T M 1919 *Report on the Head Filling of Chemical Shells*. Ministry of Munitions of War. London: HMSO

Yarnall, J 2011 *Barbed Wire Disease: British and German Prisoners of War, 1914–19*. Stroud: History Press

Young, M 2000 *Army Service Corps, 1902–1918*. Barnsley: Pen and Sword

Index

Illustrations and references in captions are in **bold** type.

A

Abel, Sir Frederick 120
Accrington (Lancs), cinema 155
acetone 125, 127–8, 129, 177
aerial photography 100
aerial training 94–5, 99–101, 117
aerial war
  deployment 95–6
  foundations 93–5, **94**
  survival and conservation 111–18, **111**, **113**, **114**, **115**
  see also airfields
agriculture
  crafts and industries 178
  crops 177–8, **177**
  food crisis 166–7, **166**
  horses 173–5, **174**, **175**
  labour force 167–9, **167**, **168**, **169**, **170**
  parks 175–7, **176**
  ploughing-up campaign 171–3, **171**, **172**
  smallholdings 175, 176, **176**
  timber 178–9, **179**
  vermin control 178
air attacks 5, 97–8, **97**, **98**, 118, 165
Air Ministry 28
aircraft
  Avro 504 101
  DH4 **104**
  DH9 106
  Handley Page 56, 118
  Maurice Farman Shorthorn 99
  pre-war 94, **95**
  RFC 99–101, **104**
  RNAS 56–7, **57**, 58, 59, 62
  SE5 101
  Short Type 184, 58
  Sopwith Camels 62, 115, 140
  see also airships; Giant bombers; Gotha bombers; seaplanes
aircraft carriers 56, 62, **62**
aircraft factories 138–40, **138**, **139**, **140**
airfields
  airfield buildings 107–10, **108**, **109**, **110**, 114, **114**, **115**

building of 93–4, **93**, 101–5, **102**, **103**, **104**, **105**
description 99–101, **99**
post-war 213–14
survival and conservation 111–17, **111**, **113**, **114**, **115**, **117**
see also individual airfields by name
airships
  manufacture 138
  origins and deployment 94, **96**
  RNAS 56, **57**, 58–9, **58**, 95
  training 101
alcohol 143–4, 155
Alderley Edge (Ches), hospital 186
Aldershot (Hants)
  Balloon Factory 138
  barracks 8, 9
  bombing school 21
  hospitals 181, 196
  signals training 24
Alderton (Suffolk), pillbox **86**
Aliens Restriction Act 14
Allen, John 171
Allison, R J 189, 191
Allix, C P and Cecily **201**
allotments 175, 176, **176**
Alton (Hants)
  hospital 183–4
  internment camp 15
Alton estate (Staffs) 175
Altrincham (G Manchester), AOC depot 29
ambulances 183
American troops
  air campaigns 59–60, 113
  Duxford 106, **106**
  hospitals 188, 189
  navy 112
  quartering 9
  YMCA 149, **150**
SS *Amerika* 46
HMS *Amphion* 181
Ampthill (Beds)
  training depot 194
  war memorials 201
SV *Amy* 64, **64**
Anderson, Alexander Ellis **155**
Anderson, H L **162**
Anderson, J McVicar **162**
Anderson, P & W 106
Anderson & Co 102

HMHS *Anglia* 43, **44**, 181
Anglo-German Chilworth Gunpowder Co 15
animal memorials 204, **204**
anti-aircraft gun emplacements 24, 97–8, **97**, **98**
Arborfield Cross (Berks), remount depot 174, **174**
architecture, civic and civilian 147–8
  commerce 158–62, **159**, **160**, **161**, **162**
  cultural heritage 163–5
  leisure 155–6, **156**, **157**
  materials and regulations 148–51, **148**, **149**, **150**, **151**
  public buildings 163, **163**
  religion 158, **158**
  see also housing
Ardeley (Herts), war memorial 201
HMS *Arethusa* **39**
HMT *Arfon* 43, **43**
Argles, Cecil 194
HMS *Argus* 56
armaments manufacture 6, 146
  explosives manufacture see explosives
  factory design 142–3, **142**, **143**
  housing 145–6
  local engineering works 140–1
  national factories **136**, 137–8, **137**
  poison gas 134–5, **135**
  post-war 214
  requirements 119
  shell manufacture and filling 130–4, **131**, **132**, **133**, **134**, **135**
  standards 120–1, **120**
  steel helmets 141
  welfare 143–5, **144**, **145**, 155
  see also aircraft factories; state arsenals; tanks
armistice 216, **216**
Armstrong, B H O 10, 103, 105, 113, 184
army
  demobilisation 34
  fighting branches 8
  nature of during war 3, 4–6, **4**, **6**, 8

quartering 8–13, **9**, **10**, **11**, **12–13**
support branches 28; see also Army Ordnance Corps; Army Service Corps; Labour Corps; Women's Army Auxiliary Corps
training 16; see also aerial training; artillery training; bombing practice; gas warfare training; Machine Gun Corps; practice trenches; rifle ranges; Royal Engineers, training; Tank Corps
Army Council 28
Army Medical Service 180
Army Ordnance Corps 28, 29–30, **29**
Army Postal Service 177
Army Service Corps 28, 30–1, **171**, 174
Arthur, Lieutenant Desmond **95**
artillery training 22–3, **23**
Ashford (Kent), tank 28, **28**
Ashton-under-Lyne (G Manchester), TNT production 122–3
Asquith, Herbert 137
Asquith, Margot 153
Atwick (E Yorks), pillbox 86
Auburn (E Yorks), pillbox 86, **86**
Australian troops
  Codford Camp 173
  hospitals 188, 189
  Leighterton 113
  quartering 9, **9**, 13
  torpedoed 44, **44**
  training 17, **18**, **108**
Avonmouth (Bristol)
  explosives factory 143, **143**
  military port 27, 31, 174

B

SMS *Baden* 62
Baines, Frank, designs by 165
  factories **123**, **138**, 142, **142**, 143
  housing 146, 152, **152**
Baker, Sir Herbert 202, 203, 209
Ball, Albert 112
Ballarat 44, **44**

Index

balloons 23, 56, 94, 95, 101, 138, 140
Bamburgh Castle (Northumb), naval gun 39, **39**
Bambury, Thomas **160**
Banbury (Northants), National Filling Factory 132–4, **132–3**, 144
Bangour (W Loth), hospital 188
Barley Rig 43
Barmston (E Yorks), pillbox **83**
Barnbow (W Yorks), National Filling Factory 132, 144
Barnsley (S Yorks), housing 151
barracks
 airfields 104–5, **105**, 106, 109, **109**, 111, 114, 115
 army **9**, 10–12, **10**, **11**, **12**, 24, 213
Barrie, J M 192
Barrington, Lady 197
Barrow-in-Furness (Cumbria)
 distillation plant 122
 housing 152
 library and museum 155
 Piel Island 204
Barton on Sea (Hants), hospital 195
Barwick (Som), flax **177**
Basil 45
basketmaking 178
Bassett-Lowke, W J **155**
Bawdsey (Suffolk), pillbox 86, **86**
Beachborough Park (Kent), hospital 189, **189**
Beacon Hill (Medway), defences 98
Beacon Hill (Wilts), practice trenches **16**
Beauchamp, Dr Sydney 192, 193
Bedford, Duchess of 191
Bekesbourne (Kent), hangar 113
Belfast trusses **101**, 102, **102**, 103, 107, 143
Belgium
 appeal for aid 1
 gratitude memorial 203
 refugees 146, 157, 178
 troops 188
Belmont (Surrey), hospital 190
Belton Park (Lincs), training centre 27
Bennett, Thomas 146
Berlage, Hendrik Petrus 159, **161**
Beverley (E Yorks), graffiti 164, **164**
Bicester (Oxon), airfield 93
Bickerdike, W E **157**
Biggin Hill (London), Wireless Experimentation Establishment 101
Billyard-Leake, Charles 189
Bing, Mr 132

Bircham Newton (Norfolk), airfield 118
Birling (Kent), defences 88, **88**
HMS *Birmingham* 47
Birmingham (W Mids)
 Austin Village 152
 Birmingham Small Arms Co 119
 Colmore Row, bank 162
 Greet, engine works 140
 Hall of Memory 211
 St Germain's Church 158
Birtley (Co Durham)
 housing 146, **146**
 National Projectile Factory 146
Bisley (Surrey), tank training 27
Blackheath (London), horse training 30
Blackpool (Lancs)
 leisure 156–7
 war memorial 207
Blay, George 198
blockhouses 82, 83
Blomfield, Sir Reginald 202
Blücher 80, 81
Blundstone, Ferdinand 208
Blyth (Northumb)
 battery **79**, 83
 Fort Coulson 75
 pillbox 83
 submarine base 46, 75
Blyth, Edmund 205
Boardman, Edward & Son 186
Bobbing (Kent), pillbox 89
Boer War 94, 141, 182–3, 200
Bolton (Lancs), post office 163
bombing practice 21
Boot, Sir Jesse 210
Bootle (Merseys), Western Packing Case Co 148, **149**
Boots the Chemist 160
Boulby (Redcar & Cleveland), sound mirror 61
Boulogne (France), hospital 180
Bournemouth (Dorset), Westbourne Carnegie Library 155
Bovington (Dorset)
 practice trenches 16
 Tank Corps 28, 213
Bracebridge Heath (Lincs), hangar **101**
Bradford (W Yorks), explosion 123
Bradgate Park (Leics), war memorial 205, **205**
Bramley (Hants), AOC depot 29
Brent (London)
 animal memorial 204, **204**
 Roe Green 146
Brentwood (Essex), Brook Street Hill 152
Bridge Farm (Redcar & Cleveland), sound mirror 61
Bridgnorth (Shrops), war

memorial 207–8, **208**
Bridlington Bay, wreck 40
Bridport (Dorset), ropemakers 175, 178
Brighton (E Sussex), hospitals 187, 188–9, **188**
HMS *Bristol* 38
Bristol
 allotments 176
 Boots 160
 Chittening, shell filling 134, 135, **135**
 Memorial Ground 204
 White City 9
 see also Avonmouth; Filton; Shirehampton
Bristol box kites 94
Bristol & Colonial Aeroplane Co 94
British Army School of Camouflage 20
British Expeditionary Force 3, 4, 5, 8, 31, 95, 121
British Red Cross Society 182, 183, 185, 186, 188, 190
Broadway (Worcs), Lifford Memorial Hall 158
Brockenhurst (Hants), hospital and crematorium 158, 189
Brocton (Staffs)
 barracks 9
 hospital 190, **190**
 POW camp 15
 practice trenches 19, **19**
 see also Cannock Chase; Rugeley
Brodie, John L 141
Bromham Hall (Beds), hospital 193
Brooklands (Surrey)
 flying displays 94
 wireless experiments 54
Broughton-in-Furness (Cumbria), graffiti 164
Brownlow, Earl of 27
SMS *Brummer* 62
Brunner Mond & Co 121, 122, 123
Bulford Camp (Wilts) 8, 34, 104, 173
Bull Sand Fort (E Yorks) 75, 77, **77**, **78**
Bunford (Som), flax factory **177**
Burston (Norfolk), Strike School 156, **157**
Burton-on-Trent (Staffs)
 machine gun factory 137, **137**, 145, **145**
 rifle range 21, **21**
Burwell (Cambs), Gardiner Memorial Hall 158
Bury (G Manchester), school war memorial 210
Bustard Inn (Wilts) 104
Bustard Trenches (Wilts) 17

C

cafés/restaurants 155, **156**
Calais (France), hospital 180
Calshot (Hants), seaplane station 59, **60**, 101, 102, **102**, 112
Cambridge (Cambs), hospital 185–6, **185**
camouflage 20, 39, 45
HMS *Campania* 56
Campbell, Kenneth F 186
Canadian Forestry Corps 178
Canadian troops
 Duxford 110
 hospitals 186, **186**, 188, 189, **189**, 196, 197, 198
 quartering 9
 YMCA 149
canals 32
Cannock Chase (Staffs)
 barracks 9, 12, **12**
 gas warfare 26
 POW camp 15, **20**
 practice trenches 17, 19–20, **19**, **20**
 railway 24
 rifle range 21, **21**
 see also Brocton; Rugeley
Canterbury (Kent), war memorial 211
Capel-le-Ferne (Kent), airship station 58, **58**
Cardiff (Glam), hospitals 187
Cardwell, Edward 4
Carisbrooke Castle **180**
Carlisle (Cumbria)
 memorial bridge 204
 post office 163
 public houses 155
HMS *Caroline* 39–40, **40**
Catfirth (Shetland) 112
Catterick (N Yorks)
 camp 9, 10, 213
 hangars 103, **103**, 112
Cattewater (Devon), seaplane station 112
Cecil family 175
Chance & Hunt 123
Channel Fleet 3, 36
charcoal production 179
Charlton (W Sussex), pub **170**
Chatham (Kent)
 hospital 181, 183
 Royal Engineers 24, 25
Chatham Land Front 56, 88–9, **89**, **90**
Chattenden (Medway), defences 84, 92
Chawton (Hants), memorial hall 204, **204**
Chelmsford (Essex)
 cinema 155
 Marconi 53, 141
Chetwynd, Viscount Godfrey 132

235

Index

Childers, Henry 4
Chilham (Kent), war memorial 201
Chilwell (Notts), National Filling Factory 132, **132**, 145
Chinese Labour Corps 34, **34**
Chipping Campden (Glos), war memorial 203, **203**
Chiseldon (Wilts)
  bombing training 21
  hospital 188
chlorine gas 26
churches
  building of 158
  memorials 201, **201**, 211
Churchill, Winston 51, 94, **102**, 129, 141, 192
Churton, Major 193
cinemas 155, **157**
Cirencester (Glos)
  bank 162
  Royal North Gloucester Militia Armoury **4**
Clark, John Pain 187
Clark, Lindsey 208
Clarke, Russell 53
Cleethorpes (Lincs), air raid shelter **97**
Clemens, Benjamin 207
Clément-Talbot works 140
Cliffe (Medway), Curtis & Harvey 125–8, **126**, **127**, **128**, 142
Clipstone (Notts), barracks 9, **10**
Clutton-Brock, Arthur 203
Coalville (Leics), Co-op 159, **160**
coast artillery
  commander 69
  development of 73–9, **75**, **76**, **77**, **78**, **79**
  Dover 69–70, **69**, **70**, 71, **72**, **73**
  Dover Barrier 78–9, **79**
  guns and emplacements 74–5
  Humber 75–7, **76**, **77**, **78**
  range-finding 71–2, 78
  Tyne turrets 77–8, **79**
coastal defences
  artillery 71–81, **75**, **76**, **77**, **78**, **79**
  before WW1 66, **67**
  defended ports and fortress system 68–71, **68**, **69**, **70**, **72**, **73**
  raids and invasion 80–2
Coatham (N Yorks), Pasley Battery 75
Cobh (Ireland) 3, 36
Codford Camp (Wilts) 173
Cody, Samuel 94
Coke, D J, painting by **176**
Colchester (Essex)
  barracks 8
  bombing training 21
  hospital 181

memorial swimming baths 204
Coleford (Glos), distillation plant 129
Connaught, Duchess of 186
conscientious objectors 34, 164, 168–9
conscription 6, 8
Constantine, Courtenay **154**
convoy system 50–1
Cooper, Edwin 196
Cornwell, Boy Jack 201
Cosham (Hants), hospital 181
Coventry (W Mids)
  Charter House Hotel 155
  housing 152
  White & Poppe's works 142–3, 144
Cowan, Colonel J H 21
Cowans, General Sir John 30
Cowtan & Sons 153
Cranwell (Lincs), flight training 101
HM *Crathie* 43
Crayford (London), gun maufacture 137
Credenhill (Herefs), AOC depot 29
crematoria 158, 189
Crewkerne (Som), war memorial 210
Cropton (N Yorks), memorial benches 204
Croydon (London), aircraft factory 139
Cullercoats (Tyne & Wear), wireless station 54
Cunard Steamship Co 139
Curragh (Ireland), barracks 8
Curtis, Ward & Hughes **201**
Cury (Cornwall), village hall 59
SS *Cyclop* 63, **63**

D

HMS *Daedalus* (Hants), hangars 59, 112
Daily Mail Active Service Exhibition 20
Dale, T Laurence **154**
Darland Banks (Kent), mining training 25, **25**
Darro 44
Dartford (Kent), hospital 188, 190
Dartmoor (Devon) 169, 178
Deal (Kent), war memorial 201
Defence of the Realm Act 6, 10, 14
Deganwy (Conwy), Royal Engineers 24
Deptford (London), Reserve Supply Depot 30
Derby (Derbys), by-law 15

Derflinger 80
Detling (Kent), defences 89
Devizes (Wilts), direction finding station 54
Devonport (Devon), naval dockyard 38, 96
Dewsbury (W Yorks), AOC depot 30
Dick, William Reid 211
Didcot (Oxon), AOC depot 29
direction finding 54
Disposals Board 12, 213
Ditchampton Farm (Wilts) 173
Donibristle (Fife), airfield 112
Donington Hall (Leics), POW camp 14
HMS *Doon* 80
Dorchester (Dorset), POW camp 14
Dorking (Surrey), building plans **148**
Dorman Long 103
Dover (Kent)
  air attack 97
  castle 54, 70, **70**, 71
  cinemas 155
  defences 69–71, **69**, **70**, **72**, **73**; see also Dover Barrier
  hospital ships 181
  Marine Station 31, **31**, 32
  Royal Flying Corps 95
Dover Barrier 49–50, **49**, 78–9, **79**
Dover Patrol 36, 69
Dowdeswell (Glos), war memorial 204–5
Doyle-Jones, Francis **209**
drainage 172
Dreadnought 37–8
SMS *Dresden* 62
drill halls 4, **4**, 8
Dunham Massey (Ches), hospital 191
Dunkirk (France), hospital 180
Dunrobin Castle (Highland), hospital 191
Duxford (Cambs)
  conservation 112
  fighter base 106–7, **106**, **107**, **108**, 110
  hangars 103, 106, **107**, 111

E

East Coast Defences 85–7, **85**, **86**
East Fortune (Fife), airfield 96, **96**, 112
East Garton (E Yorks), pillbox 86
Eastbourne (E Sussex)
  Boots 160
  hospital 195, **195**
Eastchurch (Kent), Naval Wing

HQ 56–7, 94, 95, 101, 102
Eastcote House (Northants), internment camp 15
Eastleigh (Hants), hangar 112
Eastriggs (Dum & Gall), housing 146
Edinburgh
  hospitals 187, 188, 196
  war memorial 211
Educational Supply Association of Stevenage 103, 107
Edwards, A C Morris **148**
Eisenhower, D D 189
Elgar, Edward 211
Elgood, F M **160**
Eltham (London), Well Hall 145–6, 152, **152**
Enfield (London)
  public houses 155
  Royal Small Arms Factory 119, 155
Englefield Green (Surrey), hospital 188
Enham (Hants), village centre 197
Epsom (Surrey), racecourse 191
Erith (London), gun factory 137
Ernle, Lord 169
Étaples (France), hospital 180
Eton College (Berks) 29, **169**, 176
evacuation plan 164, **164**
Evesham (Worcs), Boots 160
Ewart, Mr 193
Ewing, Sir Alfred 53
Exeter (Devon)
  Deller's Café 155, **156**
  military hospital 178
explosives 121–2
  cordite 123–5, **124**, **125**
  factories 125–30, **126**, **127**, **128**, **129**, **130**
  high explosives 122–3, **122**, **123**

F

HMS *Falmouth* 40, **40**
Falmouth (Cornwall), defences 69, 73
Fan Bay Battery (Kent), sound mirror 61, **61**
Fargo Camp Hospital (Wilts) 190
Farmiloe, Edith 211
Farnborough (Hants)
  airfield buildings 107
  Balloon Factory 94
  hangar 103
  Royal Aircraft Factory 94, 101, 121, 138–9, **138**
  School of Photography 100
Felday (Surrey), POW camp 14
Felixstowe (Suffolk)

236

defences 73, 85–6
flying boats 57
Felixstowe flying boats 57, 58, 102
Fieldhouse, William J 185
fieldworks 82, 85–92, **85**, **86**, **87**, **88**, **89**, **90–1**, **92**
Filton (Bristol), aircraft factory 94
Finchley (London), balloon manufacture 140
Firth, Thomas & Sons 141
Fisher, Jackie 3
Fishguard (Pembs), seaplane station 109, 112
flame-throwers 25
flax 177, **177**
Flers-Courcelette (France) 27
flying boats 56, 57, 58, 59, 62, 102
  Curtiss *H12* 62
Folkestone (Kent)
  air attack 97
  casualties 181
  transit port 31
Folly Hole (E Yorks), pillbox **84**
Food Production Department 167, 171, 178
Forage Corps 174–5, **175**
Ford, Henry 171
Fordington (Dorset), war memorial 207
Forest of Dean (Glos), agricultural labour 168
Forestry Commission 214
Forrester, Joseph **97**
Fort Farningham (Kent) 88
Fort Gilkicker (Hants), battery 73
Forth Patrol 36
fortress system 68–9, 71–2
Foster, William 27, 141
Fovant (Wilts), chalk-cut badges 13, **13**
Fowlmere (Cambs), airfield 106
Fox, Sir Douglas & Partners 143
France-Aimée 45
Franklin, C S 54
Franz Fischer 41
French, Field Marshal Sir John 81, 121
Friston (Suffolk), pillbox 86
Frith Hill (Surrey), POW camp 14, **14**
Frog Island (Essex), shipbreaking **214**
Frognal House (Kent), hospital 196, **196**
Fry, J H 191
Fulwell (Co Durham), sound mirror 61
HMS *Furious* 56
Furley, Sir John 185
furlough 166, 167
future research 215–16

G

Gaea 43
HMS *Ganges* 181
gardens **10**, 13, **14**
gas manufacture 134–5, **135**
gas masks 26, 134
gas warfare training 26–7, **26**
Gateshead (Tyne & Wear), Shipley art gallery 155, **157**
HMS *Ghurka* 50
Giant bombers 97, 112
Gibb, Alexander 78
Gill, A A 199
Gill, Eric 206
Glasgow
  helmet production 141
  hospital 186
Gliddon, Gerald 175–7
Glossop, Canon George 201
Godstone (Surrey), bombing school 21
Gog 121
Goldhanger (Essex), airfield 114
Goldsack, Gladys 211
Goodwick (Pembs) 109
Goschen, Lord George 46
Gosport (Hants)
  electric light school 24
  Fort Blockhouse (HMS *Dolphin*) 46, 54
  Fort George **192**
  naval depot 36, **37**
  Royal Flying Corps 95, 99–101
  St Nicholas chapel 46
Gotha bombers 97, 112, 118, 165
Gottfried 43
graffiti 17, 164, **164**
Grahame-White, Claude 94
Grand Fleet 3, 5, 36, 64
Grantham (Lincs), war memorial 27
Graudenz 80
Graves, Robert 202, **206**
Gravesend (Kent), bridge 24
Great Dixter (E Sussex), haymaking **170**
Great Wigsell (E Sussex), Cecil family 175
Great Yarmouth (Norfolk)
  flying boats 57
  German raid 5, 35, 46, 75, 80, 163
  hospital 181
  pillboxes 84, 86
Greenford (London), filling factory 135, **135**
Greenwich (London)
  hospital 189
  internment camp 15
  workhouse 30
Gretna (Dum & Gall), explosives factory 129–30, **130**, 143, 146
Grey, Sir Edward 1–3

Griffith Dr Joseph 186
Grigg, Frederick 203
Guildford (Surrey), war memorial 211, **211**

H

Hadfield, Sir Charles 141
Haig, General Douglas 28, 94
Haile Sand Fort (E Yorks) 75, 77, **77**
Hainault Farm (Essex), hangars 103–4, **104**, 112, 113, 114
Haldane, Richard Burdon 3–4
Halifax (W Yorks), King of Prussia Inn 15
Hall, E Stanley 184
Hall, Edwin T 184, 191
Hall, John 186
Halliday, J Theo 204
Halton Park (Bucks), RFC school 110
Halton Quay (Cornwall), limekilns 172
hand grenades 25
hangars
  building 101–4, **101**, **102**, **103**, **104**, **105**
  RNAS 57, 59, **60**, 94, **94**
  survival 111–13, **111**, 114, 118, **118**
  see also individual hangars by name
Harbrow, William 101
Harefield Park (Middx), hospital 189
Harlaxton Manor (Lincs), training centre 27
Harrowby Camp (Lincs), training centre 27
Hartlepool (Co Durham)
  batteries 73, 75, 80–1
  German raid 35, 75, 80–1, 163, 191
  hospital 191
  housing 152
Hartley (Northumb), Roberts Battery 78
Hartwell, Charles 207
Harwich (Essex)
  defences 66, **68**, 69
  hospital 181
  naval base 3, 36, 62, 66
  rail bridge 32, **32**
Haslar (Hants), hospital 181
Haslemere (Surrey), Hindhead Court 153, **153**
Hatfield House (Herts), tanks 27, 142
Hawkins battery (Cornwall) 83
Hayes (Middx), aero-engine factory 140
Heanor (Derbys), King of Prussia pub 15

Heaton Chapel (Ches), aircraft factory 139
Hedge End (Hants), war memorial 211, **211**
Helston (Cornwall), airship station 59
Hendon (London)
  flying school 94, 99, **99**
  RAF museum 113
  Roe Green 152
Henley Fort (Surrey) 88
Henlow (Beds), Command Repair Depot 103, 112
Henriques, E C 158
Herbert, Auberon, Baron Lucas 192, **192**
Herbert, Nan 192, 193, **193**, 194
Hereford (Herefs), filling factory 134
HMS *Hermes* 56
Herne Bay (Kent), bombing school 21
High Elms (London), war memorial 211
Hinwick House (Beds), hospital 193
Hipper, Rear Admiral Franz 80
Hippisley, Colonel Richard 53
Hollesley (Suffolk), pillbox 86
Holton Heath (Dorset), cordite factory 129, **129**, 142, 143, **143**, 214
Home Defence Early Warning System 96
Home Defence Flight Stations 103
Home Defence Stations 110, **110**, 112, 114
HMS *Hood* **38**, 39
Hooley Hill Rubber & Chemical Co 122–3
Hooton Park (Wirral), hangar 103, 111
Hornchurch (London)
  allotments 176
  hangars 112
  hospital 189
horses 22, 30, 34, 173–5, **174**
hospitals
  aftermath 196–8, 214
  allied forces and POWs 188–90, **188**, **189**, **190**
  auxiliary and convalescent 191–5, **195**
  development and growth 180–3, **181**, **182**, **183**
  hospital ships 43, 180–1, **180**, 183
  hutted **181**, 183–6, **184**, **185**, **186**
  as memorials 203–4
  territorial and war 187–8, **187**
  see also injuries, disabling
housing
  agricultural labour 168

237

Index

armaments workers 145–6, 152, **152**
  civilian 151–3, **152**, **153**, **154–5**
  post-war 213
  see also barracks
Howard, John H **153**
Howden (E Yorks), RNAS 58
Huddersfield (W Yorks), hospital 186
Hull (E Yorks)
  Paull fort 73, 75–7
  St Mary's Church 158
Humber coast defences 75–7, **76**, **77**, **78**, 86
Humber Patrol 36
Humble Bee Creek (Kent), U-boat 63, **63**
Humphreys of Knightsbridge 184
Hundred River (Suffolk) 85
Hunstanton (Norfolk), interception operations 53, **53**
Hyam & Hobgen **156**

I

identity disc **132**
HMS *Illustrious* 77
Immingham (Lincs), docks 77
Imperial (Commonwealth) War Graves Commission 200, 202
Indian Army 3, 8, 158, 188–9, **188**
Ingenohl, Admiral Friedrich von 80
Inglis, Charles Edward, bridges 24, **24**
injuries, disabling 195–7, 213
intelligence-gathering 52–3, **53**
internment camps 14–15, 169
invasion, threat of 69, 81–2, 92
Invergordon (Highld), anchorage 3
Irlam (Lancs), cinema 155
Isle of Grain (Kent)
  defences 89
  seaplane base 56
Iveagh, Lord 185
Ivels 171

J

Jackson, Sir H B 54
Jagger, Charles Sargeant 203, 207, 208
Jameson, Rear Admiral Sir William S 51
Jellicoe, Admiral Sir John 36, **36**
Jones, Capt Adrian 206–208
Jones, Private Eli 208
Jones, Robert 196
Joyce Green (Kent), airfield 97

Jutland, battle of 5, 36, 38, 39–40, 54

K

SMS *Karlsruhe* 62
Kemp Prosser, Howard 187–8
Kempton Park (Surrey), vehicles 30
Kennington, Eric 206, 211
Keogh, Sir Alfred 182
Kessingland (Suffolk), pillbox 86
Keyser, Agnes & Fanny 182–3
Killingholme (Lincs), air base 60, 77, 112
Kilnsea (E Yorks)
  Godwin Battery **76**, 77, 83
  Murray's Post 83
  sound mirror 61
Kings Weston House (Glos), plaque 214
Kingsley, Sgt Major 193
Kingsnorth (Kent), airship base 56
Kirkwood, Dr William 193
Kitchener, Field Marshall 8, 201, 211
Kleine Patent Fire-Resisting Flooring Syndicate 15
Knockaloe (IOM), internment camp 15
Knutsford, Lord 192
Kolberg 80
SMS *Köln* 62
SMS *König* 62
SS *Königin Luise* 181
Kraftmeier (Kay), Edward 15
SMS *Kronprinz Wilhelm* 62

L

Labour Corps 34, 167
Lancaster (Lancs)
  internment camp 15
  National Projectile Factory 138
  Waring & Gillow 139
Lancing (W Sussex), railway works 140
land defences 82–4, **83**, **84**, 92, **92**; *see also* Chatham Land Front; East Coast Defences; London Defence Line
Langton Wold (E Yorks), ploughing 172
Larkhill Camp (Wilts)
  airfield 95, 111
  artillery training 23
  barracks 8, 104
  bombing training 21
  hangars 57, 94, **94**, 102
  practice trenches 17, **17–18**
  railway 24

Lathom Park (Lancs), remount depot 174
Latymer Dam (Suffolk), pillbox 85
Lawrence, T E 211
Le Touquet (France), hospital 180
Leafield (Oxon), Marconi 53
Leckhampstead (Berks), war memorial 207
Ledward, Gilbert 204, 207
Lee-on-Solent (Hants), seaplane station 112, **113**
Leeming & Leeming **2**
Leicester (Leics)
  hospital 188, 198
  Prudential Assurance HQ 162
Leigh (Lancs), POW camp 14
Leighterton (Glos), airfield 113
Lelant (Cornwall), war memorial 210
Lenham (Kent), war memorial 205, **205**
Lennox Foundry Co 134
Lethaby, W R 203
Leuchars (Fife), hangars 103, 111
HMS *Leviathan* 39
Lewisham (London), Grove Park 30
Liberty 183
Libury Hall (Herts), internment camp 15
Lichfield (Staffs), raid 165
Lidcombe (Glos), timber 178
lighters 62, **62**
limekilns 172
Lincoln (Lincs), allotments 176
Livens, Capt William H, projector 25, **25**
Liverpool (Merseys)
  Aintree, aircraft factory 139–40, **140**
  Anglican Cathedral 158
  cenotaph 212, **212**
  Cunard Building 158, **159**
  Cunard's Shellworks 130–1, **131**, **144**
  Knotty Ash, American troops 9
Llanfairpwll (Anglesey), WI 170
Lloyd, Nathaniel **170**
Lloyd George, David 6–7, 22, 137, 143, 175, 202, 213
Loch Ewe (Highld), naval base 36
Lodge Hill (Medway)
  anti-aircraft battery 98, **98**
  depot defences 92, **92**
Lofthouse (W Yorks), internment camp 15
London
  Admiralty **2**, 53, 54
  air attacks 97–8, 165
  American hospitals 189
  Australia House 163, **163**
  auxiliary hospitals 191, **195**
  Battersea, AOC depot 30

Battersea Park, war memorial 206, **206**
Belgian Gratitude Memorial 203
Blackfriars House 158
British Columbia House 163
British Museum 165
Bromley-by-Bow, fermentation plant 129
Bushy Park, hospital 189
Carlton House Terrace, hospital 183, 191
Cenotaph 202, **202**
Clapham Common, trench warfare school 25
Cleopatra's Needle 165
Clerkenwell, anti-aircraft site **97**
Cockspur Street, shipping office 42, **42**
70 Coleman Street 158
County Hall 163
Cyprus Street, war memorial 201
Dollis Hill, experimental depot 28
10 Downing Street 149, 153
Empire Memorial Sailors' Hostel 45, **45**
Essex Road, South Library 155
Francis Holland School 156
Gates House (Barnet) 153, **154**
Hammersmith, Waring & Gillow 139
Heal's store 158
42–4 Hertford Street 153
Holland House 159, **161**
Hyde Park Corner, war memorials 27, 207, **207**, 208, **208**
internment camps 15
Islington, war memorial 203
Kensington Gardens, replica trenches 20
King Edward VII Hospital 182–3
Kinnaird House 162
Ladbrook Grove, engine works 140
Lambeth, Hampton & Sons 139, **139**
Lincoln's Inn chapel 165
Lyons tea rooms 155
Marylebone Town Hall 163
National Liberal Club 28
70–1 New Bond Street 158, **159**
New Bridge Street, National Restaurant **156**
New Court (Hampstead), war memorial 201
Ocean Marine Insurance Co HQ 162
Olympia 15, 29
orthopaedic hospital 196

Index

Phoenix House 160–2, **162**
Pimlico, Royal Army Clothing Depot 29, **29**
Port of London offices 163
Prudential Assurance war memorial 208–9, **209**
Queen Alexandra's Hospital 181, 191
8 Queen Anne Street 153
Radiant House 158, **160**
Regent's Park 177
Royal Albert Hall 165
Royal Institute of Architects offices **213**
St Anne Limehouse, war memorial 208
St Botolph without Bishopsgate, war memorial 201, **201**
St Dunstan's 196, 197
St James's Park **7**, 28, 165, 177
St John's Wood, war memorial 207
St Paul's Cathedral, war memorial 211
St Wilfred's Catholic Church (Newington) 158
Southwark 98, 208
territorial hospitals 187–8, **187**, 197–8, **197**
Thurloe Place, rubber and tyre co 158
Trafalgar Square 20, **20**, **216**
Trinity Square Gardens, memorial **41**
Victoria Embankment, War Office buildings 28
War Office **1**, 28, 54
1 Wardour Street 148
Wardour Street cinema 155
Water Board Offices 163
Waterloo Station, war memorial 209
Wembley, trench warfare experiments 25
West London Police Court 163
Western Synagogue (Camden) 158
19 Weymouth Street 153, **153**
White City 29
Whitehall Place 149
wooden roads 151, **151**
YMCAs 149, **150**
see also Biggin Hill; Blackheath; Brent; Crayford; Croydon; Deptford; Eltham; Enfield; Erith; Finchley; Greenford; Greenwich; Hendon; High Elms; Hornchurch; Lewisham; Norbury; Northolt; Plumstead; Purley; Putney; Roehampton; Silvertown; Upminster; Uxbridge; Wimbledon; Woolwich
London Air Defence Area 97–8

London Colney (Herts), airfield 112
London Defence Line 87–8, **87**, **88**
London Small Arms Co 120
Longmoor (Hants), railway 24
Lorimer, Sir Robert 210–11
Lostock (Ches), amatol production 123
Lough Swilly (Ireland), naval base 36
Loughborough (Leics), carillon **210**, 211
Lowe, Thomas & Sons **137**
Lowestoft (Suffolk)
  defences 85
  German raid 75
  school war memorial 210
Lubbock, Hon Eric 211
Lusitania 36, 44
Lusk (Ireland), remount depot 174
Luton (Beds), Boots 160
Lutyens, Sir Edwin **41**, 202
Lydd (Kent), artillery training 22, 23, **23**
Lyndhurst (Hants), bombing school 21
Lyons & Co 183
Lytham St Annes (Lancs), practice trenches 20

M

HMS M33 39, **39**
McCarthy, Thomas Ignatius **160**
McClean, Frank 94
Macclesfield (Ches), war memorial 208
McCudden, James 112
Machine Gun Corps 27
machine guns 27, 83, 84, 87, 137
Mackenzie, A Marshall **163**
Mackintosh, Charles Rennie 153, **155**
Maclennan, Roderick **99**
Madeley (Staffs), POW camp 14
Magog 121
Manchester
  Heaton Park, trenches 20
  hospital 186, 187
  war memorial 202
Mannock, Mick 112
Manston (Kent), hangars 104, 112
HMS Maori 50
Marconi Wireless Telegraph Co 53, 141
Marfleet (E Yorks), docks 77
Margate (Kent), German raid 35
Margaux 45
SMS Markgraf 62
Markham, Sir Arthur 189
Marlborough College (Wilts) 210

Marsden (Co Durham), Kitchener Battery 78
Maunsell, Guy 79
Mee, Arthur 204–5
Melton Mowbray (Leics), remount farm 174
memorial halls 204, **204**
SS Mendi 44
merchant navy 2, 41–6, 50–1
Messines (Belgium) 19, **20**, 25
Milburn, Lieutenant Gerald 114
Millard, John 208
Mills bombs 21
Minchinhampton (Glos), aerial gunnery training **108**
Ministry of Blockade and Shipping **6**, 7
Ministry of Information 7
Ministry of Labour 7
Ministry of Munitions
  aircraft 139
  building commandeered by 162
  building regulations 148, 150–1
  creation of 22, 28, 137, 146
  history of 119
  post-war 214
  Trench Warfare Dept 25, 26
  welfare 143
Ministry of National Service 7, 28
Ministry of Pensions **6**, 28, 195, 197
Ministry of Shipping 177
Mitchell, Shaw & Co 140
Moltke 80
Monkham's Hall (Essex), gun emplacement 98
Montrose (Angus)
  barracks 109
  hangars 95, **95**, 103, 111
Moore, Temple 158, 206
Morecambe (Lancs), filling factory 135
Morley Horder, Percy 207
Mothers' Union 178
motorised vehicles 30
Mount's Bay (Cornwall), wreck 40
mules 173, 174
Müller, W H 159
Murray, John George 194
Muslim burial ground 158, **158**
mustard gas 26
Muswell Manor (Kent), Royal Aero Club 94, 111

N

Narborough (Norfolk), airfield 118
national factories
  building of 123, 137–8, **137**, 146
  design 142–3, **142**, **143**
  distribution **136**

  post-war 214
National Restaurants 155, **156**
naval war 35–6, **36**, 64–5
  guns 39, **39**, 43, 44
  naval organisation 36; see also merchant navy; Royal Naval Air Service; Royal Naval Reserve; Royal Navy (surface fleet)
  post-war losses 64
  surviving vessels and wrecks **38**, 39–41, **39**, **40**, **41**
  undersea service 46–56, **46**, **47**, **48**, **49**, **50**, **51**
navy, German 62–3, **62**, **63**
Netheravon (Wilts)
  airfield buildings 103, **105**, 107, 111, 118, **118**
  squadron station 95, 105, **105**
Netley (Hants)
  crematorium 158
  Royal Victoria Hospital 181, **181**, **182**, 184–5, 189, 190, 196
New Zealand troops
  hospitals 188, 189, 198
  Leighterton 113
  quartering 9, 13
  riots 34
  torpedoed 44
  training 17, 19
Newark (Notts), Royal Engineers 24
Newbury (Berks)
  hospital 186
  internment camp 15
Newcastle upon Tyne (Tyne & Wear)
  St Barnabas Vicarage 158
  war memorial 207
Newhaven (E Sussex)
  coast artillery 73
  military port 31
  seaplane station 59, **60**
Newington (Kent), pillbox 89, **90**
Newton, W G 210
Nissen, Capt Peter 24, 198
Nobel Industries Ltd 214
Norbury (London), allotments **176**
Nore (Thames), naval defences 36
North Shotwick (Flints), hangars 103, 111
North Somercotes (Lincs), pillboxes 87
North Weald (Essex)
  hangar 112
  redoubt 88
Northampton (Northants)
  78 Derngate 153, **155**
  Duston Hospital 141
  post office 163
Northern Barrage 49
Northern Patrol 36

239

Index

Northfleet (Kent), war memorial 209, **209**
Northolt (London), squadron station **110**
Northwich (Ches), explosives factory 123
Northwood (W Sussex), incinerator 179
Norwich (Norfolk), hospital 186
Nottingham (Notts)
   Co-op Store 159
   Memorial Gardens 210, **210**
   Trent Bridge 191

O

O. B. Jennings 45
Oakley estate (Beds) 175
Office of Works 132, 142, 146, 148, 165, 189
Old Oswestry hillfort (Shrops) 165
Old Sarum (Wilts)
   conservation 112, 116
   hangars 103, **104**, 111, **111**
Old Warden Park (Beds), hospital 193
Oldbury (W Mids)
   national factory 123
   railway workshops 142
Oldham (Lancs), aircraft factory 140
Oliver, Rear Admiral Henry 53
Ongar (Essex), Herons House 153, **154**
Orfordness airfield (Suffolk) 34, 101, **109**
Orpington (Kent), hospital 186, **186**, 189, 197, 198, **198**
Osmington Mills (Dorset), Upton Battery 73
Ostend (Belgium) 51
Oswestry (Shrops), hospital 188, 190, 197; *see also* Old Oswestry
Oundle (Northants)
   school 141
   workhouse 168
Owen, General J F 66
Owen, Wilfred 196
Owlerton (S Yorks), memorial hall 204
Oxford (Oxon), St Hugh's College 156

P

Padiham (Lancs), memorial park 204
Palgrave, F P 159
Panmure Barracks (Angus) 109
Panshanger estate (Herts) 175

Parnell, Major Geoffrey 211
Passport Office **6**
Patcham (E Sussex), crematorium 158, 189
HMS *Patrol* 80–1
Pembroke (Pembs), naval patrol 36
Pendennis Head (Cornwall), wrecks 63
Penguins **104**
Peter Brotherhood, Messrs 141
phosgene gas 26
Pick, S Perkins 188
picric acid (Lyddite) 122, 123, 144
pillboxes
   Chatham Land Front 88–9, **90**
   coastal defences, Dover 71
   development and use of 83–4, **83**, **84**
   east coast defences 85–7, **86**
   Sheppey coast defences 89, **91**
   for use at the front 32
Pither, F L **160**
Plumley (Ches), amatol production 123
Plumstead (London), munitions factory 119
Plymouth (Devon)
   defences 36, 83
   hospitals 181
Polegate (E Sussex), airship station 58–9, **59**
Poole (Dorset), school 177
Port War Signal Stations 41, 70, **70**, 77, 80
Portishead (Som), distillation plant 122
Portland (Dorset)
   hospital 181
   naval base 36, **38**, 39, 69
Porton Down (Wilts) 24, 26, **26**, 27, 213
ports, defences 66, **67**, 68–9; *see also* Dover
Portsmouth (Hants)
   floating POW camps 14
   historic dockyard 39, **39**
   naval defences 36
   naval dockyard 38
   St Cuthbert's Church 158
   Wimborne School 156
   practice trenches 16–20, **16**, **17**–**18**, **19**, 157
Preston, E Carter 211
Preussen 41
Price, Henry 186
Priestly, J B 199
prisoners of war
   agricultural work 167, 168, **169**, 172, 178
   hospitals 190, **190**
   housing 14, **14**, 15, 213
   war memorial 207
   at Yatesbury 116

Pritchard, H E 146
public houses 155
Pudsey (W Yorks), women workers **167**
Pulbrook, Ernest 178
Purfleet (Essex), proof range 121
Purley (London), war memorial 205, **205**
Putney (London), Woolworth 160

Q

Q-ships 44, 64, **64**
Quartermaster General 3, 28
Queen Elizabeth 36
Queensferry (Flints), national factory 123, 130
Quinan, Kenneth B 130

R

rabbits 178
railways, military 24
Ramsgate (Kent)
   German raid 35, 160
   hospital 196
   Woolworths 159–60, **161**
rats 178
Rawtenstall (Lancs), war memorial **168**, 200
Reading (Berks)
   food queue **166**
   Wantage Hall 110
Redmires (S Yorks), practice trenches 16
redoubts 71, 82, 88, 89, **91**, 92, **92**
Reigate Fort (Surrey) **87**, 88
remount depots 174, **174**
Renney battery (Cornwall) 83
Reuter, Rear Admiral Ludwig von 62
HMHS *Rewa* 43
Reynolds, Edwin Francis 158
Rhind, W Birnie 157
Richardson, Albert 201
Richborough (Kent), military port 31, 32–3, **33**, 34
Richmond (N Yorks), graffiti 164, **164**
Richmond (Surrey)
   aircraft factory 140
   hospitals 189–90, 196–7
Ridley, Lieutenant Claude 114
Rievaulx Abbey (N Yorks) 165
rifle grenades 25
rifle ranges 21, **21**
rifles 82, 119, 120
Ripon (N Yorks), barracks 9, 10, **11**
Rishton (Lancs), cinema 155, **157**
Rivers, Dr W H R 196

Roberts, Mary 43
Robson, Lieutenant Colonel L 80
Robur 50
Rochford (Essex), airfield 114
Roe, A V 94
Roehampton (London), hospital 196
Rohilla 43
Rollestone Camp (Wilts) **9**
Rolls, Charles S 57
Rolls-Royce 141
Romsey (Hants), remount depot 174
rooks 178
Roslyn, L F **168**
Rosyth (Fife), naval base 3, 38, 62, 66
Rothbury (Northumb), practice trenches **17**
Rotherwas (Herefs), National Filling Factory 134, **134**, **142**, 143
Round, Henry J 54
Rousseau, Victor 203
Royal Air Force 94, 118
Royal Army Medical Corps 180, 182, 183
Royal Artillery 22, 69
Royal Engineers 23–5, **25**, 69, 187
Royal Flying Corps
   deployment 95–6, 97
   end of 118
   origins 56
   training 23, 95, 99–101, 110
   women 109
Royal Garrison Artillery 22, 71
Royal Naval Air Service 56–62, **56**, **57**, **58**, **59**, **60**, 95–6, 101, 118
Royal Naval Reserve 43–6
Royal Navy (surface fleet) 2–3, 5, 35, 37–9, **38**
Royston (Herts), war memorial 207
Rugeley Camp (Staffs) 9, 19–20, *see also* Brocton; Cannock Chase
Rushall (Norfolk), airship **57**
Rushmere (Suffolk), pillbox 85

S

S-24 63
Saffron Walden (Essex), evacuation arrow 164, **164**
St Albans (Herts), war memorials 201
St John's Ambulance Association **6**, 182
St Leonards Forest (E Sussex), vermin control 178
Salisbury Plain (Wilts)
   barracks 8, 9, **9**, 13

military railways 24
practice trenches **16**, 17, **17**–**18**
Samuelson & Co, Messrs 134
Sandbach (Ches), amatol production 123
Sandtoft (Lincs), bridge **24**
Sarisbury Court (Hants), hospital 190
Sassoon, Siegfried 196
Scafell Pike (Cumbria) 204
Scampton (Lincs), airfield 93
Scapa Flow (Orkney), naval base
 aerial cover 96
 creation of 3, 35, 66
 German fleet at 62, **62**
 Grand Fleet at 36
Scarborough (N Yorks), German raid 5, 35, 75, 80, **80**, 163–5
schools
 agricultural work 167, 169, **169**, 176, 177
 building of 156, **157**
 used as hospitals 182, 183, 187, 188
 war memorials 209–10, **209**
 war production 141
Scott, Giles Gilbert 158, 196
sea forts 75, 77, **77**, **78**
Sea Palling (Norfolk), pillbox 86
Seaford Camp (E Sussex) **12**, 27
seaplane stations 58, **96**, 109, 112, **113**
seaplanes
 deployment 96, **96**
 hangars 102, **102**
 RNAS 56, 57, **57**, 59, 60, 62
 Sopwith Baby **57**
 Sopwith Bat Boats 102
 Sopwith Pup 56
searchlights (DELs) 24, 69, 70, 96, 98
Sedgeford (Suffolk), airfield 116
Seed Testing Station 172, **172**
Selborne, Viscount 46
Selby (N Yorks), filling factory 135
Selsey (W Sussex), sound mirror 61
Seydlitz 80
Sheerness (Kent), defences 56, 66, 89, **91**
Sheffield (S Yorks)
 helmet production 141
 Telegraph & Star building 159, **160**
Shell Borneo petroleum 122
shell shock 180, 196, 197
Sheppey (Kent)
 airfields 94, 111
 bridge 24
 coast defences 89, **90**–**1**
 Fletcher Battery 75, 89, **91**
 Merryman's Hill Redoubt **91**
Shepreth (Cambs), village hall 191

Sherbrook (Staffs), practice trench **19**
Sheringham (Norfolk), defences 86
Shipping Controller 44, 45
ships, domestic 43–6; *see also* hospitals, ships; lighters; Q-ships; submarines; warships
Shirehampton (Bristol), remount depot 174
Shoeburyness (Essex), artillery training 22–3, 121
Shoreham Harbour (W Sussex) 79
Shorncliffe (Kent)
 barracks 8, 9, **13**
 Chinese Labour Corps graves **34**
Short brothers 57, 94, 111
Shotley (Suffolk), hospital 181
Shrewsbury (Shrops), hangar 112
Shrivenham (Berks), village centre 197
Silvertown (London), TNT factory 122, **122**
Singleton & East Dean WI (W Sussex) 170
Skidbrooke (Lincs), pillboxes 87
Skipper, Charles F 186, **186**
Skúli Fógeti 43
Sledmere (E Yorks)
 agriculture 173, 178
 war memorial 206, **207**
Slough (Berks), depot 30–1, **215**
Smith, George Herbert Tyson **212**
Smith-Barry, Major Robert 99–101
smoke bombs 25
Smoogroo (Orkney) 112
Smuts, General 97, 118
Solihull (W Mids), war memorial 206
Sopwith, Tommy **102**
Sorrell, Alan, *A Land Fit for Heroes* 199, **200**
sound mirrors 61, **61**, 113
South African troops 44, 188, 189–90
South Queensferry (Edinburgh), hospital 184
South Shields (Co Durham), Frenchman's Point Battery 73, **75**
Southampton (Hants)
 barracks 9
 hospital ships 181
 military port 31, 32
 war memorial 202
Southend-on-Sea (Essex)
 floating POW camps 14
 hospital **183**
Southport (Merseys), hospital 186
Southwold (Suffolk), pillbox 86
spagnum moss 177–8

Spee, Maximilian von 5
Spurn Point (E Yorks), defences 77, 83
Staines (Surrey), hospital 183
Stallingborough (Lincs), battery 77
Standford Hill (Kent), glider tests 57
Stanton Moor (Derbys), timber 179
state arsenals 119–20
steel helmets 25
Stock Force 44, 64
Stockbury (Kent), pillbox 89
Stockport (Manchester), war memorial 204
Stockton-on-Tees (Co Durham), wireless station 52–3, **52**
Stockwell, Arthur **157**
Stonehenge (Wilts), airfield 93, **93**, 100, 101
stop lines 85
Stow, war memorial 211
Stow Maries (Essex), airfield **109**, 112, 114–15, **114**, **115**
Strassburg 80
Strathord 64
Stratton St Margaret (Wilts), explosives factory 123, **123**, 143
Strauland 80
Street, A G 173
Stroβ, Kap Alfred 50
Stuart, Colonel A M 105
submarines
 A1 46
 A3 46
 A7 46
 B2 46
 C9 81
 C29 46
 D5 46, **47**
 H52 64
 use of and losses 46–7, **46**, **47**, **48**, 49, 51, 215
 see also U-boats
Sudbury (Suffolk), engine works 140
sugar beet 177
Sunderland (Co Durham)
 hospital 186
 Roker Battery 75
Sunk Island (E Yorks), battery 77
Sutherland, Duke & Duchess of 180, 191
Sutton Courtenay (Oxon), Asquith residence 153
Swaffham Prior (Cambs)
 ploughing 171
 war memorial 201, **201**
Swanage (Dorset), war memorial 210
Swaythling (Hants), remount depot 174

Swindon (Wilts)
 railway works 140
 swimming baths 191
Sykes, Sir Mark **207**
synagogues 158

T

T-189 63
Tadcaster (N Yorks), hangar 113
Tank Corps, training 27–8, **28**
tanks 141–2
Taplow (Bucks), hospital 186, 189
Tapper, Sir Walter 211
Taranaki 64
Tavistock (Devon), depot 178
Taylor, Frederick 143
Teddington (Middx), National Physical Laboratory 121
Territorial Force 4, **4**, 8
USS *Texas* 39
Thetford (Norfolk), tank training 27
HMT *Thomas W Irvin* 43
Tidworth (Wilts), barracks 8
timber 150–1, 178–9, **179**, 214
Tisdall, Arthur 201
Tiverton (Devon), Boots 160
TNT 122–3, 132, 143, 144–5
toluene 122
Torquay (Devon), Boots 160
tractors 171, **171**
Training Depot Stations 101, 103, 106, 110, 111, **113**, 118
Tredegar, Lord 183
tree memorials 204–5, **205**
Trench Warfare Department 134
Trenchard, Hugh 93, 118
Trenches 16–28, **16**, **17**, **19**, **25**, **26**, 34, 71, **72**, 82, 85, 86, 88, **88**, 89, 91, 92, **92**, 165, 173, 215–16; *see also* practice trenches
Tresco (Scilly), seaplane station 58, **96**, 112
Tritton, William 141
Trumpington (Cambs), war memorial 206
tunnelling 17, **18**, 24–5, **25**
Tyne Patrol 36
Tyne Turrets 75, 77–8, **79**
Tynemouth (Northumb)
 coast artillery 73
 range-finding system 78, **79**

U

U-boats
 film **64**
 internment 62, 63, **63**
 use of and losses 36, 40, 41, 47–56, **48**, **50**, **51**

Index

U-8 50, **50**, **51**
U-15 47
U-40 64
UB-65 47
UB-81 47
UB-122 **63**
UC-5 49
Ugley (Essex), evacuation arrow 164, **164**
Unwin, Raymond 146
Upavon (Wilts)
   airfield buildings 107
   barracks 105
   flying school 95, 99, **99**, 111
Upminster (London), Engayne Gardens 152
Upper Heyford (Oxon), airfield 93
Uppingham School (Rutland), labour 169
Uxbridge (London)
   Armament School 110
   war memorial 206

V

V-44 63
V-82 63
Varley, Fred 27
venereal disease 180, 188, 196
Verdun oaks 205
Vickers 6, 27, 137, 152
Ville d'Oran 46
Viverdon Down (Cornwall), lime 172
Voluntary Aid Detachments 183, 186
Von Der Tann 80
Voysey, Charles 146

W

Wakefield, B F G 27
Walker, A G 208
Walter, Josef 207
Waltham Abbey (Essex), Royal Gunpowder Factory 119, 124–5, **124**, **125**, 145, **145**, 214
Walthamstow (Essex)
   Associated Equipment Co 142
   filling factory 135
Walton-on-Thames (Surrey), hospital 189, 198

War Channels 40–1
war dogs 23
War Knight 45, **45**
war memorials 199, 212, **212**
   including women **168**
   institutional 207–11, **207**, **208**, **209**
   memorials of private grief 211, **211**
   monumental 206–7, **206**, **207**
   origins and emergence 199–202, **201**, **202**
   raising 202–3
   utilitarian 203–5, **203**, **204**, **205**
War Office Cinematograph Committee 155
Ward, Mrs Humphrey 177
Ward, T W **214**
Waring & Gillow 139
Warneford, Flight Sub-Lieutenant Reginald 97
warships 37–41, **38**, **39**; *see also* submarines; U-boats; wrecks
HMS *Warspite* 40, **41**
Warwick, Countess of 204
Watt, Madge 170
Weaver, Lawrence 172
Webb, Beatrice 216
Weedon Bec (Northants), depot 29
Weizmann, Chaim 129
Wellingborough (Northants), family portrait **6**
Wellington Heath (Herefs), Memorial Hall 198
Wemyss, Lord 178
West Didsbury (Manchester), hospital 190
Westminster, Duchess of 180
Westwell (Oxon), war memorial 207
Weymouth (Dorset), hospital 189
Whipsnade (Beds), war memorial 205
Whitby (N Yorks), German raid 35, **35**, 75, 80, 163
White, Sir George 94
White, W Henry 189
Whitehaven (Cumbria), German raid 35–6
Whittick, Arnold 204
William Foster Co 141–2
Wills, Anderson & Kaula **153**
Wilson, Henry 3

Wilson, Walter 141
Wimbledon (London), seaplane shed 59, **60**
Wimborne (Dorset), war memorial 211
Winchester College (Hants), war memorial 209–10, **209**
Windsor Great Park (Berks), Hut Town 178
Winney, T Herbert 158
Winnington (Ches), amatol production 123
wireless communication 24, 141
wireless stations 52–3, **52**, 54, **55**
Withernsea (E Yorks), cinema 155
Withow Gap (E Yorks), pillbox 86
Wiveliscombe (Som), war memorial 203, **203**
Woburn Abbey (Beds), hospital 191, 192, 194
Woking (Surrey), Muslim burial ground **158**
Woldingham (Surrey), defences **88**
Wolverhampton (W Mids), helmet production 141
women
   agricultural workers 167–8, **167**, **168**, 174, **175**, 177–9, **177**
   Army Ordnance Corps 29
   building workers 147, **147**
   munitions workers **6**, 119, **131**, 144–5
   scientists 120
   seed testing 172, **172**
   VADs 183, 186
   WRAF 106, **106**, **108**, 109, 115
Women's Army Auxiliary Corps 34
Women's Forestry Corps **168**, 178–9, **179**
Women's Institute 170, **170**
Women's Land Army 167–8, **168**, **177**
Women's Royal Naval Service 109
Women's War Agricultural Committees 167, 168, 176
Wood, Francis Derwent 207
Woodham Mortimer Hall (Essex) 114

woodpigeons 178
Woolwich (London)
   AOC depot 29
   hospital 181
   housing 145, 146, 152
   remount depot 174
   Royal Arsenal 119, 120, 125, 145, 152, 214
   Royal Military Academy 22
   signals training 24
Woolworths 159–60, **161**
Worcester (Worcs), Gheluvelt Park 204
Worthington, Hubert 210
wrecks
   battlefield landscape 65
   Hood **38**
   Portsmouth Harbour 63
   post-war 64–5, 214–15
   RNR and merchant vessels 40–1, **40**, 43–5, **43**, **44**, **45**
   Scapa Flow 62, 63
   submarines/U-boats 46, 47–9, **47**, **48**, 50, 51, **51**, 63, **63**
   war channels 40–1, **40**
   warships **38**
Wrest Park (Beds), hospital 192–4, **192**, **193**, **194**
Wright brothers 94, 111

Y

Yantlet Creek (Kent), Grain Firing Point **120**, 121, **121**
Yatesbury (Wilts)
   airfield 173
   conservation 112, 116–17, **117**
   hangars 103, 111, 112
   POW labour 14, 116
York (N Yorks), Minster 165
Young, Henry 173
Young, William **1**

Z

Zeebrugge (Belgium) 51, 56
Zeppelin raids 5, 61, 95, 97, 112, 151, 165
Zimmerman, Arthur 53